SEX, LAW, AND SOVEREIGNTY IN FRENCH ALGERIA, 1830–1930

CORPUS

The Humanities in Politics and Law

JURIS

Series editor: Elizabeth S. Anker, Cornell University

CORPUS JURIS: THE HUMANITIES IN POLITICS AND LAW PUBLISHES BOOKS AT THE
INTERSECTIONS BETWEEN LAW, POLITICS, AND THE HUMANITIES—INCLUDING HIS-
TORY, LITERARY CRITICISM, ANTHROPOLOGY, PHILOSOPHY, RELIGIOUS STUDIES, AND
POLITICAL THEORY. BOOKS IN THIS SERIES TACKLE NEW OR UNDER-ANALYZED ISSUES
IN POLITICS AND LAW AND DEVELOP INNOVATIVE METHODS TO UNDERTAKE THOSE
INQUIRIES. THE GOAL OF THE SERIES IS TO MULTIPLY THE INTERDISCIPLINARY JUNC-
TURES AND CONVERSATIONS THAT SHAPE THE STUDY OF LAW.

SEX, LAW, AND SOVEREIGNTY IN FRENCH ALGERIA, 1830–1930

Judith Surkis

CORNELL UNIVERSITY PRESS   ITHACA AND LONDON

First published 2019 by Cornell University Press

Library of Congress Cataloging-in-Publication Data

Names: Surkis, Judith, author.
Title: Sex, law, and sovereignty in French Algeria, 1830–1930 / Judith Surkis.
Description: Ithaca : Cornell University Press, 2019. | Series: Corpus juris | Includes bibliographical references and index.
Identifiers: LCCN 2019006301 (print) | LCCN 2019011011 (ebook) | ISBN 9781501739514 (pdf) | ISBN 9781501739521 (epub/mobi) | ISBN 9781501739491 | ISBN 9781501739491 (cloth) | ISBN 9781501739507 (pbk.)
Subjects: LCSH: Islamic law—Algeria—History. | Domestic relations (Islamic law)—Algeria—History. | Muslims—Legal status, laws, etc.—Algeria—History. | Women—Legal status, laws, etc.—Algeria—History. | Algeria—History—1830–1962.
Classification: LCC KQG469 (ebook) | LCC KQG469 .S87 2019 (print) | DDC 349.6509/034—dc23
LC record available at https://lccn.loc.gov/2019006301

For Leïla

CONTENTS

EPILOGUE

ILLUSTRATIONS

ACKNOWLEDGMENTS

Many institutions and individuals, colleagues and collaborators, friends and family have sustained this project and its author over the long years of its research and writing. It is a pleasure to finally be able to offer my thanks now. I am lucky to have completed this book at Rutgers University, where it and I have found a genuine intellectual home. Material support, including a subvention from the Rutgers Research Council, helped to finance its publication. Other institutions, including the Pembroke Center for Teaching and Research on Women at Brown University and the School of Social Science at the Institute for Advanced Study in Princeton, offered much-needed leave time and incredible intellectual community at decisive moments in the project's development. Harvard University funded early phases of my research.

The colleagues and friends that I found in all these places have been no less indispensable. The Pembroke Center, in particular, played a crucial role. I have been in conversation with Joan Scott about this book ever since she encouraged me to apply there; her engagement and brilliant insight have sustained me throughout. A year of discussions with director Elizabeth Weed, and my fellow postdocs, Timothy Bewes and our much missed friend, Dicle Koğacıoğlu, reoriented my original project in fundamental ways. Ongoing dialogues with colleagues from Harvard, especially Peter Gordon and Afsaneh Najmabadi, have continued to shape my thinking. At IAS, the theme Seminar on Secularism with Joan Scott was an incredible incubator, as were the days (and nights) of discussions with Gil Anidjar, Rita Chin, Mayanthi Fernando, and Cécile Laborde. The University of California Research Intensive Project on Sex/Gender/Religion, codirected by Mayanthi Fernando and Saba Mahmood, also played an essential role. I regret not being able to share my finished work with Saba, whose research and critical reflections inspired my own. The encouragement, insight, and wit of history department colleagues at Rutgers have been a continuous source of support. I feel particularly lucky to have codirected the Rutgers Center for Historical Analysis and the Mellon Sawyer research seminar on Ethical Subjects with Seth Koven, whose expansive intellect and marvelous wit have enriched my work before and since my arrival at Rutgers. An advanced seminar on the genealogy of family law at the Radcliffe Institute was the perfect place to finalize my arguments, alongside two scholars, Janet Halley and Julia Stephens, with whom I have been in dialogue since this book's inception. I am obliged to the many knowledgeable audiences who offered generous and judicious feedback in the course of seminars and conferences at Brown, CEMA-Oran, Chicago, Columbia, Cornell, CUNY, Drew, the EHESS, the ENS, George Washington, Harvard, IAS, Illinois, Johns Hopkins, Le Havre, Michigan, Minnesota, NYU, Paris-8, Pennsylvania, Princeton, Reid Hall, Rutgers, Santa Cruz, Sciences-Po, Sheffield, Stanford, Texas, the Triangle Area, and Yale. I am especially grateful to Michael Allen, Anjali Arondekar, Talal Asad, Leora Auslander, Ed Baring, Beth Baron, David Bell, Ben Brower, Gia Caglioti, Mary Ann Case, James Chappell, Rita Chin, Julia Clancy-Smith, Joshua Cole, Brian Connolly, Fred Cooper, Carolyn Dean, Madeleine Dobie, Thomas Dodman, J. P. Doughton, Dan Edelstein, Tarek El-Ariss, Geoff Eley, Brad Epps, Eric Fassin, Jan Goldstein, Stefanos Geroulanos, Durba Ghosh, Paul Hanebrink, Dagmar Herzog, Peter Holquist, Isabel Hull, Duncan Kennedy, Dina Khoury, Ethan Kleinberg, Lloyd Kramer, Dominick LaCapra, Lisa Leff, Patricia Lorcin, Greg Mann, Marc Matera, Tracie Matysik, Maya Mikdashi, Phil Nord, M'hamed Oualdi, Robert Parks, Bruno Perreau, David Powers, Sara Pursley, Frédéric Queguineur, Lucinda Ramberg, François Richard, Sandrine Sanos, Gisèle Sapiro, Andrew Sartori, Joshua Schreier, Bonnie Smith, Orla Smyth, Miranda Spieler, Christelle Taraud, Francesca Trivellato, Steven Vincent, Gary Wilder, Tara Zahra, and Andrew Zimmerman.

Emmanuelle Saada's close readings of many chapters helped me to clarify many essential points. Todd Shepard's feedback on the work in progress as well as detailed and incisive comments on the manuscript as a whole have made this a stronger and more tightly argued book. Camille Robcis's enthusiastic support guided me to the Corpus Juris series at Cornell University Press. I am indebted to Liz Anker for her expansive editorial vision and to managing editor Diane Berrett Brown for her critical eye. Editor-in-chief Mahinder S. Kingra has expertly guided the long process of turning the manuscript into a book. I am grateful to Bill Nelson and Julianna Teoh for their help redrawing tables and maps and to Hayv Kahraman and the Jack Shainman Gallery for granting permission for the cover art.

I have been extremely lucky to have brilliant graduate students whose own work has so productively intersected with and informed my own. I am especially grateful to Ed Baring, Philippa Herrington, Kristen Loveland, Ward Penfold, François Proulx, Sarah Shortall, and Julia Stephens, and more recently, Julia Buck, Anaïs Faurt, Hannah Frydman, Patrick Harris, Ariel Mond, and Katie Sinclair. Dear friends in Cambridge, Princeton, and Paris and many points beyond have been an incredible source of support, encouragement, and distraction. I am indebted to Karen Adler, Brian Connolly, Carolyn Dean, Juliette Cadiot, Jackie Clarke, Dan Edelstein, Serguei Emeline, Melissa Feinberg, Mayanthi Fernando, Peter Gordon, Manu Goswami, Paul Hanebrink, Karen Hong, Maya Jasanoff, Erika Kiss, Seth Koven, Maria Koznikova, Keena Lipsitz, Karuna Mantena, Jennifer Milligan, Sam Moyn, Jan-Werner Müller, Grigo Pop-Eleiches, Camille Robcis, Olivier Samour, Sandrine Sanos, Joan Scott, Todd Shepard, Suzanne Stewart-Steinberg, Cate Toscano, Francesca Trivellato, Molly Watson, Gillian Weiss, and Gary Wilder. Charly Coleman closely read, deeply considered, and discussed every line of this book with me; it would not have been the same without him. My family has been no less indispensable. My sister, Rachel Annon, is a font of sanity, good humor, and understanding; Robert Annon has offered counsel and laughter, while my nephews, Oliver and Henry, are always keen to play a competitive game. My parents, Angela and Julius Surkis, have provided myriad forms of support, as well delightful breaks in the California sunshine. I am grateful to Antoine Guitton for his patience and devoted parenting of our daughter, Leila, whose own life coincided with my years of research and writing. Her love and laughter continually inspire me. I dedicate this book to her.

NOTE ON TRANSLATION AND TRANSLITERATION

This book is based on the colonial archive of French Algeria. To consistently reflect these sources, I have maintained the colonial-era names and transliterations of places and people. Contemporary place names have been indicated in parentheses where appropriate—for example, Orléansville (Chlef). When not following French sources, transliterations from Arabic follow the guidelines of the *International Journal of Middle East Studies*. Translations from the French are my own.

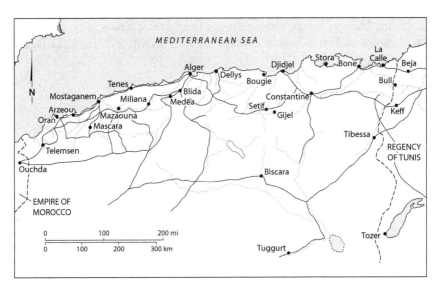

FIGURE 1 / The ex-Regency of Alger (1834). Based on a French government map in *Colonisation de l'ex-régence d'Alger. Documens [sic] officiels déposés sur le bureau de la Chambre des Députés* (Paris, 1834), redrawn by Bill Nelson. Place names rendered as in the original.

SEX, LAW, AND SOVEREIGNTY IN FRENCH ALGERIA, 1830–1930

INTRODUCTION

The French conquest of Algeria was sexualized from the outset. A contemporary caricature, *Le Sérail en émoi* (The seraglio astir), satirized the military expedition to Algiers in 1830 as an erotic adventure. Playing on fantasies of Algerian women and captive "white slaves," shut up in harems and desperate for male attention, it depicted the soldiers' seizure in carnal as well as martial terms. In the lithograph, the inhabitants of an Algerian "seraglio" are gathered on a rooftop, eagerly awaiting the French fleet's landing. With their male guardian anxiously looking on, the women spy handsome soldiers from whom they hope to receive marriage proposals. In this fantasy, Algerian women embraced the French invaders as liberators, while Algerian men responded with trepidation, since the arrival of Europeans portended the loss of exclusive sexual privileges. Other contemporary images mocked maladroit French soldiers taking Algerian women by force.[1]

According to these satires, the French mission across the Mediterranean aroused base desires, not high-minded morality. Early critics of the occupation were less sanguine than humorists about these effects. They denounced the military conquest's violent and brutalizing excesses, which risked, in the words of anticolonial deputy Xavier de Sade (Aisne), to "alter the noble character of our soldiers."[2] In response to pervasive concerns about French demoralization, advocates of the occupation endorsed a colonial rule of law. They affirmed the terms of the July 5, 1830, Treaty of Capitulation, signed between the Ottoman regent, Hussein Dey, and General Louis Bourmont, which guaranteed that "the freedom of the inhabitants of all classes, their religion, their property,

---

1. Numerous suggestive cartoons, with titles such as "La Conquête d'Alger," "L'innocence au sérail," "Les fruits de la victoire," and "L'embarras du choix," appeared in these early months. On caricatures of the conquest, including images of the harem, see Sessions, *By Sword and Plow*, 33, 50. On "white slavery" as pretext for conquest see G. L. Weiss, *Captives and Corsairs*, chap. 8.

2. Sade, Procès-verbaux, Chambre, April 28, 1834, *Archives parlémentaires*, Ser. 2, vol. 89, 408–9.

FIGURE 2 / "They have finally arrived, the nice Frenchmen! Can you see that big blond, my dear, and closer still, that handsome brunette; divine Mahomet, we are all going to be married!" Eugène-Hippolyte Forest, *Le Sérail en émoi*, lithograph, 1830. Musée Carnavalet / Roger-Viollet.

their commerce and their industry, will not be disturbed. *Their women will be respected.*"[3] Citing this precedent, the architect of Algeria's 1834 judicial organization, Deputy Justin Laurence (Landes), answered charges of French rapaciousness with promises of peaceful coexistence. He promoted the legal organization of colonization before parliament by proposing a no less fantasmatic idea of the occupation. "The environs of Algiers," he claimed, "offer the singular spectacle of the French set up next to Arab families, European dwellings facing Muslim houses, in whose interior can be found the secret of interior life and cloistered women, without there being any fear, any anxiety about this proximity [*voisinage*], which our opponents declare to be impossible."[4] For Laurence,

3. "Convention entre le général en chef de l'armée française et son Altesse le dey d'Alger, 5 Juillet 1830," in Estoublon and Lefébure, *Code de l'Algérie*, 1:1. My emphasis.
4. Laurence, Procès-verbaux, Chambre, May 21, 1835, *Archives parlémentaires*, Ser. 2, vol. 96, 286. On the history of such fascination with Muslim houses and their inhabitants see Çelik, "Framing the Colony."

FIGURE 3 / Antoine Adolphe Fonrouge, *Jean-Jean au sérail d'Alger*, lithograph, 1830.
Musée Carnavalet / Roger-Viollet.

Algeria required legal organization to establish effective colonial government and ensure the smooth transfer of property into European hands. His
1834 ordinance creating Algerian civil jurisdictions expressed this idealized
vision by separating the laws that applied to French and native inhabitants
of the ex-regency, whom he designated as *"indigènes."* As an indication of its

enduring power, this classification evolved into a defamatory epithet symbolizing Algerians' subjugation.[5] In this way, the colonial regime laid a legal fantasy
atop desires for conquest and possession that caricatures knowingly mocked.
By 1834, the architects of colonial occupation embraced the logic of the clois-
ter as the first principle of their juridical system, even as they repeatedly transgressed it.

In this book, I argue that sexual fantasies did not just inspire artwork;
they also prompted the writing and practice of law.[6] Long after the conquest,
Algeria's legal colonization remained beholden to the image of a hidden "interior life and cloistered women." French promises to preserve local gender
order worked in tandem with a concerted campaign to strip Algerians of their
land, which was also made subject to new legal classification.[7] Over the course
of a century, the law applied to desirable real estate, categorized as real property (le statut réel), was increasingly assimilated to a purportedly universal
French civil law, while the "personal status" (le statut personnel) associated
with family law and masculine privilege became a repository of Muslim legal
difference.

Once Algeria was formally declared a French possession in 1834, colonial officials instituted a plural legal order that recognized local law, while subordinating
it to French oversight. These officials regularly expressed ambivalence toward
this system of Muslim, Berber customary, and, for most Algerian Jews until 1870,
Mosaic law. Assuming a Janus-faced approach, they at once upheld and criticized local law, especially its treatment of women. In their accounts, legal sexual
privileges, including polygamy, repudiation, and child marriage, epitomized
Algerian men's difference from French men. Apparent conflicts between local
law and the French Civil Code instituted a sexualized hierarchy of civil status that

---

5. "Ordonnance du Roi concernant l'organisation de l'Ordre judiciaire et l'administration
de justice dans les Possessions françaises du Nord de l'Afrique, August 10, 1834," in *Bulletin
des Lois*, pt. 2, section 1, n. 324 (1834), 123–35. I have sought to limit my own references to
"*indigène*" to this legal usage. I favor the use of "Algerians" instead, although I do not intend it
to imply that inhabitants of the ex-regency had a fixed or stable conception of national identity
in this period. Earlier discussions of "*la question indigène*" include Saada, "La loi, le droit et
l'indigène"; Weil, "Le statut des musulmans"; Brower, *Desert Named Peace*; Blévis, "L'invention
de 'l'indigène'"; Shepard, *The invention of Decolonization*.

6. On the violence of eroticized imagery see McClintock, *Imperial Leather*; Alloula, *Colonial
Harem*; Clancy-Smith, "La Femme Arabe"; and Grigsby, "Orients and Colonies."

7. Guignard, "Les inventeurs de la tradition 'melk' et 'arch'"; Ruedy, *Land Policy in Colonial Algeria*; Sari, "Le démantèlement de la propriété foncière."

simultaneously disqualified Algerian men from citizenship and made Algerian women's legal status a recurrent problem. This French fixation on men's sexual "privileges" in Muslim marriage became a staple of colonial legal and political argument, especially after an 1865 *sénatus-consulte* (a law adopted by the Senate under the Second Empire) mandated that Muslim men, while granted French nationality, had to renounce their law in order to become full-fledged citizens. This rhetoric and policy created a rule of difference in the name of maintaining male citizens' sexual equality before the law.[8]

French jurists made Muslim law status an obstacle to Algerians' political assimilation, but not to the appropriation of their land. In 1873, major property reform (the "Warnier Law") territorialized French civil law in large swaths of the colony's richest agricultural region, the Tell. In these areas, the state nullified Muslim law with respect to property title and sale in order to "Frenchify" it.[9] At the same time, the legislation claimed to "in no way alter the personal status or rules of inheritance of natives."[10] Algerian land thus became fully French, while the Algerians living on it remained Muslim persons (albeit with French nationality). They were, that is, governed by a Muslim law that was nonetheless recognized by the French colonial state. This law supposedly stood in the way of Muslim men's adoption of French civil law for their family matters—but not for questions of real estate.

Material and political interest do not alone explain how such sexualized conceptions of Muslim legal difference endured. I argue that they were also imbued with powerful affective investments.[11] My account goes beyond showing how erotic imagery legitimated the colonization of a dissolute and "feminized" Orient in order

---

8. For the "rule of difference" see P. Chatterjee, *Nation and Its Fragments*.

9. Larcher, *Traité élémentaire*, 3:306.

10. "26 Juillet 1873, Loi relative à l'établissement et à la conservation de la propriété en Algérie," in Estoublon and Lefébure, *Code de l'Algérie*, 1:409.

11. I draw on many scholars' accounts of how gender and sexual regulation shaped imperial projects. Previous studies of Algeria include Lazreg, *Eloquence of Silence*; Clancy-Smith, "Islam, Gender, and Identities"; Sambron, *Les femmes algériennes*; Rogers, *Frenchwoman's Imperial Story*; Lorcin, *Historicizing Colonial Nostalgia*; Ghabrial, "Le 'fiqh françisé.'" For other contexts, and the British and Dutch Indies in particular, see McClintock, *Imperial Leather*; Sinha, *Colonial Masculinity*, and *Specters of Mother India*; Stoler, *Carnal Knowledge and Imperial Power*; Ghosh, *Sex and the Family in Colonial India*; Burton, "From Child Bride to 'Hindoo Lady'"; Nair, *Women and Law in Colonial India*; Levine, *Prostitution, Race, and Politics*; Sturman, *Government of Social Life in Colonial India*; Arondekar, *For the Record*; Esmeir, *Juridical Humanity*; Mahmood, *Religious Difference in a Secular Age*; Birla, *Stages of Capital*; Hussin, *Politics of Islamic Law*; Stephens, *Governing Islam*.

to expose deeply gendered logics at the heart of legal personhood and property. The sexual politics that I detail were an integral part of the shifting dynamics of French rule in the elaboration of land legislation, the administrative regulation of the Algerian population, and the fostering of "European" settlement. They determined who would be subject to what kind of law by giving form and feeling to definitions of Frenchness as well as its idealized gender and familial norms. Algerians would eventually lay claim to their personal status as, in the words of Ferhat Abbas, their "real country," or *pays réel*. My focus is not, however, on this tactical, if ironic, appropriation of a French colonial category.[12] I show instead how a colonial conception of Algerian Muslim law became part of French law in the first place.

Emotionally powerful ideas about Muslim sex and Muslim families were central to French efforts to secure sovereignty over the territory and population of France's prized settler colony. Progressively detached from land, the French colonial construction of Muslim law was bound to the bodies of Algerian persons and their families. More than just a symbol of Muslim difference, family law became an instrument of colonial rule. As in other imperial contexts, this rule of difference focused attention on the patriarchal excesses of native law and its effects on women. It also served to obscure the patriarchal structure of French civil law. This colonial legal genealogy elucidates how "the Muslim question" became a sexual question—and why it remains one, still today.

Sex, Law, and Sovereignty

This book offers a unique perspective on the history of French Algeria by foregrounding how ideas about sex and the family were integral to the development of colonial legal theory and practice. Exploring both continuity and rupture over a *longue durée*, it revises conventional periodization and reframes longstanding historical questions about the dynamic interplay between colonizers and colonized, the military and civilian settlers, metropolitan and local politics, forms of knowledge and colonial power, as well as the apparent antinomy between French universalism and colonial difference.[13] French legal assertions

---

12. Rahal, "Ferhat Abbas, de l'assimilationnisme au nationalisme," 444; McDougall, *History and the Culture of Nationalism in Algeria*, 86–96.

13. Prochaska, *Making Algeria French*; Lorcin, *Imperial Identities*; Brower, *Desert Named Peace*; Abi-Mershed, *Apostles of Modernity*; Shepard, *Invention of Decolonization*; Sessions, *By Sword and Plow*; Blais, *Mirages de la carte*; Stein, *Saharan Jews and the Fate of French Algeria*; Messaoudi, *Les arabisants et la France coloniale*.

about Muslim sexual privilege and perversion recurred across regime changes and political reconfigurations, at once justifying domination and continually troubling the coherence of colonial legal order. This is not to say that these were timeless fantasies. They operated in specific ways at specific moments over the course of a century. My analysis of the repeated redeployment of such clichés helps in understanding their resilience, while also interrogating the sexual, racial, and civilizational assumptions on which these preconceptions relied in the past, and arguably to this day.

Gender and sex directly shaped diverse aspects of colonial policy, from land law and personal status to exceptional penal law. Civil law provided a ground and framework for more overtly repressive legal forms, including the notorious punitive administrative law, the "*indigénat.*" For some critics, the arbitrary exercise of colonial power should not, in fact, be understood as *legal* force. The discretionary policing and punishment of Algerians' activities and movements nonetheless relied on legal categories: in particular, the classification of the vast majority of Algerians as "*indigènes.*"[14] Fantasies of sexual difference, I argue, sustained these categories' discriminatory and violent operation.

As legal historians have amply demonstrated, plural legal systems were a typical strategy of imperial governments. In the Algerian case as elsewhere, architects of the new juridical order claimed to be "preserving" the Ottoman state's prior plural juridical organization, at least in the domain of private law. In doing so, they sought to guarantee an effective and efficient legal order in the newly conquered territory. In my account, this legal pluralism was not opposed to state-centered law, but nor was it the intentional tool of a presumptively coherent and unified colonial state. Rather than assuming the strategic self-evidence of French Algeria's legal pluralism, I illustrate how its ground and authority remained perpetually troubled. In other words, while it appeared to solve some problems posed by colonial government, it also created new ones. A consideration of how gender both structured and complicated an ideally segmented legal order sheds new light on the immanent contradictions of such a legal system. As I show, the adjudication of questions about men's and women's legal status with respect to the family, sex, and property put French sovereignty repeatedly on trial.[15]

---

14. Merle, "Retour sur le régime de l'indigénat"; Le Cour Grandmaison, "Exception and the Rule"; Mann, "What Was the Indigénat?"; Thénault, "Le 'code de l'indigénat'"; Thénault, "L'indigénat dans l'empire français"; Guignard, *L'abus de pouvoir*; Saada, "Law in the Time of Catastrophe."

15. Benton, *Law and Colonial Cultures*; Benton and Ross, *Legal Pluralism and Empires*. For earlier formulations see Griffiths, "What Is Legal Pluralism?"; Merry, "Legal Pluralism"; Merry, "Law and Colonialism."

Within the framework of Algeria's 1834 judicial organization, local Muslim law became French state law, effectively transforming both in the process. This local law was itself plural, comprising judges (qadis) from the Maliki school of Sunni Islamic jurisprudence that was followed by the majority of the population, Hanafi school qadis of the Ottoman Turkish governors and notables, decentralized tribal and customary jurisdictions overseen by local elites and religious leaders, and rabbinic courts for Algerian Jews. The French privileged qadis as the clearest analogues to French magistrates, building local judicial organization around these state-appointed figures to administer Muslim law tribunals (*mahakmas*). After this multiform juridical organization was theoretically centralized and subordinated to French sovereignty, colonial jurists and administrators continued to negotiate the extent and limits of their own authority over local law, while Muslim jurists sought to carve out a space of relative autonomy in this highly asymmetrical structure. My account of these developments is indebted to previous scholarship on the institutional and social aspects of this history.[16]

While I trace the development of legal institutions and doctrines as well as the social dynamics of legal agency, my argument focuses on a capacious and cultural (rather than a narrowly formal or sociological) conception of law and legal history. I show, in other words, how texts and trials refracted and ramified concerns that extended beyond the confines of technical legal argumentation on the one hand, and the interests of jurists and litigants in the colonial legal field on the other.[17] I do so with a distinct aim: to illuminate how contests over the legal status of Algerian men and women were implicated in wider conflicts over French efforts to assert colonial sovereignty. As a result, my source base both includes and casts beyond official legal texts and state archives to comprise an array of journalistic, academic, and novelistic writing. Reading from a variety of theoretical perspectives, I reconstruct the "cultural life" of Algerian colonial law, which is to say the material, political, and affective resources and resonances on which its elaboration and its powerful effects depended.[18]

---

16. Christelow, *Muslim Law Courts*; Charnay, "Le rôle du juge français"; Henry and Balique, *La doctrine coloniale*; Henry, "La norme et l'imaginaire"; Shepard, *Invention of Decolonization*; Vatin, "Science juridique et institution coloniale"; Vatin, "Exotisme et rationalité"; Bontems, "Les tentatives de codification du droit musulman"; Arabi, "Orienting the Gaze"; Blévis, "Juristes et légistes"; Blévis, "Une université française en terre coloniale"; Renucci, "La doctrine coloniale en République"; Bras, *Faire l'histoire du droit colonial*; Dupret, "De l'invention du droit musulman"; Wood, *Islamic Legal Revival*; Ghabrial, "Le 'fiqh françisé.'"

17. For an account of both legal formalism and a sociological approach to law see Bourdieu, "Force of Law."

18. On the "cultural life" of law see Sarat and Kearns, *Law in the Domains of Culture*.

Conflicts over models of colonization and legal authority emerged with the conquest in 1830 and continued to trouble the territory's judicial organization for the next century. Across these struggles, sex was, in Michel Foucault's apt phrase, "a dense transfer point for relations of power."[19] Foucault's own investigation of the micropolitics of sexual regulation moved away from law in an effort to decenter state power. In directing his critique against the repressive function of law, he ironically took the discourse of sovereignty—its presumptive coherence, centralization, and uniformity of expression—at its own word.[20] By contrast, my emphasis on private law makes sovereignty's contingency manifest by highlighting legal indecision over the organization and regulation of sexual and familial order.[21] I study multiple moments of legal uncertainty: policy debates over Muslim conversion and mixed marriage; doctrine and jurisprudence that tested the French legality of Muslim polygamy and forced marriage; frustrated efforts to fix the meaning of the "Muslim family" in the creation of property titles. Because Algerians could and did exploit loopholes and inconsistencies in the law, legal efforts to shore up French sovereignty by recourse to claims about sex were never fully secure.[22] At the same time, French law, while contested, had powerful, indeed ruinous, effects on Algerians, women, men, and children alike.

By adopting a view of sovereignty as unstable rather than internally coherent, this book reads colonial law as part of the history of French law, rather than as a parenthetical exception to or anomaly within it. More specifically, I show how the colonization of Algeria troubled the French fantasy of national legal homogeneity emblematized in and by the 1804 Civil Code—and the

---

19. Foucault, *History of Sexuality*, 103.

20. For Foucault, an analytic focus on law and sovereignty projected a centralized unity onto a mobile terrain or "moving substrate" of local relations of force. He proposed instead to study "sex *without* the law, and power *without* the king." See his *History of Sexuality*, 92–93. For some critics, this focus on "micropolitics" is unhelpful for analyzing colonial contexts: see Spivak, "Can the Subaltern Speak?"; Cooper, *Colonialism in Question*, 48–49; Vaughan, *Curing Their Ills*, 8–12. Ann Stoler has meanwhile indicated how Foucault's focus on marginal people and spaces remains useful for understanding colonial history, and colonial histories of sex and desire in particular: Stoler, *Race and the Education of Desire*.

21. The reference is an intended contrast to Carl Schmitt's account of the sovereign "as he who decides the exception." Schmitt, *Political Theology*. While Giorgio Agamben's idea of the state of exception has been influential for discussions of "emergency" colonial law, it notably runs the risks stabilizing conceptions of the "rule of law." See Agamben, *State of Exception*; Hussain, *Jurisprudence of Emergency*. And for recent critiques see Benton, *Search for Sovereignty*; Saada, "Law in the Time of Catastrophe." On the simultaneous force and insecurity of colonial law to make and unmake landscapes and persons see Spieler, *Empire and Underworld*. On sovereignty's fundamental insecurity see Ben-Dor Benite, Geroulanos, and Jerr, *Scaffolding of Sovereignty*.

22. On the mutual instability of sex and politics see J. W. Scott, *Sex and Secularism*, 25.

distinctions, between men and women, property and persons, contract and status, on which it was based. In glaring contrast to the Code's stated ideal and mythology of national homogeneity, Algerian legal pluralism activated conflicts of law that were associated with the ancien régime's patchwork of status and privileges.

Postrevolutionary projects of codification were supposed to abolish this domestic legal pluralism by creating a universal framework of civil law. As Jean-Marie Portalis explained in his introduction to the first articles of the Civil Code: "Up until now the diversity of customs created, in the same state, a hundred different statuses. The law, everywhere opposed to itself, divided citizens rather than uniting them."[23] In rectifying this confusion, the Code claimed to encompass "the universality of things and persons." Its architects adopted the triumvirate Roman framework of Persons, Things, and Actions (modes of acquiring property) as a systematizing plan.[24] "Personal status" no longer managed internal legal diversity as it had in the ancien régime. It applied internationally instead, following French persons beyond the territorial borders of the nation. These principles were laid out in the Code's preliminary articles, which presumed a distinction between personal and territorial legal status. According to this framework, laws governing real property, as well as laws of police and security, were territorial. "Personal law" was an exception to territoriality that inhered in and followed persons when they traveled or lived abroad. The international legal specialist André Weiss later explained the distinction between territoriality and personality as a division within sovereignty itself: "The law has two different sovereignties: a territorial sovereignty and a personal sovereignty, one governing the ground, the other governing persons."[25] Algerian colonization posed the relationship between these two sovereignties as a recurrent domestic—at once familial and political—problem.[26]

The secularism of the Civil Code, which is to say, its separation between spiritual and temporal law, was integral to these efforts to nationally unify personal status law. Following principles established by postrevolutionary legal reform, the Code granted the state an exclusive power to oversee marriage law, thus distinguishing the civil contract of matrimony from its Catholic sacramental role. That power practically and symbolically expressed the rights of the

---

23. Portalis, *Discours, rapports et travaux*, 142.

24. Arnaud, *Les origines doctrinales du Code civil*.

25. A. Weiss, *Traité théorique et pratique*, 1:211–12.

26. On the international dimensions of "divided sovereignty" in the neighboring protectorate of Tunisia see Lewis, *Divided Rule*.

sovereign, which were for Portalis "inalienable and imprescriptible." Declaring marriage to be a "temporal object" over which the church should have no influence, he explained that "the Church can and must oversee the sanctity of the sacrament, but civil power alone must oversee the validity of the contract."[27] In 1807, the Grand Sanhedrin, a meeting of French rabbinic authorities convoked by Napoléon, adopted the same strictures for French Jews by committing themselves to following civil marriage law. In many histories of French secularism, this institutionalization of a purely civil marriage contract appears as an inclusive achievement of civil legal equality. It was, in the words of Jean Baubérot, a "first threshold" in the long march toward the attainment of a fundamentally liberal French "laïcité."[28] The history of Muslim (as well as Mosaic) personal status in Algeria exposes the limits of this progressive narrative by making manifest the double-edged operation of this universalizing civil law. The Code's emphasis on state authority over marriage contracts was, in other words, not simply about establishing civil equality. The Algerian case makes clear how it also expressed sovereign power.

As recent critics have pointed out, state assertions of secularity, including in the regulation of marriage, designate the legitimate forms, expressions, and limits of religion, in public and private space and law. Political secularism, in this view, does not have a fixed ideological orientation or necessarily progressive telos. It is a variable modality of government, which polices both majority and minority religions, albeit in different ways and toward different ends.[29] From this perspective, the French state's management of the Catholic Church's role in colonization and its administration of Muslim law (alongside Jewish and customary law) in Algeria were not exceptional contradictions to the progressive history of secular French law.[30] Rather, the history of French Algeria illuminates how French secularism underpins sovereignty and delimits religion, both in the past and still today.

By establishing state control over marriage, the Civil Code did not only regulate religion; it also managed gender and sex. In focusing on the patriarchal excesses of Muslim law, colonial jurists effectively obscured the male privileges enshrined in the Code's framework of private law. To promote national unity

---

27. "Exposé des motifs du titre du mariage," in Portalis, *Discours, rapports et travaux*, 180.

28. Baubérot, *Histoire de la laïcité en France*. See also Weil, "Why the French Laïcité Is Liberal."

29. Asad, *Formations of the Secular*; Agrama, *Questioning Secularism*; J. W. Scott, "Sexularism," and *Sex and Secularism*; Brown, "Civilizational Delusions"; Fernando, *Republic Unsettled*; Mahmood, *Religious Difference in a Secular Age*.

30. Saaïdia, *Algérie coloniale*.

and public order, it sought to eliminate domestic legal conflicts, exemplified by those between ancien régime Roman and customary law, especially within families and between husbands and wives. The firm placement of legal authority in the hands of husbands and fathers of families contributed to this aim not only by commanding the "obedience" a wife owed to her husband, but also by giving him control over their joint assets. The Code's regime of communal marital property privileged the conjugal family over the lineage family and made all management of property subject to the husband's authorization. This emphasis on the protection of family property had a direct impact on the marital organization of sex. The differential criminal treatment of adultery confined women's sexuality to marriage, while men's extramarital sex was surrounded by legal protections, exemplified by the Code's ban on paternity searches by illegitimate offspring. This same principle of marital unity also applied to international law, as women who married foreigners lost their French nationality, while foreign women who married a French man became French. The normative patriarchal family thus served practically and symbolically to unify and embody national law. The purportedly universalist Civil Code made French women's personal status distinct and distinctly subordinated to that of men.[31]

Herein lies one of the deep and persistent ironies of colonial jurists' repeated contention that the Civil Code was more advantageous to women than Muslim law. As numerous scholars have shown, Islamic law, including in Ottoman North Africa, granted women an independent legal identity and agency when it came to disposing of their property. Although the exercise of those provisions was conditioned by context, Muslim law broadly maintained married women's legal personality and property rights in ways that French civil law did not.[32] French women, not unlike Algerian Muslims, had an inferior civil as well as political status in French law. This embodied gender and sexual order was designed to protect French men's sexual, economic, and political rights. In an effort to naturalize and valorize French civil law, colonial legal experts and politicians fixated on men's sexual privileges in Muslim and customary law, while disavowing their own advantages under the Civil Code. Their doctrines and policy were both animated and unsettled by this contradiction.

---

31. Halpérin, *L'impossible code civil*; Desan, *Family on Trial*; Heuer, *Family and the Nation*; Fuchs, *Contested Paternity*.

32. Tucker, *In the House of the Law*; Doumani, *Family History in the Middle East*; Sait and Lim, "Muslim Women and Property."

Fantasies of Legal Power

French colonial policies were clearly motivated by economic, professional, and political investments. Jurists' recurrent association of Muslim law with polygamy, forced marriage, and repudiation shaped those policies in crucial ways: from legal definitions of personhood and property to tactics of civil and land registry, from exceptional regimes of punishment to the refusal of political rights. In the process, an ostensibly private Muslim family law became integral to strategies of colonial government and, eventually, a site of potential resistance to the colonial state's incursions. In order to understand these repeated deployments, we must analyze the affective dimensions of materially and politically interested claims. The fact that colonial jurists and politicians used sex to establish Algerians' legal difference does not fully explain those arguments' efficacy. Attending to the legal power of fantasy as well as the fantasy of legal power elucidates why the rhetoric of sexual difference took psychic as well as political hold.

Anticolonial psychiatrist Frantz Fanon famously analyzed the complex of sexual aggression and desire that motivated the "blanket indictment against the 'sadistic and vampirish' Algerian attitude toward women." For Fanon, the material violence and rapaciousness of the conquest also took a psychic form that came to focus on the Algerian family and women as a site of struggle between French and Algerian men. French efforts to save women could never be clearly distinguished from a desire to possess them. Sexual aggression and solicitude, covetousness and concern, lust and legality, were, in other words, two sides of the same colonial coin. Fanon notes, as symptomatic of this ambivalent attitude, a "revealing reflection" by a lawyer who denounced Algerians for "concealing so many strange beauties" and a "cache of such prizes."[33] I document the long legal history of this colonial sexual projection and disavowal.

Equivocal emotions did not only inspire artists, novelists, and travel writers; they also influenced colonial administrators and jurists. By studying what Teemu Ruskola has termed "legal Orientalism," we see how this imaginary took concrete political and social form.[34] The operation of colonial law always relies on a compensatory fantasy, which is to say a denial of the inevitable gaps and uncertainties of knowledge entailed by rule over a distant and often defiant population. In Algeria, as elsewhere, colonial jurists and magistrates, many of whom arrived fresh from law school in the metropole, drew on increasingly developed forms and institutions of

---

33. Fanon, "Algeria Unveiled," 38.
34. Ruskola, *Legal Orientalism*, 11.

knowledge production in order to overcome considerable ignorance. In the process, they created a corpus of Muslim law that was refracted through a decidedly French lens. To fill their own epistemological gaps they relied on ministerial, parliamentary, and local reports on Algeria's judicial organization, repeated translations of canonical texts of Islamic jurisprudence or *fiqh*, compendia of customary law, new colonial legal journals, geographical surveys, the creation of a Law Faculty in Algiers in 1879, and, eventually, in 1905, a monumental project to "codify" Algerian Muslim law along lines similar to the Civil Code.[35] Despite persistent challenges, jurists, administrators, and politicians regularly enacted a colonial legal fantasy: they issued judgments and policies *as if* they knew "Muslim law."[36]

It is helpful to recall here that, as Edward Said noted in his classic text, the discursive construction of Orientalism was as much based on "desires, repressions, investments, and projections" as it was on knowledge of empirical reality.[37] Critics of Said have pointed to the risk of reproducing a totalizing and Manichean opposition between the Orient and the West.[38] In exploring the fantasmatic aspect of legal Orientalism, I do not seek to reify and homogenize French and Muslim law, or to suggest that Muslim law was simply a projection of French jurists' heated legal imaginations. Indeed, my account of the instability of French sovereignty—its long history of legal pluralism, the confusions of colonial jurisprudence, and the incomplete project of systematizing Algerian Muslim law—indicates precisely the opposite. Understanding these projects *as* fantasies in a psychoanalytic sense elucidates their tenuousness, while also explaining their tenacious and violent effects. As critic Jacqueline Rose has suggested, "The modern state enacts its authority as ghostly, fantasmatic authority. But it would be wrong to deduce from this—like those who misread Freud's attention to fantasy as essentially trivializing—that the state is any less real for that."[39] By demonstrating the recursive efforts to secure French colonial sovereignty through appeals to the no less certain ground of sexual difference, we better comprehend both the uncertainty and force of its discriminatory law.

Feminist scholars and historians have found the analytic framework of fantasy to be productive precisely because it accounts for how structures of power,

---

35. See note 16. For other contexts, most notably South Asia, see Cohn, *Colonialism and Its Forms of Knowledge*; Kugle, "Framed, Blamed and Renamed"; Hallaq, *Sharīʿa*; Hussin, *Politics of Islamic Law*; Stephens, *Governing Islam*.

36. "To be in fantasy is to live as if." Riley, *Words of Selves*, 13. On colonial epistemic uncertainty see Stoler, *Along the Archival Grain*, 4.

37. Said, *Orientalism*, 8. See also Grosrichard, *Sultan's Court*.

38. Prakash, "Orientalism Now"; Burke and Prochaska, *Genealogies of Orientalism*.

39. Rose, *States of Fantasy*, 9. And Laplanche and Pontalis, "Fantasy and the Origins of Sexuality."

even when precarious, produce real effects.[40] To be sure, economic interests in Algerian land prompted French jurists' creation of a legal order that sequestered personal status from property law. Debates over the legal status of Muslim women shaped how colonial jurists constructed new jurisdictions and claimed their own legal authority. But to grasp how these arguments took hold in the juridical realm and beyond it, we must also grapple with these officials' libidinal and affective investments in law. Such sentiments are not simply ideological veils for real material interests, nor are they mere metaphors of rule. They are, rather, as Ann Stoler has suggested, at the "heart" of colonial governmentality.[41] The policies and practices of Algerian colonial officials were guided not only by *raison d'état*, but also by powerful desires. Juridical discussions of sexual relations and rights were, from this perspective, not just covers for other interests. They mattered because they mobilized and managed visceral and violent emotions connected to sex.

Affects are palpable across the colonial archive that I survey: in voluminous treatises written by jurists as well as in their tortured case law, in anxious reports written by land surveyors, and in speeches by parliamentarians, no less than in sensational copy written by journalists and sentimental prose written by novelists, including some who were also jurists. This diverse body of sources illustrates a deeply ambivalent relationship between the authors and their purported subjects, one that displays a simultaneous fascination with and repulsion toward the sexual privileges associated with Muslim law. These defensive reactions can be understood in psychoanalytic terms as denial, disavowal, and foreclosure, which is to say the repression, rejection, and refusal of their own thoughts, feelings, and desires.[42] They reveal, in other words, unrecognized desires and fantasies that were regularly displaced or projected onto Algerian men and women.[43]

Over and over again across a century of colonization, French jurists and journalists, politicians and publicists ritually rehearsed Algerian men's purported privileges in their denunciation of the "intimate" sexual excesses of Muslim law, including polygamy, prepubescent marriage, and repudiation. Remarks by Marcel Savoyant, a jurist who graduated from the Law Faculty in

---

40. Yeğenoğlu, *Colonial Fantasies*; J. W. Scott, *Fantasy of Feminist History*; Dean, *Frail Social Body*; Sanos, *Aesthetics of Hate.*

41. Stoler, *Along the Archival Grain*, 58–59.

42. In psychoanalytic terms, denial, disavowal, and foreclosure are distinct psychic processes of negation. I draw on all three in my analysis. For a helpful account see Shepardson, "Lacan and Philosophy," 123–24.

43. Fantasy is a "favored spot for the most primitive defensive reactions, such as turning against oneself, or into an opposite, projection, negation." Laplanche and Pontalis, "Fantasy and the Origins of Sexuality," 17.

Algiers and became political editor of the *Courrier de Tlemcen*, exemplify the dynamic of projective identification and disavowal on which these arguments relied. Assuming the position of the Algerian who benefited from the presumptive privileges of Muslim law, he thus explained why he would prefer these sexual advantages to full French citizenship, which required their renunciation: "The naturalized Muslim would no longer enjoy [*ne jouirait plus*] his personal status, which he prefers to the problematic advantages of voting rights [*la carte d'électeur*]." For Savoyant, these sexual rights were incompatible with Algerians' accession to French men's political rights. In his view, the difference—and indeed, inequality—between Algerians and French men would violate "public order" and hence grant them "incontestable advantages over us; they would enjoy all the prerogatives implied by the quality of the citizen ... while benefiting from their 'personal status': polygamy, forced marriage, concubinage, repudiation, paternity searches."[44] Savoyant both imagined Algerian men's sexual license and refused it as irreconcilable with the sexual limits of citizenship.

Savoyant's fantasmatic relation to Muslim subjects, like that of jurists and journalists before and after him, can be described in the paradoxical parlance of Jacques Lacan as "extimate." It displays, that is, a fascination with and jealousy of an Other's excessive sexual pleasure that reveals deep-seated but unrecognizable desires within the self. As an "alien kernel" that points to the subject's own incompletion and undoing, desire for this transgressive pleasure or *jouissance* cannot be expressed in the language of the law (the Symbolic). That unacknowledged desire represents an intimate foreignness that is actually created, by the structure of social and psychic rules, as an internal excess.[45] Its avowal would rupture, to use the terminology of the Civil Code, both "public order" and the subject of the law. Fixation on the other's pleasure, instead, expresses and exteriorizes those desires and thus preserves a fantasmatic sense of (masculine) wholeness or totality by establishing the other's sexual difference from the self, while simultaneously indulging in their imagined fulfillment.[46] This conception of "extimacy"

---

44. Marcel Savoyant, "La Conscription des indigènes," *Le Courrier de Tlemcen*, October 16, 1908.

45. Dolar, "Beyond Interpellation," 80.

46. For Jacques-Alain Miller, such extimacy animates racism and hatred of "our Islamic neighbor." It "is founded on what one imagines about the Other's *jouissance*; it is hatred of the particular way, of the Other's own way of experiencing *jouissance*." Miller, "Extimacy," 237. As described by Slavoj Žižek, extimate projection often takes form as the Other's purported "theft of enjoyment," which offers "satisfaction by means of the very supposition that the Other enjoys in ways inaccessible to us." It is not sufficient, he argues, to merely suggest that the "racist's Other" is a threat to "our" identity. The relationship is more complicated than mere opposition. Rather, "the fascinating image of the Other gives a body to our own innermost split, to what is 'in us more than ourselves' and thus prevents us from achieving full identity with ourselves. *The hatred of the Other is the hatred of our own excess of enjoyment.*" Žižek, *Tarrying with the Negative*, 206. On racial extimacy see also Seshadri, *Desiring Whiteness*, 58–60.

offers insight into the repetitive litany of charges against men's sexual advantages in Muslim law. As Savoyant's editorial suggests, these privileges embodied a reservoir of potential sexual powers and pleasures supposedly denied to French men, who, as citizens, were bound by the Civil Code. Muslim personal status in Algeria represented an inside/outside of the presumptive sovereign totality of French civil law, at once securing its purportedly superior coherence and risking to undo it at the same time.

This "extimate" projective (dis)identification was never stable. At moments, jurists and politicians let the apparently oppositional structure slip, revealing their identification with rather than repudiation of Muslim men's pleasure. Indeed, French law itself left ample room for French men's extramarital sex (and, one might add, marital rape), despite the Civil Code's professed commitment to monogamous marriage. In one parliamentary debate in 1913, the Catholic monarchist deputy and lawyer Christian de Villebois-Mareuil jokingly pointed out that polygamy remained something of an unwritten—and hence unrecognized—French law. In a rejoinder to deputies' protestations against Algerians' polygamy, he proclaimed: "We apply it in France without a decree." The quip registered a moment of recognition. According to the transcript, the chamber responded with laughter (*On rit*).[47] Such moments illuminate the revealing negation at work in the frequency of French men's projection and denunciation of Muslim men's sexual pleasures.

I argue that a totalizing and gendered fantasy of the Civil Code prompted such extimate projections. It was, after all, the Code's legal imaginary that helped to shape Lacan's own profoundly patriarchal conception of the Symbolic as a universal structure of "the law of kinship."[48] To this day, the Civil Code operates, in the words of the celebrated late twentieth-century civil jurist Jean Carbonnier, as "an unforgettable symbolic system." In his article devoted to the Code as a "realm of memory," Carbonnier tellingly juxtaposed it to the Qur'an, as a parallel system of universal and imperial law: "Never since the appearance of the Qur'an had a book of laws shown such an ability to spread abroad—a feat all the

---

47. Vicomte de Villebois-Mareuil, *Journal Officiel* (hereafter *JO*), Débats, Chambre, December 23, 1913, 4026.

48. Robcis, *Law of Kinship*. On the contemporary exclusionary fantasy of the Civil Code see Robcis, "Liberté, Égalité, Hétérosexualité." The history of the Freudian unconscious suggests another point of connection, namely in Sigmund Freud's elaboration of the theory of parapraxis, which linked a story of his own unconscious repression—the forgetting of the Italian painter Signorelli—to ideas about Muslim sexual customs. Freud, *Psychopathology of Everyday Life*, 12; Anidjar, *Jew, the Arab*, 134. In Lacan's reading, Freud's repression of the "ideas concerning the sexual stories of the Muslims" showed how language expresses unconscious truths, albeit in a "deformed" way. Lacan, *Seminar I*, 48–49.

more remarkable when one considers that the Code lacked the spur of religious faith that had driven the spread of Qur'anic law."[49] According to Carbonnier, the secular French Code has remained "a symbol of unity," so much so that he wondered "whether civil laws outside the Civil Code do not run the risk of remaining outside memory as well."[50] My history of French Algeria counteracts that work of historical forgetting in order to reveal the negated memory of Muslim law in French law.

A Century of Legal Colonization

The official centenary of French Algeria (1830–1930) that frames this book's chronology was a retrospective fiction that presented Algeria's colonization as a monumental historical achievement of French domination and Algerian subjection. For Algerians, the event had a starkly opposite meaning: it symbolized French imperial hubris and tragic loss. Taking the artifice of this colonial century as my point of departure, I show how France's fantasmatic sovereignty over the colony, in contrast to the mythic historical projections of the official celebration, was contested.[51]

Law was as important to Algeria's colonization as military might, not least because France's claim to the former possessions of the Ottoman regency remained uncertain after an initial victory in 1830. The leader of the regency, Hussein Dey, capitulated on July 5 to French forces under the leadership of General Bourmont. The territory's fate nonetheless remained far from settled. Initiated by the politically embattled reactionary French monarch, Charles X, this military "conquest" was not motivated by a coherent colonial plan. When the Revolution of 1830 broke out in Paris three weeks after the Ottoman regency's capitulation, France also underwent a regime change, making the status of French sovereignty in the ex-regency doubly insecure. This political and legal confusion did not diminish the violence and rapaciousness of the French army's actions and exactions in the first years of the occupation under Louis Philippe's July Monarchy (1830–1848). It did, however, pose challenges to establishing a stable system of rule, in light of Algerians' forceful resistance as

---

49. Carbonnier, "French Civil Code," 337–38.
50. Ibid., 348.
51. Oulebsir, *Les usages du patrimoine*.

well as ambivalence toward colonization on the part of skeptical metropolitan politicians.[52]

Proponents of colonization soon realized that securing French sovereignty depended on law. They thus returned to the arrangement of the Treaty of Capitulation and the legal protections—of religion, property, and "women"—that it offered.[53] These terms were regularly violated and renegotiated (property was violently seized and religious edifices desecrated, for example). The treaty nonetheless provided a framework for creating the colony's juridical structure. Beginning in 1834, the French colonial state assumed authority over local tribunals. It directly employed qadis (judges) and muftis (jurists), regulating them and increasingly circumscribing their jurisdiction in successive reforms. In doing so, it wrought fundamental transformations in the structure of their authority and in the nature of legal procedure, as well as in the scope of Muslim law.[54]

As I show in chapter 1, questions about religious and sexual difference, especially with respect to Algerian women's status, instantiated the legal challenges posed by colonization. During the first four years of French occupation, metropolitan politicians engaged in contentious debates over the viability of the colony and the prospect of establishing a colonial rule of law. At the same time in Algiers, several women sought French legal protection by converting from Islam to Christianity. Their efforts caused widespread public consternation, prompting official efforts to clarify their legal status. By refusing their requests, French colonial officials renewed a commitment to "respecting Algerian women" and hence the purported authority (but not the autonomy) of a presumptively patriarchal Muslim law.

These cases demonstrate how assumptions about gender and the family were central to the government by plural civil law established at the outset of colonization. This history of legal pluralism unsettles conventional accounts of French colonial assimilationism.[55] As I show, the French colonial state consistently sought the assimilation not of Algerian people, but of Algerian land. Following the Revolution of 1848 and under the Second Republic (1848–1851), Algeria became "an integral part of French territory"—a legal extension of France. The creation of the three new departments of Alger, Oran, and Constantine granted

---

52. My overview draws on several excellent surveys of Algerian history, including McDougall, *History of Algeria*; Ruedy, *Modern Algeria*; Ageron, *Modern Algeria*.

53. "Convention entre le général en chef de l'armée française et son Altesse le dey d'Alger, 5 Juillet 1830," in Estoublon and Lefébure, *Code de l'Algérie*, 1:1.

54. Henry and Balique, *La doctrine coloniale*; Christelow, *Muslim Law Courts*.

55. For the classic statement see Betts, *Assimilation and Association*. Recent reassessments include Abi-Mershed, *Apostles of Modernity*; Belmessous, *Assimilation and Empire*.

a growing population of settlers of French origin (roughly 42,000 out of a combined "European" population of close to 110,000) access to parliamentary representation.[56] Algerian natives were not included. In the Second Empire (1852–1870), Napoléon III pursued a policy (the so-called Arab Kingdom) that both maintained and regulated Algerians' legal difference. The 1865 *sénatus-consulte* played a decisive role in this organization. It recognized Algerians as French nationals, while mandating that they renounce their local law as a condition of citizenship.

French legislation adopted a different approach to Algerian people's land, transforming and truncating Muslim legal jurisdiction over it in order to speed the transfer of property into French hands. The state took charge of distributing expropriated land to settlers. Subsequent policies of official colonization came to rely on legal land classifications, determining those territories that would be open to state seizure and private purchase and those where Algerians' property rights and law remained intact. Algerian territory was thus divided into distinct categories: the "public domain" or *beylik* lands, which supposedly belonged to the former Ottoman regent and were claimed by the French state; religious trusts (*habous*), to which the state also eventually laid claim; collectively owned tribal lands (*arch*), which could not be purchased but whose size was limited by successive reforms; and finally, private property (*melk*), which was made available for purchase by European settlers.[57] The state and military oversaw this oftentimes chaotic process of legal appropriation, thus controlling settler access to land. By the middle of the century, advocates of civilian settlement launched new projects of colonization. Contesting the state monopoly, which they associated with the authoritarian Second Empire, they clamored to extend their rights to acquire property privately. As a result, many became fierce critics of Napoléon III's "Arab Kingdom" policy, which relied on military-run Arab Bureaus to administer much of Algeria's territory and population. In their view, the emperor's land policy, and an 1863 *sénatus-consulte* in particular, extended too much protection to tribal lands that were held in common under Muslim law. These campaigns against the empire called for the extension of French civil law to Algerian land.

Chapter 2 analyzes how debates over the persistence of polygamy in the colony were directly linked to these efforts to appropriate and settle Algerian land. As I show, early approaches to colonial government did not uniformly represent polygamy as integral to a timeless Muslim law. They instead linked polygamy

---

56. For population estimates see Kateb, *Européens, "indigènes" et juifs*, 29.

57. Ruedy, *Land Policy in Colonial Algeria*; Bendjillali, "L'histoire de la propriété foncière en Algérie"; Grangaud, "Dépossession et disqualification"; Guignard, "Les inventeurs de la tradition 'melk' et 'arch.'"

to Algerians' nomadic social organization and viewed it as amenable to economic (i.e., property) reform as imagined by Saint-Simonian military men and
administrators. This began to change in the 1860s, when, during debates over
the nationality and citizenship of Algerian Jews and Muslims, polygamy came to
symbolize the alien status of their religious law. While roughly thirty-five thousand Algerian Jews were granted full citizenship by the Crémieux Decree in 1870,
an estimated population of three million Muslims continued to be governed by
their local law. New concepts and categories of Muslim legal, religious, and sexual difference emerged at this moment and in connection with property reform
that consolidated the legal construction of the "Muslim family."

In 1870, the defeat of the Second Empire in the Franco-Prussian War brought
an end to military rule in Algeria, opening the way for civilian government and
greater settler influence under the Third Republic (1870–1940). Settler ascendency was further assured by the repression of the 1871 Moqrani Rebellion, a
massive uprising in the areas of greater and lesser Kabylia (Kabylie). Measures
of collective punishment exacted in its aftermath devastated these populations,
sequestering and confiscating 446,000 hectares (1,102,090 acres) of land and
charging 36 million francs in indemnities from rebel tribes.[58] The passage of the
1873 Warnier Law, which opened up Muslim land to purchase by settlers, further
secured the material as well as political basis of settler domination. The law's provisions encouraged a massive transfer of arable Algerian land into settler hands,
some 563,762 hectares (1,393,086 acres) between 1878 and 1898.[59] Designed to
dismantle Algerians' collective and family real estate holdings by applying the
Civil Code to land, the Warnier legislation at the same time promised to leave the
Algerian people's "Muslim law" intact.

While the history of expropriation in the colony is familiar to historians,
chapter 3 offers new insight into how "Muslim family law" —as the purportedly
intimate core of Muslim personal status law—was legally and ideologically distinguished from property law. Focusing on the devastating effects of the 1873 law,
I show how French colonial interpretations of Muslim law unavoidably elided
and confused questions of property and family, government and religion, even
as the law's structure appeared to distinguish between them. In the disingenuous rhetoric of these reformers, the law claimed to preserve "the intimate life" of
Muslim families and religion, even as it carved up "family property."[60] As I show,

---

58. Ageron, *Modern Algeria*, 52.
59. Bennoune, *Making of Contemporary Algeria*, 49.
60. Rapport fait par M. Warnier in "26 Juillet 1873, Loi relative à l'établissement et à la conservation de la propriété en Algérie," in Estoublon and Lefébure, *Code de l'Algérie*, 1:399.

the designation of some domains of life (i.e., property) as extra-intimate legally disrupted Algerians' ties to land while concentrating the regulation of intimacy on a new object: the "Muslim family."

The end of the Second Empire and advent of the Third Republic appeared to secure the stability of civilian settler rule through the passage of new legislation governing both Algerian land and people. As part of the effort to secure the territory against revolt in the wake of the Moqrani Rebellion, an 1874 judicial reform granted French justices (*juges de paix*) extended jurisdiction in areas governed by Berber customary law. In 1881, the so-called law of the *indigénat* accorded punitive disciplinary power similar to that possessed by the military to civilian administrators of "mixed communes" (*communes mixtes*), in order to subjugate and terrorize the vast majority of Algerians who lived in these areas recently transferred from military to civilian control. These exceptional measures—a list of forty-one "special" infractions not included in common penal law—were supposedly only provisional, but the law was regularly renewed.

These new punitive powers abetted the application of land reform law that, while confused and chaotic, continued to dispossess Algerians of their property. Indeed, failure to comply with the 1873 law was one of the infractions punished by the *indigénat*. In 1882, the institution of a native civil registry (*état civil*) imposed patronymic family names on Algerians in order to assure the transparency of property titles and other legal documents. New laws on Algeria's judicial organization in 1886 and 1889 further restricted the competency of qadis, enhancing the power of French magistrates to shape and interpret Muslim law. This massive expansion of legal policy and practice produced a voluminous record of doctrine and jurisprudence that was increasingly cataloged in new compendia and colonial legal reviews.

The purported preservation of local personal status and jurisdiction alongside the creation of new domains of competency for French magistrates multiplied sites of legal conflict that tested the extent and limits of French sovereignty. In chapter 4, I focus on the development of one highly charged site of contestation in order to show how gender and sex were at the core of these debates: the legality of the *wilayat al-ijbar*, or what the French called the "*droit de djebr*," the father's "right to force" a minor's marriage in Islamic and Berber customary law. The question of "child marriage" was deployed in a variety of contexts in order to underwrite and explain why the French needed to intervene in and regulate Muslim law and Berber custom despite vows to preserve them. A defense of Algerian women's marital consent thus became a linchpin in arguments for French legal sovereignty, both with respect to the desirability of French civil law and the exceptional legal treatment of "*indigènes*." Trials brought before French courts and officials eventually helped to spur state projects to codify Muslim law and reform customary law.

Alongside conflicts between French and local civil law, tensions between military and civilian law and authority persisted in Algeria even after the transfer to civilian rule in 1870. Given that war (so-called pacification) continued in the southernmost reaches of the territory, a considerable military presence was maintained in garrisons in the civilian-administered north. The overlap between military and civilian legal regimes gave rise to their own jurisdictional conflicts, including debates over the legitimacy of exceptional military justice. In chapter 5 I show how sex, gender, and civilizational difference inflected these contests. An 1891 case involving a military doctor's charges of sexual misconduct against a fellow officer in the native cavalry unit (called "spahis") showcases how the fantasmatic integrity of colonial legality, masculinity, and racial dignity remained precarious, vulnerable to charges of perversion and corruption, even as French domination appeared to be reaching its height.

Fears of sexual and racial corruption also informed the biopolitics of colonial settlement. Legal measures contributed to efforts to foster and secure the European (and largely Catholic) population, including an 1889 law that granted French nationality to the children of migrants from Spain, Italy, and Malta. The law was designed to increase the overall size of the French settler population and to counteract separatist sentiment among foreign nationals. In 1898, Governor-General Édouard Lafferière estimated that of a total French population of 384,000, there were 109,000 who had been recently naturalized, including 53,000 Jews.[61] The prominent presence of these "*néo*" French gave rise to new anxieties about a "foreign peril," a powerful wave of antisemitic agitation, and a concerted effort to integrate them, especially through marriage. In response, demographers actively promoted unions among Catholic "Europeans" as a privileged modality of racial and national "fusion." At the same time, jurists and administrators denounced unions between Europeans and Muslim Algerians as threatening to the integrity of French laws and French bodies. The law thus granted official recognition to a new idea of Algeria's uniquely vigorous and virile "Latin" settler identity, one that was increasingly defiant of metropolitan authority and Muslim Algerians. The granting of budgetary independence to Algeria in 1901 and the creation of the *délégations financières* gave institutional and political expression to, while also curbing, Algerian settlers' claims to autonomy.

---

61. Julien, *Histoire de l'Algérie contemporaine*, 121.

Chapter 6 explores the demographic and legal treatment of so-called mixed marriages, especially between Muslim Algerians and European women, as integral to the history of these concerns over Algeria's population and settlement. It traces how ideas of personal law were corporealized as the expression of bodies and desires, both Muslim and European. Although rare according to official statistics of the civil registry, these marriages provoked extensive juridical discussion about the sexual conflicts between Muslim and French law. In pondering these cases, jurists elaborated an embodied and civilizational account of personal law. Their agonizing over the legal effects of marriage for citizenship and nationality defined the exigencies of "public order," the presumptive "dignity" of the Civil Code, and the secularity that it was supposed to enshrine.

This corporealized conception of Muslim law provided an impetus for denying Algerian subjects their full rights as citizens. The legal existence of polygamy alongside the question of marital constraint fueled jurists' and politicians' imagination of Muslim men's sexual prerogatives, inciting extimate expressions of jealous condemnation. These emotionally charged accusations opposed new arguments for civic and political inclusion made by French-educated elites and their metropolitan advocates. Algerian military conscription, adopted in 1912 despite considerable resistance on the part of both settlers and Algerians, raised the stakes of this debate. Proposals to extend citizenship to a select elite of men who nonetheless maintained their Muslim personal status proliferated during the First World War. So-called Young Algerians insisted that cynical claims about Muslim law obscured how Algerians were, in fact, legally French. But even after the sacrifices of some 173,000 Algerians under the French flag, colonial jurists and politicians refused to recognize this apparent legal contradiction.[62] The intolerable prospect of the polygamous citizen again blocked political rights. In limiting a 1919 law that was supposed to facilitate Algerians men's access to full citizenship, Governor-General Charles Jonnart explained that "it is hard to admit that there might be polygamous citizens given that French law forbids polygamy."[63]

Chapter 7 returns to "child marriage" and polygamy in order to analyze why they remained such powerful features of political and legal argument. The chapter focuses on two reform debates: a project to codify Muslim law (the so-called Code Morand) and the proposed revisions to Algerians' political status during and after the First World War. I analyze the political and psychic denials at work

---

62. McDougall, *History of Algeria*, 136.
63. Gov. Gen. to Pres. du Conseil, "Envoi d'un projet de loi," April 19, 1918, 7, in AN 19950167/2.

in assertions about the sexual superiority of French civil and political law. I further show how Young Algerians identified and answered these extimate fantasies about Muslim law by denouncing, in the words of the prominent lawyer Taleb Abdesselem, "the malicious insinuations of immorality and barbarism that are so generously attributed to it."[64] My account restores a fuller sense of how intellectuals like Abdesselem did not fetishize French law but were, rather, its most incisive critics.

Although the 1919 Jonnart Law did not grant citizenship to men with Muslim status, it extended new political rights to selected noncitizens in local Algerian elections. This expansion of the political field raised new questions about the extent of Algerians' political representation, as well as the meaning of their legal status and its prospective modernization, especially in the field of Berber customary law. This reformist project culminated in the adoption of two laws intended to ameliorate Kabyle women's legal status with respect to marriage age as well as divorce and inheritance rights. Elaborated through a process of compromise and conciliation between French colonial jurists, politicians, and Kabyle representatives in the *délégations financières*, the laws seemed to present a colonial consensus that coincided with the official centenary celebrations of 1930 and its rhetoric of the civilizing mission. Meanwhile, even modest efforts to secure Algerian men's political rights, such as those reclaimed by the Fédération des élus musulmans in 1927 and outlined in legislation drafted by the former governor-general and liberal senator Maurice Viollette, did not have the same success. Given the rejection of these initiatives, the events of the centenary appeared to be an elaborate spectacle of political and psychic refusal.

In order to understand these dynamics of denial, chapter 8 explores the connection between discussions of political representation and efforts at customary-law reform by following the career of Ferdinand Duchêne, a colonial magistrate whose prize-winning novels sentimentalized the sufferings of Algerian women, especially from Kabylia, where he had long served. The chapter charts the success of Duchêne's novels in the interwar period, his role on commissions drawn up to reform Berber customary law, and the critical ire that his fiction drew on the part of Algerian intellectuals. In their journalism, the Young Algerians countered these political emotions by offering up their own sentimentalized vision of Algerian women. Together, these competing visions illustrate an intimate and supplementary relationship between law and fiction on the eve of the 1930 centenary.

---

64. Abdesselem, "Le statut personnel des musulmans français," 1516.

In the epilogue I analyze the centenary itself as a compensatory fantasy that revealed by denying the affective underpinnings of French claims to sovereignty in Algeria. If government officials and politicians clung to a rhetoric of exclusion, French feminists and Algerian intellectuals challenged that fantasy in an effort to reconceive the legal and sexual ground of political inclusion. Although unsuccessful at the time, their arguments remain touchstones of an alternative conception of French law that does not draw on fears of Muslim sex in order to secure its sovereignty.

1

BODIES OF FRENCH ALGERIAN LAW

In January 1832, an Algerian notable lodged a complaint before the chief French military commander of the newly conquered territory, General Anne Jean Marie René Savary, the Duke of Rovigo. The man was clearly in a state of emotional distress. According to Rovigo's report to the minister of war, the man was "in tears and complained of the abduction [*rapt*] of his two sisters and his wife by a European who had been holding them for three days." Accompanied by the French-appointed *agha* (chief) of Arabs, El Hadj Mahiddin, the betrayed husband beseeched the general to return his wife to him. In his notorious military policy, Rovigo systematically violated Algerian lives, beliefs, and belongings, but he displayed remarkable solicitude in this case. The suspected seducer, called in for interrogation alongside the women, admitted to conducting a clandestine affair with the man's wife, having gone as far as to rent the house next door. The seducer, Rovigo was dismayed to learn, was a judge on the Court of Appeals of Algiers, a certain M. Colombon.[1]

The infamously violent French military commander rapidly responded to the scandal. A Napoleonic war hero who had served in the Egyptian campaign, he pursued a policy of extensive military colonization with little heed for the niceties of law: he authorized extralegal massacres and summary executions, most notoriously of the El Ouffia tribe; converted mosques into cathedrals; destroyed cemeteries to create roads across the capital; and expropriated buildings without regard for titles.[2] His actions regularly contravened the protections extended to Algerians by the July 5, 1830, Convention of Capitulation. In this case, however, Rovigo acted against the French official, "forced by the general interest to enact a harsh measure and to treat the natives with equity." He put Colombon under house arrest and soon deported him to the metropole. Leaving the judge unpunished would, he claimed, disrupt "all of the *Maures*' authority over their women."

---

1. Letter 54, Rovigo to Min. of War, January 27, 1832, in Savary, *Correspondance*, 1:140.
2. Julien, *Histoire de l'Algérie contemporaine*, 90.

In his view, they sought "vengeance for the assault on a law that remains a matter of religion."[3]

Rovigo acted quickly to correct the French magistrate's sexual affront to local "religious" law by restoring patriarchal authority. In doing so, he worked to reverse the widespread images of French soldiers as agents of sexual license and plunder in the earliest days of the conquest. One contemporary lithograph playfully drew a direct connection between Algerian women's apostasy and sexual corruption in its depiction of two naïve soldiers competing for the affections of a faithless woman, "*une infidèle*." Rovigo, by contrast, presented himself as a defender of Algerian women's religious and sexual honor. The case illustrates how French officials variably constructed the boundaries of religious belief and practice in an effort to secure sovereignty. Rovigo had considerable latitude in determining what mattered for the Muslim religion, viewing the assault on the husband's sexual rights as particularly sensitive. It represented a challenge not only to local men's authority, but also to his own. As he explained, "Had I not accorded them a dazzling [*éclatant*] justice, all that I had accomplished with the Arabs would be forever lost."[4] In affirming an intimate connection between religion and patriarchal rights, Rovigo sought to buttress his own legitimacy and power. As this chapter makes clear, his gesture presumed that Muslim religion was bound to Algerian women and their legal status.

This dramatic contest between military, civil, and local authority condensed broader struggles over how to establish French sovereignty and law in the ex-regency. Because the ultimate fate of the territory as a French possession remained insecure, these early years are often characterized as a "period of uncertainty."[5] In this chapter, I show how this insecurity extended beyond military planning to shape debates about law in the nascent colony. "Uncertainty" was, in other words, an epistemological and legal problem, precisely because the very meaning of "law" in the territory was unclear. Between the signing of the July 5, 1830, convention and the July 22, 1834, ordinance that annexed Algerian territory to France, military commanders, civilian officials, metropolitan politicians, and local notables struggled to assert and preserve their authority by

3. Savary, *Correspondance*, 1:140.

4. Letter 54, Rovigo to Min. of War and Président du Conseil, January 27, 1832, ibid., 142. Also, Lekéal, "Entre séduction charnelle et spirituelle."

5. Julien, *Histoire de l'Algérie contemporaine*, 64; Heggoy, "Looking Back," 59; McDougall, *History of Algeria*, 58.

FIGURE 4 / Cornille (Victor Auguste Laurent), *Une infidèle*, lithograph, 1830. Musée Carnavalet / Roger-Viollet.

making competing claims about legality. Over the course of four years, gendered fantasies of law, religion, and religious law worked to ground an otherwise uncertain colonial order. Far from converting or "liberating" women, these fantasies located Algerian women in the presumptively private domain of their family.

Official concerns with legality emerged in response to the wanton destruction wrought by unchecked military force. The Convention of 1830 signed between General Bourmont and the Ottoman regent Hussein Dey was supposed to bring hostilities to an end, extending protections to a diverse local population of an estimated four million Arabs, Berbers, and Jews.[6] It dissolved the "foreign" Turkish government, while promising to respect the territory's indigenous residents, proclaiming: "The freedom of the inhabitants of all classes, their religion,

---

6. Kateb, *Européens, "indigènes" et juifs*, 16.

their property, their commerce and their industry, will not be disturbed. Their women will be respected."[7] The French army immediately violated this law of peace. The pillaging of the ex-regency's capital continued long after the convention's signing, as soldiers seized private and public belongings, destroyed buildings, and laid claim to pious foundations (*habous*). Terrorized, thousands of residents fled the capital city. War continued as the army sought to extend French control beyond Algiers. In November 1830, General Bertrand Clauzel ordered the nearby town of Blida to be sacked in response to local resistance. This massacre of hundreds of inhabitants, including women and children, made it clear that the army had no intention of respecting the terms of the convention. While Clauzel's successor, General Pierre Berthezène, promised to act with greater respect toward the local population, his tenure was short-lived. With Rovigo, violent exactions and terror returned as the order of the day.[8]

When Rovigo assumed command in late 1831, the army had conquered Algiers and some of the surrounding coastal plains, but only provisional structures of government were in place. Alongside the military commander, a civil intendant, Louis André Pichon, was named to oversee civil matters, thus giving rise to chronic conflicts over authority. In this moment of political indecision, the future of the territory's relationship to France was tenuous, under vigorous assault from local resistance and metropolitan ambivalence toward a confused and costly colonial project.

Unfolding in this chaotic context, the apparently minor incident regarding Colombon's sexual dalliance raised larger questions about the relationship between French and local "religious" law, military and civil power, force and right. The limits of brute military violence of the kind exercised by Rovigo became increasingly clear to politicians in Paris who sought to institute a durable colonial government. Intendant Pichon pursued the stabilization of French sovereignty through regularized laws, not personal military rule. He denounced Rovigo's Napoleonic military fantasy of domination, which remained inadequate "for Algiers as for Egypt." For Pichon and other critics of military excess, the government had been misled by Napoleonic myths, which amounted to nothing more than a "novel of Algiers."[9] As these contemporary controversies made clear, such fictions had real, indeed devastating, effects.

---

7. "Convention entre le général en chef de l'armée française [Bourmont] et son Altesse le dey d'Alger, 5 Juillet 1830," in Estoublon and Lefébure, *Code de l'Algérie*, 1:1.

8. Brower, *Desert Named Peace*, 15–17.

9. Pichon, *Alger sous la domination française*, x.

French officials sought a viable legal solution to the military and epistemological problem of the ex-regency's fate. Erupting in this uncertain context, the
Colombon Affair symptomatically inspired its own novel, staged as a fantasy
about men's sexual and legal control of Algerian women. Fantasy, as I understand
it here, both enacts and seeks to answer fundamental epistemological problems.
The novel sheds light on the Colombon Affair as a "primal scene" of colonial
legal fantasy. That is to say, it demonstrates how gendered fantasies were generated in response to originary questions in the colony—including about the
structure and organization of law.[10]

From the incident of the kidnapped wife in the Colombon Affair to controversies over women's efforts to escape Muslim law by conversion to Catholicism,
Algerian women provoked French officials' legal thought and desire. They came
to embody broader concerns about the prospects of French colonization. As
scenes of affective and erotic investment, gendered fantasies about women's
place in Muslim law and religion came to ground a regime of colonial law that
was eventually adopted in 1834. By focusing on gender, this chapter offers new
insight into how the "period of uncertainty" was fantasmatically staged and pro-
visionally resolved in law.

Originary Fantasies

Fantasies about Muslim men's patriarchal rights evidently shaped Rovigo's
response to the Algerian husband's plea. The general decided to release the
women, who were from a prominent family, to their brother and husband,
after receiving assurances from the city's principal Muslim qadi and the Agha
Mahiddin that they would not be harmed under "Turkish law." Concerned about
rumors that the women had been imprisoned and even killed, the agha assured
Rovigo that their "isolation" had "shielded them from insults," given how the
affair "dishonored the family." Confirming Rovigo's conception of Algerian
patriarchy, Mahiddin expressed gratitude for the "good action that conformed
to our religious principles."[11] In disciplining both Colombon and the women,
the general shaped the official meaning of "religion" and lent it the backing of

---

10. On fantasy and the staging of originary conflicts see Pontalis and Laplanche, "Fantasy and
the Origins of Sexuality."

11. Agha to Rovigo, February 3, 1832, in Savary, *Correspondance*, 3:59–60. Letter 39 in Pichon,
Alger sous la domination française, 446–49.

French armed force. With the apparent restoration of religious and social order, the women disappear from the state record.[12]

Rovigo's punitive force demonstrated masculine and military authority not only to the Algerian notables and tribal leaders, but also to French civil officials whose competing authority he rejected. The women's uncertain jurisdiction troubled the relationship not just between the general and the indigenous male elite, but also between French officials. They were, in other words, a "ground" for struggles between men.[13]

The general's disciplinary actions exacerbated a brewing conflict with the civil intendant, Pichon. Appointed by President Casimir Périer, Pichon had just arrived in Algiers. The ordinance creating his office separated "military and civil powers" in order that "justice could, in this country, assume a regular operation."[14] This attempt to divide civil law and military force created a new terrain of conflict. Rovigo resented the imposition of civilian authority, warning Périer against creating a "rival power" that was ill-adapted to the local context: "I repeat, the action of executive power cannot be divided here. To attempt to do so would be to misunderstand the Turks and Arabs."[15] Pichon had a decidedly different perspective on how law should operate in the conquered territory, based on a lifelong career as diplomat and colonial official in Martinique and Guadeloupe. Proclaiming himself a defender of the 1830 convention's principles, Pichon denounced Rovigo's violent actions against the Algerian population. His memoir catalogs the wanton destruction and "terror" sown by Rovigo's brutal policies: the conversion of the spectacular Ketchoua mosque into a cathedral, the destruction of cemeteries to build roads, the imposition of an exorbitant wool tax on local merchants, the wanton demolition of buildings in Algiers, and the massacre of the El Ouffia tribe in April 1832. When critics charged him with being "anticolonial," Pichon responded, "No, I do not want a colonization like that desired by the Party of pillage and extermination."[16]

While apparently minor, Colombon's case cast the conflict between civil and military authority as a contest between different models of masculinity and law. For Pichon, Rovigo's actions instantiated an abuse of power. He claimed

---

12. Letter 63, Rovigo to Président du Conseil, January 30, 1832, in Savary, *Correspondance*, 1:159.

13. Mani, "Contentious Traditions," 79.

14. "Ordonnance du roi qui confie à un Intendant civil, en Alger, la Direction et la Surveillance des services civils et financiers et de l'administration de la justice," December 1, 1831, *Bulletin des Lois*, vol. 3, 2ᵉ partie, no. 126, 603–4. See also Julien, *Histoire de l'Algérie contemporaine*, 87–88.

15. Letter 63, Rovigo to Min. of War, January 30, 1832, in Savary, *Correspondance*, 1:163.

16. Pichon, *Alger sous la domination française*, 94.

that the Napoleonic veteran had no right to "proceed militarily" in what was a "purely judicial matter" or to take such "arbitrary actions toward women."[17] Pichon denounced Colombon for immorality, but more pointedly condemned Rovigo for the "palpable irregularities" in his exercise of power. Pichon claimed to advocate for the women, who, in his view, had been turned over to "a man who had no right over them." In overstepping the boundaries of his authority, Rovigo did "damage to the personal security no less of the natives than of our nationals."[18] Pichon thought that legal procedure rather than military authority would provide better guarantees for all, including Algerian women. For Rovigo, by contrast, "there could be nothing in greater conformity with their religious law and that of humanity than to return these women to their family, while tempering by my influence the most rigorous aspect of their domestic justice."[19]

The Colombon Affair illustrates how debates over the legal form of colonial power were bound to the status of Algerian women, and more specifically whether they should be subject to Muslim law. This primal scene of imperial rescue enacted originary conflicts of Algerian colonial government that would continue for more than a century. As a fantasy, it held apparently contradictory positions together: Colombon expressed a French jurist's eroticized legal desire to "save" women from Muslim patriarchy; Mahiddin secured a position as colonial intermediary by guaranteeing women's submission to their male kin; Rovigo assured martial masculine authority by shoring up local gendered hierarchies; and Pichon upheld the rule of law as the best way to protect women and the nascent colonial order.[20] Rather than resolving them, this drama of transgressive sexual desire and punishment staged these political contests as an affectively laden scene.

The affair's dramatic intrigue was symptomatically refracted in one of the earliest novels about colonial Algeria: *Mœurs d'Alger: Juive et Mauresque*. Published in 1833, it was written by a liberal man of letters, Hippolyte Bonnellier, who worked in the civil affairs office in Algiers, alongside Pichon.[21] His anticlerical and antimilitarist novel depicted the confused landscape of the newly conquered Algeria as legally and libidinally treacherous. The fictionalized account sought

---

17. Ibid., 68.

18. Pichon to Rovigo, January 29, 1832, in Savary, *Correspondance*, 3:40–41.

19. Letter 64, Rovigo to Pichon, January 30, 1832, in Savary, *Correspondance*, 1:166. For a related account of these competing conceptions of law see Lekéal, "Justice et pacification."

20. I am extending here the Freudian reference in Gayatri Spivak's famous formulation of the fantasy of imperial rescue, "white men saving brown women from brown men." Spivak, "Can the Subaltern Speak?," 93; Freud, "Child Is Being Beaten."

21. Julien, *Histoire de l'Algérie contemporaine*, 89.

to lay bare the truth of Rovigo's mistreatment of both the judge and the women in the case. It made a brief for a colonial rule of law by mobilizing "the noise of opinion asking for justice."[22]

To enhance Colombon's story, Bonnellier added a Jewish love plot to the Muslim one. Such juxtapositions of Jews and Muslims characterized many early depictions of Algiers after the conquest, in fiction and painting as well as law.[23] In the novel, the magistrate Robert Cowel (Colombon's alias) falls in love both with Johane, the Jewess, and a beautiful *Mauresque*, Fatma, who is trapped in an unhappy polygamous marriage. By desiring both women simultaneously, Cowel himself succumbs to the confused temptations of polygamy, thus "absorb[ing] the religious prejudices of these two opposing religions." While his heart drives him toward amorous and assimilationist passion, Cowel's intellect remembers the legal limits on his desire, set by the Convention of 1830: he "still had enough reason not to misrecognize the rights even of the vanquished, and too much probity to fearlessly offend defenseless virtue." He worried that local men's "vindictiveness" was "implacable in the protection that it grants to the servile virtue of women."[24]

Cowel's anxieties appear to be well founded. Fatma's vengeful husband, Sidi Taleb, denounces the French judge for encroaching on his domestic rights: "The sanctity of our customs guaranteed by our laws make the secret asylum of our homes inviolable to any stranger, to any man, to any Christian."[25] Fatma and her two co-wives escape their husband's murderous rage. Helped by a scheming translator, they arrive at Cowel's door, awakening him from a dream. With his wishes fulfilled by their apparition, Cowel cannot distinguish reality from fantasy, proclaiming "my uncertainty is frightening." When the women ask for "asylum and protection," he hesitates. At the translator's urging, he admits that it would be a "stupid cruelty" to force them to return home—and to their death. Cowel resolves to shield them in his house, but never consummates his love.[26]

When the betrayed husband reports the incident—"with sobs, and great cries, begging justice and vengeance"—to Rovigo, the general issues a "punishment of exemplary severity" that is supposed "to reassure the Algerians that their most valuable property would be conserved, that of the honor they invested in

22. Bonnellier, *Mœurs d'Alger*, x.

23. J. Pharaon, *De la législation française, musulmane, et juive*. Also, Samuels, "Philosemitism and the *Mission Civilisatrice*"; Schreier, *Arabs of the Jewish Faith*; Grigsby, "Orients and Colonies."

24. Bonnellier, *Mœurs d'Alger*, 177–78.

25. Ibid., 214.

26. Ibid., 224.

their women."[27] While Cowel is sentenced to deportation, "justice and vengeance" come at an even higher cost to the women: Fatma and her co-wives are beheaded in Koléa. The novel's last scene takes place inside the mosque that Rovigo had violently turned into a cathedral. Johane has converted in order to marry Cowel, only to be disappointed. Cowel, now married in France, has renounced his wayward desires in submission to the monogamous discipline of French civil law. Johane dies brokenhearted.

Herein lies the interest of Bonnellier's novel as a refraction of two intimately linked legal fantasies: Fatma's eroticized rescue and Johane's assimilation. In fact as in fiction, Rovigo's actions, which Bonnellier describes as having all "the logical force of a saber," severed the fictional jurist from his objects of desire. This act of symbolic castration by military power at once prompted these legal fantasies and allowed them to persist. Rovigo's action as reprised in the novel set the stage for this scene to be repeated. As we will see throughout this book, jurists continued to dream of liberating Algerian women. The Colombon Affair and its retelling in Bonnellier's novel illustrates how this fantasy was not merely a projective trope of Orientalist fiction.[28] It also became integral to the early policy and practice of Algerian colonial law.

Observing Local Law

A contemporary review in Le Figaro praised Bonnellier's novel for its vivid depiction of the "mœurs of the country's inhabitants."[29] Curious metropolitan readers of exotic fiction were not the only people interested in such details. Government officials were also keen to garner this information in order to evaluate the territory's colonial prospects. Their efforts to map local law focused on "the family" as integral to Algerians' presumptively private, religious domain.

A rash effort to abolish local courts entirely on September 9, 1830, was quickly corrected by an ordinance signed by General Clauzel on October 22, which instituted French tribunals and reestablished indigenous counterparts. This hasty provisional organization only raised further questions and generated considerable local consternation.[30] In an effort to address this precarious

---

27. Ibid., 232.

28. Said, Orientalism; Yeğenoğlu, Colonial Fantasies; Lazreg, Eloquence of Silence.

29. Le Figaro, September 23, 1833.

30. "Arrêté portant institution et détermination de la juridiction et de la compétence du qadi maure, du tribunal israélite, de la cour de justice et du tribunal correctionnel," October 22, 1830, in Collection des actes du gouvernement, 24–26.

situation, the Ministry of Justice sent Charles Paravey, a legal adviser to the Conseil d'État, to Algiers to survey the existing legal system and offer thoughts on its reform.

Paravey approached the problem of Algerian law philosophically. A member of the "Generation of 1820," he had followed Victor Cousin's lectures on moral philosophy at the Sorbonne.[31] As a student, Paravey grappled with the question of the respective role of sensibility and reason in the formation of moral laws, concluding in a prize-winning essay from 1818 that "one can never derive any fixed law from the system of sensibility."[32] Following Cousin, he concluded that only "scientific observation" based on reason could tame the passions and thus derive the "absolute principle" that would "allow the law to be itself, and nothing but itself."[33] Upon arriving in Algiers, Paravey drew on this observational method in order to understand local law. His sixty-seven-page report professed to be a dispassionate account, supposedly based solely on the "study of facts," untainted by sensational prejudices about Oriental despotism. He flatly rejected "ideas in this vein about Oriental justice," confessing to the justice minister, "I must admit that nothing could have been more inexact than the notions with which I arrived." He studied the ex-regency's judicial system and concluded that the deposed dey had been "very *legal*."[34]

Using translators, Paravey interviewed local Islamic legal scholars, qadis and muftis of the Hanafi and Maliki schools of Islamic jurisprudence, both of which had tribunals in Algiers.[35] He explained that qadis were not merely "judges," but also notaries and social mediators whose primary aim was "to reconcile the parties concerned." Qadis made rulings only occasionally, and when they did, they "judged according to the law." Litigants followed such judgments voluntarily or made appeals to the Medjeles (Majlis) council, whose qadis and muftis weighed in on controversial questions. In contrast to the hierarchical French appellate system, ultimate legal authority resided in the community of scholars ('ulama'). As the mufti in Algiers explained to him, "The Judge fears only his equals, only scholars like himself, only the Ulama."[36]

31. Spitzer, *French Generation of 1820*; Goldstein, *Post-Revolutionary Self.*

32. Cousin, *Fragments philosophiques*, 415.

33. Ibid., 422.

34. C. H. Paravey, "Rapport à Monsieur le Garde des Sceaux sur l'Organisation judiciaire à Alger," October 3, 1832, AN BB30/616. Emphasis in the original. On liberal accounts of the dey see Sessions, *By Sword and Plow*, 58–59. On the vicissitudes of ideas of Oriental despotism see Pitts, *Boundaries of the International.*

35. See Hoexter, "Qadi, Mufti and Ruler." On translators see Messaoudi, "Renseigner, enseigner."

36. Paravey, "Rapport à Monsieur le Garde des Sceaux," AN BB30/616.

Based on this positive assessment, Paravey recommended that existing insti-tutions be left in place. What he did criticize was their current, unsystematic administration by the French. Given his rigorous philosophical and legal bent, Paravey roundly rejected the military administration's approach to justice. The October 22, 1830, ordinance established an initial basis of judicial organization by recognizing the Maliki qadi and instituting a rabbinic tribunal alongside new French courts. However, by reducing the Hanafi qadi to a mere advisory role, the measure had significantly alienated the city's Turkish elite, many of whom were important mediators for the French. Subsequent efforts to correct these over-sights and straighten out jurisdictional conflicts only exacerbated confusions, creating an ongoing source of local discontent.[37]

Paravey proposed a comprehensive system of separate tribunals for each community for civil matters and misdemeanors. A committed liberal, he delib-erately set aside the private lives of families. As he explained, the local popula-tion would "find it very strange that [the sovereign] would attempt to mix in their private affairs, in their family relations, while visibly completely ignorant of the law that applied to them."[38] He also maintained local law for real property transactions (*droits réels*), even in cases where litigants were French. In cordon-ing the Algerian family off from direct intervention by French state sovereignty, the report did more than simply "preserve" the Algerian family as legal domain. Paravey's account contributed to the production of privatized domesticity—in law, but also in the psychic landscape of jurists and colonists.

Paravey dismissed full legal assimilation as theoretically and practically flawed for family and religious matters. In his view, "our dignity as Sovereigns" did not authorize the French to "impose on the country our judges and our laws," as if "natives have no say and that after all they would benefit." In a telling footnote, he questioned whether a colonial judge could "obtain the authority" or "inspire the necessary confidence to be a conciliator" in applying "Moorish law." How, he wondered, "could he get mixed up in questions of family . . . and that host of questions in which religious law is mixed with civil law"? It fol-lowed that only a qadi would be fit for the task. Mosaic law, meanwhile, would be maintained for matters of marriage, divorce, and inheritance, as "these questions are attached to the social constitution of a people and penetrate all the details, and all the secrets, of private life." He believed that this system would reinforce rather than threaten French authority. In making native judges "our judges," he

37. Khodja, *Le miroir*, 207.
38. Paravey, "Rapport à Monsieur le Garde des Sceaux," AN BB30/616.

argued, "their authority will give homage to our sovereignty because they will be instituted by us." As he explained, "their special jurisdiction will not undermine the unity of political power any more than do commercial tribunals [*tribunaux de commerce*] in France."[39]

Paravey's commitment to multiple jurisdictions nonetheless presumed civilizational hierarchy and legal teleology. He here followed Cousin, whose early lectures on Kant traced a disjuncture between reason's higher law and written law's historical instantiations. In Cousin's Hegelian account, "Saint Liberty" does not "uncover her face all at once; she only lifts her veils successively."[40] Professing similar faith in the progressive work of history, Paravey cautioned the ministry against pursuing assimilationist aspirations all at once, calling instead for "more accommodations, delicacy, and time." While motivated by a "natural and laudable desire to hasten by all means the progress of civilization," such reforms, especially with respect to "certain acts of domestic authority, of paternal or marital power," needed time. Paravey echoed Cousin's feminine allegory of historical progress to illustrate his point. He claimed that Algerian women's veils would "fall by themselves in a few years (if we can believe sensible *Maures*)." By contrast, "If we wanted to tear them away today, they will be tied that much more tightly around their heads."[41]

This liberal legal vision stood in stark contrast to the violent and disorganized tactics of military commanders such as Rovigo. Paravey's ideal of legal evolution, requiring patience and time, was, however, no less fantasmatic. It too presumed that local "religious" law, especially with respect to women and the family, had to be accommodated. In Paravey's estimation, the recognition of local civil law would enhance rather than undermine French sovereignty.

To Colonize or Not to Colonize

Paravey's report was only a blueprint, as the legal form and fate of the ex-regency remained very much in question. In October 1832, the Ministry of War, under the leadership of Maréchal Jean-de-Dieu Soult, took charge of the conquered territory's future, while the military's extralegal actions preoccupied metropolitan political debate. The prospect of establishing a stable system of law played a crucial role in efforts to guarantee the viability of the future colony.

---

39. Ibid.

40. Cousin, *Cours d'histoire de la philosophie morale*, 20–21.

41. Paravey, "Rapport à Monsieur le Garde des Sceaux," AN BB30/616.

Some colonial publicists overtly defended the army's most brutal tactics. In one bellicose pamphlet, P. Carpentier endorsed Rovigo's use of force, mocking Pichon's pretensions to legality. "We proceed," he wrote, "law in hand. We speak of the constitution, we want legality. Well, good God! What law! What legality! A mix of French laws, local customs, circumstantial measures, the amalgamation of which produces a bastard system, which is mortal for creative activity." Dismissing this confused and "bastard" law as deficient, he instead promoted the singularly redemptive power of violence. Praising Rovigo's Egyptian heroism, he proclaimed: "We must tear down, clear away, and rebuild; with a strong will, with a singular will, we must destroy and create."[42] Victor-Arman Hain, a founder of the Colonial Society of Algiers, likewise defended Rovigo's use of ruthless tactics against a "savage" native population, claiming that the extermination of the El Ouffia tribe was not only "justified but necessary."[43] According to his corporealized conception of Algerians' civilizational difference, these "brutes, with their ferocious *mœurs*, who understand no others," could only comprehend "the brutal and vigorous [*nerveuse*] action of force."[44] For Hain, this was a principle of "legitimate defense," and he appealed to the tale of a gruesome murder of a young French girl by two "Kabyles" to make his point. While Pichon claimed that the assault against the victim, a Miss Renaux, was a rare exception, for Hain it explained why "the government should not fear to act energetically against these barbarians."[45]

These pamphleteers celebrated military violence as a precondition of colonial success. In parliament, however, pro-colonial politicians took another tack in defending the military's budget authorization against critics who questioned whether the spending was worthwhile. Rather than overtly embracing violence, they suggested that colonization could be made viable and cost-effective as long as it was based on a rule of law.

The government itself remained hesitant. At parliament's urging, Maréchal Soult convoked a commission to study the ex-regency in July 1833.[46] Its members traveled across the territory, interviewing military and civilian officials as well as Algerian notables. Even sympathetic politicians questioned the Algerian endeavor and sought to resolve the prospective colony's legal status and judicial

---

42. Carpentier, *Alger, M. le Duc Rovigo, et M. Pichon,* 4–5.
43. Hain, *À la Nation, sur Alger,* 21–22.
44. Ibid., 89.
45. Ibid., 91. Pichon, *Alger sous la domination française,* 290.
46. Baron Mounier recommended the appointment of a commission of "disinterested men" on April 19, 1833: *Archives parlémentaires,* ser. 2, vol. 82 (1833), 670.

organization. According to the commission's instructions, the capitulation of July 5, 1830, which was aimed at "the submission rather than the expulsion of the natives," placed "the inhabitants of Algiers" in a "peculiar position." Their legal status had to be clarified.[47]

The parliamentary interventions of Frédéric Gaëtan de La Rochefoucauld highlight the pressing nature of these legal questions. A deputy from the Cher, he took a firm stand against Rovigo's systematic violations of the 1830 treaty. He called on the minister of war "to halt now and for good . . . the barbarous system that has been tested out in Algiers." The massacre and dispossession of the El Ouffia tribe emblematized Rovigo's deviant violence. As La Rochefoucauld sardonically noted, "This is how we have respected the individual liberty guaranteed by the Capitulation." As a liberal Catholic defender of the freedom of conscience, he deplored the destruction of sacred sites, and especially the conversion of the Ketchoua mosque into a cathedral. In his view, these regressive policies made the exercise of religion "as exclusionary and intolerant as it was under the Restoration."[48] A champion of civilian authority, he expressed sympathy for the magistrate Colombon, deploring the jurist's unjust deportation, merely under the suspicion of "a love intrigue that had not even been proven." While his colleagues laughed at the reference, La Rochefoucauld saw it to be a telling example of the military's unbridled power: "Imposing its arbitrary authority on all in Africa, the military can even remove a magistrate from his functions, without any form of trial. And you want to colonize a country?!" La Rochefoucauld wanted to reconcile colonization with the "principles of 1789" and the constitutional legal order of the July Monarchy. The military government had failed to realize these lofty ideals, thereby leaving "our administration in Algiers . . . illegal and despotic, in opposition to our Charter and our laws."[49]

These quandaries about the relationship between military and civilian legal authority weighed on the Soult Commission members as they tried to sort out whether "the necessary regularity, moderation, and stability of the civil administration" could be guaranteed.[50] They set themselves the task of establishing a framework for colonization based on legality, rather than spectacular military force.

---

47. See the official instructions, *Programme des instructions pour la commission spéciale à envoyer en Afrique, 22 juin 1833*, 2. See also Julien, *Histoire de l'Algérie contemporaine*, 106–10; Yacono, "La Régence d'Alger en 1830"; Blais, "Qu'est-ce qu'Alger?"

48. La Rochefoucauld, Procès-verbaux, Chambre, *Archives parlémentaires*, ser. 2, vol. 82 (March 30 to April 20, 1833), 271–72.

49. Ibid., 273. On anticolonial argument see Pitts, "Republicanism, Liberalism, and Empire."

50. *Programme des instructions pour la commission spéciale à envoyer en Afrique, 22 juin 1833*, 4.

A majority of the commission's members supported the territory's "definitive occupation by France." In an effort to clarify the legal status of the conquest as established by the Convention of 1830, they debated its territorial purview and disputed the Ottoman dey's authority at the time of its signing (as a representative "not of indigenous sovereignty, but of a foreign occupying power"). The commission decided to limit the guaranteed protections exclusively to the inhabitants of Algiers.[51] Beyond the question of territorial reach, however, they debated how far allowances for religion should be extended to the domain of law. As we saw in the Colombon Affair, the sense and spatial boundaries of religion, for French officials as well as for Muslim and Jewish inhabitants of the ex-regency, became an explicitly political problem.[52]

For some members of the commission, the treaty's meaning was restricted to "the exercise of religion and respect for mosques." For others, granting religious protection to "institutions and civil laws" was tantamount to renouncing French sovereignty. It seemed inconceivable, in this view, that France would have "given up [aliéné] its right to make laws, a right inseparable from sovereignty." For still another official, guarantees of "the free exercise of religion" necessarily encompassed "laws, institutions, and customs." Paralyzed by these contrasting viewpoints, the commission effectively postponed the question, only agreeing that "the letter" of the convention agreement needed to be observed.[53] The problem of how and where to separate "justice from religion" would require further study.[54]

The commission toured Algiers, interviewing French as well as Muslim and Jewish jurists in September and October, to gather facts on the ground.[55] These interlocutors, French and indigenous alike, expressed deep reservations about extending French law to the former regency's inhabitants.[56] Justin Laurence (Landes), the deputy who had raised the question in the first place, admitted as much in his report on judicial organization. Promoting "the dignity of justice" as well as the "maintenance of French sovereignty," Laurence recommended limiting Muslim tribunals to civil jurisdiction and rabbinical courts to mediation,

---

51. Ibid., 30–31.

52. For a discussion of other controversies see Schley, "Tyranny of Tolerance."

53. *Programme des instructions pour la commission spéciale à envoyer en Afrique, 22 juin 1833*, 32–33.

54. Ibid., 35.

55. Ibid., 134.

56. The jurists interviewed included R. Vincent, Roland de Bussy, and the *procureur du roi* Hautefeuille, as well as Maliki mufti Mustapha ben Kebabti, the rabbinical judge Aron Moatti, and the translator Samuda. See Guénoun, *L'ordonnance du 10 août 1834*, 35.

marriage, and religious disputes. He proposed that all criminal law cases be transferred to French tribunals and, beyond the army's southernmost outposts, to military courts or "*conseils de guerre.*" According to the commission, the recognition of Muslim and Mosaic tribunals appeared to be a "realistic" solution to the territories' legal problem.[57] This appeal to realism bolstered their claim to found the new legal order on a structure of distinct religious communities, each with its own law.

In an effort to address persistent questions about the colony's viability, the commission expanded from eight to nineteen members, including two noted opponents of colonization, Hippolyte Passy (Eure) and Xavier de Sade (Aisne). The new "Commission d'Afrique" held further hearings that called on fierce critics of the military's policy to testify. Among those witnesses, former civil intendant Pichon and his associate, the cosmopolitan notable Hamdan ben Othman Khodja, claimed to counterpose legal fact to the fiction and fantasies of military conquest and occupation.

Pichon's commentary drew on his long career abroad as a diplomat, engineer of the Louisiana Purchase, and eventual ambassador to the United States. He was a strong critic of the military mishandling of Saint-Domingue and more broadly of imperial overreach. He thus argued for a "restrained" approach to Algerian colonization that would remain limited to trade ports along the coast. Opposing extensive settlement, he urged that Algeria was not America. In contrast to the Amerindian population, Algerians had a clear conception of landed property rights, as "farmers and pastoralists" who "occupy and possess the ground." Pichon affirmed that Algerians "see themselves as owners of the land that they occupy."[58] To believe otherwise, he suggested, was to mistake fiction for truth. He had raised similar concerns in an exchange with Rovigo in January 1832, in the midst of the Colombon Affair. "On this question of colonization and the concession of lands," he wrote, "we must manage to distinguish between what is real and practicable from the doomed projects and *fictions* [*romans*] that have, here as in America, created so many victims."[59] For Pichon, these dreams of unoccupied productive land put lives and fortunes at risk.[60]

---

57. *Programme des instructions pour la commission spéciale à envoyer en Afrique, 22 juin 1833*, 162.

58. *Procès-verbaux et rapports de la Commission d'Afrique*, 67–68.

59. Pichon, *Alger sous la domination française*, 88. For the complete exchange, 362–73. And Letter 50, Rovigo to Pichon, February 16, 1832, in Savary, *Correspondance*, 1:163.

60. On the conflict between Pichon and Rovigo see Dumasy, "Propriété foncière, libéralisme économique et gouvernement colonial," 50. On the rhetoric of "illusion" and "fantasy" in the parliamentary debates see Sessions, *By Sword and Plow*, 213.

Pichon's ally Hamdan Khodja also sought to set the record straight in his "historical and statistical account of the Regency." A legally trained former adviser to Hussein Dey, Khodja claimed to give a "faithful rendering" (*un tableau fidèle*) of conditions in Algeria before and after the arrival of the French. Ironically invoking the genre of the mirror of princes, his *Mirror* gave a distinctly unflattering picture of the occupation. France's treatment of the ex-regency appeared as a hypocritical violation of "the liberal principles and advantages that one might have expected from its government."[61] Like many contemporary critics, Khodja invoked liberal principles in order to point up the French government's deviation from them: "We thought that an honorable nation would not violate its treaties, that we would enjoy liberty and that we would be treated with justice."[62] As he explained to the commission, the very opposite came to pass.

According to Khodja, the French had violated the rule of law from the outset of the occupation. The inhabitants of Algiers initially welcomed Louis Philippe and the July Monarchy. Hailing the regime's commitment to liberty and law in the Charter of 1830, they regarded the new king as a dutiful *père de famille* who would "never separate husband from wife and children."[63] When the army's actions violated these liberal principles, the urban elite in Algiers grew disillusioned. Khodja expressed this disappointment with ironic apostrophe: "The extortion of property, the shedding of blood, plunder and crimes, these are the acts that have been accomplished in Algiers!! What a Constitution! What inhuman laws, opposed to all system of peace and equality! What a Charter we have!!!"[64]

The *Mirror*'s liberal rhetoric clearly touched a nerve.[65] Concerned members of the commission pressed Hamdan Khodja to provide more "evidence" for his charges. The Ministry of War itself drafted an internal rejoinder to his criticisms of the French army. Drawn up by none other than Paravey, the memorandum assented to many of Khodja's objections, noting that his "memoir is important; it repeats the warnings that the government has already received and it cannot

---

61. Khodja, *Le miroir*, 38; Temimi, "L'activité de Hamdan Khudja à Paris"; Pitts, "Liberalism and Empire"; Pitts, *Boundaries of the International*, 138–41.

62. Khodja, *Le miroir*, 174.

63. On gendered representation of Louis Philippe see Margadant, "Gender, Vice, and the Political Imaginary"; Surkis, "Carnival Balls and Penal Codes."

64. Khodja, *Le miroir*, 205–7.

65. *Procès-verbaux et rapports de la Commission d'Afrique*, 56. See also *Réfutation de l'ouvrage de sidy Hamdan-Ben-Othman-Khoja*; Khoja, *Réponse à la "Réfutation de l'ouvrage d'Hamdan-Khoja."* And Khodja, *Le miroir*, 265–314. For Khodja's impact on the commissions see Pitts, "Liberalism and Empire," 291.

be neglected." Paravey, who had now moved to a position in the Ministry of War, again called for a legal framework for Algerian rule. In his view, France could not "govern by force without recognizing any rights of the inhabitants." The expulsion of the native population and "their substitution pure and simple by a European population" was both "unjust and extremely costly." He thus urged the government to return "completely to the principle of respect for the Capitulation," and "in a manner convincing to the local population and authorities."[66]

The Ministry of War's response was never published. Nor was it sent to Khodja himself. It nonetheless indicates how his pointed criticisms registered at the highest levels of the government. The commission's final report and ensuing debates in parliament over whether or not to colonize the ex-regency reflected a renewed concern to respect the terms of the 1830 convention, especially regarding its inhabitants' "religion" and "their women."

A Legal Colonization?

The commission's deliberations in 1834 reflected this renewed emphasis on legality. As we have seen, the preliminary Soult Commission had limited the 1830 convention's legal application to Algiers. By 1834, the expanded Commission d'Afrique shifted its position. It would now extend to the territory as a whole. Critics of military occupation, Sade and Passy in particular, emphasized its ironically brutalizing and corrupting effects on the French army. Speaking about the El Ouffia massacre, Sade noted with dismay that "rather than bringing lessons of civilization to this people, we should fear taking lessons in barbarism from them."[67] The commission nonetheless voted 17–2 in favor of colonization. But now even its most fervent advocates admitted that blatant violations of the convention had been a grave mistake.

The report on colonization by the deputy Alexis de La Pinsonnière (Indre et Loire) clearly articulated these new concerns, acknowledging the irony of the French army's recourse to "savage" tactics. He admitted that the military's violence "exceeded the barbarousness of the barbarians we wanted to civilize, and now we complain about not having succeeded! But we were our own worst

---

66. "Analyse et observation sommaire sur le mémoire remis au Ministre le 3 juin 1833 par Sidi Hamdan Bin Othman Khodja," in Temimi, *Recherches et documents d'histoire maghrébine*, 139–40.

67. Sade, Procès-verbaux, Chambre, April 28, 1834, *Archives parlémentaires*, ser. 2, vol. 89, 408–9. On the medical dimension of these concerns about the degenerative effects of the military campaign see Dodman, *What Nostalgia Was*, 151.

enemies in Africa!"[68] He thus sought a different way forward: "The errors of the past," he declared, "are destined to serve as instruction for the future." While his anticolonial colleagues lingered on these harsh facts, La Pinsonnière insisted that they were now "nothing but history, and could no longer be attributed to the current administration."[69]

His report gave a comprehensive list of the government's initial missteps, lamenting in particular the defilement of sacred spaces, including family homes: "We have carelessly profaned temples, tombs, and domestic interiors, that sacred asylum of Muslims."[70] But now it was time to march ahead by replacing brute violence with the more the refined work of law. "We know that the necessities of war are sometimes difficult to resist," La Pinsonnière conceded, "but it is possible to find, in the application of extreme measures, delicate forms, even of justice, that mask what is most odious about them." Covering over atrocity, this "lawfare" would allow war to continue by other means.[71]

La Pinsonnière thus recommended that the French should "always have rectitude [bon droit] on our side." By unnecessarily violating the terms of the convention, the military had "offended beyond measure" those inhabitants who placed "faith in our loyalty and counted on us to bring about better times." In showing disdain for Muslim practice, the army ended up "injuring" the prospective Algerian subject "in all that he holds most dear." Initially claimed by force, French sovereignty in the ex-regency now had to be imposed "decently," which in turn required an adequate system of law.[72] Commission members clearly framed these legalistic efforts as protections to Muslim religious and domestic sentiments.

Deputy Laurence's report outlined the structure of law in more precise terms. Having learned of the "disasters and harms" caused by French actions during the commission's visit to Algiers, he concurred that the French had injured local sensibilities. Before the Chamber, he testified to the emotional reactions of the local qadi and mufti, who "in their expressive language reminded me, with tears in their eyes, of the promises that had been made to them, giving me the documents, the proclamations that were published to reassure them. Next to

---

68. La Pinsonnière, "Rapport sur la Colonisation de l'ex-Régence d'Alger," in Chambre des députés, *Colonisation de l'ex-régence d'Alger*, 9. And Pitts, "Republicanism, Liberalism, and Empire," 278.

69. La Pinsonnière, "Discours de la Pinsonnière, April 29, 1834," in Chambre des députés, *Colonisation de l'ex-régence d'Alger*, 203.

70. La Pinsonnière, "Rapport sur la Colonisation," ibid., 7.

71. On colonial law as "lawfare" see Comaroff, "Colonialism, Culture, and the Law," 306.

72. La Pinsonnière, "Rapport sur la Colonisation," Chambre des députés, *Colonisation de l'ex-régence d'Alger*, 39–40.

these now illusory guarantees, they unfurled their long list of complaints and the betrayals [*manques de foi*] of which they accused the French administration. Sadly, all of these charges were well founded."[73] As for La Pinsonnière, Laurence wanted this past to "shed light on the organization of the present" and "serve as a lesson for the future."[74]

Laurence encouraged settlement, but promised to spare natives from "expulsion" and "extermination." Reversing past practice, he defended native property titles in order to allow colonization to proceed as a legal process. In his view, "Nowhere is possession better founded on more regular titles." He praised qadis for their notarial skills, highlighting "the regularity and clarity of their titles," as well as their knowledge of law, "which they apply with wisdom and intelligence." Respect for their law would, he implied, promote a smooth and orderly transmission of land. As Laurence explained, "If the ground has masters, one can conclude that they can change and that someone who acquires a title will be able to transfer that title in turn." Laurence thus fostered a fantasy of native removal by economic transaction rather than forceful banishment or annihilation. As he explained, "When the Arab or *Maure* finds it impossible to live near us, he will sell and buy further away."[75]

La Pinsonnière made similar propositions, drawing on the example of the United States. He explained that the French "should profit, as have the Americans, from all of the occasions that present themselves to obtain the progressive transfer of their territory for a small bit of gold."[76] Critics of settlement, including Pichon and Passy, had invoked the American case as a negative exemplar of "extermination."[77] La Pinsonnière, by contrast, upheld the no less devastating tactics of expropriation as a positive model. These advocates substituted the tarnished image of Algeria's disorderly and destructive occupation with an idealized plan for legal property exchange. The affirmation of Algerians' property rights meant that the land would be available for purchase, as long as proper legal mechanisms were put into place. Over the course of the next four decades, recurrent efforts to fix Algerian property titles demonstrated the limits of this

73. Laurence, Procès-verbaux, Chambre, April 30, 1834, *Archives parlémentaires*, ser. 2, vol. 89, 622.

74. Ibid., 624.

75. Ibid., 627.

76. La Pinsonnière, "Rapport sur la Colonisation," Chambre des députés, *Colonisation de l'ex-régence d'Alger*, 37.

77. See, for example, Passy's invocation of the "trail of tears." He concluded: "There is no modern colonization that did not result in the natives' expulsion, extermination, or reduction to servitude." In Procès-verbaux, Chambre, May 1, 1834, *Archives parlémentaires*, ser. 2, vol. 89, 646.

fantasy of seamless legal settlement.[78] In 1834, however, these arguments underwrote the July Monarchy's liberal imperial project by granting it an appearance of lawful coherence.

The commission thus claimed that the ex-regency needed a more secure legal foundation. An 1833 law had established parliamentary authority over the "particular laws" of the colonies.[79] Because the ex-regency had not yet become a colony, it did not fall under this law's regulatory ambit. Instead, Algeria's presumptive legal difference from the "old colonies" underwrote political arguments in favor of government by sovereign decree. As the president of the Chamber, André Dupin, a jurist close to Louis Philippe, explained, its population was made up not of citizens, but of legally diverse subjects. The territory's internal diversity rendered a universal law "absurd" and ultimately inapplicable. In his view, laws voted by the parliament could not and should not apply: "When you vote a law for Algiers, for some portion of Africa, for the Bedouin, the Kabyle, the Arab, the inhabitant of this locality, will he be touched by your law? To what extent and up to what point will he be touched? Will you grant him the political rights of the citizen? Probably not. With no fixed territory and no recognized subjects, your legislation cannot apply."[80] Without a claim to popular sovereignty, Algeria would thus be subject to royal as opposed to parliamentary authority. The "legal" protections extended to native inhabitants were thus based on their subordinated status as noncitizens. A royal ordinance of July 22, 1834, annexed the ex-regency to France, placing it under the singular authority of a governor-general. It was at this moment that the colony was legally born.[81]

Within weeks of this official birth, another royal ordinance created the "judicial organization of the French possessions in North Africa." Bringing the ex-regency's legal uncertainty to an end, the new arrangement appeared to "preserve" old jurisdictions. The measure outlined a new system of tribunals to be implemented, including the selection and investiture of magistrates. Following the proposals set forth initially by Paravey and later by Laurence, the legislation of August 10, 1834, "maintained" Muslim tribunals, with "muftis and qadis named and instituted by the King, or in his name, by the Governor" (article 25). It thus made the judges French government officials, albeit of a distinct jurisdiction.

---

78. On the instability in French conceptions of Algerian property and the problem of proof see Grangaud, "Prouver par l'écriture."

79. "Loi concernant l'exercice des droits civils et des droits politiques dans les colonies" and "Loi concernant le régime législative des colonies," April 24, 1833, in *Collection complète des lois*, 33:104–14.

80. Dupin, in Procès-verbaux, Chambre, May 1, 1834, *Archives parlémentaires*, ser. 2, vol. 89, 690.

81. "Ordonnance qui crée le commandement général," in Estoublon and Lefébure, *Code de l'Algérie*, 1:7–8.

The same was true of the rabbis named to Mosaic courts, whose jurisdiction was more restricted than that of the Muslim tribunals, which continued to rule in matters of both civil and criminal law for members of the "Muslim" community (article 38).[82]

The question of how to recognize Muslim faith and practice while simultaneously subjecting them to French oversight would persist long after 1834.[83] Under the regency, the sovereign remained bound by Qur'anic prescription. Its French counterpart, Laurence noted, was not similarly limited.[84] Asserting the prerogative to overturn qadis' judgments, he expanded French authority and influence over the tribunals.[85] Other members of the commission had shown more wariness on this point. "It is necessary to allow the already existing customs [*usages*] to remain in place," one member noted, so as "not to upset the qadis' jurisdiction and follow the Arabs' *mœurs*."[86] Insisting on such differences only underscored a potentially disruptive shift. The 1834 ordinance, by placing Muslim tribunals within a French juridical hierarchy, effectively made "Muslim law" a French law.

As in other colonial contexts, this plural legal structure reified the coherence of native communities, families, and laws.[87] But it did not prevent conflicts over the legal status of persons and property. On the contrary, it gave rise to them. Establishing strict lines of religio-legal community could not accommodate individuals, women in particular, whose desires and actions transgressed those bounds.

Aïcha's Case

On September 2, 1834, mere weeks after the new judicial apparatus had been adopted, a "Moorish woman" named Aïcha bent Mohammed appeared before Alexandre Pierre Cottin, the *commissaire du roi* and acting mayor of Algiers. She declared her solemn intention to convert to Christianity. Cottin questioned her motives. According to an account by the translator Joanny Pharaon, her husband

---

82. "Ordonnance du Roi concernant l'organisation de l'Ordre judiciaire et l'administration de justice dans les Possessions françaises du Nord de l'Afrique, August 10, 1834," in *Bulletin des Lois*, pt. 2, section 1, no. 324 (1834), 123–35.

83. Christelow, *Muslim Law Courts*; Barrière, *Le statut personnel des musulmans*.

84. *Procès-verbaux et rapports de la Commission d'Afrique*, 283.

85. Ibid., 286.

86. The member is not named in the procès-verbaux; see ibid., 305.

87. Cohn, *Colonialism and Its Forms of Knowledge*; Merry, "Law and Colonialism"; Benton, "Colonial Law and Cultural Difference"; Stephens, *Governing Islam*.

had beaten and divorced her after she had made herself too visible to Europeans.[88] Aïcha admitted to Cottin that she had been mistreated, but claimed that the abuse had not inspired her new faith. A divorced woman, she asserted that her husband "no longer has any power over me." Cottin nonetheless sought to dissuade her, insisting that "even if you remain Muslim, you will be no less protected by French authority than if you become Christian." The woman remained adamant, insisting on her heartfelt conviction: "I repeat, I fear nothing. I want to become Christian to be Christian; it is my heart that wants it this way [*c'est mon coeur qui l'exige ainsi*]." Her pleadings apparently persuaded Cottin. In his report to the interim governor-general Théophile Voirol, he recommended that Aïcha be allowed to convert after a few days of considered reflection.[89]

As in the Colombon Affair, controversy over Aïcha's conversion distilled jurisdictional conflicts between civil and military authority as well as between French and Muslim law. Her case further demonstrates how the newly adopted legal order was tested and transformed by the colony's new subjects, including women. Presuming reified religious communities and families, jurists and politicians overlooked the question of conversion. In revealing this blind spot in their fantasy of legal coherence, Aïcha created a quandary that rose to the highest levels of the administration, from the governor-general to the minister of war. While she was a socially marginal subject, her legal status became "symbolically central" to the organization of Algeria's new colonial legal order."[90]

Following the paper trail of Aïcha's case reveals dramatic plot twists, local conflict, administrative incomprehension, and ministerial backtracking, all in a desperate effort to remedy a vexing situation from afar.[91] While based on the presumption of discrete religious communities, official policy on legal and religious status was not clearly worked out in advance. Aïcha's predicament shows how contingency and uncertainty, as much as strategic planning, shaped Algeria's legal order.

As the interim governor-general and other officials soon learned, the legal implications of Aïcha's change in belief quickly became a source of local scandal, provoking, much like the Colombon Affair, strong emotions and visceral reactions. According to a report by Civil Intendant Pierre Genty de Bussy, "the event created a sensation and became the pretext for two or three outbursts that

---

88. J. Pharaon, *De la législation française, musulmane, et juive*, 179.

89. Alexandre Pierre Cottin to Governor General Théophile Voirol, September 3, 1834, SHD 1 H 28.

90. Benton, *Law and Colonial Cultures*, 209.

91. On the incoherencies of colonial administration see Stoler, *Along the Archival Grain*.

reached a fever pitch [*scènes poussées de part et d'autre au dernier degré*]."[92] The incident reignited conflict between civilian and military authorities, as Genty de Bussy blamed Voirol for the furor. As Voirol served in an interim position, his authority was insecure.

Voirol explained to the minister of war that he had urged Cottin to dissuade the woman from her spiritual project.[93] But Aïcha had seemed to justify the conversion by insisting on her personal belief. Voirol thought that to deny her protection would represent an "abdication of authority." In his view, the government, while abstaining from proselytism, had to allow "complete liberty to individual determinations." In his own meeting with her, Voirol concluded that Aïcha "was free in all her actions." At the same time, he noted that in Algeria's judicial organization "religion engendered a kind of nationality."[94] Acting in the name of religious freedom, he felt that he could not stand in her way, even if the legal effects of her action remained unclear. By his own admission, he had granted permission to the abbé Spitz, chaplain of the army's garrison in Algiers, to act as her spiritual adviser.[95] Had Voirol obeyed the law, or had he violated it? If the latter, which law or laws had been broken?

The problem was that Muslim law was *also* French law. After the 1834 ordinance, religio-legal status was an attribute of French sovereignty, and not merely a matter of personal conviction. "Muslim" tribunals were indeed "maintained" for natives, but the governor-general appointed their qadis and muftis "in the name of the King."[96] Once they were appointed by Voirol on September 12, these magistrates had legal authority over all "Muslim" subjects in Algiers.[97] Assuming that individuals would retain allegiance to their confessional communities, the law made no provision for individuals who, like Aïcha, chose to convert.

News of Aïcha's apostasy spread throughout the city, creating legal and social chaos. The recently named Maliki qadi Abdel Aziz wanted to dissuade Aïcha from realizing her plans. According to Voirol, she feared being subjected to the physical punishment of the *bastonnade*, which the French regularly denounced as emblematic of Algerian cruelty. She cried out for help when she was brought

---

92. Genty to Min. of War, September 13, 1834, SHD 1 H 28. J. Pharaon, *De la législation française, musulmane, et juive*, 179–81.

93. Ibid.

94. Voirol to Min. of War, September 11, 1834, in Voirol, *Correspondance*, 787.

95. Voirol to Min. of War, September 11, 1834, ibid., 784. On early debates over Muslim conversion see Francis, "Civilizing Settlers," chap. 1.

96. Ordonnance du Roi concernant l'organisation de l'Ordre judiciaire, August 10, 1834, article 25.

97. Note, September 12, 1834 SHD 1 H 28.

before the qadi.[98] "Freed" by several French military translators, including the Syrian-born priest Jean-Charles Zaccar, Aïcha took refuge in a church.[99] With the help of the abbé Larue, she converted on the spot, hoping, according to Genty, to escape the clutches of her "*juges naturels*."[100]

The newly named Muslim jurists were scandalized. Abdel Aziz threatened to kidnap her and return her to her husband. In a public protest, he closed his tribunal, leaving the local population without their judge and notary. Notables addressed petitions to the Ministry of War in support of the qadi. They explained that, while divorced, Aïcha had violated her prescribed three-month waiting period or *idda*, during which time she remained under the qadi's authority and that of her husband. Citing the qadi, one petition denounced the government for violating the terms of the Convention of 1830, condemning its actions as "tyrannical." Seizing on the legal guarantees granted by the French state to the recently named Muslim justices, it urged that "for everything that touches on our religious law, we cannot tolerate any tyranny." Grasping the political power of claims to religious liberty, Abdel Aziz underscored how "the Sultan of France has promised us, through his representatives, that our religion, our women, our children would be respected." When the government failed to honor its word, he reportedly declared, "I can no longer sit at this tribunal, I cannot consent to see justice scorned."[101] The qadi and the notables who penned these petitions had a clear sense of what the convention's language of religious freedom entailed: Muslim men's authority over women as a legal right.

Claiming that Voirol's decision had done irreparable damage, Intendant Genty registered his complaints with the Ministry of War. "In this one affair," he observed, "the Commander-in-Chief has lost in the eyes of the *Maures* all that he had accomplished in two years of paternalist government. . . . This woman should have been left in the hands of her *juges naturels*; her conversion should not have been so carelessly permitted."[102] In this contest, in contrast to the Colombon Affair, the civil intendant sided with the qadi and the petitioners, while the governor-general appeared to take the side of the woman.

The Ministry of War concurred with the civil intendant. An internal report, again written by Paravey, denounced Voirol's failure to respect the "independence

98. Voirol, *Correspondance*, 785. On the punishment see Lanjuinais, *La bastonnade*, 1.

99. Féraud, *Les interprètes de l'Armée d'Afrique*, 182–84. On political divisions among translators see Messaoudi, "Renseigner, enseigner."

100. Genty to Min. of War, September 13, 1834, SHD 1 H 28.

101. Translation of the "Requête des habitants d'Alger," September 13, 1834, SHD 1 H 28. For other examples of petitions see Schley, "Tyranny of Tolerance," chap. 3.

102. Genty to the Min. of War, September 13, 1834, SHD 1 H 28.

of the Muslim magistrates."[103] The political bind was clear: the young woman's actions, by violating Muslim officials' jurisdiction, also compromised secular legal authority and French rule. In his previous report on the organization of Muslim justice, Paravey had held that "family matters" should remain private and free of French intervention. This principle also informed the policy that he elaborated as legal adviser to the Ministry of War.

Upon arrival in the colony later in the month, the permanent governor-general, Jean-Baptiste Drouet, comte d'Erlon, rectified Voirol's misguided policy. As Paravey's internal report explained, "the administration has other things to do than to offer up commonplaces about religious liberty." The Ministry of War clearly indicated to the governor-general that conversions should be opposed in order to prevent "anything that might trouble order."[104] To justify its volte-face, the ministry cast doubt on the purity of Aïcha's motives. According to rumors detailed in several anonymous letters and hinted at by Genty, the *real* reason that Aïcha wanted to convert was that she was having an affair with a European.[105] Taken in by her claims, Voirol had mistakenly "protected debauchery in the name of the freedom of conscience."[106] This focus on supposed sexual misconduct highlights the vulnerability of Aïcha's claim to freedom. Working in concert with the qadi, the ministry and new governor-general reasserted sexual and legal order. While there is no specific indication of Aïcha's individual fate in the archive, her actions ultimately had significant, if less than emancipatory, effects in that the ministry's decision set a precedent for subsequent policy.

Confused and contradictory missives from all concerned communicated the intensity of emotions provoked by Aïcha's conversion. Forced to sort out dissonant and competing narratives by civil and military authorities as well as local notables, the Ministry of War relied on gender hierarchy to structure and confirm the new legal order. Faced with epistemic confusion, French authorities drew on patriarchal fantasy to enforce women's subordination. The ministry's policy reinforced legal and religious as well as sexual boundaries between communities. Doing so entrenched the legal and religious differences that simultaneously authorized and confounded the Algerian colonial project.

---

103. Min. of War, "Rapport au Ministre le 13 octobre 1834 sur la conversion d'une mauresque à Alger." See also the correspondence based on the report between the minister of war and Governor-General d'Erlon, October 13, 1834, SHD 1 H 30.

104. Min. of War, "Rapport au Ministre le 13 octobre 1834, sur la conversion d'une mauresque à Alger," SHD 1 H 30.

105. Min. of War, "Rapport au Ministre le 13 octobre 1834" mentions "two private letters." See also the "Bulletin analytique," which alludes to a "curieuse lettre d'un arabe racontant l'affaire de la mauresque." And Genty to Min. of War, September 13, 1834, in SHD 1 H 30.

106. Min. of War, "Rapport au Ministre le 13 octobre 1834," SHD 1 H 30.

In the months that followed, more women came forward to convert. The handling of their requests illuminates how gender structured emerging policy. A second woman named Aïcha bent Mohammed (or perhaps it was the same petitioner?) came before Governor-General d'Erlon in February 1835. According to local officials, she was an orphan and prostitute. Claiming that the qadi had imprisoned and beaten her on learning of her intentions, she sought French protection. Seeking to avoid the disorder created by Voirol's earlier efforts, d'Erlon adopted an alternative solution: he sent her to Marseille aboard a government vessel.[107] As in the Colombon Affair, deportation effectively eliminated challenges to the new colony's segmented juridical order. (It was also a policy that Rovigo had adopted for prostitutes who refused to submit to medical surveillance.)[108] In May, yet another woman approached d'Erlon with a conversion request. She wanted to escape her mother-in-law's mistreatment and her father's excessive authority. The governor-general refused to extend protection to her and returned her to her family. "Conversion," he explained, would "in no way absolve her of the obedience she owed her father." Technically free to follow her conscience, she remained subject to her father's law.[109] The Ministry of War endorsed d'Erlon's decisions in both cases. In response to the threat posed by these women's conversions, it reasserted the new order's fragile integrity. When the public prosecutor allowed a *mauresque* widow, suspected of being a prostitute, to appeal a qadi's judgment to the French tribunal, ministerial officials clearly indicated in the margin of the prosecutor's report that "he was wrong."[110] The ministry's policy thus anchored Algerian women in their family and "Muslim" jurisdiction.

While advocates of "religious freedom" came to these women's defense, the ministry's policy firmly endorsed Algerian women's subjection to local law. La Rochefoucauld, who, as we have seen, denounced earlier violations of the 1830 Convention and Rovigo's seemingly arbitrary treatment of Colombon, lamented authorities' treatment of these women. Endorsing Voirol's gesture of protection, La Rochefoucauld granted women confessional autonomy. In his view, "the future prosperity of the colony" would be "founded on conversions."[111] His ideal

---

107. Gov. Gen. to the Min. of War, February 1, 1835, and Minute, Min. of War to d'Erlon, February 27, 1835, SHD 1 H 30.

108. Letter 51, Rovigo to Min. of War, February 17, 1832, in Savary, *Correspondance*, 1:159.

109. D'Erlon to Min. of War, May 14, 1835, SHD 1 H 32.

110. Compte rendu de l'administration de justice, 3rd trimester, 1835–36, in AN BB30/616.

111. La Rochefoucauld-Liancourt, *Note sur l'administration d'Alger*, 27. See also Pellissier de Reynaud, *Annales algériennes*, 2:206. On Catholic conversion and women's autonomy see C. C. Ford, *Divided Houses*.

of a Catholic *mission civilisatrice* would not win out.[112] In an effort to secure French sovereignty and guarantee the stability of the colony's nascent legal order, the Ministry of War's apparently more "secular" model of colonization enforced a patriarchal vision of "Muslim law."[113]

As the decisions taken in these conversion cases indicate, the Ministry of War tried to limit the Catholic Church's meddling in colonization by blocking it from proselytizing to native Algerians. The government wanted to secure a nascent, but still quite precarious, order. French authorities went beyond simply tolerating and "preserving" religious and family power. Authorized by military as well as judicial force, familial power dynamics within Algerian households became instruments and extensions of French rule.

Algeria's early colonial judicial organization did not simply "maintain" the ex-regency's legal system. It sought to grant the colony a more certain legal foundation in order to better govern Algeria's population and its land, securing it for colonization. As Laurence made clear in his parliamentary report, the recognition of "Muslim law" with respect to property and property titles was imagined as a way to peacefully promote settlement, allowing seizure to proceed smoothly rather than violently. This fantasy of easy land transfer also entailed a patriarchal fantasy about the intimate relationship between the family and religion in Muslim as well as French law.

As Aïcha's case makes clear, questions about the legal attributes of both persons and things persisted beyond the moment of the colony's legal "birth." As we will see throughout this book, women's legal status continued to represent a troublesome node of colonial government. These conflicts were embedded in the colony's judicial organization from the outset precisely because it was founded on an uneasy association between Muslim religion and law. Colonial officials imagined that they could appease Muslim men's religious sentiments by enforcing women's legal subordination. As a result, the French administration did not seek to disrupt local patriarchal power, even if some magistrates imagined that they could liberate Algerian women. Few early efforts were made to "assimilate" Algerian natives—either Muslim or Jew—to French civil law. Colonial officials invested military and legal force behind an ideally segregated and gendered juridical system. Jurists' fantasies of liberating and possessing Algerian women sustained rather than undermined these legally entrenched differences.

---

112. Curtis, *Civilizing Habits*; Francis, "Civilizing Settlers."
113. J. W. Scott, *Sex and Secularism*. On women's conversion as a challenge to the state regulation of religion see Mahmood, *Religious Difference in a Secular Age*.

2

POLYGAMY, PUBLIC ORDER, AND PROPERTY

An early draft of the 1834 ordinance on judicial organization sought to reconcile the new plural legal order with the French Civil Code. One proposed article asserted that nothing authorized in Algeria should "contravene the law with respect to public order and good morals" (article 6 of the Civil Code). A marginal annotation highlighted how the legality of polygamy in Muslim and Jewish law violated this idea of "public order." Registering broader concerns about placing limitations on Muslim law, the drafters removed the article from the final version.[1] The polygamy of local law would be preserved alongside the Civil Code and its monogamous ideal. As the Ministry of War explained, a hasty application of "French" law would have decidedly negative effects, because "sovereignty, imposed in this way, will either be nominal or it will be despised."[2] For French jurists, polygamy nonetheless remained a sexualized symbol of native legal difference.

These views predated Algerian colonization. The preparatory documents of the Civil Code clearly marked polygamy as an unnatural, tyrannical custom outside the modern French legal order. In his preliminary discourse on the Code, Jean-Marie Portalis upheld monogamy as a legal principle grounded in nature, which "placed in our own hearts, the rule and limit" on men's otherwise "irresistible penchants." He and the Civil Code's article 147 affirmed that "marriage can only be an engagement of two individuals; as long as one marriage exists, it is not possible to contract a second one."[3] Drawing on Enlightenment anthropologies of "Oriental despotism," Portalis avowed polygamy's existence elsewhere: "The multiplicity of husbands or wives may be authorized in certain climates,

---

1. *Projet d'Ordonnance royale*, art. 34, in AN BB30/616. For the final version see *Bulletin des lois du Royaume de France*, 2ᵉ partie, 1ʳᵉ section, no. 324, 1834.
2. Rapport, Ministère de la Guerre, "Observations sur le projet d'ordonnance royale relative à l'organisation de la Justice en Afrique," in AN BB30/616.
3. "Discours préliminaire," in Portalis, *Discours, rapports et travaux*, 22.

but is legitimate in none; it brings about the servitude of one sex and the despotism of the other." Unnatural and antisocial, polygamy did not, in his view, correspond to "the real needs of man" and "introduced into families a confusion and disorder that soon spreads to the entire social body." Reprising the familiar Orientalist fantasy of the despotic patriarch's deviant sexual excess, Portalis associated plural marriage with the "stupid brutishness of certain at once corrupt and semi-barbarous nations of Asia." In contrast to the practice of these disordered societies, monogamy, he claimed, "was a universal law of all well-governed nations [*nations policées*]."[4] This rejection of polygamy as decadent and primitive nonetheless underwrote women's legal subordination in the "sexual contract" of the Civil Code.[5]

Transgressing natural and positive law, polygamy violated the principles of "public order and good morals [*bonne mœurs*]" enshrined in article 6 of the Civil Code. By forbidding private conventions that violated "the general will," this article upheld a "supreme law" and stood in the way of the "dissolution of the State." The "good morals" that "supplemented good laws" were a hallmark of "well-governed nations."[6] These precepts were supposed to protect the integrity of the Civil Code and French sovereignty, while establishing a civilizational standard of belonging in the "family of nations."[7]

The 1865 law—the *sénatus-consulte*—that established a categorical distinction between French citizens and "indigenous" subjects drew on related arguments indexing civilization to sexual law. Its different categories of legal personhood were tautologically grounded on a distinction between French civil law on the one hand and Qur'anic, customary, and Mosaic personal status law on the other. In order to explain the incompatibility and incommensurability between these legal systems, the measure's advocates pointed to the privileged "rights" of polygamy and divorce in indigenous law as core features of difference. In defending the proposed law before the Senate, the *conseiller d'état* Louis-Hughes Flandin explained that "the full exercise of French citizenship rights is incompatible with the maintenance of Muslim status and its dispositions, which are contrary to our laws and our *mœurs* for marriage, repudiation,

---

4. "Exposé des motifs," ibid., 173–74. On Oriental despotism see Grosrichard, *Sultan's Court*, 114–19; Dobie, *Foreign Bodies*.

5. On the sexual and social contract imagined as a sacrifice of primitive patriarchy and polygamy see Pateman, *Sexual Contract*.

6. "Exposé des motifs," in Portalis, *Discours, rapports et travaux*, 160.

7. Gong, *Standard of "Civilization"*; Lorca, "Universal International Law."

divorce, the status of children."[8] The *sénatus-consulte* established a rule of Algerian difference by outlining the terms and conditions of legal assimilation. French citizenship, French civil law, and indissoluble, monogamous marriage were of a piece.[9]

This projective Orientalist fantasy was a durable facet of French legal and broader cultural imagination. Premised on the timeless and unchanging character of "the Orient," it appeared to resist historical change.[10] Behind this apparently timeless screen, however, the legal, social, and political meanings attributed to polygamy across the nineteenth century were, in fact, multiple and conflicting, especially as France's engagement with Algeria intensified. This chapter traces that change over time. As I show, colonial interests did not exclusively view indigenous polygamy as an expression of religious law. They also linked it to the disposition of property.

In the earliest decades of Algerian colonization, Saint-Simonian-inspired military officers understood polygamy to be an economic institution that could be reformed by social engineering. In debating colonization schemes, military officials, settler advocates, metropolitan publicists, Jewish philanthropists, Muslim notables, and juridical experts alternately denounced or denied polygamy's status as an entrenched cultural practice. The eventual identification of polygamy as an intractable—and intolerable—Qur'anic "right" emerged out of politically charged debates about the place of Algerian natives in the colonial order. This genealogy clarifies how the difference between "French" and "native" law surrounding the family became a linchpin of the Algerian colonial order.

Prior to the collective naturalization of indigenous Jews by the Crémieux Decree in 1870, polygamy was protected in both Muslim and Mosaic personal status law. After that date, polygamy indeed became almost exclusively an attribute of the *indigène musulman*, an emblem of his inassimilable religious and legal difference, which justified exceptional legal treatment and political exclusion.[11]

---

8. Flandrin cited in Estoublon and Lefébure, *Code de l'Algérie*, 1:303.

9. Henry, "La norme et l'imaginaire"; Brett, "Legislating for Inequality"; Blévis, "Les avatars de la citoyenneté"; Saada, *Empire's Children*; Barrière, *Le statut personnel des musulmans*; Merle, "Retour sur le régime de l'indigénat"; Shepard, *Invention of Decolonization*; Yerri, *L'indigène dans le droit colonial*.

10. Said, *Orientalism*. On fantasy and history see J. W. Scott, *Fantasy of Feminist History*. On the historical and literary inversions of the "harem fantasy" see Apter, "Female Trouble in the Colonial Harem."

11. Mosaic law did remain in place for Jews of the Mzab, which was annexed to Algerian territory in 1884. Stein, *Saharan Jews*.

This development was not, however, as inevitable or as coherent as it might seem in retrospect. This chapter restores to view the fragmentary components out of which this politically potent but by no means stable image of Algerian Muslim legal difference was fashioned.

A Familiar Fantasy

Algeria had been associated with polygamy since the Enlightenment, most notably in the writings of Montesquieu.[12] After 1830, Romantic painters such as Eugène Delacroix and Théodore Chassériau depicted mythic harems filled with idle and languorous inhabitants, whose apparently tranquil timelessness occluded the violence and political uncertainty of the conquest.[13] Such fantasies of the unadulterated harem would not, however, survive the brutal reality of colonial penetration intact, as numerous contemporary caricatures of its invasion by French soldiers mockingly made clear.

Citing Delacroix, an 1837 article in the recently founded *La revue africaine* on dancing women indicates a widespread awareness of this fantasy as a cliché. The author offers an "opinion on the harem" based on a spectacle, "a painting of physical pleasure," that he viewed while visiting Algiers in the company of Genty de Bussy.[14] Describing the dream induced by the lascivious dance, the author literalizes a scopophilic and extimate fantasy of "becoming Muslim" as a "sensation [*mouvement*] of pride, an instinctive action which makes you enjoy your superiority. Like a real Muslim, one gives oneself a soul, while refusing one to women."[15] In the thrall of this enjoyment of male domination, he proclaims: "O harem! O harem! There at least you will no longer escape us; your body, your spirit, we will enclose them in a narrow prison. Only there will we calmly enjoy all the happiness that they each give us."[16]

In this account, the sensual dance induced an identification with the Muslim and his law that granted the French observer a sense of mastery despite the

---

12. Montesquieu cites Laugier de Tassy, *Histoire du royaume d'Alger* (1720) in Montesquieu, *Spirit of the Laws*, pt. 3, bk. 16, chap. 6, "On polygamy itself," 268. See also Grosrichard, *Sultan's Court*.

13. Grigsby, "Orients and Colonies." Also, "*Women of Algiers*" in Porterfield, *Allure of Empire*, 117–41. For a later period see Alloula, *Colonial Harem*.

14. Ch. de L., "Danses maures—Opinion sur les harems," 61, 63. For contemporary accounts see Duchesne, *De la prostitution dans la ville d'Alger*, 22–34; Bertherand, *Médecine et hygiène des arabes*. See also the invaluable history, Taraud, *La prostitution coloniale*.

15. Ch. de L., "Danses maures—Opinion sur les harems," 641.

16. Ibid., 68.

tenuousness of colonial domination. Its ethnographic pretext cast dancing as an expression of local culture, its "relations between men and women," and hence an index of their "morality and legislation."[17] Travelogues, in turn, reproduced this cliché of the *mauresque* dancer, creating a tourist market for women who worked as dancers-cum-prostitutes throughout the colony. An entry on "L'algérien français" in one famous July Monarchy tableau depicts this bespangled figure, writhing before an excited crowd.[18]

Moral condemnation was the flip side of this eroticized compensatory fantasy.[19] Familiar denunciations of polygamy's political and economic vices dovetailed with religious critiques. An overtly Catholic perspective animated contributors to the *Revue de l'Orient*, a journal that promoted a French and Christian perspective on the "Eastern Question" in the 1840s. The *Revue*'s sponsor, the Société orientale, focused on religious matters, and especially on cataloging the effects of Islam on "Oriental civilization." Its program proposed to investigate polygamy "as an obstacle to civilization." The authors highlighted "its effect on the family and society," and they worried that divorce in Europe might have "consequences analogous to those of polygamy."[20] Family matters were at the heart of this Catholic politico-religious vision.

Théodore Fortin d'Ivry, an advocate of colonial settlement, laid out the content of this critique in detail. In what became a familiar colonial trope, Fortin condemned how Islam "justifies instincts and legalizes the most atrocious fantasies and the most revolting passions."[21] Viewed as a corporealized rather than properly spiritual religion, Islam was assumed to promote "men's capacity [*faculté*] to develop his sensual appetites, and the consecration of these appetites by doctrine."[22] Polygamy epitomized this sensualism; the "multiplicity of women, their inferiority, and men's near absolute freedom over them" constituted Islam's lure and lore.[23]

In the same journal ten years later, another author, a sub-prefect in the newly created department of Constantine, André Pierre Charles Lamouroux,

---

17. Ibid., 57.

18. Mornand, "L'algérien français," 207. See also Duchesne, *De la prostitution dans la ville d'Alger*, 87–90. And Lazreg, *Eloquence of Silence*, 29–33.

19. See, for example, Eusèbe de Salle, "Mémoire sur la polygamie musulmane," *Journal des économistes*, 1842.

20. See "Actes de la Société orientale," *Revue de l'Orient* 1 (1843): 223–25.

21. Fortin d'Ivry, "Orient et Occident," *Revue de l'Orient* 4 (1844): 211.

22. Ibid., 212.

23. Ibid., 221. He goes on to list numerous citations from the Qur'an that are intended to prove this argument.

argued that the French should abolish polygamy altogether in order to eliminate antagonism between Christians and Muslims. For Lamouroux, the advantages were numerous: poor men would have ample opportunities to marry;
women and children's lives would improve; and the temptation of sodomy
would be eliminated. These reforms would, in turn, benefit French domination
and the security of the country. Extending French civil law throughout
the colony would create legal uniformity and bring settler and Muslim populations closer together. But his closing paragraph also hints at another motivation.
Abolishing polygamy would, he claimed, stop Europeans from "allowing themselves to be seduced by Muslim doctrines, which are largely given over to sensuality."[24] The prospect of polygamy, in other words, might tempt European
men into converting.

This brief survey indicates the prevalence of the projective fantasies of Muslim
sensuality and decadence that bolstered European claims to cultural superiority
and domination, at once desiring and fearing the seductions of polygamy. But
they were by no means universal, especially among those who put French domination into practice. The French military men responsible for implementing
colonial government in the colony's newly established Arab Bureaus (*bureaux
arabes*) adopted an apparently less moralizing perspective—one that did not pre-
sume the immediate extension of civilian colonization and with it French law.
Initially created in 1837 and formalized in 1844, the Directorate of Arab Affairs
was under the authority of the governor-general, with virtually no civilian oversight. It relied on extensive intelligence-gathering measures, including detailed
studies of indigenous culture, to secure the military's control. Placed within a
bureaucratic hierarchy, military officers were appointed to positions at the head
of offices located in each of the territory's provinces (Alger, Oran, Constantine) as
well as at intermediate-level "subdivisions" and smaller "circles." They observed
the local population and regularly filed extensive reports that traveled up the
chain of command.[25] Army officers' claims to expertise served, in turn, to authorize military rather than civilian control over colonization. Their studies of subject tribes and towns notably downplayed cultural and legal antagonism, even as
their writings perpetuated stereotypes of Algerian difference. An analysis of their
accounts of polygamy complicates a monolithic conception of how sexual and
cultural difference informed early debates over Algerian colonization.

---

24. Lamouroux, "De la polygamie en Algérie," *Revue de l'Orient* 10 (1851): 44. Lamouroux eventually served as a *conseiller* in Philippeville, but his measure was never adopted.

25. Abi-Mershed, *Apostles of Modernity*, 76–84.

Similar Subjects

Administrators in Algeria immediately confronted the problem of how to "harmonize" French laws with local ones.[26] As we saw in the last chapter, the judicial organization of 1834 established distinct frameworks of law for civil matters.[27] While French penal law was territorialized on February 28, 1841, a September 26, 1842, ordinance maintained "religious law" for the "civil status" matters of natives, both Muslim and Jewish. In Muslim law courts, government-appointed qadis and muftis were responsible for civil and commercial affairs "between Muslims" (article 31). This legislation did, however, abolish rabbinic tribunals. While Mosaic law still applied, rabbis no longer had "any jurisdiction over their coreligionists" (article 32). They were reduced to a consultative role regarding questions of "civil status, marriage, and repudiation" (article 49). The same ordinance also maintained military officials' discretionary disciplinary powers in the territories that they administered, while granting "French" and "European" inhabitants a limited right of judicial appeal. No such appeal was open to those who belonged to the legal category of *indigènes* or that of "non-European" foreigner (article 43).[28]

This policy of multiple jurisdictions was entrenched by the formal establishment in 1844 of the system of Arab Bureaus, which administered much of the newly conquered territory in the first decades of French rule. Relying as they did on native chiefs and native justice to maintain their control, the military men who assumed these roles adopted a tactical attitude toward Muslim law. Written at the behest of Governor-General Thomas Robert Bugeaud, the official government "handbook" for these officers on "the current state of Arab society" outlined this orientation. The preface explained that because the Qur'an linked religious and civil law, it would "always be difficult to substitute an entirely French system of administration for one developed by habits, *mœurs*, and beliefs in Africa without profoundly disturbing the population."[29] As the instructions made clear, the guarantee of justice remained reliant on the expertise of local qadis. From the perspective of the Arab Bureaus, native society suffered less from an excess of Islamic law than from its uneven and incomplete application. It was accordingly seen not as a source of decadence, but as a font of native social renewal.[30]

---

26. J. Pharaon, *De la législation française, musulmane, et juive*, iv.

27. *Exposé de l'état actuel de la société arabe*.

28. "Ordonnance sur l'organisation de la justice en Algérie (26 septembre 1842)," in Estoublon and Lefébure, *Code de l'Algérie*, 1:22–30.

29. *Exposé de l'état actuel de la société arabe*, v. See also Lorcin, *Imperial Identities*, 54.

30. Brett, "Legislating for Inequality," 445–61; Jean-Loup Amselle, *Affirmative Exclusion*.

This pragmatic attitude was borne out in Arab Bureau officers' published writings. Given their schemes for radically transforming rural tribes' nomadic ways of life, these administrators often emphasized the economic rather than religious bases of polygamy and generally downplayed "Islamic law" as a source of women's suffering. This approach carried all the hallmarks of their training at the elite military engineering academy, the *École polytechnique*, which has been so well analyzed by Osama Abi-Mershed and Patricia Lorcin.[31] The Arab Bureau "intellectual" Charles Richard was, on this count, a case in point. When he was not actually testing out new settlement schemes in the district of his Arab Bureau of Orléansville (Chlef), he devoted his time and energy to planning native reform by penning a number of well-known pamphlets.[32]

According to Richard, the colony's subjects embodied moral disarray, as "three million souls living in the confusion of all imaginable abominations, an orgy of all known immoralities, from those of Sodom to those of [the bandit] Mandrin."[33] He predictably castigated polygamy as "the most shameful immorality existing under the cover of legality."[34] Richard's approach to native government nonetheless suggested that Muslim law, properly interpreted, could operate in the service of French domination. He detailed Qur'anic provisions protecting married women's property and curbing the tyranny of fathers and husbands. For Richard, the French should awaken Muslim women to the rights outlined for them in the Qur'an: "No longer beaten as a beast of burden, her condition will improve in her own eyes; astonished to have rights, she will dream of claiming them in full; she will want to reign alone in the tent, and will be pleasantly surprised to learn, once again from us, that the law allows her to do so and that she can stamp out the polygamy, which is her most cruel enemy."[35] Richard suggested that the administration of native Muslim justice under proper French authority would bring about social and moral reform. French rule, he claimed, "will improve *mœurs* and morality with the aid of the intelligent interpretation of Muslim law itself; it will stamp out old barbarous customs, and polygamy in particular, with the help of that law."[36]

Richard opposed the application of French law to Algeria's subject populations on both moral and practical grounds. Polygamy theoretically violated

---

31. Abi-Mershed, *Apostles of Modernity*. Lorcin, *Imperial Identities*, 99–117.
32. Yacono, *Les bureaux arabes*, 136–45.
33. Richard, *De la civilisation du peuple arabe*, 7.
34. Richard, *Du gouvernement arabe*, 53.
35. Ibid., 56.
36. Richard, *De la civilisation du peuple arabe*, 29.

the territoriality of French penal law, most pointedly its article 340, which out-lawed bigamy. But the prosecution of bigamy would, in his view, test the lim-ited resources of the French administration, especially in isolated Arab Bureaus. As in discussions of Algeria's original judicial organization, polygamy served as a linchpin in Richard's case. It emblematized the impossible legal conflict that would arise from any attempt to territorialize French civil law.[37] As that which had to be reformed and yet could not be legally abolished, polygamy thus under-lined the necessity of "leaving the Arab people its Muslim law, while submitting it to intelligent surveillance."[38] The Arab Bureau system asserted its legitimacy by claiming to ensure this regular surveillance.

This regulatory principle underwrote the Arab Bureau system and its con-tinued application in territories that were turned over to civil rule. As Ferdinand Lapasset, an Arab Bureau chief at Ténès, explained in his 1850 brief for the institution, "Far be it from us to apply our ideas and our French form. . . . It is impossible to straighten a tree, which is twisted and already thick; too much force would break it. We should follow the judicial forms and customs which are already in place and straighten only that which is too egregious [mauvais]."[39] Albert Javary, a captain in the Zouaves, likewise explained that "civilizing a peo-ple does not mean leading them to no longer have any religion, to no longer be held back by any moral limit."[40] Preserving "religion" was, in other words, a strategy of military administration.

Army officer Henri Pellissier de Reynaud, who headed the early Arab Bureau of Algiers in 1833 and 1834, justified this approach to Muslim law by arguing that "Arab" husbands were "not worse than others."[41] In his 1854 *Mémoire sur les mœurs et les institutions sociales des populations indigènes du nord de l'Afrique*, Pellissier adopted an apparent universalism: "Humanity is one; the differences that can be seen among the different societies that make them up are more apparent than real; while forms vary, the foundation is always the same."[42] He disputed painters' fantasmatic images of Muslim women "as piled up in great number in a harem, waiting, with the abnegation of a prostitute, for their hus-bands to throw them a sign." Polygamy, he argued, while "tolerated by the law, which even restricts it to four women," was "far from taken advantage of by everyone." Algerian women were not mere "beasts of burden." As he sardonically

---

37. Richard, *Du gouvernement arabe*, 77.
38. Ibid., 81.
39. Lapasset, *Aperçu sur l'organisation des indigènes*, 32.
40. Javary, *Études sur le gouvernement militaire*, 151.
41. Pellissier de Reynaud, *Annales algériennes*, 3:456.
42. Ibid., 3:426.

commented, "It is not as if the wives of our peasants and workers pass their lives in the lap of luxury."[43] In a subsequent essay, Pellissier suggested that Muslim polygamy compared favorably to the "plurality of women" in the Christian world, which was "less decent and more productive [*féconde*] of disorders."[44] Viewed from this perspective, polygamy could curtail adultery and hence serve public and familial order rather than disrupting it.

This relativism illuminates military officials' endorsement of Muslim law courts' autonomy in 1854, when a decree removed qadis' decisions from French appellate oversight. For army officers, maintaining separate jurisdictions avoided unnecessary confusion and sped the progress of colonization. Advocates of civilian settlement disagreed. Increasingly vocal in their criticism of the Arab Bureaus, they sought to extend French civil jurisdiction and scale back military control. Given the professional interests at stake, civilian magistrates lent settlers their support.[45] In this contest, the moral evaluation of Arab Bureau heads was linked to that of the Muslim law whose "independence" they sought to preserve.

Chafing against the military resistance to free settlement, civilians contested the army's fitness to carry out large-scale colonization. In making their case for "European" expansion, settler advocates once again mobilized a rhetoric of the rule of law against the army's rule of force. They heaped ridicule on utopian projects of military colonization, of turning soldiers into farmers, and they charged officers who headed up Arab Bureaus with violent excess, corruption, and moral disarray.[46] The 1856 trial of Captain Auguste Doineau, head of the Arab Bureau of Tlemcen, for murder and corruption encapsulated this crisis in the moral authority of the military. By bringing public attention to the purportedly illegal methods and rapacious habits of military rule, it provided a perfect occasion for civilian magistrates to expand their influence. Jules Favre, an ardently republican lawyer and politician, spearheaded the attack. He charged the army captain with having fallen prey to the vices of Oriental rule, with behaving as a "sultan" and

---

43. Ibid., 3:440–41.

44. Ibid., 3:500–501.

45. "Décret portant organisation de la justice musulmane (1 octobre 1854)," in Estoublon and Lefébure, *Code de l'Algérie*, 1:173–78. See also Christelow, *Muslim Law Courts*, and Brett, "Legislating for Inequality in Algeria," 443–51. Brett describes the adoption of the 1854 legislation as a combination of "cultural perception, practical advantage, moral duty and legal commitment" to the protection of Islamic law in civil matters (445).

46. See, for example, Feuillide's mocking account of the military colonies: Capo de Feuillide [Jean Gabriel Cappot], *L'Algérie française*, 34–41; and C. Duvernois, *L'Algérie ce qu'elle est*, 248. On the longer history of this conflict see Sessions, *By Sword and Plow*.

becoming "inebriated with power," hence wanting to "perpetuate the pleasures and profits of domination."[47]

In answer to such charges of violence and mismanagement, Arab Bureau officer Ferdinand Hugonnet's memoirs, published in 1858, depicted military officials as preoccupied with questions of justice, at once uniquely fit to adjudicate native conflicts and to carry out their reform. Hugonnet aimed to bolster his argument by correcting "current opinion" about Muslim women. While depicting Muslim "fanaticism" as an obstacle to civilizing progress, he disputed "current opinion in Europe with respect to the Muslim woman, which is based on information given in the Qur'an granting men the right to have four legal wives." For Hugonnet, oft-cited stories of the "harems of great oriental lords" and the figuration of women as a mere instrument of men's sensual needs contributed to these misconceptions.[48] He instead assumed a position of knowledgeable detachment and expertise, over and above the inflamed romantic imaginations of artists and armchair tourists.

Like Richard, Hugonnet viewed polygamy as a sign of "a truly inferior social state."[49] And he attacked the "plurality of women" as the "greatest vice" and "radical defect" of native society. He nonetheless attributed its persistence not to "Islamic law" or even to "sensual tastes" (although he did mention them in passing), but rather to material exigency: the need for multiple women's labor "under the tent." This economic interpretation of polygamy in turn shaped his reformist vision. He claimed that the material progress sponsored by the Arab Bureaus, such as the introduction of grain mills and bakeries, would eliminate the need for so many women's hands. Like many Arab Bureau heads, he hoped public works would tie nomadic native tribes to the land and inspire loyalty to French rule. The happy result, according to Hugonnet, would be that the "farmer will realize that one woman will suffice."[50]

The Saint-Simonian historian, librarian, and archaeologist Louis Adrien Berbrugger made similar arguments in the *Revue africaine*, the journal of his Société archéologique et historique d'Algérie. As Patricia Lorcin has shown, he and the *Revue* more generally helped to construct the "Kabyle myth," or myth of

---

47. Armand Fouquier, "Le Capitaine Doineau." Also, Delayen, *Les deux affaires du capitaine Doineau*. On the competing interests at work in the case see Albert de Broglie, *Une réforme administrative en Afrique*, 135–39. On Favre, republicanism, and the *bureaux arabes* see Rey-Goldzeiguer, *Le royaume arabe*, 113; Abi-Mershed, *Apostles of Modernity*, 160–62; Bowler, "'It Is Not in a Day.'"
48. Hugonnet, *Souvenirs d'un chef de Bureau arabe*, 91.
49. Ibid., 96.
50. Ibid., 117.

Berber assimilability, that rested on accounts of their difference from tribal and nomadic Arabs.[51] In this colonial anthropology, Berbers were depicted as sedentary, domestic, democratic, agrarian, and even as ancient Christians—hence closer to the French.[52] An article devoted to "Muslim polygamy" elaborated on this distinction by underscoring the relationship between polygamy and the nomadic existence of Arabs. Drawing out the connection, Berbrugger reported a conversation that he mediated between "a European woman" who denounced the "vile custom" of polygamy and an Arab chief, who responded that she had no idea what "a nomadic household is like." The chief wagered that, given the labor involved, she would have "no repugnance in being joined by three legal companions, and might even regret that her husband could not have any more." While Berbrugger assumed men's universal desire for polygamy as "an effect of original sin," his story countered a myth of a timeless or even specifically "Muslim polygamy." He instead claimed that "despite the legal means and the innate penchant that men have for polygamy," Muslims turned to it only when it was economically feasible. According to this civilizing narrative, a stable home, the division of labor, and the development of monogamous domesticity were of a piece. In attempting to understand polygamy's "fatal causes and the means of destroying them," Berbrugger, like Hugonnet, sought to engineer an "economic" solution to it. "Even the nomad," he wrote, "when he settles in a town, turns monogamous, and often remains single, because being very calculating, he sees in the tally of four simultaneous households an excess of cost and bother, which he holds in horror."[53] While Berbrugger's article supposedly answered distorted fiction with anthropological fact, it was no less of a fantasy, one that was based on the social and economic engineering of Algerian households and families.

This story helped military officers to elaborate a counter-myth that offset images of the "Arab woman" as odalisque on the one hand, and beast of burden on the other. Eugène Daumas, the head of the Directorate of Arab Affairs under Bugeaud, also recounted it in his posthumously published *La femme arabe*.[54] Daumas, who served as an Arab Bureau head before being promoted to general, proposed to tear away the proverbial "veil" that shielded Arab women's lives. His rhetoric thus played on the trope of sexual revelation, even as he claimed to

---

51. On Berbrugger and *La Revue africaine* see Lorcin, *Imperial Identities*, 141–43. On Saint-Simonians and colonization see Abi-Mershed, *Apostles of Modernity*; Pilbeam, *Saint-Simonians in Nineteenth-Century France*; Marçot, "Les premiers socialistes français," and *Comment est née l'Algérie française*.

52. For a discussion of this mythology see Lorcin, *Imperial Identities*, 65–67.

53. Berbrugger, "La polygamie musulmane," 256–57.

54. Daumas, *La femme arabe*, 20–21.

dispense with overheated fictions. Adopting a posture of impartiality, he claimed to be fighting "reciprocal prejudices" between French and Arab in order to promote their reconciliation or "rapprochement."[55]

This model of harmony downplayed religious and racial enmity, despite the army's ongoing repression of resistance to French rule.[56] Sidelining conflict, it appears as powerful compensatory fantasy. The harmonious ideal was grounded in a revisionist assessment of the "Arab" family and prospects for its reform. According to Daumas, the differences between classes of Arab women resembled that between "our rich women and poor *paysannes* of our countryside."[57] Their suffering was the product of ameliorable economic conditions, not tyrannical and unchanging Islamic law. While unscrupulous fathers might take advantage of their daughters, and husbands their wives, the qadi was for Daumas a protector of women's well-defined rights. In his concluding remarks, Daumas thus praised the Prophet Muhammad for introducing progressive sexual reform by regularizing marriage and placing limits on polygamy and repudiation. In doing so, according to Daumas, "he achieved great progress. Creating what did not exist before him, he gave his people marriage and constituted the family."[58] The military officers of the Arab Bureaus imagined themselves as capable of bringing about analogous reform by drawing upon, rather than rejecting, "Muslim law."

Unsettling Muslim Law

Civilian settlers and their advocates, by contrast, pointed to polygamy as a symptom of the failure of the Arab Bureaus—and more generally of military colonial policy. In their view, Algeria's divided territory and distinct jurisdictions "isolated" Arab populations and worked against colonial integration. In an effort to expand opportunities for colonization, settler advocates pushed for "free" colonization by Europeans and "legal assimilation," which is to say a uniform application of a "common law," especially as it related to questions of property. An 1851 land law legitimated state seizures of Algerian property, while declaring tribal lands inalienable and forbidding land sales in military territory. To the consternation of civilian settlers, the law made individual land purchase difficult. In their efforts to expand the purview of French civil law, they, too, addressed the

55. Ibid., 2.
56. Clancy-Smith, *Rebel and Saint*, "La Femme Arabe," and "Islam, Gender, and Identities."
57. Daumas, *La femme arabe*, 25, 141.
58. Ibid., 53.

apparent legal anomaly of polygamy. It thus became a crucial node in debates over the place of Muslims in the colonial legal order.

Settler advocates were increasingly optimistic about achieving reform when Napoléon III instituted a civilian-led Ministry of Algeria headed by his cousin Prince Jérôme in 1858. Rather than resolving their differences, however, the creation of the ministry exacerbated them, intensifying conflicts between defenders and critics of military rule.[59] There was no more vocal advocate for the "liberal" settler position than the ambitious young publicist and prolific pamphleteer Clément Duvernois. Published in the wake of the Doineau affair, his writings insistently argued against the "special" military administration of Algeria and its exceptional legal regime. "Religious differences" did not, in his view, necessitate "different administrations." Positioning himself as a consummate patriot even as he assumed an oppositional stance, he urged: "Algeria is either French or it is not; if it is not French, then we should have nothing to do with it; if it is French, all the populations which inhabit it should respect our laws or leave. We should respect Muslim faith, like we do that of the Israelites, nothing more."[60] Duvernois was confident that a separation of the civil and religious aspects of Qur'anic law would be possible, along lines similar to that pursued by French Jews after the Revolution and Napoléon's Grand Sanhedrin. In this account, the French Israélite came to exemplify an idealized separation between private faith and civil law.[61]

Against the military's central planning, settlers' liberalism applied to land and family law alike. In his reform-minded pamphlets, Duvernois invoked polygamy as an apparent obstacle to Algeria's legal uniformity only to explain it away. Not unlike his military adversaries, he saw such marital arrangements to be primarily economic rather than sexual or "sensual." "Tolerated" rather than "commanded" by the Qur'an, it was also not, he argued, a core religious principle.[62] In his view, polygamy could not serve as a pretext for separating civilian and military authority or French and Muslim jurisdictions.[63] In keeping with his liberal vision, he proposed that civil marriage be suppressed in order to allow "the Arab to marry two or three times if that is what he desires." This was, he admitted, a rather radical solution, but it carried further advantages. Settlers from diverse backgrounds

59. Moulis, "Le Ministère de l'Algérie."

60. C. Duvernois, L'Algérie ce qu'elle est, 252, 53. See also Murray-Miller, "Imagining the Trans-Mediterranean Republic."

61. See Schreier, "Napoléon's Long Shadow," and Arabs of the Jewish Faith.

62. C. Duvernois, L'Algérie ce qu'elle est, 101, 254.

63. C. Duvernois, L'Akhbar, 11.

could also marry according to their own national laws. In doing away with oppressive military rule, Algeria would, he proclaimed, finally become "a land of liberty, the refuge of all those who love to breathe freely."[64] Duvernois further argued that increased European settlement and "industry" in "Arab territory" would reduce women's labor, hence eliminating polygamy's economic causes. The military and settler positions coincided on this point, but remained opposed in their projected solutions.

Critics of Napoléon III, such as Jean-Gabriel Cappot de Feuillide, depicted the persistence of polygamy as a symptom of despotism. In his view, the Arab Bureaus' effective separation of Arabs and Europeans artificially reinforced differences.[65] Feuillide instead advocated legal assimilation—the universal application of French law—as an "immediate agent of Franco-Arab fusion." His claims were manifestly republican: "Where there is unity of law, there are equal rights; where this equality reigns, it matters little if there are diverse races: there will soon be a single nation."[66] "Israélites" again provided a model. As he explained, "The Muslim's inner being [for intérieur] will remain in submission to the Qur'an, just as the Israelite's is to the Bible; but as in his case, the Muslim will be submitted to French law for his external being."[67] According to this secularizing template, the inner religious self would be cleaved from legal personality. Dismantling Arab tribes, he argued, would meanwhile promote private property and, by reducing polygamy, encourage intermixing—including marriages—with "Europeans." In this fantasy, women would "complete Franco-Arab fusion."[68]

Similar to these advocates of civilian settlement, French magistrates criticized the system of divided jurisdictions and dangerous independence of qadis under the 1854 law on judicial organization. In the wake of a series of corruption scandals, jurists pressed for more French appellate oversight of Muslim law.[69] The contrast between military and civilian positions was most extreme in Oran, the seat of the worst scandals involving the independent Muslim judiciary. At one end was the head of the division of Oran, General Jean Louis Marie Ladislas Walsin-Esterhazy, who argued forcefully against extending civil administration and law by promoting the reformist potential of Muslim law, which in his view

---

64. C. Duvernois, *La réorganisation de l'Algérie*, 14.
65. Feuillide, *L'Algérie française*, 75.
66. Ibid., 248.
67. Ibid., 250.
68. Ibid., 246.
69. See Secretary General to Minister, "Résumé des rapports de généraux et des Préfets, du Premier Président et du Procureur Général sur la reorganisation de la Justice Musulmane," in ANOM 17 H 2. Christelow, *Muslim Law Courts*, 164–66; Moulis, "Le Ministère de l'Algérie," 234–45.

FIGURE 5 / Félix-Jacques-Antoine Moulin, *Midjeles [Majlis], Tribunal supérieur musulman (Tlemcen)*, from *L'Algérie photographiée: Province d'Oran* (1856–1857). Bibliothèque nationale de France.

"offered, to anyone who knows how to interpret it, precious texts for the amelioration of Muslim society." He regarded it as "the most useful tool for bringing about the progress of these masses toward our civilization."[70] By contrast, the prefect of Oran wanted to do away with the Muslim appellate council, the Majlis, entirely, replacing it with a French tribunal.[71] As depicted in a contemporary photograph by Félix Moulin, these councils appeared to operate independently of French oversight or intervention.

The judicial reform adopted in 1859 made concessions to these advocates of civilian rule. Drawn up by Jêrome's replacement, Prosper Chasseloup-Loubat, the ministry's report denounced how the "retrograde" disjuncture between French and Muslim jurisdictions under the 1854 decree created "yet another obstacle against the assimilation of the two populations."[72] By reinstituting French

70. Gen. Com. d'Oran to Minister, August 11, 1859, in ANOM 17 H 2.
71. Secretary General to Minister, "Résumé des rapports," in ANOM 17 H 2.
72. "Rapport à l'empereur sur le décret qui organise la justice musulmane (31 décembre 1859)," in Estoublon and Lefébure, *Code de l'Algérie*, 1:231.

appellate oversight of Muslim courts, the 1859 reform curbed their autonomy, while also maintaining their separation from French civil jurisdiction. In these fraught debates about Algeria's legal organization, "polygamy" increasingly symbolized how and whether "Muslims" fit into the categories of French law.

Property and Propriety

This flurry of reformist activity renewed conflicts over France's imperial philosophy and strategy, conflicts that refracted contradictory tendencies of the Second Empire itself: between centralization and decentralization; authoritarianism and liberalism; clericalism and anticlericalism. With the suppression of the Ministry of Algeria in 1860, Napoléon III returned Algeria's government to military hands while elaborating a new, apparently conciliatory policy of the "Arab Kingdom." Drawing on the assistance of advisers such as Ismayl Urbain, Ferdinand Lepasset, and Frédéric Lacroix, he developed new policies that defined and delimited the extent of indigenous rights, while supposedly securing "Arabs" from the rapacious designs of civilian settlers. After traveling to Algeria in 1861 and 1865, he initiated two major legislative reforms, the *sénatus-consultes* of 1863 and 1865. Together these laws established a framework for the government of Algerian property and personhood. Advocates of civilian settlement criticized these legal frameworks because they maintained centralized state control over the legal status of land and its acquisition. The problem of polygamy continued to inform these debates over Algeria's "legal assimilation."

The Saint-Simonian intellectual Urbain was one of Napoléon's closest advisers on the Algerian question. After traveling to Egypt in 1833 with Prosper Enfantin, Urbain had converted to Islam and married a Muslim woman.[73] Committed to defusing the "Eastern Question," he was a longtime advocate of tolerance between Christians and Muslims.[74] In Algeria, he defended the native population against aggressive claims by settlers, most famously in a pseudonymous pamphlet, "Algeria for the Algerians." Written under the name Georges Voisin in 1861, it took distance from the former Ministry of Algeria's pro-settler policies, including the 1859 justice reform.[75] His intervention spurred a pamphlet

---

73. A. Levallois, *Les écrits autobiographiques d'Ismayl Urbain*, 38. M. Levallois, *Ismaÿl Urbain*.

74. See Urbain, "Chrétiens et musulmans, Français et Algériens," *Revue de l'Orient*, ser. 2, vol. 2 (1847): 351–59.

75. Voisin, *L'Algérie pour les algériens*, 58.

war between advocates and critics of Napoléon's policies that continued over the course of the decade.[76]

In contrast to "indigenophiles" such as Urbain, settler advocates like Clément Duvernois argued for a "common law" (*droit commun*) in Algeria. Their rhetoric of postrevolutionary legality aimed to abolish the "feudal" privilege that, in their view, was maintained by Algeria's exceptional legal regime. In its place, they sought "the application to Arab society of the principles of 1789; rights of property, the abolition of *la dîme* and *la corvée*; the abolition of exceptional jurisdictions, the abolition, in a word, of feudalism, and all its consequences."[77] This proposed "common law" would, they claimed, facilitate the Europeans' purchase of "Arab" land and effect a secularization of Muslim law. As one author explained, "It is only a matter of separating the spiritual from the temporal in the Qur'an; property must be submitted to the Napoleonic Code."[78] These arguments in favor of a "common law" did not, however, cast polygamy as an inassimilable feature of native religious difference. They actually minimized its significance, while actively promoting the civilizational advantages of French property law.

These claims became more pointed in response to the 1863 *sénatus-consulte*, which promised to protect collective property (classified by the French as *arch*), while introducing "individual" property holding to a limited extent. Its provisions presumed that communal property or native "indivision" was "not only in conformity with their seminomadic habits, but also with their religious precepts."[79] Indigenous real estate, under this regime, remained a matter of religious law. While purporting to "preserve" tribal property, the law's numerous conditions and exceptions effectively promoted its loss. The translation of indigenous classifications into French legal categories and norms had particularly disruptive effects.[80] Opposed to the legislation's purported protection of native land titles, settler advocates continued to press for the creation of individualized property

76. Rey-Goldzeiguer, *Le royaume arabe*, 233. See, for example, the anonymously published pamphlet, Urbain, *L'Algérie française: Indigènes et immigrants*. And the response that it provoked, *Algérie: Immigrants et indigènes*. Urbain's close associate Frédéric Lacroix attacked the proliferation of pamphlets in defense of settler interests, condemning their anti-Arab "racism." He upheld a conception of "civilization" as something distinct from "assimilation." In [Frédéric Lacroix], *L'Algérie et la lettre de l'Empereur*, 43. See also Murray-Miller, *Cult of the Modern*, 105–14.

77. C. Duvernois, *Les autolatres*, 18.

78. *Algérie: Immigrants et indigènes*, 22.

79. "Rapport Casabianca, 8 avril 1863," on the "Sénatus-consulte relatif à la constitution de la propriété en Algérie, dans les territoires occupés par les Arabes," in Estoublon and Lefébure, *Code de l'Algérie*, 1:273. See also Autin, "La législation foncière"; Guignard, "Les inventeurs de la tradition 'melk' et 'arch.'"

80. Guignard, "Conservatoire ou révolutionnaire?"

ownership, claiming that private property was "the most powerful means of civilization, of fusion between the two races, and of progress."[81]

Debates over the law in the spring of 1863 mobilized settler opposition to Napoléon's policies, giving rise to petition campaigns, virulent press coverage, and more pamphlets. Auguste Warnier, the former Saint-Simonian military doctor who became a large Algerian landowner, vigorously criticized the legislation and its "indigenophile" defenders in his 1863 pamphlet, *L'Algérie devant le Sénat*. As part of his effort to defend the extension of the Civil Code to indigenous property, Warnier promoted European colonization's positive effects, especially on Algerian women. Economic modernization introduced by European grain mills and goods reduced women's labor "under the tent": "as a natural consequence, there has been a decrease in polygamy; a single woman is now sufficient to carry out household tasks."[82] While optimistic about these purportedly civilizing effects of European settlement, he also recognized how "serious the substitution of the Napoleonic Code for customary law" would be, not least in its effects on the "constitution of the family." At the same time, he suggested (as he proposed ten years later in the 1873 property reform) that "the application of the Napoleonic Code, in limiting it to property, would not hurt any of the fundamental bases of Islamism."[83] On this view, property could be removed from "Muslim law" jurisdiction without doing damage to Muslim religion.

Clément Duvernois's brother, Alexandre, a former Arab Bureau official and translator, made a similar argument in favor of French property law in a pamphlet purportedly penned "from a Muslim point of view." Calling for individualized property titles to be instituted throughout the rich agricultural region of the Tell, it claimed that it was unjust to deny Algerians access to French law, while Napoléon's government sought to "take them back to Muslim law."[84] This ventriloquized text begged that Algeria be placed "under common law immediately, except for that which concerns *l'état-civil*, marriage, and repudiation." While family matters appeared here as a durable core of Muslim legal difference, Duvernois did not make that difference into an obstacle to further legal reform. He also proposed that Algeria's native inhabitants could be recognized

---

81. Minority opinion in "Rapport Casabianca, 8 avril 1863" on the "Sénatus-consulte relatif à la constitution de la propriété en Algérie, dans les territoires occupés par les Arabes," in Estoublon and Lefébure, *Code de l'Algérie*, 1:274.

82. Warnier, *L'Algérie devant le Sénat*, 55.

83. Ibid., 150.

84. A. Duvernois, *La question algérienne*, 23.

as "French subjects," albeit without the "rights of citizens"—precisely the frame-work adopted by the *sénatus-consulte* in 1865.[85]

The question of extending French property law to Algeria thus intersected with contemporary arguments about the "Frenchness" of Algerian natives and hence how "French law" would apply to them. The General Councils of the departments of Alger, Oran, and Constantine regularly discussed the matter in their meetings. Alongside calls to facilitate naturalization requirements for Spanish, Italian, and Maltese settlers, the departmental governing bodies sought legislation that would allow individual Algerians to become French citizens. In 1860, the president of the General Council of Alger, Pierre-Charles de Vaulx, who had been named the first president of the Cour imperial d'Alger in 1858, outlined a plan of "voluntary" naturalization for both "Europeans" and native Algerians.[86]

De Vaulx wanted to preserve the exclusivity and dignity of French citizen-ship by attracting "choice" European elements. He meanwhile proposed an "individualized" path for Jews and Muslims. He clearly stated that Muslims did not immediately qualify, because citizenship was "incompatible with the state of their society, which essentially differs from ours in its *mœurs* and its habits, as in its constitution."[87] While acknowledging the achievements of indigenous Jews, he did not believe that their "personal status" should be collectively abolished either. The voluntary system that he proposed required individuals to adopt French civil law.[88]

Answering the requests for collective "naturalization" made by Jewish dele-gates to the General Council, this "individual" route to citizenship also addressed the concerns of Muslim representatives who resisted it. Concerned about further encroachments on an already limited set of legal rights, Muslim representatives claimed that naturalization, even if voluntary, would violate their "religious" law. As one Muslim council member explained, "The Muslim who becomes natural-ized must accept the French Civil Code and will hence be obligated to renounce our law, which is, above all, essentially religious." This delegate claimed polygamy as a stumbling block to "naturalization." He asserted that the urban *Maure* was monogamous ("attached to the society of one woman, who shares her life with him, and faithfully fulfills her duties as spouse and mother"). By contrast, he

---

85. Ibid., 30.
86. Conseil général d'Alger, *Procès-verbaux* (1860), 120. See also Conseil général d'Oran, October 18, 1859, *Procès-verbaux* (1859), 170–74.
87. Conseil général d'Alger, *Procès-verbaux* (1860), 104.
88. Ibid., 120.

claimed, the "nomadic Arab who lives in a tent" posed a problem. It would be impossible "to convince him to abandon a condition that the law does not prohibit and that is so ensconced in the *mœurs* of the country where he lives."[89] Mirroring the logic of French juridical thinking, the representative strategically used the nomadic Arab's presumptive polygamy to reject naturalization and the implicit extension of French law.

Jews and Muslims were in the minority on the council, however. Denouncing the recalcitrant minority's "illiberalism," the majority adopted a measure in favor of individual naturalization by a vote of 16–4. The council's "liberal" solution was based on voluntarism.[90] Appealing to this same idea of individual will, the 1865 *sénatus-consulte* eventually made choosing the Civil Code a precondition of full citizenship.

The Legal Problem of Jewish Personal Status

While their status as "French" remained a question, Muslim and Jewish Algerians could contract under French civil law, an option that was outlined in the September 26, 1842, ordinance on judicial organization. Jews did occasionally make use of the provision, especially given that the same ordinance obliged them to appear before French courts, even though matters of their civil status [*l'état civil*] continued to follow "religious law" (article 37).[91] French judges began to hear Mosaic law marital and inheritance cases and hence to adjudicate questions that were foreign to French civil law—including polygamy, levirate marriage, and repudiation. This delicate arrangement created confusion between the required forum (French tribunals) and the litigants' "choice of law." Algerian Jews' "personal status" thus emerged as specific site of legal struggle.

Instigated in part by metropolitan Jewish reformers, many of the first questions about the legal status of Algerian natives concerned not Muslims, but Jews. In metropolitan France, the secularization of family law was integral to Jewish national inclusion and citizenship. The Grand Sanhedrin convoked by Napoléon in 1807 eliminated Jews' "special customs" and framed submission to French civil law as a preeminent religious duty. The Assembly of Jewish Notables declared polygamy to be a violation of the "*mœurs* of Nations." They also renounced

89. Ibid., 115.

90. Ibid., 121–22.

91. "Ordonnance sur l'organisation de la justice en Algérie (26 septembre 1842)," in Estoublon and Lefébure, *Code de l'Algérie*, 1:22–30.

repudiation and required all Jewish marriages to be conducted before a French civil officer.[92] This model of Jewish legal assimilation constructed a division between a "private" realm of religion and a universal "public" law of the state, instantiated by the Civil Code. It created and symbolized that split by asserting state sovereignty over family matters.[93]

Even after the rabbinic tribunals had been abolished, Algerian Jews were not subject to this same regime, since the colony's judicial organization maintained their "religious law" for questions of personal status. For metropolitan Jews who took up a "civilizing mission" on their behalf, family reform through the application of French civil law contributed to a broader project of social and moral uplift.[94] Questions about the difference of Jewish marriage law, and polygamy in particular, played a significant role in discussions of Algerian Jews' assimilation, even when the cases were not overtly focused on "family law."

No one better emblematized Algerian Jews' ambivalent relationship to French law than Elie-Léon Enos, who fought a protracted struggle for admission to the bar (the "Ordre des avocats") in Algiers after having been a member of the Parisian order. In 1862, the appellate Cour impériale d'Alger (Imperial Court of Algiers) took up the question of whether Enos, as a "nonnaturalized" Algerian Jew, possessed, if not citizenship, then at the very least the requisite civil and national status or "*qualité de Français*" to practice law.[95] The Ordre claimed that Enos was not French but a "subject of the French nation," a status that was at once "foreign and inferior to that of citizenship." The Imperial Appeals Court, by contrast, confirmed Enos's French nationality or *qualité de Français* as an effect of Algeria's annexation by France. It upheld his right to work as a lawyer, even if he could not become a magistrate.

The decision, written by President de Vaulx, created a sharp distinction between subject and citizen, grounding this political division on cultural differences of "religion, *mœurs*, the constitution of marriage, and the organization of the family." Algerian natives' "exceptional" rights were, it held, incompatible with "the great principle of the equality of the law that the revolution of 1789

92. Gutman, *Les décisions doctrinales du Grand Sanhédrin*, 29–33.

93. Brown, *Regulating Aversion*, 52.

94. See, for example, an article criticizing indigenous rabbis for performing polygamous marriages and divorce, in *L'Univers israélite*, no. 10 (June 1864): 184–85. And the defensive reaction on the part of the secretary of the Consistoire d'Alger in *L'Univers israélite*, no. 11 (July 1864): 532. See also Leff, *Sacred Bonds of Solidarity*; Schreier, *Arabs of the Jewish Faith*; Assan, *Les consistoires israélites d'Algérie*.

95. On the "qualité de français" understood by article 7 of the Civil Code see Heuer, *Family and the Nation*, 129.

inscribed at the head of our institutions." For de Vaulx, "the rights conferred by Muslim and Israélite personal status cannot be reconciled with the duties imposed on French citizens, duties whose yoke cannot be shaken without contravening the principles of public order and even those penal laws, under whose double protection the French nation lives."[96] Implicitly targeting polygamy, de Vaulx here upheld marital monogamy as a symbolic "yoke of citizenship."[97]

The Ordre des avocats refused to accept the decision, appealing it to the Cour de cassation. In making this case, the Ordre's counsel Aubin asserted that the "incompatibilities" between "Muslim and Mosaic law" and "French civil law" disqualified Algerian natives from Frenchness as well as from citizenship. For Aubin, there was "no legal difference between Muslims and Israélites; they are equally far removed from the French." By contrast, Enos's lawyer Philippe Larnac sharply distinguished Mosaic law from Muslim law, advocating the inclusion of Jews, but not Muslims, as "compatriots." He based his argument on French Jewish history and the fact that Judaism, like Catholicism and Protestantism, was practiced on French soil "without offending its laws, public order, or good morals."[98] The same could not be claimed for Islam.

The Cour de cassation ultimately found that Israélites, and indeed all Algerian "*indigènes*," were French nationals. They were hence apt to serve as lawyers, even if they were not full citizens. This difference-splitting decision did not meet with universal approval. One account by Auguste Bourguignat in the jurisprudential *Recueil Sirey* lambasted the court's logic by focusing on how Mosaic and Muslim law differed from French family law: "Do we need to recall that the family, as it is constituted by these laws, which are exclusively religious, is not submitted to the same rules as ours; that on so many points, native *mœurs* are repugnant to our public morals; and that such deeds are recognized as legitimate in the eyes of the Talmud and the Qur'an, while they are rejected by our laws." Bourguignat cited the myriad offending differences—repudiation, inequitable inheritance laws, annulment based on impotence, and, of course, polygamy—as so many legal offenses that demonstrated that for "Algerian natives" the "good morals of private life are not what we understand the word civilization to represent."[99] The sexual difference of their law wed Algerians to a regime of legal exclusion.

---

96. See Enos Cour d'Alger (February 24, 1862), in *Journal de la jurisprudence de la Cour impériale d'Alger* [hereafter *Robe*] (1862), 93.

97. On the Enos case as a precedent for the 1865 *sénatus-consulte* see Cherchari, "Indigènes et citoyens"; Schley, "Tyranny of Tolerance," 272–78.

98. *L'Akhbar*, March 17, 1864, 1–2.

99. Avocats d'Alger v. Aïnos ou Enos, *Receuil général des lois et des arrêts* (Receuil Sirey), 1864, pt. 1, 113–14.

Enos responded in the *Journal de jurisprudence de la Cour impériale d'Alger*, claiming that by virtue of the law of conquest, Algerian Jews should be considered not only as subjects, but as full citizens. In his view, this inclusion would be much more consistent with French legal principle, citing de Vaulx's own language regarding the "principle of equality before the law" of "the revolution of 1789" to make the case.[100] Ultimately, the argument about the radical disjuncture between subject and citizen prevailed, in jurisprudence and eventually in law.

The presumptive cultural differences highlighted by the Enos decision resonated with the concerns of French magistrates who heard Mosaic law cases. Significant jurisdictional confusion arose after an 1851 decree encouraged Jews to marry before French civil officers rather than rabbis.[101] The ambivalent implications of the decree would be seized upon by litigants who tried to claim that they had contracted under the Civil Code. Lower courts like the Tribunal of Algiers often affirmed the choice of French law, while the appellate Court of Algiers was more cautious. Its decisions, many of them presided over by de Vaulx, were guided by two connected principles: on the one hand the protection of indigenous belief and *mœurs*, and on the other the preservation of the "dignity" of French citizenship.[102]

These cases puzzled over whether appearing before the French civil officer represented a choice of forum or a choice of law. Algerian Jews (and their lawyers) took advantage of this ambiguity. By seeking out the protections of French law, husbands and wives made Jews' marital affairs a concern of public order for metropolitan reformers, journalists, and jurists. At stake in these cases was whether personal status could be decided by choice.

Many Mosaic law cases focused on divorce. For example, in 1861 Mardochée Tingé claimed that his marriage, while conducted by the civil registrar of Algiers, was contracted under the Mosaic law that allowed him to divorce his sterile wife, Messaouda ben Kenoun. She meanwhile claimed the protection of French law, which forbade divorce. The Tribunal of Algiers's decision refused Tingé's demand, claiming that to allow the marital bond to be broken by recourse to another law would be "something strange and abnormal that a French tribunal

---

100. Enos, "Quelle est la condition juridique des israélites algériens? Sont-ils Français?," *Robe* (1864), 70.

101. See "Décret qui affranchit des droits de timbres et d'enregistrement (5 September 1851)," in Estoublon and Lefébure, *Code de l'Algérie*, 1:144.

102. See, for example, Attali v. Attali, Cour d'Alger (January 29, 1857), in Estoublon, *Jurisprudence algérienne*, 2:6–9

could not endorse." Finding for his wife, the tribunal upheld the integrity and supremacy of French law.[103]

Men also claimed the protections of French law. The contest between Simon Courcheyia and Guenouma Strock, for example, revolved around his sexual impotence—a condition that no longer constituted grounds for annulment in French civil law.[104] The couple had married before the civil registrar of Oran in 1854. When Guenouma sought a Mosaic law divorce, Simon claimed French law status.[105] While the Tribunal of Oran sided with Simon, the Appeals Court of Algiers resisted the lower court's assimilationist argument. It refused to accept that the couple had renounced their personal status simply by appearing before a French official. After his appeal to the Cour de cassation, Simon's case was reconsidered by the Court of Aix in 1864. In its view, the civil registry officer had indeed spoken in the name of French civil law.[106] A member of the prominent Crémieux family, acting as Simon's lawyer, convinced the court that "the progressive assimilation of native Israélites is evident in the thought of the French government." Reflecting the reformer's assimilationist line, the decision claimed that the couple's marriage before a French official demonstrated their "will to place that contract under the empire of French law." Refusing to sanction Guenouma's divorce claim, the Supreme Court presented the Israélites' assimilation as already well on its way.[107]

While these decisions confirmed Algerian Jews' legal assimilation, the Appeals Court of Algiers maintained their Mosaic law status in subsequent cases. In the 1865 case of Judas Zermati, for example, it explicitly maintained polygamy as a protected practice under Mosaic law. Appearing first before the Tribunal of Algiers in 1862, this acrimonious trial opposed the children of Zermati's first marriage to Zermati himself, his second wife, and their children. Zermati's first marriage had been contracted under Mosaic law to Ricca bent Zermati in 1832. She and her family had "looked askance" at his subsequent second marriage to Ricca Tabet and "did everything in their power to prevent Zermati

---

103. Tingé v. Messaouda Ben Kenoun, Tribunal d'Alger (June 29, 1861), in Estoublon, *Jurisprudence algérienne*, 3:43–45.

104. See Dame Courcheyia v. Courcheyia, Cour d'Alger (January 19, 1860), ibid., 3:1–4; Dame Courcheyia v. Courcheyia, Cour d'Alger (May 18, 1860), 3:27–29; Courcheyia v. Dame Courcheyia, Cour de cassation (April 15, 1862), ibid., 3:25–26.

105. On the "scandalousness" of impotence trials see Moussaud, *Précis pratique des maladies des organes génito-urinaires*, 345–46.

106. Courcheyia v. Dame Courcheyia, Cour de cassation (April 15, 1862), in Estoublon, *Jurisprudence algérienne*, vol. 3 (1862), 25–26. For the previous case, Tingé v. Messaouda Ben Kenoun, Tribunal d'Alger (June 29, 1861), in Estoublon, 3:43–45.

107. Dame Courcheyia v. Courcheyia, Cour d'Aix (June 2, 1864), in Estoublon, 3:19–21

from contracting the new union."[108] Five of the six children of the second marriage were not declared to be his on the civil registry, appearing only as "*enfants naturels*." When Zermati approached the Tribunal of Algiers in order to recognize them, the children of the first marriage vociferously contested the second union's legality, given that it had been conducted in clandestine circumstances.

Resentment-filled accusations of adultery and concubinage multiplied in the course of this rancorous legal struggle over filiation and inheritance. The contest took on wider significance in the context of debates over Algerian Jews' legal status. As arguments in the case made clear, the uncertainty of the second marriage resulted from communal misgivings about Zermati's bigamy. The Tribunal of Algiers was sympathetic to the children of the first marriage, and its decision was partly based on a refusal to give an apparent juridical "consecration of polygamy." According to the lower court, it was the "duty" of French tribunals to outlaw "all that in *mœurs* and customs is contrary to morality and public order." Polygamy, the decision recalled, was outlawed not only by the Civil Code, but also by the Penal Code. As a matter of public order, the principles at stake were of "greatest interest to the State, the family, and good morals."[109]

Described as a "*négociant*" in the published trial transcripts, Zermati was a wealthy landowner as well, so he had ample resources to pay for skilled legal counsel on appeal. His lawyer was Jules Chabert-Moreau, who had made these suits something of a specialty, having also acted as counsel in the Courcheyia and Enos cases, while Ricca Tabet was represented by Joseph Guérin, and the six children from the second marriage, all minors, were represented by Eugène Robe, the prominent editor of the *Journal de jurisprudence de la Cour impériale d'Alger*. The case tellingly received extensive coverage in Robe's journal, which reproduced the argument made in Zermati's favor in its entirety.

In making his case before the court, the general counsel of the Cour d'Alger Benjamin Mazel expressed reluctance at granting polygamy's legality, not only for Muslims, but also for Jews. He acknowledged Algerian Jews' increasing claims for assimilation, noting that bigamy had "become shameful" for them, in implicit contrast to Muslims. Despite these caveats, he asserted that "from a purely doctrinal position" bigamy was legal, based on the history of Mosaic law, the Convention of 1830, Algeria's subsequent juridical organization, and rabbinical opinion consulted in the case.[110] With the dispositions of the 1807 Grand Sanhedrin applicable

---

108. In Zermati v. Zermati, Cour d'Alger (May 22, 1865), *Robe* (1865), 31.

109. Judgment of Tribunal d'Alger, July 7, 1864, cited ibid., 35–36.

110. Among other sources, he drew on Salvador, *Histoire des institutions de Moïse et du peuple hébreu*, 2:157–66.

only to "European," and not to Algerian Jews, the proper resolution of this messy matter awaited the attentions of "imperial wisdom."[111] Following this argument, the court upheld the integrity of Mosaic law for Jews' "personal status," explaining that, until new legislation was adopted, tribunals would continue "to apply Mosaic law, just as, every day, in instances between Muslims, they apply Muslim law, despite the sharp differences that divide these laws from French civil law."[112] Only legislation could "regularize" Algerian Jews' confused situation.

Advocates of assimilation took up this call to reform. The Jewish Consistory, for example, actively supported Casimir Frégier, the president of the Tribunal of Sétif, who published widely on the oddities of Algerian law.[113] Frégier made a case for the "special" character of Algerian law, but also argued that it should be organized and codified. In his view, this "Janus-faced" law was turned "today toward the past, tomorrow toward the future, here toward the Orient, there toward the Occident."[114] Frégier drew clear distinctions between native Jews and Muslims, citing their different attitudes toward assimilation and most notably their imagined attachment to polygamy as an index of that difference. He proclaimed: "Although they [Jews] too practice or can practice polygamy, have they, like the Muslims of Algiers, claimed, by way of their representatives on the Conseil général, a 'right to a harem'?"[115] For Frégier and other advocates of Jews' legal assimilation, Muslims' greater attachment to polygamy justified the Jews' qualification for French citizenship.[116]

Frégier meanwhile reserved his harshest judgment for misguided jurisprudence. He opposed the recent court decisions that addressed individual cases and argued for collective naturalization instead. As he explained, Jews' "personal status" entailed an established group of "rights, capacities, qualities, and attributes." Drawing on ancien régime jurists such as Robert Pothier and Philippe Merlin, he underscored that legal personality should not be confused with individual will. Following Roman law, legal personhood could not be simply cast off by will or convention. The inalterability of "personal status" that was the cornerstone of

---

111. Mazel in Zermati v. Zermati, Cour d'Alger (May 22, 1865), *Robe* (1865), 41. And "La bigamie chez les Israélites algériens," *L'Akhbar*, May 25, 1865.

112. Decision of the Cour d'Alger in *Robe* (1865), 49.

113. Rey-Goldzeiguer, *Le royaume arabe*, 114.

114. Frégier, *Du droit algérien*, 20. As well as *L'Akhbar*, July 23, July 29, and August 11, 1864. See also Renucci, "Les juifs d'Algérie et la citoyenneté."

115. Frégier, *Juifs algériens*, 352.

116. See Adolphe Franck, "Rapport verbal sur un ouvrage de M. Frégier," *Bulletin de l'Académie des sciences morales et politiques*, September 23 (1865), 465–70. See also Schreier, "Napoléon's Long Shadow."

ancien régime law had been upheld by article 6 of the Civil Code.[117] Allowing Algerian Jews to alter their legal status simply by appearing before the civil registry clearly violated these terms of legal personhood.

Frégier did not deny that the laws of Algerian Jews contained "precepts and interdictions which are contrary to our ideas, our institutions, our laws, and even our *ordre public*."[118] In his view, however, it was "vain to cry out against the immorality, in the eyes of French law, of the effects of Israélite marriage, such as polygamy, divorce, etc." This "immorality" was, in fact, written into the hybrid structure of Algerian law: "Hasn't Algerian law allowed for these effects? If so (and how could one deny it), then the law itself should be put on trial."[119] His volume on *Les juifs algériens* was intended to do precisely that.

In his text devoted to the confused juridical condition of *les indigènes algériens*, a lawyer at the Cour d'Alger, Aimé Poivre, likewise called for the reform of Israélite civil status and marriage.[120] He supported Algerian Jews' legal assimilation but also believed, like Frégier, that this transformation could come about only by way of comprehensive legislation, not piecemeal jurisprudence. He too was skeptical of the decisions in the Tingé and Courcheyia cases, which made Algerian Jews' status individually mutable. For Poivre, these cases undermined the sovereign hold of law, which "imposes itself on persons, without leaving them free to seek it out or abdicate it." In his view, this voluntarist conception of civil status would "facilitate the intrusion into each state of subjects who could be dangerous for it."[121]

Contradictory jurisprudence regarding Jews' personal status galvanized metropolitan reformers as well as local advocates to pursue a legislative solution to the confusion created by the ambiguities of Algerian law. The end result would be the *sénatus-consulte* of 1865.

The Impossible Choice of Law

Advocates of assimilation were optimistic that a much-awaited reform would follow in the wake of Napoléon III's second visit to Algeria in 1865. Rabbis in Algiers and Constantine called on the emperor to redress a legal situation in

---

117. Frégier, *Juifs algériens*, 141.
118. Ibid., 142.
119. Ibid., 165.
120. Poivre, *Les indigènes algériens*, 24.
121. Ibid., 32.

which "marriage, which is the basis of the family, has become a source of disruption and scandal."[122] The 1865 *sénatus-consulte* was designed, in part, to remedy the disordered state of Jewish marriage law.

Following the departmental councils' recommendations and the jurisprudence in the Enos case, the legislation outlined procedures for the "naturalization" of foreigners as well as indigenous Muslims and Jews. It confirmed that Muslim and Jewish natives of Algeria were French nationals. It also adopted the General Council of Alger's "liberal" legal solution. According to its terms, Muslims who followed their "religious law" and Jews who maintained their "personal status" law would remain subjects rather than citizens. Full citizenship, by contrast, entailed a renunciation of local civil status and the adoption of the Civil Code in its place.

For the legislation's sponsors, the conflict between local codes and French citizenship was a matter of public order. For the *conseiller d'état* Louis-Hughes Flandin, polygamy was a particular obstacle. In his view, the precedent set by the Grand Sanhedrin explained why neither Muslims nor Jews who continued to claim their personal status could be citizens.[123] Senator Claude Delangle's presentation likewise highlighted the conflict between polygamy and French law as a question of public order. In his view, its renunciation was a matter of individual choice. As Delangle explained, "If, from the status that they abandon are derived rights and customs which are incompatible with public decency, with morality, with the good order of families, these rights are abolished [*anéantis*]. The acceptance of the quality of French citizen constitutes the most formal abdication. There cannot exist on the soil of the nation [*patrie*] citizens who have contradictory rights."[124] By conceiving of polygamy as a privilege, Delangle opposed indigenous legal status to the "equal" rights of citizens. Citizenship required male citizens to relinquish special sexual rights. According to this extimate logic, Algerians could not reasonably have access to a sexual privilege that was denied to French men. The settler advocate Wilfred de Fonvielle elaborated on this principle, drawing on an implicitly republican argument that presented Algerian men's polygamy as an aristocratic privilege: "the right to a harem, that

---

122. "Adresse des Israélites d'Alger à sa Majesté Napoléon III," *L'Akhbar*, May 19, 1865. And Frégier, *Juifs algériens*, 446.

123. See "Exposé des motifs de M. Flandin, conseiller d'État, le 22 juin 1865," in Estoublon and Lefébure, *Code de l'Algérie*, 1:303. See the analogous discussion in Brett, "Legislating for Inequality in Algeria"; Schreier, "Napoléon's Long Shadow."

124. "Rapport présenté par M. Delangle le 30 juin 1865," in Estoublon and Lefébure, *Code de l'Algérie*, 1:304.

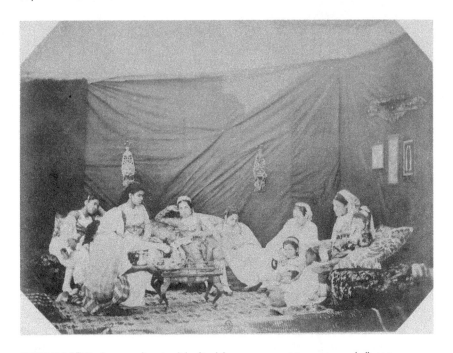

FIGURE 6 / Félix-Jacques-Antoine Moulin, *Mauresques en visite, costume de l'intérieur (Alger)*, from *Colonisation française de l'Algérie et voyage de Napoléon III en 1865*. Bibliothèque nationale de France.

is what separates the great Arab chiefs from our civilization. A people has to be enslaved in order to permit a few hundred aristocrats to escape from the bonds of monogamy that are uncomfortable [*liens souvents gênants*] even for the best French men."[125]

Defenders of the *sénatus-consulte* embraced this framework and the deliberate "choice" that it offered indigenous Jews, Muslims, and foreigners alike. In his commentary on the legislation, Joseph Sartor, a lawyer from Oran, upheld the logic of sexual sacrifice as a crucible of citizenship. Celebrating the integrity of the Civil Code, he rejected any "conciliation" between the "unity and magnificent linkages [*enchaînement*] of our legislation" on the one hand and the "either rival, or bastardized laws" on the other.[126] According to Sartor, opting for French law was premised on and performed by the renunciation of polygamy. "Isn't it grand [*beau*]," he commented, "to see a man, in the presence of a passion that pushes

125. Wilfred de Fonvielle, "Le Droit au sérail," *Revue du monde colonial* 7, no. 14 (January 1865): 67.
126. Sartor, *De la naturalisation en Algérie*, 8.

him and of a duty, which in turn imposes itself on his spirit, break with what custom and religion allow him to do with difficulty, in order to follow the sage laws of reason."[127] Sexual self-renunciation conferred and confirmed the dignity of French citizenship.

Other politicians and publicists criticized the framework of individual sexual sacrifice as unrealistic. The Saint-Simonian economist Michel Chevalier drew on the example of the Grand Sanhedrin and argued instead for a "collective" measure to eliminate polygamy, which he viewed as a "source of radical inferiority, the cause of debasement, and an obstacle to progress."[128] Less optimistic about the prospects of such reform, Chevalier's parliamentary colleagues ridiculed his vision for Algeria's legal assimilation. Provoking "general hilarity" in the Assembly, Comte General Aristide de la Ruë explained why the project was doomed to failure: "If we propose to them that they can become French citizens at the price of this sacrifice, to not be able to take a young wife when the one that they have has gotten old, they will not be very tempted to use this right under such a condition."[129] Advocates of Algeria's legal assimilation, especially among the settlers, were inclined to agree.

Other critics of the 1865 *sénatus-consulte* used a similar logic to attack the privileges left in place by the law. Polygamy again served as a linchpin of their arguments against granting natives access to civil and military posts. For liberal-leaning senator Vicomte Victor Ambroise Lanjuinais, it maintained unfair legal distinctions that violated "all notions of justice and reason." He protested against granting rights to Algerian natives that were denied to citizens. Muslim sexual privilege exemplified that difference: "In this way, everyone knows that under Muslim law, every Muslim can have several legitimate wives and he can, in addition, have an indefinite number of concubines inhabiting his conjugal home. That's Muslim law."[130] Drawing on Delangle's argument about the equality of citizens before the law, Lanjuinais held that all those who possessed the "*qualité de français*" should be forced to follow the Civil Code.

Assessments of the *sénatus-consulte* all ultimately converged on this point. They viewed the "right to a harem" as an exorbitant and aristocratic sexual privilege that could not be tolerated within the legal framework of French citizenship.

---

127. Ibid., 26–27.
128. See "Délibération sur le projet de Sénatus-consulte relatif à l'état des personnes et à la naturalisation en Algérie," *Procès-verbaux des séances du Sénat* 5, no. 35–39 (July 1–7, 1865): 219
129. Ibid., 229–30.
130. *Annales du Sénat et du Corps législatif* 2 (March 3, 1866): 93.

Separating Property and Personal Status

While the *sénatus-consulte* formalized the distinction between French colonial subjects and French citizens, settlers and assimilationist Jews remained dissatisfied with the law and pressed for the extension of civilian power and, with it, the Civil Code.[131] Settlers sought this reform not to eliminate the privilege of polygamy, but to submit Algerian Muslims to French property law, while preserving, as was the case with Jews, their "personal status." Writing in his newspaper *L'Akhbar*, Joseph Guérin responded skeptically to calls like Chevalier's for the suppression of polygamy, which, he suggested, went too far: "We wouldn't have asked for so much. We would have wished that in becoming French, Muslims, instead of remaining entirely under Muslim law, would be under French law for all that is outside of their personal status." According to the settlers' preferred argument, property law reform would prepare the subsequent progress, which was "more complete and more desirable."[132]

Unsatisfied with the results of the *sénatus-consulte*, the General Council of Alger resumed discussions of "naturalization" in 1866. Its new head, Augustin de Vialar, focused on social conditions rather than "religious law" per se as the source of indigenous difference. Citing fellow council member Berbrugger's social and economic analysis, he presented polygamy as amenable to eventual reform. In his view, polygamy was "excusable for current Arab life" and even analogous to "certain tolerances that civilization is obliged to support in order to preserve marriage and family honor." In other words, he saw polygamy as roughly equivalent to adultery and prostitution. According to this social logic, Vialar suggested that "in order to abolish divorce and polygamy, we need to make certain causes disappear before we can try to abolish their effects."[133] Property reform was one such technology of social reengineering.

Settler advocates were willing to compromise the purported purity of French civil law in order to legally assimilate Algerian property. The prolific Duvernois again proposed that while a "single law" should be introduced in Algeria, all those who were not French citizens should be permitted to marry according to the precepts of their religion.[134] An opinion column in *L'Akhbar* by Arnold Thomson

---

131. See, for example, "Appel aux Israélites de l'Algérie, au sujet de leur naturalisation," and Arnold Thomson, "Des députations israélites se sont présentées à sa Majesté à chacun de ses voyages, pour demander la naturalisation," *L'Akhbar*, May 18, 1866.

132. See Joseph Guérin, "Le sénatus-consulte I," *L'Akhbar*, July 27, 1865. They proposed, in other words, to make marriage an exception; see C. Duvernois, "La question algérienne II," *L'Akhbar*, December 14, 1865.

133. Conseil général d'Alger, *Procès-verbaux* (1866), 11–12.

134. C. Duvernois, "La question algérienne II," *L'Akhbar*, December 14, 1865.

likewise suggested, "Why don't we introduce a moderation into our law that will satisfy the practices of the people we want to assimilate?"[135] One tract attacking how Muslim law limited free property transactions between Europeans and natives minimized the significance of polygamy, comparing it positively to adultery. "I don't know," he wrote, "if French customs are more moral than those of Arabs, but at the very least they are more expensive and, from the point of view of the surveillance of such women, I prefer the Oriental system."[136]

Settler attacks on government policy became even more vocal in the wake of the massive famine of 1868.[137] The crisis provided an occasion to again denounce the Arab Bureaus. Advocates of civil government claimed that maintaining the native population's primitive customs, habits, and laws, by blocking assimilation, had contributed to the devastation. The editor of the *Independant* of Constantine, Jules Vinet, was typical in this respect. In his view, "Muslim" and "French" law were largely comparable, except for matters of "marriage and more generally personal status." Drawing on Frégier's work, he argued in favor of "placing the Arabs under the Civil Code, while reserving for them certain special questions, such as divorce and polygamy."[138] These matters aside, wrote Vinet, "there should be only one right [*droit*] to recognize, and one law [*loi*] to apply, French right, French law."[139] He proposed the creation of a "*statut personnel musulman*" law that would be cleaved from the "*statut réel.*" Doing so would, effectively, separate family law from real property in Muslim law.

A bailiff from Mascara and self-proclaimed expert on Islamic law, François Cadoz, outlined such a system in his critical commentary *Droit musulman Malékite.* Written after the institution of civilian rule in 1870, Cadoz's pro-settler text was designed as a guide for administrators. It argued that Muslim law was amenable to "civilizing" transformation. More specifically, he claimed that "the principles of Muslim law and Islamic dogma are not at all opposed to the application of the Civil Code to the Arabs of Algeria." He advocated for the extension of French civil law to fertile areas that had been targeted for colonization. At the same time, he suggested that "Muslim personal status" would need to remain in place "for a long time," if only for questions of "the status of persons, juridical capacity and incapacity, guardianship, marriage, divorce, wills and inheritance."[140] This limited legal assimilation would not entail political rights.[141]

---

135. Arnold Thomson, "Assimilation (suite et fin)," *L'Akhbar*, November 20, 1866.
136. Ballue, *La question algérienne à vol d'oiseau*, 47.
137. On the famine and its aftermath see Taithe, "Algerian Orphans and Colonial Christianity."
138. Vinet, *Le droit commun pour les indigènes*, 8.
139. Ibid., 11.
140. Cadoz, *Droit musulman Malékite*, 185.
141. Ibid., 195.

Cadoz meanwhile approved Jews' collective naturalization by the Crémieux Decree in 1870. The measure realized the civil and political assimilation of Jews that had been long sought by metropolitan reformers, including by its noted author, Alfred Crémieux. For Cadoz, that inclusion assumed Algerian Jews' adoption of French "family values." As we have seen, legal debates in the 1860s had worried over the differences between Jewish law and French law. In 1871, Cadoz depicted "Jewish Algerian youth" as "deserving of all of our sympathy." In his account, "the men are hardworking, economical, good fathers and husbands; the women are virtuous and excel at domestic tasks; many of them, by their education, their talent, their simple and elegant garb, could rival French women in salons."[142] Subsequent critics of the decree disputed these claims about the extent and success of the civilizing mission on Algerian Jews. What matters here, however, is how Cadoz closely associated Jews' new political rights with the abolition of Mosaic personal status law and its polygamy.[143]

As we will see in the next chapter, it was at this same moment that "Muslim personal status" assumed legal existence. The shift from military to civilian rule that accompanied the advent of the Third Republic in Algeria created a new opportunity for property law reform and the extension of French civil law to areas targeted for colonization. This juridical innovation assumed legal force in 1873, as a result of the reform drawn up by longtime settler advocate Warnier. Following the logic laid out by settler publicists and jurists, it instituted the separation of "personal status" from a territorialized real estate law based on the French Civil Code.

Within the framework established by the Civil Code, the *statut personnel* regulates persons, while the *statut réel* regulates transactions of landed property. Their domain of application differs accordingly: one is national, while the other is territorial. Their respective objects and jurisdictions are both mutually constituting and mutually exclusive.[144] Because Algerian natives had French nationality after 1865, their personal status had an uncertain ground. Algerian Jews, who sought the protections of French law, exploited the legal and political conflicts between their status, their religion, and their nationality. The resulting debates about Mosaic law focused jurists' attention on polygamy as a violation of French civil law and its "public order." These debates provided a vocabulary and legal

---

142. Ibid.
143. Décret du 24 Octobre 1870, *Bullétin officiel du gouvernement d'Algérie*, 1871, 336. S. B. Roberts, *Citizenship and Antisemitism.*
144. Maurice Block, *Dictionnaire de l'administration française* (Paris, 1856), s.v. Statut, 1488.

framework for denouncing polygamy as incompatible with French citizenship. This was as true for Muslims as it was for Jews.

The legislators' discussion of Muslim polygamy thus appeared to parallel that of Jewish polygamy. But there was a crucial difference between the seeming legal equivalence of the *statut musulman* and the *statut personnel israélite*: property law. As I have suggested here, discussions of Muslim polygamy were historically linked to disputes about property and colonization that were virtually absent from discussions of the Algerian Jews' legal situation. While the language of polygamy as a moral and legal scandal was shared, the stakes involved in its mobilization by Arab Bureau officers and advocates of settler colonization were quite different from those of Jewish assimilationists.

In order to understand how polygamy came to instantiate the incompatibility of *Muslim* personal status with French citizenship, we must attend to the transformations that took place, not only in Algerian citizenship and nationality law, but also in property law. We have seen that in the 1850s and 1860s, settler advocates contended that property law reform would effect the moral and social reform of Algerian natives, including an eventual disappearance of polygamy and a purported fusion of populations. In framing polygamy in economic rather than in religious terms, they saw it as amenable to social reform. Some settler advocates were even willing to grant Muslim marriage an exceptional status in order to otherwise universalize French civil law.

Once a partial territorialization of French property law was achieved in 1873, settler interest in Muslim assimilation predictably all but vanished. Instead, the political preservation of the purity of French citizenship—and with it French law—became paramount. In the process, the newly defined Muslim personal status and its presumptive "right to polygamy" came to represent an extimate exception that both confirmed French legal sovereignty and the exclusive dignity of French citizenship.

3

MAKING THE "MUSLIM FAMILY"

The 1865 *sénatus-consulte* was a watershed moment in the history of French Algeria and in French legal history *tout court*. By drawing a novel separation between French nationality and French citizenship, the law established a categorical distinction between citizens and "indigenous" subjects that continued to serve as a basis for a discriminatory legal system in colonial Algeria and beyond it. This political differentiation between persons was tautologically grounded on a distinction between civil jurisdictions: between French civil law on the one hand and native law on the other. In order to explain the incompatibility and incommensurability between these legal systems, the measure's advocates famously pointed to indigenous legal "rights" of polygamy and divorce as core features of difference.[1]

Why did the sexual privileges associated with indigenous "family law" figure so prominently as an obstacle to French citizenship? As we saw in the last chapter, the Napoleonic precedent of Jewish legal assimilation, which was contingent on the renunciation of polygamy and similar customs, served as a model. For those who sought to regenerate Algeria's Jews and make them French citizens, family morality became constitutive of the Algerian *mission civilisatrice*. Napoleonic legal categories, and debates over Jews' "personal status law" in particular, played an important role in the development of Algerian colonial law.[2] The connection between civil law status and citizenship that was cemented by the 1865 *sénatus-consulte* was, however, neither necessary nor inevitable, as the existence of colonials who, after 1848, were granted citizenship even though they maintained a distinct civil law status (namely, in the four communes of Senegal and the five *comptoirs* of French India) famously shows.[3]

---

1. Henry, "La norme et l'imaginaire"; Brett, "Legislating for Inequality"; Blévis, "Les avatars de la citoyenneté"; Saada, *Empire's Children*; Barrière, *Le statut personnel des musulmans*; Merle, "Retour sur le régime de l'indigénat"; Shepard, *Invention of Decolonization*.

2. Schreier, "Napoléon's Long Shadow," and *Arabs of the Jewish Faith*.

3. On this point see Weil, *Qu'est-ce qu'un Français?*, 235. Subsequent measures nonetheless worked to limit the extent to which these colonial citizens could exercise their rights; see Deschamps, "Une citoyenneté différée"; Coquery-Vidrovitch, "Nationalité et citoyenneté"; Yerri, *L'indigène dans le droit colonial*.

Why then did "Muslim" family law come to instantiate the Algerian native's specifically *legal* difference at this decisive moment of colonization? In order to understand the import of the Civil Code's model of the family we need to explore not just the history of Algerian Muslim legal personhood, but of Muslim property as well. While these are often treated separately in historiography, I argue that the legal regulation of the population cannot be told apart from heated debates over indigenous property rights and competing strategies of colonization. The link between citizenship and family law was, in fact, cemented by a separation of Muslim personal status from real property law, of the "*statut personnel*" from the colony's "*statut réel.*" For Algerian Muslims, this legal separation of persons and property was enacted not in 1865, but in 1873, by the Warnier Law to "Establish and Conserve Property in Algeria." The colonial legal construction of the "Muslim family" was an effect of this ideological cleavage.

For Karl Marx, the Warnier Law's project to introduce private property "masked fraud" under "the supposedly eternal laws of political economy." The purported universalism of the French Civil Code's property law had a very specific aim: to "uproot Arabs from their natural ties to the land, breaking what remained of powerful tribal ties." Attacking Algerians' "kinship ties," it pursued a simultaneously economic and political goal: "to destroy the bases of this society."[4] As Marx's late observations on Algerian land law indicated, the settler colonial project necessarily focused attention on the Algerian family and its property. "Family law" thus emerged in tandem with a land law that sought to dismantle undivided Algerian "communal" or "family property." The Warnier Law contributed to a broader global legal reconfiguration of the relation between market law and marriage law. In this transformation, the family was supposed to become a repository of affectively invested moral and cultural values, rather than economic ones.[5]

This connection between Algerian personal law and property law sheds light on how and why family morality became the locus of Algerians' different legal status. Seen from a genealogical perspective, personal law was not a preexisting domain in Muslim law. It was legally constituted in and by Algerian colonization. Historians have amply documented the devastating effects of colonial land

---

4. From Marx's notes on Maxim Kovalevsky's 1879 book on communal land ownership, which had an extensive chapter on the history of land and land law in Algeria. See Marx, "Le système foncier en Algérie," 396, 400.

5. Halley and Rittich, "Critical Directions in Comparative Family Law"; Halley, "What Is Family Law?"

expropriation in Algeria.[6] Others have charted the elaboration of the system of Muslim personal status law, whose restricted jurisdiction encompassed matters of "marriage, divorce, and inheritance."[7] In this chapter, I draw these two histories together in order to show how property reform relied on and shaped Muslim personal status, despite its claims to the contrary.

Much like settler colonial projects elsewhere, land reform constituted family law as a distinct domain of cultural difference that not only coexisted with but also justified the emerging property regime. This reform organized "Muslim" economic and emotional investments in landed property on the one hand, and in persons on the other. The colonial legal enterprise administered material and affective economies as if they were distinct. The legislation designed by settler advocate Auguste Warnier constructed property as a divisible economic abstraction, devoid of collective affective investments, and hence amenable to administrative partition by French law. It simultaneously imagined the "Muslim family" as a repository of intimate and religious sentiments.[8]

This ideological opposition between property and family was belied in practice. As we will see, the 1873 law's purportedly neat categories created confusion rather than clarity—to the considerable frustration of the French administrators who were charged with implementing it. They were confronted over and over again with an inadequation between their legal categories and the social form—and life—of property. And they realized, as well, that "the family," far from being a stable and fixed entity, was subject to interpretation and contestation. The procedural challenges of applying the law, and jurisdictional disputes over what would remain in the province of Muslim law, revealed the legislation's oversights. In the aftermath of its passage, politicians, jurists, and administrators quickly proposed measures to reform the reform.

---

6. Ageron, *Les Algériens musulmans*, 1; Sainte-Marie, "Législation foncière et société rurale"; Christelow, *Muslim Law Courts*; Yacono, *La colonisation des plaines du Chélif*; Sari, "Le démantèlement de la propriété foncière"; Djerbal, "Processus de colonisation et évolution de la propriété foncière"; Guignard, "Le sénatus-consulte de 1863."

7. Barrière, *Le statut personnel des musulmans*; Weil, "Le statut des musulmans en Algérie coloniale"; Saada, *Empire's Children*; Shepard, *Invention of Decolonization*; Belmessous, *Assimilation and Empire*. David Powers, in his pathbreaking account of the French legal attack on family endowments, draws attention to the connection between the two as well as their inadequacy in Muslim law. Powers, "Orientalism, Colonialism, and Legal History," 541.

8. For a contemporary account of the attributes of the "Muslim family" see Morand, *La famille musulmane*.

The implementation of land reform revealed that what was separable in theory remained entangled on the ground. The execution of land reform continued to imbricate real estate and personal estate—and hence French and Muslim law. More specifically, the government agents charged with implementing the law realized that they could not do so without a clear definition of the "Muslim family" and its presumptively patriarchal structure. The law's application revealed deep confusion over the exact meaning of this family. Fantasmatically presumed to be a site of phallic potency, the Muslim family was a paradoxical lacuna in the ordinary language of the law. Both the law's regulatory linchpin and its fundamental blind spot, the Muslim family became a site of contestation. French jurists and Algerian property holders struggled over how to define its shape and size in allotting individual titles. Multiple follow-up circulars alongside numerous reports pointed to the originary lack of definition. In continually seeking to fill the loophole through administrative and bureaucratic procedure, these efforts revealed the psychic and social limits of the law as well as the totalizing fantasies that sustained its operations.

Maintaining Muslim Law

As we have seen, the Muslim law jurisdiction established by the 1834 ordinance comprised more than "personal status." According to that law, French and native tribunals assumed reified categories of personhood—French, European, indigène musulman, and indigène israélite—whose distinctive attributions continued to shift in the early decades of colonization.[9] The formal establishment of military-run Arab Bureaus in the 1840s reinforced this system of multiple jurisdictions.[10] Relying on native chiefs and native justice to maintain control, military men adopted a tactical attitude toward Muslim law, even as they sought to circumscribe its effects both legally and territorially. Muslim legal constraints on properties sold to Europeans were increasingly curtailed, for example, by the October 1, 1844, ordinance, which disallowed indigenous claims that certain properties were "inalienable" because they were held in religious trusts (habous).[11] Projects

---

9. Henry, "La norme et l'imaginaire."
10. Abi-Mershed, Apostles of Modernity; Frémeaux, Les Bureaux arabes; Lorcin, Imperial Identities.
11. On the colonial attack on habous see Powers, "Orientalism, Colonialism, and Legal History."

of "cantonment," beginning in the late 1840s, delimited tribes' territories sup-posedly based on their needs, in order to free up lands for settlement. Part of Emperor Louis Napoléon's project of an Algerian "Arab Kingdom," the 1863 *sénatus-consulte* on the "constitution of property in territories occupied by Arabs" circumscribed lands on which colonization could be pursued. Despite its claims to conservation, it promoted disaggregation of collective tribal lands, albeit based on principles of Muslim property law.[12] While subject to such rein-vention, Muslim law continued to regulate native property titles and transac-tions until the Warnier Law established French titles on selected "family" proper-ties and collectively held lands in 1873.[13]

In these initial decades, interpretations of Muslim land law were bound up with competing models of colonization: whether it should be military or civil-ian, state-directed or based on private initiatives, focused on European settlers or native Algerians.[14] Treatises debated the fine points of local land law and outlined the categories and concepts that structured successive approaches to land policy. Claiming to merely describe traditional forms of land tenure, they elaborated the nature of individual or "private" property (*melk*) and collec-tive titles (*arch*), the status of pre-conquest "state lands" (*beylik* or *Makhzen*), and the complex legal construction of religious endowments (*habous*).[15] In his defense of European colonization, Alexis de Tocqueville drew on these interpretations to claim that it was easier to settle in a territory like Algeria "that is owned only communally than onto land where every inch of soil is protected by right and a particular interest."[16] As John Ruedy has point-edly shown, "Muslim law" was, in these years, mobilized as an instrument of expropriation.[17]

---

12. Sainte-Marie, "L'application du sénatus consulte"; Guignard, "Le sénatus-consulte de 1863."

13. Sainte-Marie, "Législation foncière et société rurale."

14. See, for example, Enfantin, *La colonisation de l'Algérie*; Worms, *Recherches sur la constitution*; and, more generally, Sessions, *By Sword and Plow*.

15. Worms, *Recherches sur la constitution*. On the "invention" of these categories as traditional by French jurists see Guignard, "Les inventeurs de la tradition 'melk' et 'arch.'" For an overview see Ruedy, *Land Policy in Colonial Algeria*, 4–12; Dumasy, "Propriété foncière"; Grangaud, "Dépossession et disqualification des droits de propriété"; Nouschi, "La dépossession foncière et la paupérisation" and *Enquête sur le niveau de vie*. For the broader political significance of the debates see Abi-Mershed, *Apostles of Modernity*, 154–58.

16. "Second Report on Algeria (1847)," in Tocqueville, *Writings on Empire and Slavery*, 175.

17. Ruedy, *Land Policy in Colonial Algeria*, 103.

As we saw in the last chapter, the civilian settlers who began to arrive from metropolitan France in the 1840s bristled against Algeria's exceptional regime of land law. They denied the existence of indigenous property rights and titles, while boldly asserting their own. Citing King Louis Philippe's speech to parliament on December 23, 1839, in which he declared "Africa" to be "forever French," civilian settlers lobbied to make Algeria's legal status conform to that of metropolitan France. They denounced violations of their property and personal freedom as so many "exceptions to the Charter"—the constitution of the July Monarchy—and called for a legal affirmation of their "civil rights." Petitions and memoirs signed by wealthy and influential *colons* such as Baron Augustin de Vialar condemned military government and colonization schemes, asserting their rights as citizens whose rights were protected by the charter.[18] Tocqueville's writings and parliamentary reports on Algeria are just one prominent example of these appeals for greater legal guarantees on settlers' land and political rights. Lesser-known authors similarly denounced the arbitrary regime, demanding that Algeria become legally part of France so that settlers might recover their "rights, so long trampled underfoot by an antinational administration."[19]

Focused on promoting civilian colonization, settlers lobbied to make Algeria's real estate regime conform to the Civil Code, thus facilitating the sale of "Muslim" lands to Europeans. The provisional government's revolutionary promise in 1848 to defend Algeria "as French soil" and to extend political rights to French settlers (but not native Algerians) gave official sanction to these demands and galvanized *colon* interests.[20] But the Second Republic was short-lived. During the Second Empire, Louis Napoléon's model of the "Arab Kingdom" exacerbated the conflicts between the military regime and settler advocates. Over the course of the next two decades, the latter continued to combat centralized military policy and the exceptionality of Algerian land law in the name of their rights as French citizens. While the revolution of 1848 confirmed the settlers' political citizenship, the nationality of native Algerians as well as that of foreign settlers remained unclear. The *sénatus-consulte* of 1865 was designed to address this legal lacuna.

---

18. *Mémoire au roi et aux Chambres*, 14–15.

19. Franclieu, *Encore l'Algérie devant les Chambres*, 12.

20. Proclamation du Gouvernement provisoire aux colons, March 2, 1848, in Sirey, *Receuil général des lois et arrêts*, 2ᵉ serie (1848), 13.

Producing "Muslim Personal Status"

In declaring that all native Algerians were French nationals but not citizens, the 1865 *sénatus-consulte* sought legal clarification, not assimilation. One of the measure's framers, Ismayl Urbain, a Saint-Simonian convert to Islam and adviser to Louis Napoléon, hoped to protect indigenous interests from erosion by increasingly vocal settlers. In order to do so, he rejected Algeria's full legal assimilation to the metropole.[21] Settlers, by contrast, called for "assimilation"—not of the population, but of Algerian *property*. They wanted, in other words, to make Algerian land—not Algerian persons—French. They achieved a partial victory with the passage of the 1873 Warnier Law. While territorializing French civil law for "real property" in the prized and fertile region of the Tell, it guaranteed that "personal status and inheritance" would be left intact (article 7).[22] In its wake, colonial jurists asserted that Algerian Muslims maintained a traditional attachment to this novel legal entity, their "personal status." These jurists obscured how that status was an artifact of the legal division between personhood and property created by the law. Purportedly traditional "Muslim personal status" was, in other words, a wholly French legal category. It was French not only because it was subordinated to sovereign French authority. The category itself was *French*.[23]

Derived from the Roman law of persons, "personal status" fixed an individual's legal identity and capacity, including how and when he or she could acquire or lose legal autonomy, marry and divorce, control property and create trusts. Following ancien régime treatises, nineteenth-century French jurists traced the history of personality to Frankish invasions of Gaul. The personality of law in Europe in this account emerged out of conquests and the ensuing confrontation between "Roman" and "Germanic" systems. Bound to a deep European history of empire, personal law governed diverse peoples who lived in a territory under a single political power. Histories of European legal development sketched a shift from the predominance of personality to the ascendance of territoriality. Personality nonetheless continued to exist alongside territoriality, albeit as an "exception" to increasingly territorial legal and political orders.[24]

---

21. Abi-Mershed, *Apostles of Modernity*, 175–76.

22. "26 Juillet 1873, Loi relative à l'établissement et à la conservation de la propriété en Algérie," in Estoublon and Lefébure, *Code de l'Algérie*, 1:399.

23. For related arguments on the colonial construction of "personal status" see Hallaq, *Sharī'a*; Asad, "Reconfigurations of Law and Ethics in Colonial Egypt," in *Formations of the Secular*; Agrama, *Questioning Secularism*; Cuno, *Modernizing Marriage*; Mahmood, *Religious Difference in a Secular Age*; Stephens, *Governing Islam*.

24. Lainé, "Le droit international privé en France," 137. See also the discussion of the "personality of law" in Lupoi, *Origins of the European Legal Order*. For an account of competing theories of the emergence of personal law and its supplanting by territoriality see Guterman, "Principle of the Personality of Law"; R. T. Ford, "Law's Territory."

Personality organized important aspects of private law in the ancien régime. Multiple regional customs—of Brittany, Normandy, Paris, and Burgundy—existed alongside written Roman law in southern France, as well as canon law.[25] Established on the basis of domicile, personal laws determined the "estate and condition of the person." While the jurisdiction of real laws regulating real estate transactions was confined to a given territory, personal law remained in effect everywhere a person traveled. Ancien régime jurists described it as metonymically attached to bodies. According to Charles Loyseau, it clung "like leprosy to the skin [adherent lepra cuti]."[26] For Henri de Boullenois, personal law "penetrated" the person.[27] In this legal imaginary, personal law was a corporeal supplement or "second nature."

Postrevolutionary projects of codification were designed to abolish internal legal pluralism. In his speech introducing the first articles of the new Civil Code, Jean-Marie Portalis described how "up until now the diversity of customs created, in the same state, a hundred different statuses. The law, everywhere opposed to itself, divided citizens rather than uniting them."[28] The Civil Code aimed to undo this confusion. One of its principal architects, Portalis explained its totalizing project to encompass "the universality of things and persons." Following ancien régime jurists, architects of the Code adopted the triumvirate Roman framework of persons, things, and actions (modes of acquiring property) as an organizing framework.[29] "Personal laws" regulating status and capacity presumed mobility beyond the territorial borders of the nation. As Portalis explained, "In this way, French law, with the eyes of a mother, follows the French to farthest regions; it follows them to the extremity of the globe."[30] With unified civil legislation, personality became a feature and function of the citizen's nationality, rather than religion or domicile.[31] Preliminary article 3 of the Civil Code held that all laws governing the "status and capacity of the person" governed French nationals even when "they resided in a foreign country." Based on a principle of reciprocity between nations, subsequent codification projects in Europe and beyond adopted this model of personality.[32]

---

25. Schneider, *King's Bench*; Kelley, "'Second Nature.'" On territorialization see Maier, *Once within Borders*.

26. Loyseau, *Les œuvres de maistre Charles Loyseau*, 29.

27. Boullenois, *Traité de la personnalité*, 173 (Titre 1, chap. 3, obs. 12).

28. Portalis, *Discours, rapports et travaux*, 142.

29. Arnaud, *Les origines doctrinales du Code civil*.

30. Portalis, *Discours, rapports et travaux*, 154.

31. Foelix, *Traité du droit international privé*.

32. For Italy see Mancini, "Rapport," *Revue de droit international privé et de législation comparée* 1, no. 7 (1874): 294, and Italian Civil Code of 1865, article 6; for Egypt see *Codes des tribunaux mixtes d'Égypte*, 28, and Code Civil, article 4.

Following older jurists, commentators in the late nineteenth century drew on corporeal metaphors to articulate nationality and personal status. The Belgian jurist François Laurent, a leading continental interpreter of international private law in the personalist school, for example, commented that "there are statutes which are part of our being, of our blood and which cannot be detached from our personality, because they [the statutes] are identified with it."[33] Following Laurent's bodily metaphorics, Louis Barde claimed that "the personal status of foreigners is, like that of the French, in the blood of individuals. Personal status is the juridical physiognomy of peoples."[34] Both Laurent's and Barde's analyses drew links between nineteenth-century legal personality and that which existed in the Middle Ages. The Civil Code was supposed to abolish the last traces of this system in domestic or "internal" law. As we have seen, Algerian colonization re-created a plural legal structure and an internal diversity of status under French sovereignty.

Laurent and Barde asserted a historical continuity between modern and pre-modern theories. Armand Lainé, a professor of international law in Paris, posited a historical rupture between these older forms and a modern personal status based on territorial jurisdictions. In his view, "the new personality of law signified, no longer the application of a particular law to a race of men, but rather the application of a local law in a place other than its jurisdiction [ressort]."[35] Lainé thus distinguished between the earlier "racial" attachment to law that characterized the Franks and Gauls, and the modern national and territorial one. While this "racial" conception of law was supposed to be a thing of the past, Algeria represented an exception.

In Lainé's historical narrative, Algerian personal status was a palimpsest in which ancient and modern were overlaid. On the one hand there were foreigners, who "maintain the usage of their national laws when it comes to their état, their relations with their family, and their capacity." On the other hand, Algerians who had been declared French nationals were made categorically distinct from these foreigners, whose "personal status" was a function of nationality. As he explained: "The application of Muslim and Kabyle law in these conditions resembles more or less the regime of the personality of law as it was practiced in Gaul in Barbarian times. There is not perfect identity, since only indigenous Arabs and Kabyles benefit and not in an absolute manner;

---

33. Laurent, Droit civil international, 1:531 §368.
34. Barde, Théorie traditionnelle des statuts, 169.
35. Lainé, "Le droit international privé en France," 140. See also Lainé, Introduction au droit international privé.

but the analogy is striking."[36] This supposed "analogy" to an earlier form of racialized law was, of course, ideologically laden. For Lainé, "Muslim personal status" in Algeria recalled an antiquated, transitory legal and social condition. In drawing this comparison to "barbarian" times, Lainé depicted "Muslim personal status" to be at once a historical throwback and an organic emanation of archaic Muslim tradition.[37] His argument obscured the Roman and early modern European genealogy of the category. He instead asserted a political and social difference between modern "European" and traditional "indigenous" law that structured the differential juridical treatment of the two. This difference also distinguished international law, based on principles of territoriality and extraterritoriality, from colonial legal concerns.[38] Foreigners had a national territory that served as the seat of their law. In the case of Algerians, whose nationality *was* French, personal status became tautologically anchored, not in a national land, but in their embodied persons. "Muslim personal status" was, in other words, corporealized.

This genealogy clarifies how Muslim personal status continued to be closely associated with a fantasmatic—and specifically embodied—conception of Islam.[39] As a distinct corpus of law, it would apply only to particularized Muslims, investing Muslim *bodies*—rather than property or territory—as the locus of law. Ideas about "Muslim" sex were integral to this specifically embodied conception of law. As we saw in chapter 2, French jurists associated it with a sexualized account of Muslim law, in which polygamy was a potent symbol of masculine privilege and libidinal excess. This legal organization of sex became central to how the law distinguished property from persons. It underwrote the assimilation of Algerian real estate, while particularizing the Algerian persons that lived on that land.

While the 1865 *sénatus-consulte* presumed specific sexual and family arrangements as an unassimilable core of Muslim legal difference, the actual legal cleavage of personhood from property occurred eight years later in the Warnier Law. As Warnier explained in his report to parliament, "we must distinguish between the 'personal status' and 'real property status' of Algerian Muslims." Citing article 3 of the Civil Code, he underscored that "immobile property, even that possessed

---

36. Lainé, "Le droit international privé en France," 142.
37. On the connected temporalization of the "feudal" and the colonial see Davis, *Periodization and Sovereignty*, and Fabian, *Time and the Other*.
38. A. Weiss, *Traité élémentaire de droit international privé*, 245.
39. On the "embodied" conception of Islam and its ethnicized particularism see Masuzawa, *Invention of World Religions*, chap. 6. On "French Islam" and embodiment see Davidson, *Only Muslim*.

by foreigners, is governed by French law."[40] As one jurist explained after the law's passage, this French "real property status, once imprinted on the land, would remain immutable."[41]

French real estate law was inscribed onto Algerian land, while Muslim personal status was attached to Algerian bodies and families. As Warnier explained in his report, "We respect personal status, which touches on diverse matters of the freedom of conscience, of religion, of the intimate life of families; but, because it touches on real-estate interests, it is our duty to restrain real property law [*le statut réel*] in order to submit it to French law, to the fundamental principles of our public law which is in place wherever our national flag flies."[42] The law claimed to protect the "intimate life of families" and religion, as if these were the core elements of "Muslim law." Article 7 of the law promised to "in no way alter the personal status or rules of inheritance of natives." It was supposed to affect the legal status of land alone, not that of families, whose inheritance rules and "intimacy" would remain intact.

The law entailed a twin project of economic and emotional government. By casting landed property beyond the sphere of familial and religious intimacy, it separated the enjoyment of property rights from sexual rights. The colonial regulation of intimacy thus also carved out some domains of law and life as extra-intimate.[43] This structure of sentiment legitimated indigenous dispossession by denying an intimate attachment to land. It is an essential aspect of what Mark Rifkin describes as "settler common sense."[44]

The Warnier Law's claims to conserve family and religious intimacy were evidently disingenuous. Indeed, the architects of the Warnier Law explicitly intended to convert what were "familial" or "communal" landholdings into individual property titles under French civil law. It had a devastating effect on actual families. While supposedly preserving "intimate" concerns, the law affected their radical transformation by constituting a novel legal domain.[45] "Muslim personal status" was produced by this cleavage from what was supposedly "improper" to it, property.

---

40. Rapport Warnier in "26 Juillet 1873, Loi relative à l'établissement et à la conservation de la propriété en Algérie," in Estoublon and Lefébure, *Code de l'Algérie*, 1:399.

41. Eyssautier, *Le statut réel français en Algérie*, 87.

42. Rapport Warnier, in Estoublon and Lefébure, *Code de l'Algérie*, 1:399.

43. On the regulation of colonial intimacy see Stoler, *Carnal Knowledge and Imperial Power*.

44. Rifkin, "Settler Common Sense."

45. For a parallel discussion of the transformative effects of reducing shari'a to a law of "personal status" see Asad, "Reconfigurations of Law and Ethics in Colonial Egypt," 205–56.

What Is a Family?

The 1873 law territorialized French civil law in piecemeal fashion by designating select areas to be surveyed and partitioned by government-appointed *commissaire-enquêteurs*. In these areas, the commissioners allocated individual title holdings for all those who could demonstrate "current possession" (*jouissance effective*) of privately held (classified as *melk*) land. Even more significantly, the law broke up collective lands (classified as *arch*) that were held in common by extended families and tribes, in order to facilitate the sale of property to European settlers. The economic liberalism of the law had limits. It allowed "indivision" to persist at the level of the family because, according to Warnier, Algerian "family ties are still strong enough to incite members to remain in indivision, even at the expense of their own interests."[46] While claiming not to impinge on "the intimate life of families," the reform placed the definition of the "Muslim family" at its core.

Critics of the law in the National Assembly, and most notably Alexandre Clapier, foresaw the difficulty of substituting individual holdings for familial and communal ones. He remained skeptical of this effort to change *mœurs* by decree, to substitute the "house for the tent," and "individualism for the family."[47] Article 4 of the legislation indeed allowed individual family members to sell off their parts of a collective holding by a judicially mandated auction or "licitation." The provision was based on article 815 of the Civil Code, which held that no individual could be forced to remain in "indivision." Warnier assumed a universal *homo economicus*, claiming that "one would have to be unfamiliar with man to doubt that before long, in each family, there will be someone who will ask for a share in order to better assure his independence and give greater force to his activity."[48] The text of the law did not however specify what constituted "a family" and hence which family members would be granted titles. This blind spot gave rise to considerable administrative and legal confusion.

Once jurists detected the oversight, government officials tried to fill the definitional lacuna. Eugène Robe, a prominent lawyer at the Cour d'Alger and deputy on the Conseil général d'Alger, formulated the problem succinctly: "What is a family? Where does it begin and where does it end?"[49] Aiming to clarify matters, Governor-General Antoine Chanzy's Instructions of July 1, 1875, explained

---

46. Rapport Warnier, in Estoublon and Lefébure, *Code de l'Algérie*, 1:400.
47. In *Annales de l'assemblée générale*, vol. 18 (June 30, 1873): 641.
48. Rapport Warnier, in Estoublon and Lefébure, *Code de l'Algérie*, 1:400.
49. Robe, *Propriété immobilière en Algérie*, 67.

that the law was designed "to constitute property not by the individual, but by the family unit." Begging the question, he left the "family unit" undefined.[50] The Conseil supérieur de gouvernement revisited the question six months later, when Robe, now a deputy from the department of Alger, reported on proposed modifications. A fierce advocate of opening Algerian property to sale, Robe observed that the definition of "the family" directly impacted how the law would apply to land. As he explained, "Since what matters here is to divide the land between family units, what must be determined is the relation of the indigenous family to the land in order to say where it begins and where it ends. If it takes blood ties as its basis, the number of co-owners will be too large; it could even be a *ferka* [faction], a *douar* [circle], a tribe; the parts will be too small and, in this case, the ties of persistent indivision will be too difficult to break." In other words, extended families would be more likely to maintain a collective holding, thus keeping their land off the market. By contrast, Robe believed that the bonds of indivision would be much weaker "if the unit of interest and possession is reduced to descendants of a single line." Robe made the desired result brutally clear: if the "family unit" were reduced in size, "the wedge of division [*le coin du partage*] would penetrate easily." Of course, single family lines were no less of an abstraction. It required painstaking work on the part of the *commissaire-enquêteur* to register these family members by drawing on "his knowledge and experience of Arab things." This was, as Robe avowed, the very heart of the difficulty ("C'est là où la difficulté se trouvera"). He here underscored the governor-general's 1875 instructions: "'One of the most important things for the *commissaire-enquêteur* IS TO FIRMLY GRASP WHERE THE REAL FAMILY UNIT IS FORMED.'"[51]

Other politicians and jurists remained unsatisfied by this definition of the "family unit." Rémy Jacques, deputy of Oran, the department where much of the "Frenchification" of land was taking place, found it too vague. Jacques wanted land to be broken up into distinct units and thus argued for a more restricted definition of the family. Making his case in a debate over the 1876 budget, Jacques explained how the delimitation of families would dismantle collective holdings, while also reconfirming the rights of the "*père de famille*." Jacques here endorsed a nuclear model of the family. "How should one understand the family unit?" he asked rhetorically. "Is it the European family made up of a father, a mother, and

---

50. *Instructions du Gouverneur Général de l'Algérie pour l'exécution de la loi sur la propriété*, 29. See also Ageron, *Les Algériens musulmans*, 1:84–5; Djerbal, "Processus de colonisation et évolution de la propriété foncière," 202–4.

51. Conseil supérieur de l'Algérie, *Procès verbaux* (December 1875), 436. Capitalization in the original. For the text see *Instructions du Gouverneur Général de l'Algérie pour l'exécution de la loi sur la propriété*, 33.

their children, with the unit of property in the hands of the father? If it is that, if you give the title to the father of the family, we agree."[52]

While *commissaire-enquêteurs* worked to implement the law, government representatives continued to debate its foundational categories. In 1877 and 1878, discussions by the Conseil supérieur de l'Algérie generated reform projects, including one authored by Jacques and his fellow deputies Gaston Thomson (Constantine) and François Gastu (Alger). According to Jacques, the law needed to be altered because Algerian families could have as many as 100 or 150 members. A government adviser, Évariste Vignard, defended the law, claiming that these figures were exaggerated, "more of a legend than reality." In his view, "the Arab family, in its greatest extent cannot stretch beyond the degrees conferred by inheritance" and hence never took on "the biblical proportions" imagined by Jacques. For Vignard, proceeding with the application of the law would demonstrate that, especially in the case of large holdings, possession was in fact held by "distinct families."[53]

Despite these assurances, the question of how to define "the family unit" continued to plague officials and the commissaires, in particular. Over the next decade and a half, they had to determine who belonged to "a family" and which family members would be granted titles. They consulted village councils (*djemmas*), qadis, and family members in order to map families and apply Muslim rules of inheritance.

Early directives tried to provide guidance. Following a discussion in the Conseil supérieur, a September 22, 1876, circular to departmental prefects explained that the commissaire's mission was to find "the real owners of the ground." "Current possession" (*jouissance effective*) was to be the sole criterion on which titles would be assigned, "without worrying about either the sex or the condition of the occupants." The circular rejected a hereditary definition of family membership, as it would lead to "inevitable confusion." The hereditary conception risked including all of those who descended from a single progenitor—"present or absent, blood relations and in-laws [*directs ou alliés*]"— rather than those who "lived in the same tent." In making possession rather than heredity the central criterion, "no woman nor any minor who effectively participated in exploitation of the land was excluded."[54] Effective possession rather than heredity was supposed to determine rights to collectively held land.

---

52. *Annales du Sénat et de la Chambre des Députés, Débats et Documents*, Session extraordinaire de 1876 (November 17, 1876), 1:284.

53. *Étude sur la propriété indigène*, 15.

54. Circular Gov. Gen. to Prefects, September 22, 1876, "Propriété indigène—sujet des droits des femmes aux terrains de propriété collective," dossier Pref. d'Oran; Section de la Propriété; 1876; Circulaires et décisions in ANOM 92/1N/4. And, Conseil supérieur de l'Algérie, *Procès verbaux* (November 1876), 30-31.

"Inevitable confusion" nonetheless persisted. While working closer to the ground, commissaires remained beholden to bureaucratic fantasies of the Algerian family and the power of state officials to apprehend it. The law assumed that local inhabitants would remain fixed in place, patiently waiting for colonial officials to survey their lands. This was not to be the case. When Commissaire François Gourgeot was sent to the *douar* of Messer in the department of Oran in 1874, he found that property possession was in a considerable state of flux. The passage of the law had sown chaos, rather than creating order.

Adding Disorder to Disorder

Immediately after the passage of the 1873 law, the Conseil général of Oran recommended that Messer along with the areas of Tirenat and Sidi Yacoub be converted to French law. The zones were chosen because of their proximity to Sidi Bel Abbès and its population of 8,786 Europeans. The operations would, according to council member Adolphe Pelliat, "make land transactions possible" and "facilitate in the most regular and legal manner the extension of French colonization." Unsurprisingly, the measures targeted the "richest lands," especially those that lent themselves to "industrial agriculture."[55] That was the plan. But once on site, the commissaire reported that he suffered a "long and cruel perplexity." Inhabitants moved around incessantly, claiming areas "that had never been cultivated by anyone" and selling these plots to Europeans. The law naïvely presumed that, prior to the commissaire's arrival, "no one would move." It imagined, in the commissaire's telling visual metaphor, that he could "take a photograph of the lands and give them to those who cultivated them."[56]

This fantasy of the aerial photograph captures a bureaucratic desire for visual mastery and the immediate projection of French law onto Algerian land. The governor-general's Instructions of 1875 underscored the need for rapid and uniform application, urging commissaires to work "methodically in order that, everywhere in Algeria, from the department in the East, to those in the West and Center, nothing deviates from the precise rules that are indispensable to follow." Otherwise, affairs would risk falling into "the inextricable chaos in which indigenous property finds itself, because we will add disorder to a preexisting

---

55. Procès-Verbaux, Conseil général d'Oran, October 18, 1873, 269–71. And Gov. Gen., Arrêté relatif à trois douars-communes du département d'Oran, May 19, 1874, in *BOGGA* 14 (1874): 364.

56. Exécution de la loi du 26 Juillet 1873, Douar-Commune de Messer, Tribu des Oulad Brahim. In dossier Propriété Indigène, Tribu des Oulad Brahim, ANOM 92/2N77.

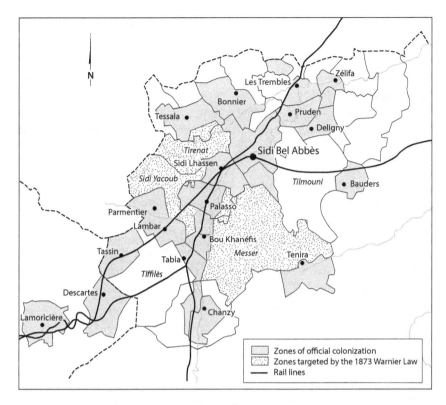

FIGURE 7 / Detail of area of colonization around Sidi Bel Abbès. Based on *Algérie—Carte de la Colonisation officielle* (1902), redrawn by Bill Nelson.

disorder."[57] Such claims about the "chaotic" character of local property title had long been part of settler arguments for reform. In a report to parliament in 1847, Alexis de Tocqueville lamented that property in Algeria that remained under native title was "confused and unproductive": "the same fields have been sold to several Europeans at once, by sellers whose right was either doubtful or nonexistent, and who in addition never indicated their boundaries."[58] The 1873 law was supposed to straighten out this purported disorder.

Legal fantasies of immediate application did not last long. Local conditions thwarted the governor-general's demand for speed and precision. These

---

57. *Instructions du Gouverneur Général de l'Algérie pour l'exécution de la loi sur la propriété*, 11. On "seeing like a state" and aerial photography see J. C. Scott, *Seeing Like a State*; Haffner, *View from Above*.

58. Tocqueville, *Writings on Empire and Slavery*, 163.

frustrations were symptomatic of a founding contradiction of modern (French) paperwork. As Ben Kafka has suggested, the unfulfillable desire for bureaucratic immediacy can be understood in a psychoanalytic sense "as a desire that is not reducible to a need or demand." Precisely because bureaucracy relies on the messy mediation of paperwork, it can never fully deliver the order, efficiency, and transparency that it promises. The impossibility of immediacy paradoxically produces at once a desire for and a frustration with the mechanisms of the state.[59]

The 1873 law produced just such bureaucratic frustration. Now endowed with greater political power, settlers placed more faith in the state to secure and guarantee property transactions. The fantasy of bureaucratic omnipotence entailed in legally remapping the territory was, however, inevitably compromised by its necessary mediation: the recourse to translators, informants, and the sheer complexity of the titling process itself. The commissaires' work was haunted by uncertainty and anxiety.[60] Their often exasperated reports clearly express unfulfilled bureaucratic desires.

Critics of the law such as Clapier worried about the excessive power of the commissaire, who was poised to become the "sovereign arbiter of Arab property."[61] In fact, these "sovereign" land surveyors were relatively low-level officials who were entirely dependent on intermediaries—translators and qadis, members of municipal councils or the village elders appointed to *djemmas* to assemble written, oral, and eyewitness evidence of property ownership. As emissaries of the colonial state, the commissaires both wielded an extraordinary amount of power over local inhabitants and remained subject to manipulation by them, as subsequent trials made clear.[62] These efforts produced the opposite of efficient order. As the commissaire who carried out the operations in Messer ironically noted, the law provoked "complete anarchy" instead.[63]

Rather than organizing property titles out of native disarray, the law's "method" created disorder. A marginal note by an inspector on the divisions carried out in Harrar in 1876 was, for example, succinct in its verdict: "very

---

59. On this contradiction see Kafka, *Demon of Writing*, 57.

60. On affect and contingency in the colonial archive see Stoler, *Along the Archival Grain*. On the instability of colonial bureaucracy and its dependency on mediators see Raman, *Document Raj*. Also Bayly, *Empire and Information*.

61. Clapier in *Annales de l'assemblée générale* 18 (June 30, 1873): 644.

62. See, for example, Mediahed v. Veuve El Hachemi, Cour d'Alger (May 4, 1899), *RA*, 1900, pt. 2, 92–94.

63. Exécution de la loi du 26 Juillet 1873, Douar-Commune de Messer, Tribu des Ouled Brahim. In dossier Propriété Indigène, Tribu des Oulad Brahim, in ANOM 92/2N77.

confused."[64] On one level, this is unsurprising. After all, the law was designed to disrupt native property titles as a tactic of dispossession. Warnier's report and subsequent commentaries made this clear. But these apparently straightforward economic aims do not entirely explain how the law's form and tactics took shape, nor do they account for the struggles of commissaires and local property owners as they negotiated the confusion provoked by its implementation. The legal reshaping of Algerian property did not and could not correspond to fantasies of projecting civil law onto Algerian land. Instead, these operations produced considerable psychic as well as social "friction."[65] The limits of the colonial state became perceptible at the very moment that these officials sought to render Algerian land and Algerian families visible to French officials.

The operations pursued in two villages close to Messer, Tirenat and Sidi Yacoub, illustrate the conflicts produced by efforts to determine the "current possession" of "existing family units."[66] A heated exchange between Inspector Louis Gourgeot and Commissaire Louis Pontet over how to divide property demonstrates the contested meanings of both possession and "the family unit." According to Gourgeot, Pontet's operations had caused a local scandal by denying women and children's property claims in Tirenat. The widow Fatima bent El-Kadi claimed that she was cheated out of her rightful ownership of lot 362, worth some 1,500 francs, by her husband's nephew, Bou Medine ben Arricha, even though (or rather because) he was the president of the *douar* and her legal representative. After interviewing Fatima and other inhabitants of the village, Gourgeot asserted that Bou Medine had manipulated Pontet by claiming the parcel as his own. According to Gourgeot, Fatima denounced Bou Medine in his presence, explaining that "as a woman," she "did not know the size of a hectare." In her view, it was easy to take advantage of her, "because I am a woman and my children are still young, we were sure to end up victims."[67] For Gourgeot, Commissaire Pontet erred in accepting Bou Medine's verbal assertions of possession.[68] Pontet, meanwhile, offered an alternative interpretation of "current possession." He claimed that minors who were too young to work the land "could not be considered as having effective possession of any land at all." In Gourgeot's

---

64. Dossier Harrar, 1876–79, Register 1, Division of Parcel 12, in ANOM 91/6N/6.

65. These conflicts exemplify what, in another context of disappropriation, anthropologist Anna Tsing describes as "friction." As with the opening of Indonesian forests studied by Tsing in the 1990s, the dynamics of dispossession in Algeria were highly uneven and "messy." Tsing, *Friction*, 2.

66. *Instructions du Gouverneur Général de l'Algérie pour l'exécution de la loi sur la propriété*, 10.

67. "Rapport de l'Inspecteur des commissions d'enquête ... dans les deux douars de Sidi-Yacoub et Tirenat," 11–14, in ANOM 92/2N77.

68. Ibid., 20, in ANOM 92/2N77.

eyes, this policy resulted in nothing less than the "dispossession of minors, women, and absent family members."[69]

The section of Gourgeot's report devoted to properties that remained in "indivision" sheds light on his apparently indulgent attitude toward Fatima's claim: he favored breaking large properties up into smaller units. In his view, Pontet did not sufficiently dismantle large familial property holdings, mistakenly allowing collective holdings to remain in place among brothers, who "in order to ensure their independence ask that their part be delimited." For Gourgeot, "each brother, who is the head of a family [chef de famille], which is to say, who has children and a household of his own and whose name figures on the tax rolls, should have his own lot, delimited and demarcated."[70]

Pontet wrote a fifty-four-page report to the prefect of Oran in response. He underscored the trying climatic conditions of winter rain that had made his operation particularly difficult. He avowed that Fatima's rights had been denied, but stated that she should have alerted him. "A word or letter," he claimed, would have sufficed.[71] Pontet fiercely contested Gourgeot's depiction of him as "an incapable agent, who became an instrument of hatreds, sympathies, rapacity and covetousness" and who allowed "intermediaries to give any information with impunity and to prepare as they wanted—literally 'à leur fantasie'—solutions to questions of property."[72] Far from being matters of cold calculation, property claims solicited intense emotions. Gourgeot's charge that Pontet was merely a tool of these passions gave rise to its own intense conflict between the two agents. Not least they struggled over how to define the "family."

In the section of his response devoted to "Questions of Principle: Current Possession and the Rights of Women and Minors," Pontet explained that he had been guided not by "personal opinion" but by the governor-general's September 22, 1876, circular, which insisted that "current possession" rather than "heredity" determined land rights.[73] More broadly, he explained that his response was motivated "not by self-regard [amour propre], but inspired by the

---

69. Ibid., 21, in ANOM 92/2N77.

70. "Rapport de l'Inspecteur des commissions d'enquête ... dans les deux douars de Sidi-Yacoub et Tirenat, L'Indivision," in ANOM 92/2N77.

71. Response to "Rapport de l'Inspecteur des commissions d'enquête ... dans les deux douars de Sidi-Yacoub et Tirenat, §8, n. 362 (15 October 1879)," in ANOM 92/2N77.

72. Response to "Rapport de l'Inspecteur des commissions d'enquête ... dans les deux douars de Sidi-Yacoub et Tirenat, §13 De ma manière de procéder (15 October 1879)," in ANOM 92/2N77.

73. Response to "Rapport de l'Inspecteur des commissions d'enquête ... dans les deux douars de Sidi-Yacoub et Tirenat, §14 Questions de principe (15 October 1879)," in ANOM 92/2N77.

observation of the method followed by colleagues, with the support of the superior authority."[74] Pontet presented himself as hewing to the rules, rather than as subject to folly or passion. In his view, the division of property held in common by families posed the greatest challenge. Citing Robe, he explained that he did not bother proceeding with unnecessary divisions when family members chose to maintain communal property. Gourgeot underscored his frustration in a marginal note on the report: "It all depends on the meaning of the word family." For the inspector, the family should be limited and "not be extended to comprise several families."[75] In his view, Pontet left too many families—and hence properties—intact.

Gourgeot developed these criticisms further in a virulent (and antisemitic) diatribe against the administration's mishandling of Algerian affairs. He privileged Deputy Jacques's limited definition of the family, which was based on the Civil Code's *père de famille*.[76] Suffering, as we have seen, from "long and cruel perplexity," commissaires frequently followed the instructions provided to them by the government in 1875 and again in an 1879 manual that outlined how to assign shares of collectively owned land. For Gourgeot, these repeated attempts at clarification simply sewed further confusion.[77] Commissaires were encouraged to calculate elaborate fractions in which the common denominator represented the entirety of the collective possession, and the numerator represented each of the individuated parts. When many family members were included as titleholders, the "quote parts" became infinitely small, while the common denominator grew in size. Strict adherence to this arithmetic created new difficulties rather than resolving them.

Insisting on the need for rule-bound conformity, the governor-general's 1875 *Instructions* had also cautioned against the risk of its excess. These directives explained that, "in desiring to observe the law in its most absolute sense and to arrive at a mathematical determination of the parts belonging to each, some have gone so far as to the translate them into seven-figure fractions and, in one case, a nine-figure fraction, which, evidently cannot be represented in thought." The governor-general warned against the dangers of these sublime fractions. The problem, of course, was that an "abstract right" could not be "translated by

---

74. Response to "Rapport de l'Inspecteur des commissions d'enquête . . . dans les deux douars de Sidi-Yacoub et Tirenat, §15 De l'emploi des qadis (15 October 1879)," in ANOM 92/2N77.

75. Response to "Rapport de l'Inspecteur des commissions d'enquête . . . dans les deux douars de Sidi-Yacoub et Tirenat, 3ᵉ partie: Indivision (15 October 1879)," in ANOM 92/2N77.

76. Gourgeot, *Les sept plaies d'Algérie*, 105.

77. Ibid., 117.

any measurement on the ground."[78] In other words, the mathematical symbol, while impeccably calculated, had no terrestrial referent. Unable to close this gap in signification, the commissaires fixated on precise arithmetic. They devised a round sum on paper, even if it was impossible to arrive at on the land. This was bureaucratic fantasy at work.

The infinitely small fraction became a source of bureaucratic madness. In the commune of Messer, for example, the reason of state risked creating "anarchy." While subsequent efforts to remedy the situation with further regularization only made it worse, the administration saw no other alternative than to (compulsively) repeat a call for order.

The 1879 *Manuel du Commissaire Enquêteur* once again outlined procedures. The document, in its first line, underscored how the "methodical work" of applying the law depended on "regularity and uniformity."[79] It sought to impose standardized forms and procedures, down to the manner in which names should be abbreviated in the documents, the graph paper on which genealogical trees should be traced, and the kind of boxes in which the twenty-two distinct elements of the dossier were to be transported (reinforced and tied up with string).[80]

Intended to regularize the actions of the commissaires, the instructions had perverse effects. Many continued to follow this template not just to the letter, but also to the number in establishing the division of shares in communally held property. For undivided property, the commissaire was supposed to trace back to the "ancestor from whom the property originally came" (*l'aïeul d'où provient primitivement la propriété*), enumerating successive generations until he arrived at living heirs. Once the order of inheritance had been established and shares apportioned "following Muslim law," the sum for every living heir could be calculated. That sum would be represented as a fraction of the whole. In order to do so, the commissaire had to derive the lowest common denominator, sometimes dividing families into distinct branches in order to better determine the whole. For large, extended families, the denominator was very high, resulting, as the previous instructions had noted, in "numbers that are hard to read and hard to comprehend." In order to address the problem, the manual determined that "denominators should not be more than five figures, or 99,999."[81] Pages outlining how to proceed with these elaborate calculations followed.

78. *Instructions du Gouverneur Général de l'Algérie pour l'exécution de la loi sur la propriété*, 21.
79. *Manuel du Commissaire Enquêteur*, 1.
80. Ibid., 16.
81. Ibid., 79.

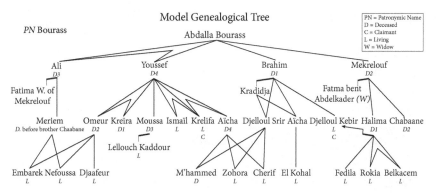

Those beneficiaries belonging to a single generation are located in the same row.
A line drawn from one name to another, from above to below, indicates that the one written above is deceased and is the father or mother of the one written below.
Two lines joined by an internal angle of those indicated above designate first cousins or children of a single bed.
A line drawn from two ascendants to the same descendants signifies that the first two are married and indicates their children in common.
A broken line ⌐ indicates widows or widowers who inherit.
A line ↘ designates that the person towards whom the line points is married to the person from whom it departs and has inherited. Unless otherwise indicated, if it is a male, this sign also indicates that he is the father of the deceased woman's children.
For descendants in a feminine line or their kin by marriage, when indication is given of the tree in which their parents figure, their patronym can be found on that tree. If these parents are not found in any tree, their patronymic is placed below their names.

FIGURE 8 / Official model of genealogical tree. Adapted from *Manuel du commissaire enquêteur pour l'application de la loi du 26 juillet 1873* (Alger, 1879). Redrawn by Julianna Teoh.

The most challenging case presented in the manual was for the inheritance of Mohammed Krodja, which spanned five generations, detailed in an extensive genealogical tree, which served as a model for the commissaires. The accompanying text demonstrated how to establish the lowest common denominator for the shares of this enormous family. Once all the calculations for the different branches of the family were added up, the number came to the round sum of 34,560! And this was the instruction manual that was designed to establish a bureaucratic norm. This effort to make the process more orderly and exact produced the opposite effect.

This official model gave rise to greater confusion for men who were sent into the field. Seeking to trace the history of property ownership back to "a primitive ancestor" (*l'auteur commun*), the commissaires went in search of a primal father. According to Gourgeot, they "believed that they had to go back centuries in order to discover the *chef de famille*. This is what led to the construction of gigantic genealogical trees, whose principal default was that they were false."[82] The painstaking effort to achieve knowing mastery of persons and property resulted

---

82. Gourgeot, *Les sept plaies d'Algérie*, 102.

in elaborate fictions. For many, the practical effects of this painstaking exercise were no less disappointing. Critics charged the commissaires with unwittingly encouraging large families to maintain communal property rather than dismantling it. Incomprehensible fractional shares could not be mapped onto the land and assigned to individuals, so families remained in indivision instead.

The execution of the law also took a toll on the commissaires, as Gourgeot's own dyspeptic report and subsequent writing attests. The labor was exhausting and the results apparently pointless. The *procureur général* Jean Baptiste Fourcade lamented the commissaire's travails before the Conseil supérieur de gouvernement in 1877: "We have required him to use genealogical trees and calculations to establish infinitesimal fractions of property. We have as a result found the impossibility of application, which we have tried to solve by half measures that remedy nothing and further slow things down."[83] Commissaires themselves complained about the task. In his final report for the Commission d'enquête de Sidi Bel Abbès, an official charged with apportioning titles for the Amarna tribe listed some of the preposterous fractions that he had calculated, including numbers such as 154,903/406,950 and 3,369/10,720. He went on to write: "It was impossible to find other fractional expressions that would allow each beneficiary the share assigned by Muslim inheritance." The fixed procedures were wholly inefficient, given that "the time it takes to do the calculations causes the expense to be greater than the value of the shares."[84]

Politicians like Fourcade recommended doing away with this pointless and costly exercise. Other jurists defended the practice as essential to realizing the true aims of the law. In their view, it allowed Europeans to "penetrate" properties held in common by families. As the *directeur des finances* Charles le Myre de Vilers explained, the apportioning of shares allowed "the European to penetrate, though licitation, into the undivided property which, in its current state, remains immobile in the hands of the Arab family."[85] Using a similarly violent rhetoric of dispossession, Deputy Robe concurred that doing away with fractional division would weaken "the law's most essential principle," namely "to wrench Arab property from the impenetrable obscurity that the constitution of the Arab family has covered it with." As these statements made starkly clear, the Warnier Law aimed to separate the "Arab family" from "Arab property."[86] In theory, the

---

83. Fourcade, Conseil supérieur de l'Algérie, *Procès verbaux* (December 1877), 315.

84. "Rapport sur l'ensemble des travaux concernant la Constitution de la propriété individuelle dans le tribu des Amarna," Propriété Indigène, dossier Ouled Brahim El Amarna, in ANOM 92/2N/78. And Arrêté du 22 September 1876 in *BOGGA* 16 (1876): 791.

85. Myre de Vilers, Conseil supérieur de l'Algérie, *Procès verbaux* (December 1877), 317.

86. Robe, Conseil supérieur de l'Algérie, *Procès verbaux* (December 1877), 315.

family remained "impenetrable" because still enveloped in its obscure Muslim law. Once submitted to French law, property ideally become visible and hence divisible.

In order to map property, however, families also had to be mapped—and named. This was the purpose of the genealogical tree as well as the assignment of patronyms to property holders. In order to distinguish family members—and their property titles—the law required commissaires to give family names alongside unique first names to each title holder. The 1875 instructions outlined the desired procedure: "every family whose property has been confirmed [*constatée*] should be assigned a name that will be for each a way to recognize his individuality in indigenous society, just as the title delivered is a way to recognize individualized properties on Algerian soil." The attribution of patronymic family names located individuals within a patriarchal family structure. The same name was given to "the family group, descendant from a common ancestor [*l'auteur commun*]."[87] The insistence on patronymics indicates how the Warnier Law, while theoretically focused on property to the exclusion of "personal status," had a fantasmatic patriarchal model of the family at its core.

The 1873 law elaborated individual names and titles. Its procedures nonetheless produced what Elizabeth Povinelli has described as a "genealogical" conception of indigenous society. While supposedly breaking up "family communism," this genealogical model grounded Algerians' legal identity in the family and "Muslim law."[88] As in the case of the widow Fatima, the presumptions and procedures built into this patriarchal model risked subsuming individuals, and especially individual women, in a fixed framework of the "Muslim family," and occasionally divesting them of their property.

Women periodically addressed themselves to colonial officials in search of redress. In the spring of 1881, for example, Sultana bent El Hadj ben Ez-Zahaf petitioned the prefect of Alger. Written in broken French, her letter made a modest request. She wanted an official map of her extended family's brush-covered property, located near the town of Ménerville (Thénia), where she claimed to have "a part a parcel." "Having cleared" the plot, she had made "all the necessary expenditures to have a garden," which she "planted with fruits." Named "Tourtite Kebaïly," the orchard was surrounded by Barbary figs.[89] Sultana's note indicated a direct personal investment in the property and hence her current possession. To her dismay, another family member had claimed the land as his own, based

---

87. *Instructions du Gouverneur Général de l'Algérie pour l'exécution de la loi sur la propriété*, 31.
88. Povinelli, *Empire of Love*.
89. Petition from Sultana bent El Hadj Mohammed to Préfet of Alger in ANOM 91/6 N 23.

on title documents issued by the commissaire. The quiet pathos of the letter in which Sultana lamented her lost garden did not stir the prefect to act on her behalf. Upholding the just application of French real estate law, he dismissed her plea. In this case, as in so many others, he classified the property matter as one of "private interest," beyond the purview of state intervention.[90]

Some jurists even sought to restrict married women's property rights. A reform drafted by Robe and the president of the Cour d'appel d'Alger, Édouard Sautayra, went so far as to propose that Algerian women should, like French women, be made subject to marital authorization for all property matters. Article 5 of their reform held that "the married indigenous woman can no longer assume obligations [s'obliger] or testify in court without the authorization of her husband or a court."[91] In the end, the measure was rejected, even though many other elements of their proposal were integrated into the law's 1887 reform. A committee of jurists charged with reviewing the proposal questioned whether it made sense to introduce "married women's incapacity" into Muslim society, given that this legal inequality was "the work of centuries" and "the result of a particular conception [une conception particulière]."[92] For these colonial legal experts, French wives' subordinate "personal status" appeared to be a mark not of backwardness but of civilized distinction.

The 1873 law was evidently riven by contradictions at the levels of both theory and practice. Not least, and most tragically, it was, despite its apparently costly and notoriously inefficient procedures, highly effective as an instrument of dispossession.[93] The administrative morass that the procedures created and the prohibitively high legal fees that they entailed put native titleholders at a distinct disadvantage, making them vulnerable to exploitation. The law played on and produced conflicts in and between families. And it contributed in no small part to the disaggregation of communities when and where it was applied. In the face of this thoroughgoing legal and administrative onslaught, Algerian families sought to maintain control over their properties in the Muslim law courts that had been maintained for matters of personal status and inheritance.

---

90. Minute de Préfet, ANOM 91/6 N 23. For other cases see Réclamations des indigènes: correspondance in ANOM 91/6N/22 and 6N/23. Also, Alger, Service de la propriété indigène. Réclamations des indigènes pour des propriétés dont ils auraient été dépossédées, 1885–1926, in ANOM 91/8/N/1–3.

91. Modifications à apporter à la loi du 26 Juillet 1873, 11.

92. Dain, Rapport sur les modifications à apporter à la loi du 26 juillet 1873, 24.

93. On the productivity of failure in land and family colonial policy see Zimmerman, Alabama in Africa, 169–70.

An early and much contested ruling by Charles-François Bastien, president of the Court of Appeals of Algiers, upheld their rights to do so. In this complex inheritance case, the majority of Mahmoud ben Abd Eltif's family resisted the efforts of his brother, Ali, to force the sale of a group of properties of which he was only a partial owner. At Mahmoud's death in October 1875, their succession was overseen by the Maliki qadi of Algiers. Ali had sold off the majority of his inheritance share before Mahmoud's death, maintaining possession in only one house. He nonetheless sought, with the aid of his European creditor Giroud, to force the rest of the family to sell all their holdings. To do so, he contested the qadi's jurisdiction in the case in order to bring the matter before a French court. The family—which included Mahmoud's sister Mimi, as well as cousins, fellow grandchildren of their "common ancestor" El Hadj Ahmed ben Abd Eltif—resisted Ali's claim.

The question before the court was whether the 1873 law now required French courts to oversee inheritance cases such as this one. President Bastien refused to grant Ali's appeal. As he explained, the 1873 law "expressly maintained the rules of Muslim inheritance in its article 7." In his view, "everything in the management of estates [*les successions*] is attached to the family, to personal status, and thus requires particular care [*ménagements*]." For Bastien, in other words, the 1873 law drew a clear distinction between property matters and personal ones. The former comprised "contracts, which are always voluntary acts," that would be treated by French courts and estate sales. In the latter domain were "events which are integral [*nécessaire*] and intimate to the indigenous family, and are reserved for Muslim judges."[94] Robe, in his commentary on the case in his journal, noted that the findings on this "delicate question" directly contradicted his own.[95] Systematically privileging French law, he regularly denounced decisions that gave precedence to Muslim law jurisdiction for inheritance.[96]

Given these provisions, local inhabitants regularly took recourse to Muslim law to thwart the operations of the commissaires prior to their completion.[97] They founded Muslim law trusts (*habous*) and appealed to their right to preemptively buy family property put up for sale (*chefaa*) in order to protect their land

---

94. Ch. des app. mus. (June 28, 1876), *Robe*, 1876, 131–32.

95. Ibid., 126–27.

96. Robe, "16ᵉ Question de droit," *Robe*, 1876, 27–31. And, *RA*, 1886, pt. 2, 68–73.

97. Mahmoud ben Belkassem Saïdji et autres v. Mohamed ben Tahar et cons., Ch. des app. mus. (March 22, 1880), *Robe*, 1880, 233–40.

from French incursion. Colonial jurists continually worked to restrain these legal strategies in order to extend the territorial reach of French civil law.[98]

More notably still, local inhabitants seized on the lability of the law's language of the family, appropriating it for their own uses. For example, when Commissaire Eugène Houdas arrived in the town of Ouarizane in the Oranais in 1882, he learned that three large property-owning families, headed by El Hadj Mohammed ben Chehida, Si El Arbi, and Si Djelloul, declared themselves to be members of a single family.[99] Their doing so certainly made Houdas's mission easier. They got to maintain their collective property, and he did not have to divide land up into infinitesimal fractions between a hundred or so kin.

In his inspection report on the operation, Gourgeot predictably raised questions about this outsize family property. In his view, it demonstrated the natives' "absolute ignorance of the new law's principles and of their own interests."[100] In fact, it illustrated precisely the opposite. They understood very well that the "family" imagined by the Warnier Law was a colonial legal construction that they could mobilize toward their own ends. Other members of the family, including five women, Yajout bent El Hadj El Miloud ben Chehida, Fathma bent Si Ahmed ben Chehida, Zohra bent si B. Khedda, Helima bent Moammar Ben Arrer, and Meriem bent Mahi el Tourari, in turn adopted a different definition. In a petition to the prefect of Oran, they asserted that Houdas's inquiry had violated their rights by assigning titles exclusively to men. As an advocate of maximal property division, Gourgeot endorsed the women's claims—alongside those of another family member, Mohammed ben Bou Dehedj, and, most notably, a European landowner, Thullier, who also laid claim to a parcel. The three heads of family had used the legal uncertainty of "the family" in order to consolidate and protect their land.[101] Colonial administrators, on the other hand, marshaled the details of Muslim inheritance law in order to counter those claims. In the conclusion to his report, Gourgeot instructed the commissaire "to end collectivity not only in

---

98. All the proposed projects for the reform of the law sought to limit the legal reach of *habous* and other protections afforded by Muslim law; see *Modifications à apporter à la loi du 26 Juillet 1873.* On strategies of resistance see Guignard, "L'affaire Beni Urjin." And Powers, "Orientalism, Colonialism, and Legal History."

99. Dossier Ouarizane, ANOM 92/2NN/603.

100. "Inspection des travaux de la propriété indigène. N. 60. Objet: Vérification sur le terrain des opérations de constatation de la propriété foncière privée au douar commune de Ouarizane. Rapport, Oran, 7 April 1882," in ANOM 92/2NN/603.

101. Translation of petition Yajout bent El Hadj El Miloud ben Chehida et al.; Translation of petition Mohammed ben Bou Dehedj, ANOM 92/2NN/603.

the lots signaled in the present report but everywhere that it encompasses in a single lot parcels belonging to different families."[102]

Warnier's initial defense of the law had focused on its advantages for entrepreneurial Muslim heirs. European settlers were nonetheless its true beneficiaries, despite its critics' claims that its application was too costly and consuming. Robe and his colleagues thus lamented that, by 1882, only 295,891 hectares out of 12 million hectares in the Tell had been granted titles.[103] In the end, the law in its original and reformed versions significantly opened up the territory of the Tell to sale. According to an official report on colonization, between the years of 1877 and 1898, Europeans purchased 563,762 hectares of Algerian land, averaging, between 1877 and 1888, 28,721 hectares a year.[104]

The 1873 reform was designed to progressively extract Algerian land from the "disorder" of Muslim law and assimilate it to the universal economic principles of contract enshrined in French civil law. According to the colonial jurist Alfred Dain, the law's aims were clear: "to allow for the circulation of real estate wealth, until now immobilized in the confusion of family communism."[105] "Personal status" law was, by contrast, supposed to remain a distinct and embodied domain of Muslim difference. Property reform imagined a separation of economy from religious and familial intimacy by making them subject to different laws. Inheritance occupied an uneasy position in this scheme. In using Muslim inheritance rules to map families and assign property titles, the law bound property and family law together in practice. In the face of persistent bureaucratic confusion over how to define "the family unit" and "current possession," inheritance became the linchpin of the law's implementation and hence a source of bureaucratic breakdown. As the law's absent center, the "Muslim family" was a site of contradiction and hence also contestation.

Politicians and administrators, settler advocates and jurists approached these contradictions as loopholes that could ideally be closed by procedural reform. Critics compulsively diagnosed the law's shortcomings and lamented its agents'

---

102. "Inspection des travaux de la propriété indigène. N. 60. Objet: Vérification sur le terrain des opérations de constatation de la propriété foncière privée au douar commune de Ouarizane. Rapport, Oran, 7 April 1882," in ANOM 92/2NN/603.

103. *Modifications à apporter à la loi du 26 Juillet 1873*, 2.

104. Peyerimhoff de Fontenelle, *Enquête sur les résultats de la colonisation officielle*, 191. According to Ruedy, Europeans took ownership of 1.75 million hectares (or 4,322,500 acres) between 1877 and 1920. Ruedy, *Land Policy in Colonial Algeria*, 81.

105. Dain, *Rapport sur les modifications à apporter à la loi du 26 juillet 1873*, 8.

inability to follow through on its provisions. Despite apparent efforts to follow the letter (and number) of the law, the *commissaire-enquêteurs'* precise—and indeed sublime—fractions could not be mapped onto the ground. In other words, the law's own mechanisms could not realize settlers' and administrators' desire for the unmediated application of French property law, even as those same measures effectively dispossessed Algerian landowners. Wealthy Muslim landowners took advantage of these slippages when they could, in turn seizing on the law's impossible separation between property law and family law. They mobilized the protection of their personal status in order to counter the imposition of French property law. Their doing so relied, however, on the very legal category that divided their personal estate from their real estate.

Dissatisfaction with the law revealed more than administrative oversight. Jurists and politicians who were deeply invested in a totalizing idea of the Civil Code continued to fantasize about the law's eventual completion. That project remained haunted by the structural contradictions revealed by challenges to its practical implementation. The definition of the "Muslim family" as embodied in the intimate affairs of personal status was supposedly beyond the purview of the law and yet central to it. Its privileges embodied Muslim difference and justified Algerian political exclusion as well as the legitimacy of land appropriation. At the same time, the law's application depended on the definition of the "Muslim family"—its structure and size as well as the nature of its inheritance law. In order to extend the law's territory further, jurists and politicians continued to tinker with it.[106] Not least, they repeatedly sought to reform "Muslim personal status" and hence the Muslim family. The "Muslim family" was, in this sense, both inside and outside the Warnier Law.

---

106. See Conseil supérieur de l'Algérie, *Procès verbaux* (December 1882). And Viviani, *Étude sur les réformes proposées à la loi du 26 juillet 1873.*

4

CIVILIZATION, THE CIVIL CODE, AND "CHILD MARRIAGE"

The promise of preserving local personal status for Muslim and Kabyle customary law soon posed its own problems. Assuming a Janus-faced approach, colonial jurists simultaneously upheld and criticized local law, focusing in particular on the "forced marriage" of girls and women. In 1874, the general counsel of the Appeals Court of Algiers Paul Piette issued a forceful condemnation of the practice: "All too often, in the exercise of our functions, we have occasion to see the deplorable consequences; and there is nothing sadder than the role imposed on justice, which is obliged to respect for natives, as a right, what it is obliged to forbid to Europeans as a crime." Speaking directly in the wake of the Warnier Law's passage, Piette rebuked in emotionally forceful terms the very "personal status" whose provisions had been maintained as integral to the "intimate life of families." Focused on Muslim men's sexual prerogatives, this moral outrage underwrote legal differences between "Europeans" and "natives," even as it deplored them. According to Piette, "we should never have engaged to respect laws that reject the least sentiment of human dignity." In his view, "to not do what is in our power to change them, would be to desert the cause of civilization that we represent in this country."[1] French sexual fascination and horror marked Algerian law as barbaric, thus justifying sovereign intervention into that law.

Piette's discourse targeted provisions in Muslim law and Kabyle customary law for a father to select marriage partners for his children—and especially daughters. French colonial jurists increasingly attacked this paternal prerogative—the *wilayat al-ijbar*, or what French jurists referred to as the *droit de djebr*—as "contrary to the fundamental principles of our legislation,

---

1. Piette, *De l'influence de la magistrature algérienne sur la civilisation des indigènes*, 19–20.

contrary to morality and to human liberty."[2] Algerian colonial law, in sanctioning and supposedly preserving "Muslim personal status," both upheld and condemned this "right."[3]

In this chapter, I trace how this apparently paradoxical situation came about. In doing so, I draw out several broader observations about colonial legal culture in Algeria—and beyond it. First, I show how, beyond operating as an Orientalist fantasy, the question of "forced marriage" was a specific node of French colonial government. Jurists' persistent concern with fathers' "right to force" exemplified the ambivalent logic on which the simultaneous preservation *and* surveillance of Qur'anic and customary law depended. Marital consent trials both highlighted and managed conflicts between a supposedly "civilized" French law and "barbaric" local codes. Contested marriages illustrated the fraught fields of colonial "intimacy" that, as Ann Stoler has suggested, incarnated colonial relations in addition to symbolizing them.[4] In studying the politics of the *droit de djebr*, I interrogate how these vexed intimacies were constituted as such in the first place—and by whom. In other words, I show how juridical attention to marital arrangements focused the regulation of intimacy on Muslim families.

This line of inquiry follows the colonial genealogy of Muslim and customary law over the course of the nineteenth century. As we saw chapter 3, after 1873, the jurisdiction of local law was limited to "intimate" matters of "personal status" and inheritance, while commercial and property transactions were increasingly supposed to be conducted under French civil law. These developments illuminate how family matters became a vexed core of colonial questioning about Muslim and customary law. Rather than presuming the self-evidence of "personal status," I argue that these trials elaborated the novel domain of Algerian family law as extimate—at once intimate *and* foreign—to French civil law.

French juridical interest in the problem of marital coercion drew Algerian women into the purview of colonial law, thus configuring women's legal agency in very specific and circumscribed ways: namely, as an expression and extension

---

2. Larcher, *Traité élémentaire*, 2:419. On the absence of age limits on marriage and the patriarchal principles of guardianship, especially in the Maliki school of jurisprudence that was predominant in colonial Algeria, see Charrad, *States and Women's Rights*, 33–34. See also Sonbol, "Adults and Minors in Ottoman Shari'a Courts."

3. I will continue to refer to it as the *droit de djebr* because I am interested in it as a French colonial legal construction.

4. Stoler, *Carnal Knowledge and Imperial Power*, 44–45.

of marital desire. Women's marital consent became hitched to the legitimacy of French law. Attending to these dynamics complicates what it means to locate women's legal agency in these trials, even as it demonstrates the significance of these questions—and the role played by women—in the ongoing elaboration and contestation of colonial legal culture in French Algeria.[5]

Child Marriage on Trial

Piette's speech indicates how French colonial critics focused on "prepubescent marriages" (mariages impubères) as exemplary of the civilizational differences between European and native law in Algeria. This legal disjuncture was not, in fact, as great as many colonial jurists claimed. The Civil Code actually contained multiple provisions requiring that parents consent to children's marriages, up until the age of twenty-five for girls and thirty for boys. According to Portalis, these conditions were in the children's interest, based on "parental love" and rec- ognized by "all ancient laws." Rather than "limiting the freedom of spouses," they protected children "from the violence of their own penchants." Casting the rules as an expression of affective rather than financial investment, he downplayed how parental consent functioned in effect to protect family property. Parents who, out of "avarice," "abuse their parental authority," were, in his view, unfor- tunate exceptions.[6]

By contrast, French jurists viewed the provisions for parental control in Muslim and customary law as an exorbitant patriarchal power. Islamic law set clear limits to this power, forbidding consummation before puberty and requiring women's consent. These conditions had long played a role in the adju- dication of marital and family disputes in which qadis intervened to annul mar- riages.[7] French jurists, even when they acknowledged these legal limits, regularly

5. On "colonial legal cultures" and the role of seemingly legally "marginal" subjects and marginal territories in their elaboration see Benton, Law and Colonial Cultures. As Julia Clancy-Smith notes, analysis of gender is largely absent from Benton's discussion. Clancy-Smith's own work calls attention to the importance of gender in the jurisdictional politics of plural and colonial legal orders: see "The Intimate, the Familial, and the Local," and Mediterraneans, 390. For a critique of historians' celebra- tion of agency see Johnson, "On Agency."

6. Portalis, Discours, rapports et travaux, 168–69. The strictures were only moderately scaled back in 1897 and again in 1907, when the age of marital majority was established as twenty-one. On the relative stringency of these provisions see Glendon, Transformation of Family Law, 41–43.

7. For an annulment case from eighteenth-century Constantine see Grangaud, "Prouver par l'écriture." On women's use of Ottoman courts see Tucker, In the House of the Law.

recounted in lurid detail how girls, cynically "sold" by their fathers, were married before puberty and subjected to rape and sexual torture by their lust-filled husbands. By the last decades of the nineteenth century, the *droit de djebr*, like polygamy, came to embody the cultural and sexual difference of indigenous personal status. French colonial jurists ceaselessly invoked it as both obstacle to and an explanation for urgently needed legal reform.

This double discourse made women's marital consent into a productive site for elaborating colonial law and governance. While posing a seeming moral quandary for French jurists who applied local law, it also asserted the superiority of French law over indigenous codes and culture. Images of the child brides and young women forced to submit to a father's will were trans-imperial clichés. However, in contrast to their counterparts in British India, French administrators did not attempt to pass laws banning the practice outright, at least before 1930, and then only with respect to Kabyle customary law. Because Muslim personal status was, in principle, protected from legislative intervention, colonial legal experts focused on jurisprudence and bureaucratic regulation instead.[8]

Administrative and juridical preoccupation with marital consent repeatedly resurfaced from the 1850s through the 1930s, and indeed up until the Algerian war. In serving to negotiate and regulate the relationship between French civil and local law, marital consent trials were a recurrent node of colonial governmentality.[9] They condensed and contained the challenges posed by a colonial legal order that depended on apparently conflicting systems of law: the French Civil Code on the one hand, and Muslim, Mosaic, and customary law on the other.[10] As in other colonial contexts, court appearances gave some women a chance to voice domestic grievances. By focusing on women's marital suffering and desire, they also framed their legal agency in constrained ways.[11]

---

8. For discussions of the 1891 and 1929 laws in British India see Pande, "'Listen to the Child'"; Sinha, *Colonial Masculinity*, and *Specters of Mother India*; Burton, "From Child Bride to 'Hindoo Lady.'"

9. See D. Scott, "Colonial Governmentality," and, more recently, Pierce and Rao, *Discipline and the Other Body*; Stephens, *Governing Islam*. On twentieth-century developments see Sambron, *Les femmes algériennes pendant la colonisation*; MacMaster, *Burning the Veil*.

10. New categories of personhood thus became "a place of contest among diverse interest groups in colonial society." See Merry, "Law and Colonialism," 891.

11. On women's use of colonial courts, especially in cases of divorce, see R. Roberts, "Representation, Structure, and Agency"; Lydon, "Obtaining Freedom." On women and forum shopping see Sharafi, "Marital Patchwork of Colonial South Asia."

Archival Traces

French concern with "child marriage" began early on during the military's period of "moral conquest" in the 1850s and 1860s. As Allan Christelow has shown, these efforts to intervene on behalf of the weak and socially disadvantaged, namely orphans and children, fit into a wider project of French colonial legitimation. They occurred in the context of two decades of brutal military conquest that intentionally targeted civilian populations in order to repress resistance to French rule.[12] At the same time, French military officers tried to establish a reputation for justice by punishing parents, husbands, and qadis who perpetrated marriages with "non-nubile" girls.[13] Military officers like Arab Bureau chief Ferdinand Hugonnet indicated their concern for young girls who rejected their father's efforts to marry them.[14] According to Arab Bureau reports from the 1850s, some French officers incited Muslim jurists to clamp down on cases of marital abuse.

By focusing on the sensitive question of child marriage, officers sought to exert control over local justices. The head of the Arab Bureau circle of Orléansville (Chlef), for example, explained in January 1852 that "several marriages contracted with underage girls were broken off. The most severe orders were given to diverse qadis that they follow in this matter the will of the law [which proscribed consummation before puberty], not the desire of certain parents."[15] Officers backed up their orders to follow the letter of the law by fining qadis who transgressed the rules for amounts as high as 300 francs. As a report from 1856 explained, the disciplinary measures were supposed to shine a "salutary light" on the shady dealings of certain Muslim jurists.[16]

The rules of shari'a forbade consummation before puberty even if they did not specify a legal marriage age.[17] Working in concert with local councils of jurisprudence, or Majlis, officers urged qadis to act within the framework of Islamic law. According to one report, a girl who succumbed to "the first efforts

---

12. Brower, *Desert Named Peace*.

13. Christelow, *Muslim Law Courts*.

14. Hugonnet, *Souvenirs d'un chef de Bureau arabe*, 22–26.

15. Rapport Cercle d'Orléansville / Div. d'Alger (January 1852), in ANOM 103 I 5 (71 MIOM 504).

16. Rapport Cercle d'Orléansville / Div. d'Alger (July 1856), in ANOM F 80 475. It mentions four different qadis who were issued this fine. The report explicitly invokes a rhetoric of "enlightenment."

17. See "İdne's Story" in Peirce, *Morality Tales*. This account, which focuses on the importance of social consensus in the deliberations of the Ottoman court of Aintab, is obviously distinct from how French officers administered colonial government. See also Sonbol, "Adults and Minors in Ottoman Shari'a."

of marriage" in June 1852 had died because of her "tender youth." The Majlis council garnered the officer's support by issuing "a judgment that forbids, in conformity with the spirit of the law, all marriages prior to the epoch of puberty, and which renders fathers responsible for exercising their authority in the matter."[18] Writing in August 1856, an officer from Orléansville again hailed the advisory judicial body, whose pronouncements backed up his own actions. He meted out punishments against husbands whose wives were too young to be married, while the Majlis pronounced the dissolution of their marriages. As the officer explained, "With its powerful help we have every reason to hope that the tribal qadis will promptly follow the example that is given them."[19]

The Majlis had expanded influence after the 1854 law on judicial organization, which granted Muslim jurists greater autonomy. While not reviewed by a French instance of appeal, qadis and the Majlis nonetheless were subject to administrative oversight by Arab Bureau officers. In order to regularize its administration, the colonial government also established an official Council of Jurisprudence in 1854 to fix Muslim legal doctrine. It advised French authorities on Muslim legal matters and hence also lent legitimacy to official directives.[20] In 1856, Governor-General Jacques Louis Randon asked the body to fix a marriage age. In a notable departure from shari'a, they established a numerical threshold. At age fifteen, they concluded, "young women are inclined toward men and can enjoy themselves in the company of a spouse."[21] With this recommendation in hand, Randon issued a circular in 1857 that declared qadis responsible for enforcing the new age limit.[22]

Disciplinary measures did not always stop early marriages and their occasionally tragic consequences. One report from the circle of Blidah in 1856 described a murder accompanied by a rape of an eight-year-old girl by her fifteen-year-old husband. While "marital rape" did not exist in French criminal law, the French officer claimed that their marriage lent the crime a "character that inspires the most profound horror."[23] In response, the officer issued "an energetic accusation against all vices and shameful customs contained by a society which tolerates such guilty unions, and illustrates the urgency of imposing reforms of a nature

18. Rapport Cercle d'Orléansville / Div. d'Alger (June 1852), in ANOM 103 I 5 (71 MIOM 504).

19. Rapport Cercle d'Orléansville / Div. d'Alger (August 1856), in ANOM 103 I 5 (71 MIOM 504).

20. On the Council of Jurisprudence see Christelow, *Muslim Law Courts*, 110–12.

21. Proceedings of the *Conseil de jurisprudence musulmane* (1855/56), in AN 19950167/12.

22. On the decision and Randon's circular see Christelow, *Muslim Law Courts*, 126–27.

23. The French Cour de cassation only recognized "marital rape" as a crime in 1990.

to lift it out of the degradation into which it has fallen." Both the husband and the marabout who oversaw the marriage were punished.[24]

Muslim jurists' relative autonomy was significantly curtailed by the 1859 law on judicial organization. As we saw in chapter 2, civilian settlers had pressed for this reform as part of their broader agenda of extending the reach of French civil law over Algerian territory. It made Muslim jurists' decisions subject to appeal before the Imperial Court of Algiers. In addition to curtailing their legal authority, the new process was costly and time-consuming. It provoked immediate resistance. In Orléansville, tribal chiefs exhibited a "*vive émotion*" when they heard that the local instance of appeal, the Majlis, would be abolished. Like other military men, the head of the circle worried that the hasty measure would provoke "profound discontent."[25] A subsequent report noted the "distrust and alarm" with which the legislation had been met.[26] The 1859 law's disruptive effects on local religious elites contributed in no small part to the major wave of rebellions against French authority that took place in 1864.[27]

The new appellate structure did allow litigants to "forum shop" by playing Muslim and French jurists off one another (even if the French jurists were supposed to rule according to "Muslim law"). In the 1860s, cases involving women's marital consent made the novel implications of French oversight increasingly visible.[28] The Imperial Court of Algiers now exercised a new power to discipline "qadi justice." The protection of women's "right" to marital consent became a linchpin of much of its jurisprudence. Women's marital consent, in turn, became an anchor for French discourse on the fate of Muslim law in Algeria.

---

24. Cercle de Blidah / Div. d'Alger, 3rd trimester, 1856, and Annual Report, 1856. And condemnations of qadis, in Rapport Cercle de Ténès / Div. d'Alger (January–February 1856), in F80 475.

25. Rapport Cercle d'Orléansville / Div. d'Alger (October 1859), in ANOM 103 I 5.

26. Rapport Cercle d'Orléansville / Div. d'Alger (June 1860), in ANOM 103 I 5.

27. Christelow, *Muslim Law Courts*, 178. Napoléon III's "*royaume arabe*" policy was based on a promise to reform the organization. A new decree was passed in 1866.

28. The reform also appears to have had a significant effect on women's claims to inheritance rights. Women contested the formation of religious family endowments (*habous*), which effectively barred them from claiming their shares. See, for example, Aicha bent Mohamed v. Allal ben El Sid Mohamed, Cour d'Alger (April 9, 1862), Estoublon, *Jurisprudence algérienne*, vol. 3 (1862), 23–24; Aïcha bent Messaoud v. Abderrahman el Bourguerrami, Cour d'Alger (July 30, 1862), ibid., vol. 3 (1862), 42–43. In other words, women's inheritance rights played a large role in the "attack on Muslim family endowments." Of course, women could be found on both sides of these legal battles, but the terms in which they were presented before the courts were as battles for women's inheritance. See Powers, "Orientalism, Colonialism, and Legal History"; Lazreg, *Eloquence of Silence*, 46, 100.

Women's Appeals

Many of the early cases brought before the Court of Algiers involved the *droit de djebr* only obliquely. They featured men who asserted marital rights to a young woman based on claims of a prior convention with her deceased father (a *promesse de mariage*). Without directly challenging paternal power, these cases sought to correct the appropriation of that authority by mercenary family members, unscrupulous qadis, and manipulative prospective husbands. Most of the trials hinged on the unreliability of witness testimony—and hence on conflicts between French and Islamic legal procedures and standards of evidence. These cases were as concerned with transforming the procedural aspects of "Muslim law" as with modifying its presumptive content.[29]

Women who contested their marriage arrangements usually had considerable family support, including, occasionally, from their fathers. French legal opinion nonetheless focused on women's individual consent. While these were technically "Muslim law" cases, they also drew on elements of the Civil Code, both the principle of "public order and good morals" (article 6) and the nullity of nonconsensual marriage (article 146). In one decision on June 11, 1862, the court held that "it is important for public order and good morals that marriages be freely contracted; and, as a result, that promises of marriage should not be obligatory, in the sense that a marriage must, of necessity, follow from them." The qadi who first heard the case judged the engagement to be valid. In overturning his decision, the French court found that the witnesses called by Mohammed ben Amir did not "inspire the necessary confidence."[30]

Some of the cases heard by the Imperial Court of Algiers were strikingly implausible. The court thus expressed skepticism regarding El Abassi ben Ahmed's claim that, because Keltoun had been previously promised to him by her father Mohamed ben Ali, she was now his rightful wife. Keltoun had since been living "in perfect union" with another man, El Seïd ben Abderrahman, and was pregnant. El Abassi had even attended their wedding party without contesting the union's legitimacy. Siding with El Seïd, the court found that the prior engagement could not "prevail" over a consummated marriage, a decision that was both "proclaimed by morality and existed in conformity with Muslim law." Keltoun appeared here to be an object of contestation between two men,

---

29. On the importance of colonial debates about procedure see Benton, "Colonial Law and Cultural Difference." On their significance for transforming shariʿa see Hallaq, *Sharīʿa*. For parallel developments in a noncolonial context see Messick, *Calligraphic State*.

30. Ahmed ben Abderrahman v. Mohamed ben Amir, Cour d'Alger (June 11, 1862), *Jurisprudence algérienne*, vol. 3 (1862), 34–35.

a contest that was adjudicated by a French court. With its decision, the court claimed to enforce both French morality and Muslim law. Under its watchful eye, the two were made to coincide even as its decisions also implicitly undermined the autonomy—and hence authority—of Islamic justice and its qadis.[31]

In the colonialist press, reports on the Imperial Court's "Arab affairs" cases foregrounded the dissimilarity between French and local law, especially with respect to "family organization," and thus helped to legitimate increased oversight of Muslim law. In *L'Akhbar*, an 1863 trial in which the French court overturned a qadi's decision to find in favor of a woman (and her father) illustrated "the superiority of European civilization over Muslim civilization." The article's generic characters—"an Arab," a "young woman," and "the father"—made the trial into an expression of cultural difference. The author avowed that even "if our laws are more protective of young woman," contemporary "mercantile tendencies" reduced marriage to an "act of commerce." But in the end, he sought to restore the dignity and difference of French law.[32]

These cases did not merely present women as hapless victims who served as the ground for contests between men.[33] Marital consent trials also constituted women *as* desiring (or just as importantly, as *non-desiring*) persons. In 1863, Messaoud bent Ahmed "formally denied the existence of a marriage" that El Taïeb sought to prove based on less than credible witness testimony. Overturning the qadi's decision in his favor, the French court held that the conditions under which "testimonial proof" could be admitted had to be particularly stringent "when an act as important as marriage" was at stake.[34] Similarly, in an 1866 case, Alia bent Caddour rejected an arranged marriage based on the claim that she had been previously married. In the eyes of the court, proof of her consent to the union was insufficiently established.[35]

In 1867, the court refused to allow a brother to make marital arrangements for his sister, Khadidja, finding his opposition to her stated desires to be "purely arbitrary and troublesome." In the course of the trial, Khadidja asserted her own wishes, declaring "for her part, that she wanted no other husband than Hamed

---

31. El Abassi ben Ahmed v. El Seïd ben Abderrahaman, Cour d'Alger (July 30, 1862), ibid., vol. 3 (1862), 46–47.

32. "Courrier du Palais," *L'Akhbar*, December 13, 1863, 2–3.

33. Mani, "Contentious Traditions." Also, Spivak, "Can the Subaltern Speak?"; Lazreg, *Eloquence of Silence*, 46.

34. Messaoud bent Ahmed v. El Taïeb, Cour d'Alger (June 2, 1863), Estoublon, *Jurisprudence Algérienne*, vol. 3 (1863), 18–19. Women's families also made less than plausible claims regarding marriage promises. They were also turned down by the court. See Sliman v. Khadidja bent Mohamed (April 17, 1867), ibid., vol. 3 (1867), 13–14.

35. Alia bent Caddour v. Saïd ben el Milliani, Cour d'Alger (June 27, 1867), ibid., vol. 3 (1866), 35.

ben Bakhta; that she freely consented to the institution of her [other] brother Bel Kassem as her legal representative [walī]; and that she gave her full adhesion to the contract realized under his auspices."[36] By recognizing Khadidja's marital desire, the court effectively linked women's marital consent to their acceptance of the Cour d'Alger's jurisdiction. Women's marital desire thus worked to legitimate the French court's oversight of "Muslim law."

The number of cases on appeal before French courts seems to have slowed once Napoléon III introduced a new judicial organization in 1866. In an effort to rectify the defects and discontents of the 1859 law, this reform reaffirmed the Majlis as an optional instance of appeal. A limited number of litigants opted instead for the French court, especially when it leaned in their favor.[37] Cases of marital consent nonetheless made a strong impression on contemporary commentators. Stereotypical accounts of "Muslim" marriage written at the time predictably praised French officers and magistrates for limiting abuse. Condemning underage marriage as both immoral and unnatural, military officer Étienne Villot hailed these officials' sensitivity: "Despite the deep mystery surrounding the Muslim, the cries of these young children, married before the age of puberty, have been heard, and the authority has forbidden the marriage of non-nubile girls." This affective and moral appeal, in turn, justified new forms of intervention and oversight. As Villot exclaimed, "there is here a reform to be completed."[38]

Individual Properties / Properties of the Individual

Created by the shift to civilian rule, legal transformations in the 1870s opened the way for reform. The government renewed its commitment to banning underage marriages in a circular issued by Governor-General Louis Henri de Gueydon on September 19, 1872. It called for "severe repression," condemning "the spouses who consummate these barbarous unions and the parents who consent to them," as well as the "Muslim magistrates who give them their sanction." Part of Gueydon's broader plan to curtail the power of Muslim justices, the directive threatened qadis with revocation and husbands with criminal charges for indecent assault.[39]

---

36. Ben Barka ben Kouïder v. Saïd ben el Miliani, Cour d'Alger (May 1, 1867), ibid., vol. 3 (1867), 16–17.

37. See, for example, Bernou ben Selimi v. Bourahla ben Mohammed, Ch. des appels entre musulmans (February 22, 1869), *Bulletin judiciaire d'Algérie*, 1869, 39–42 (hereafter *BJA*). In this case, the girl's father brought the case before the French courts, rather than the Majlis.

38. Villot, "Études algériennes," 406–7.

39. L.-M. Eyssautier, "Projet de loi sur le mariage indigène," *Revue algérienne et tunisienne de jurisprudence* [hereafter *RA*], pt. 1, 1897, 94. Ageron, *Les Algériens musulmans*, 1:210.

This new stringency coincided with the violent repression of the 1871 insur-
rections against French authority, the so-called Moqrani Rebellion. Settler advocates seized on the moment to enact legal reforms that they had been unable
to achieve under Napoléon III's Arab Kingdom. They justified these reforms by
hailing the advantages and appeal of French law. In his inaugural speech in 1874
to what had now become, after the fall of the Second Empire, the Cour d'appel
d'Alger (the Appeals Court of Algiers) on the "influence of the Algerian judiciary on the civilization of indigenes," General Counsel Paul Piette pursued this
argument. He praised the Warnier Law, which in applying French law in select
areas of the Tell region converted communal property into what jurist Ernest
Mercier described as an "available and marketable good [*une valeur disponible
et marchande*]."[40] The benefit of the law, according to Piette, was that Algerians
would "lose their collective character" to become "what they have never been,
individualities."[41] As we saw in chapter 3, the Warnier Law actually presumed a
patriarchal Muslim family structure, inscribing "individualities" in genealogies
and mandating proper "family names" or patronymics in order to guarantee the
security of property titles.

Piette meanwhile proclaimed the need to curtail patriarchal excess, including
how "natives can submit children less than thirteen years of age to their brutality." He urged fellow magistrates to suppress "Muslim" laws that were "an affront
to the dignity of justice [*qui portent atteinte à la dignité de la justice*]." In his view,
forced marriages confused personhood and property, as children were "given
over by greedy parents, without decency [*pudeur*] or pity."[42] In a lengthy end-
note on "premature marriages," he praised Gueydon's 1872 circular as well as
decisions by the Cour d'appel d'Alger that annulled suspicious unions. Citing
reforms undertaken in British India on sati and widow remarriage as successful
precedents, he urged the adoption of a legal marriage age to eliminate abuse.[43]

This call for legislation was, however, stymied by the construction of "personal status" by the 1873 land reform. While aiming to dismantle family property, French jurists continued to claim that the law had left what mattered most
to Algerian Muslims—namely religion and the family—intact. The promise to
maintain "personal status" did not, however, interrupt ongoing efforts to reform
the "Muslim family" by making it more transparent to the French state and to
prospective purchasers of Algerian land. Toward this end, settler advocates and
politicians sought to extend the imposition of fixed family names initiated by

---

40. E. Mercier, *La propriété foncière musulmane en Algérie*, 48. On the trans-imperial circulation
of this French colonial legal theory see Pravilova, "Property of Empire."

41. Piette, *De l'influence de la magistrature algérienne sur la civilisation des indigènes*, 15.

42. Ibid., 19.

43. Ibid., 33.

the Warnier Law to the whole population. As Alexandre Bellemare explained in a report to the Conseil supérieur de gouvernement in 1877, "the civil registry [*état civil*], which is the point of departure for the patronymic name, cannot be limited to property holders alone, as the patronymic name must extend to all non-property-owning members of a family, whose one member is a property holder."[44] Patronymics became the focus of subsequent discussions of the civil registry.[45] Acting Governor-General Albert Grévy explained why the names needed to be established by law: "When it comes to knowing who has the right to take or to give a name, when it comes to the status of the person and the constitution of the family, can these questions be simple matters of administration? The status of persons, in our law, is a question of the first order which takes precedence above all other interests."[46] The proposed legislation established the "Name of the Father" as integral to French sovereignty and law.[47]

Governor-General Grévy worked hard to advance this project in the National Assembly. In his report to the Chamber, Justice Minister Jules Cazot outlined why regularizing indigenous names was so urgent. The Warnier Law, by granting patronymics only to property holders, "created a real danger from the point of view of persons; in seeking to create order in property, it managed to create disorder in the family." A "native civil registry" would, he claimed, "establish order in the Arab family."[48] Deputy Rémy Jacques from Oran, the reporter for the parliamentary commission, likewise explained how the registry would extend French administrative knowledge and authority over Muslim subjects and hence guarantee transparency and traceability in property transactions between "Europeans" and Muslims.[49] As one contemporary observer remarked, "How is it possible to follow the transformations in a family and hence in the destiny of a property when every child has a unique name and it is unknown when he is born, when he marries, and when he dies?"[50]

---

44. Conseil supérieur de gouvernement, *Procès-verbaux* (November 1877), 326. And the earlier discussion, Conseil supérieur de gouvernement, *Procès-verbaux* (January 1875), 236–44.

45. Conseil supérieur de gouvernement, *Procès-verbaux* (November 1878), 205–6.

46. Report and Discussion in Conseil supérieur de gouvernement, *Procès-verbaux* (December 1879), 395–435.

47. On family names as an attribute of sovereignty see Scott, Tehranian, and Mathias, "Production of Legal Identities Proper to States." In France, Noiriel, "L'identification des citoyens." For an instructive comparison see Messick, "Written Identities."

48. "Projet de loi sur l'état civil des indigènes musulmans de l'Algérie," *JO*, Doc. Parl., Chambre, March 18, 1880, annexe 2469, 165.

49. Jacques, "Rapport fait au nom de la commission chargée d'examiner le projet de loi sur l'état civil des indigènes musulmans de l'Algérie," *JO*, Doc. Parl., Chambre, February 12, 1881, annexe 3326, 154–59. See also Ageron, *Les Algériens musulmans*, 1:176–83. And Ghabrial, "Le 'fiqh françisé.'"

50. Bourde, *À travers l'Algérie*, 256.

After considerable discussion, the law creating a civil registry for all "*indigènes musulmans*" was passed on March 23, 1882. Like the 1873 property reform, it soon encountered difficulties. One major obstacle was the fact that "Muslim law" marriages did not require sanctification by a qadi. The private nature of the contracts made the public surveillance of marriage, including "child marriage," difficult.[51] Theoretically, the civil registry allowed the secular state to track the marriages without altering their private and "religious" form. As Deputy Jacques explained, "Marriage is, among them [i.e., *indigènes*], a religious act—polygamy is in their *mœurs*, as is divorce; let's not touch it; but let's not infer that this forbids us from applying our laws when they do not harm these principles in any way."[52] The law's final version indeed required marriages and divorces to be registered, but the provision was almost impossible to enforce.

This inability to publicly document Muslim marriage remained an obstacle to administrative efforts to map Algerian families and assign proper names to their members, especially women. One solution was to give married women their fathers' patronymic, rather than their husband's. Over the course of the law's application, however, administrators remained unsure of how to name married women who did not live close to their paternal family. This bureaucratic quandary brought new questions to the fore about what model of the family—an extended patriarchal one or limited, conjugal one—the law sought to inculcate and impose.[53]

Official characterization of the "indigenous" family thus shifted depending on the premises and stakes of the policy at hand. It could be legally conceived as either analogous to or incommensurably different from the "French" family. As we have seen, the 1873 legislation gave rise to bureaucratic chaos and legal debate over how to define the Muslim "family unit." An 1887 law sought to remedy that disarray by again revising the definition.[54] Deputy and large property owner Charles Bourlier

---

51. Zeys, *Essai d'un traité méthodique de droit musulman*, 1:11. For an example of jurisprudence on the question see Min. pub. v. Baza (Zine ben Taïeb) et Merine (Abdelkader ben Zenouki), Tribunal de Sidi Bel Abbès (Ch. Corr.), *RA*, pt. 2, 1892, 197–201. The court concluded that there was no legal sanction for failing to register a marriage or divorce. See also Barrière, *Le statut personnel des musulmans*, 302–9. On marriage as a private matter, independent of the state in Islamic law, see Charrad, *States and Women's Rights*, 32–33.

52. Jacques, "Rapport fait au nom de la commission chargée d'examiner le projet de loi sur l'état civil des indigènes musulmans de l'Algérie," *JO*, Doc. Parl., Chambre, annexe 3326, February 12, 1881, 157.

53. On married women's names see "Commission centrale (Constantine). État civil. Indigènes musulmans. Procès-verbal," November 12, 1885; and Gov. Gen. to Garde des Sceaux "Recensement des femmes mariées," December 24, 1885, dossier État Civil, in AN 199950167/10.

54. See "28 Avril 1887, Loi ayant pour objet de modifier et de compléter la loi du 26 juillet 1873 sur l'établissement et la conservation de la propriété en Algérie," in Estoublon and Lefébure, *Code de l'Algérie*, 1:727–42.

(Alger) explained how delimiting "the family unit" would prevent the division of property into impossibly small, fractional parcels. He proposed breaking with the earlier definition: "The familial unit [unité familiale] on which property should be based could be found neither in the family as understood by General Chanzy [in his instructions of July 1, 1875], nor in the Islamic family." In his view, the appropriate model had to be based on "indigenous society" itself.

In an effort to curtail the excesses of the 1873 reform, Bourlier proposed a much more restricted model as more accurate: "If one penetrates into indigenous territories, one recognizes that, whether under a tent or the roof of a hut [gourbi] or house, there are only ever a small number of beings, gathered around the same fire, bound together by the most intimate ties: a husband, a wife, children, and more rarely, sisters. . . . Never two households. In this milieu, one does not find any outstandingly different characteristic between a peasant family in France and that of an Algerian fellah, aside from bigamy, from polygamy, which are exceptions." In other words, Bourlier claimed that the indigenous family barely differed from a traditional French family, headed by a père de famille: "The family, the hearth [feu], is the group formed by the adult [majeur], master of his rights, with the women, children, and incompetents who depend on his fortune." For Bourlier, the division of communal property should take this model of the family—the hearth—as its guiding legal norm.[55] After 1887, land surveyors were supposed to follow this definition in implementing property reform.[56]

According to its many critics, the new law again failed to forge an appropriately individuated, property-holding subject and family.[57] Indigenous resistance to dispossession, alongside persistent confusion over the meaning of the "family" or "hearth," could not be rectified by further legislative tinkering. By the 1890s, metropolitan politicians and concerned Algerian jurists took increasing distance from the unconsidered application of French property law.[58] In 1897, yet another

---

55. Ibid., 1:739.

56. "10 November 1887, Instruction du Gouverneur Général sur le mode de reconnaissance des biens indivis entre familles indigènes et sur le partage de ces biens, en exécution de la loi du 28 avril 1887," ibid., 1:781. For a critique of this creative, and according to some, illegal definition of the "family" see Pouyanne, La propriété foncière en Algérie, 219–22.

57. See, for example, Maurice Collin, professor of administrative law at the law faculty of Algiers, in Pensa, L'Algérie, 148–51. E. Mercier, La propriété foncière musulmane en Algérie; Larcher, Traité élémentaire (1903), 2:330–39; Boyer-Banse, "La propriété indigène dans l'arrondissement d'Orléansville." On the long-term effects of the destruction of native property institutions see Sari, La dépossession des fellahs; Lazreg, Emergence of Classes in Algeria.

58. See Burdeau, L'Algérie en 1891, 167. And, Franck-Chauveau, "Propriété foncière en Algérie," JO, Doc. Parl., Sénat, March 29, 1893, annexe 121, 270–82. On these criticisms see Sessions, "Débattre de la licitation."

law abrogated the two previous reforms. Bringing an end to the generalized "operations" over large swaths of territory, it instituted more targeted "partial inquiries" instead. In his report on the legislation, Deputy Joseph Pourquéry de Boisserin (Vaucluse) explained that whatever care had gone in to better describing the shape of the indigenous family by "carefully explaining what 'hearth' should mean," the results of the 1887 law were no less disastrous. He concluded that "in reality, natives are not in a condition which calls for the constitution and conservation of individual property." In his view, the stubborn social and material reality of the indigenous family remained an obstacle to the administrative fantasy of the Warnier Law: "Property is familial, and these *mœurs* were not modified by the passage of the land surveyor."[59] This increasingly common argument presented local resistance to the law as a sign of indigenous social failure.

By the 1890s, metropolitan politicians and settler advocates pointed to Algerians' opposition to land reform as evidence of their legal and political inassimilability. The history of property reforms revealed that "personal status" questions of marriage, divorce, and inheritance could not be easily cleaved from other domains of administrative and property law. Colonial jurists and politicians nonetheless continued to insist that the implicitly religious laws of this "intimate" and familial domain had been preserved, while the extra-intimate concerns of property and administration were subject to ongoing efforts of colonial reform.[60] The apparent failures of the Warnier Law created new colonial "alibis" and discriminatory effects.[61]

A Law of Indigenous Exception

The idea of the intransigent "Muslim family" that emerged out of the property reform debates informed jurists' approach to questions of personal status, including the *droit de djebr*, from the 1870s onward. Once the new civil government began to reduce qadi and customary law jurisdiction, more of these cases came before French judges. The harsh administrative response to the Moqrani Rebellion of 1871 was an important factor in this shift. After 1874, French *juges de paix* replaced locally elected *djemaa* councils and notables as judges in Kabyle

---

59. "Loi relative à la propriété foncière en Algérie, 16 fevrier 1897," in Estoublon and Lefébure, *Code de l'Algérie*, 2:61–62.

60. For parallel arguments about the difficult separation of "market" and "family" law in colonial India see Birla, *Stages of Capital*; Sturman, "Property and Attachments," and *Government of Social Life in Colonial India*; Stephens, *Governing Islam*.

61. On liberal failure and new colonial alibis see Mantena, *Alibis of Empire*.

customary law cases. Two subsequent laws on judicial organization, in 1886 and 1889, further expanded French jurists' jurisdiction, reducing the number of qadi courts and giving *juges de paix* greater purview over Muslim law matters as well.[62]

In this jurisdictional transformation, the Appellate Court of Algiers made a frontal assault on parental authority and the risk of marital brutality symbolized by the *droit de djebr*. The court's decisions simultaneously attacked the legal authority of qadis and the familial authority of fathers, husbands, and brothers. By undermining the extended family, this jurisprudence coincided with the aims of the Warnier Law.[63] More specifically, "child marriage" cases supplemented economic arguments against collective property with emotionally charged ones against the dangerous excesses of Muslim law and patriarchal power.

Judges sought to claim the moral high ground for French law and courts. In one case, the thirteen-year-old Kheïra bent Mohamed fell victim to the "odious lubricity" of her sixteen-year-old husband Ahmed ben Mohamed, from whose "abuse [*mauvais traitements*]" she escaped by returning to her parents' home. Citing Gueydon's 1872 circular, the court condemned the qadi of Aumale for failing to protect Kheïra. It further issued a sweeping condemnation of "the qadis of Algeria, who in most cases neglect to protect the children whose marriages they celebrate." The court's decision upheld the superiority and civilization of French justice.[64]

Fathers' potential abuse of the *droit de djebr* thus justified French oversight of local law, despite its "protected" status. In its decisions, the Court of Algiers urged that "in no case can a jurisdiction that has ideas of morality and justice order that a woman should be handed over to a man against her will; it would be the same thing as ordering a rape." Even in an instance where a woman's father sought to break the marriage promise in order to honor his daughter's wishes, the decision condemned the *droit de djebr* as an "exorbitant right."[65] In calling for its abolition, judges claimed to restore "natural right."[66]

---

62. On these shifts see Gentil, "Administration de la justice musulmane"; Collot, *Les institutions de l'Algérie*, 181–90; Christelow, *Muslim Law Courts*. On the administrative challenges that accompanied these shifts see AN 20020495/8, 9, 10.

63. I am indebted to Julia Clancy-Smith's help in thinking through this point.

64. Kheïra bent Mohamed v. Ahmed ben Mohamed, Cour d'appel d'Alger (January 29, 1878), *BJA*, 1878, 235–36. On women's use of French courts in such cases see Charnay, *La vie musulmane en Algérie*, 22–32.

65. Ahmed ben Ali ben Yklef v. Abd-el-Kader ben Mohamed, Cour d'appel d'Alger (December 10, 1877), *BJA*, 1878, 28–29.

66. This was the position taken by Charles Marchal's *Bulletin judiciaire d'Algérie*. See, for example, the note on Ahmed ben Ali ben Yklef v. Abd-el-Kader ben Mohamed, Cour d'appel d'Alger (December 10, 1877), *BJA*, 1878, 28–29.

In arguing these cases, jurists drew on new instruments of colonial legal administration, including the compendium of *Droit musulman* composed by Édouard Sautayra and Eugène Cherbonneau in 1873. As the authors explained, since the Warnier property reform had "definitively maintained personal status and inheritance, it would be useful, and in the interest of good administration and justice," to make Islamic legal principles more accessible to French jurists. The authors followed the handbook or *Mukhtasar* of Maliki school jurisprudence drawn up by fifteenth-century jurist Sidi-Khalîl ibn Ishâq, but made no effort at a literal rendering of the text. They proudly announced instead that they had "gotten rid of all that was unnecessary or superfluous, and arranged the remaining text in the order of the Civil Code." They aimed "to make research and comparison with other legislations much easier."[67]

In the absence of an official code, their eclectic combination of Qur'anic text and commentary, jurisprudence and ethnographic description, operated *as if* it were a code, especially for jurists who had an extremely limited knowledge of Islamic law. This treatise gave, in the words of one historian, "a more or less definitive form to Muslim law in Algeria."[68] And it clearly shaped how French magistrates judged cases involving the *droit de djebr*.

Women's marital consent figured prominently in Sautayra and Cherbonneau's account. The authors' introduction recapitulated the jurisprudence of the 1860s, which limited the exercise of the "right."[69] In the text that followed, they sought to codify the conditions under which marriage contracts became valid, devoting over fifty pages to the intricacies of the *droit de djebr* alone. In the process, they offered an extended critique of paternal abuse, especially of fathers who confused personhood and property by supposedly "selling" their daughters.[70] Citing the Imperial Court of Algiers's prior decisions regarding invalid "marriage promises," they reiterated that qadis would be subject to administrative punishment if they did not follow official procedures for drawing up marriage contracts. The authors noted an entry in the official newspaper, the *Mobacher*, from

---

67. Sautayra and Cherbonneau, *Droit musulman*, 1:ii–iii. For a critical discussion of the juridical uses of their text see Bontems, "Les tentatives de codification du droit musulman." David Powers nonetheless suggests that their attitudes were more sympathetic to the tenets of Islamic law than some of their successors, such as Zeys, in Powers, "Orientalism, Colonialism, and Legal History." On the effects of "textualization" on Muslim law see Hallaq, *Sharī'a*; Messick, *Calligraphic State*; Emon, "Codification and Islamic Law"; Hussin, *Politics of Islamic Law*; Cohn, *Colonialism and Its Forms of Knowledge*; Stephens, *Governing Islam*.

68. Flory and Henry, *L'Enseignement du droit musulman*, 116.

69. Sautayra and Cherbonneau, *Droit musulman*, 1:vi–vii.

70. Ibid., 1:70–73.

September 12, 1863, punishing a qadi with a 200 franc fine "for marrying a girl who was not yet nubile."[71]

Subsequent decisions by the Appellate Court of Algiers followed Sautayra and Cherbonneau's guidelines, while frequently conflating two kinds of cases: prepubescent girls who were supposedly forced to consummate marriages when they were still too young, and older women who were forced into marriages with men other than those of their own choosing. This conflation supplemented arguments about women's legal violation with affective force. The *Bulletin judiciaire d'Algérie* thus described the *droit de djebr* as a "disgusting right [*droit révoltant*]."[72] Court decisions, meanwhile, focused on emotionally charged depictions of women's martyrdom in order to nullify marriages. Mixing sexual fascination with moral horror, they justified sovereign intervention into a supposedly protected "Muslim law."

Sentimental description supplemented juridical argumentation. A telling illustration can be found in the appeal brought by Fathma bent El Arbi before the Court of Algiers in 1881 in an effort to avoid an undesirable Muslim law marriage that had been arranged by her estranged and unethical father, El Arbi ben el Haouari. The objectionable union was to a man, El Mouloud ben el Arbi, "who already had a wife and for whom Fathma showed [*avait témoigné*] an extreme antipathy." Protesting against the arrangement, she brought the matter before the qadi of Duperré (Aïn Defla), who defended the father's actions based on his interpretation of Sidi-Khalîl. She appealed to the Court of Algiers, which instead found that her father had effectively "abdicated" his paternal rights when he abandoned his daughter and wife. When her mother approved her marriage to a man who "would have pleased her and made her happy," her father intervened, instead arranging her union with El Mouloud.

The Court of Algiers registered moral horror at her father, who "acting in his own interest," had sought out "a sum of money in exchange for the violence done to his daughter, without caring in any way about the aversion that Fathma felt for the man into whose arms he threw her, thus violating [*outrageant*] her most intimate sentiments as a woman."[73] French jurists overturned the qadi's decision in order to "intervene and emancipate [*affranchir*] Fathma from the marriage ties against which she protested." Drawing on affectively charged imagery of sexual slavery, it represented the marriage as a shocking violation of her "intimate

---

71. Ibid., 1:129.
72. Hadja Kamla bent El-Hadj v. El-Menouar ben Ahmed, Cour d'appel d'Alger (April 26, 1880), *BJA* 1881, 77.
73. Fatima bent El Arbi v. Mouloud ben El Arbi, Cour d'appel d'Alger (June 27, 1881), *BJA*, 1882, 79.

sentiments" and, by extension, its own. As Victor Mallarmé wrote in his commentary, the case exemplified French jurists' struggle to "reconcile Muslim law with the most elementary principles of natural law."[74]

The motives of Fathma's father were no doubt questionable and her aversions palpable. What the decision also reveals is how the Court of Algiers appealed to emotions—of sexual disgust and violation—in explaining why it annulled the qadi's marriage of Fathma to El Mouloud. This affective supplement underwrote French magistrates' discretionary interpretations of Muslim law.

The legal argument adopted in a dispute between "Demoiselle Kheira" and her father in 1884 was similarly emotionally and morally charged. According to testimony cited in the case, Kheira strongly opposed a union that he arranged, apparently threatening to "end her days" if forced to consummate the unsavory marriage. She was supported both by her mother and by a qadi, who decided in her favor. Hoping for a different outcome, her father appealed the decision to the French court. Seizing the occasion to shore up a reformist legal principle, the French judge endorsed the qadi's position. He conceded that because "*indigènes*" were allowed to maintain their law, a French court could not "refuse a *père de famille* the right to matrimonial constraint, given that this right, as exorbitant as it is, is one of the foundational principles of Muslim law." At the same time, the decision adopted the Hanafi, rather than the Maliki rules regarding the right, according to which fathers had to obtain their children's (both male and female) explicit consent to marriage once they had reached puberty.[75] According to the court, "this eminently orthodox solution had the additional merit of coming close to French law, in which matrimonial constraint is considered, with good reason, to be a veritable assault on the human person."[76] The opinion followed arguments elaborated by the presiding judge in the case, Ernest Zeys, in his *Essai d'un traité méthodique de droit musulman*. Zeys's reformist program sought a veritable upheaval in custom through the strict application of the principles of Islamic law. Through intervention on the part of the French, he claimed, "the woman will have more and more consciousness of her dignity, she will want to resemble the French spouse, the French mother, more and more, because goodness is as contagious as evil." This civilizing project also had an explicitly political function. In transforming Muslim women and marriage, he proclaimed, "France will have legitimated its conquest of Algeria."[77]

74. Ibid., 76.

75. Esposito, *Women in Muslim Family Law*, 16–17.

76. Demoiselle Kheira v. Kheira père, Cour d'appel d'Alger (April 9, 1884), *BJA*, 1884, 131–33.

77. Zeys, *Essai d'un traité méthodique de droit musulman*, 1:11. On Zeys's career see Renucci, "Le meilleur d'entre nous?"

In cases that alleged sexual violence, French magistrates pursued a more overtly repressive tack by criminally charging husbands who consummated marriages with "underage" wives.[78] The new prosecutorial strategy coincided with the elaboration of the notorious *indigénat* or native penal code that applied to subjects who were legally classified as *indigène*. This exceptional law was both logically and institutionally dependent on the distinctiveness of indigenous "Muslim" civil status.[79] While "prepubescent marriage" was not targeted by the *indigénat* (husbands were rather tried for indecent assault under articles 331 and 332 of the regular penal code), the presumption of native criminality underwrote the exceptional code. According to the jurist Émile Larcher, the policing of prepubescent marriage justified the *indigénat*'s article 15, which regulated meetings of twenty-five people or more and events in which arms would be fired, namely "marriages, births, and circumcisions." Occulting the evidently political function of the regulation, Larcher suggested that the article allowed "the administration to continue its effort to stamp out the detestable practice of prepubescent marriage"[80]

This focus on "child marriage" consolidated and corporealized the legal meaning of *"indigène"* by highlighting a practice that, because supposedly shared by all Algerians, appeared to distinguish them from "Europeans." The "exorbitant" patriarchal right protected by Muslim and customary personal status law underwrote the "exorbitant" operations of French extrajudicial justice. In his account of the *indigénat*, Larcher thus explained: "We see here a kind of seesaw effect [*jeu de bascule*]; for, on the one hand, personal status permits certain things to the *indigène* that are forbidden by our Penal Code; while we see, on the other hand, laws and decrees which strike the same *indigène* with correctional punishment for deeds that are permitted to Europeans." In other words, the *indigène*'s supposedly extraordinary sexual rights—both the *droit de djebr* and polygamy—justified the French system of extraordinary punishment.[81] Trials focused on "child marriage" thus contributed to a broader effort to consolidate the legal, cultural, and sexual differences between "Europeans" and *indigènes*.

---

78. Mohammed ou Saïd v. Min. pub., Cour d'appel d'Alger, Ch. Corr. (May 2, 1887), *RA*, pt. 2, 1888, 10–12, and El Aïb ben Aïssa v. Min. pub., Conseil permanent de révision d'Alger (February 12, 1891), *RA*, pt. 2, 1891, 197–201. See also *JTA*, July 26, 1896; May 9, 1897; January 29, 1902. These condemnations appeared to be more frequent before military tribunals. See, for example, the records of the military tribunal of the division of Constantine in 1891, Service Historique de la Défense 5J 499.

79. On the history of the *indigénat* see Merle, "Retour sur le régime de l'indigénat"; Mann, "What Was the Indigénat?"; Thénault, "Le 'code de l'indigénat'"; Saada, "Law in the Time of Catastrophe."

80. Larcher, *Traité élémentaire* (1903), 2:121. Subsequent texts made the same argument; see Aumont-Thiéville, *De l'indigénat en Algérie*, 165; Marneur, "L'indigénat en Algérie," 50.

81. Larcher, *Traité élémentaire* (1903), 2:99.

The Tragic Kabyle Woman

As part of this effort to confirm the legal difference of the *indigène*, French jurists' new attention to child marriage cases played an important role in the waning of the "Kabyle myth." During the early decades of colonization, Algeria's Berber population had been celebrated as more sedentary, more secularized, and less apt to practice polygamy, and hence more assimilable to French laws and *mœurs* than nomadic Arab tribes. In the course of these marriage trials, jurists began to argue that the fate of Kabyle women was perhaps even worse than that of the "Arab woman."[82]

The 1873 compendium of Kabyle customary law by Adolphe Hanoteau, an army general who was stationed in Kabylie in the 1850s and '60s, and Aristide Letourneux, a lawyer at the Court of Algiers, sought to correct aspects of the myth, especially with respect to Kabyle women. For French magistrates who oversaw customary law cases, the work functioned much like Sautayra and Cherbonneau's Muslim law treatise. The authors dismissed earlier depictions of Kabyle women as "errors propagated by the brilliant paradoxes of eminent writers" and insisted instead on how customary law stripped women of legal personhood by subjecting them to forced marriage: "Bought and handed over, most often without the intervention of her will, the Kabyle woman is not a legal personality; she is a human thing [*c'est une chose humaine*]."[83] For these colonial judicial ethnographers, forced marriage exemplified Kabyle women's social and legal debasement. They continued: "The laws of humanity and decency are not even respected in the deal. Custom fixes no legal age for the consummation of marriage and fathers have the right to hand their prepubescent child over to the buyer's caresses."[84] In the eyes of French jurists, these marriage contracts problematically confused property and personhood by treating women as goods to be bought and sold.[85]

The new consensus view of the Kabyle women's legal plight had largely taken hold by the end of the century. In 1894, Emmanuel Besson, the author of a prize-winning doctoral thesis on civil law in Algeria, drew on British colonial jurist Henry Maine's model of primitive law to make the point. Structured by status rather than the modern principles of contract, Kabyle customary law

---

82. For examples of the earlier vision of the Kabyle woman as having greater freedom see Baudicour, "Des indigènes de l'Algérie," 168–69; Daumas, *Moeurs et coutumes de l'Algérie*. On these broad shifts see Ageron, *Les Algériens musulmans*, 2:885–86; Lorcin, *Imperial Identities*, 213.

83. Hanoteau and Letourneux, *La Kabylie et les coutumes kabyles*, 2:148. On the history of the works see Hannemann, "La mise en place du droit kabyle."

84. Hanoteau and Letourneux, *La Kabylie et les coutumes kabyles*, 2:149.

85. I thank Janet Halley for helping me to think through this connection.

annihilated women's individual wills, especially in forced marriage. In his view, "the Kabyle woman, deprived of personality, is purchased and delivered without the intervention of her will. . . . Fathers even have the right to give their prepubescent daughter over to her purchaser."[86] A frequently reedited reference work on Algeria by Maurice Wahl similarly highlighted the lamentable status of the "Berber woman," given that "she has no fortune of her own, and is assaulted in her interests, her dignity, and even her security by the *mœurs* and laws of a brutal society."[87] This increasingly prevalent view of Kabyle women encouraged French jurists to interpret the customary laws or *qanouns* transcribed by Hanoteau and Letourneux literally.

Alongside the "Arab" woman, the tragic Kabyle woman thus became a staple of journalistic and juridical writing on child marriage. The semipopular *Journal des tribunaux algériens* regularly reported on trials of husbands charged with indecent assault against their prepubescent wives. Citing graphic forensic reports, medico-legal experts testified to the Algerians' propensity for child marriage (and hence rape), while magistrates lamented juries' leniency in cases of husbands who consummated marriages with their ten- and eleven-year-old wives. According to one author, "these acquittals would continue as long as these precipitous unions, allowed and tolerated by Kabyle custom, are not formally forbidden in the name of the most elementary humanity."[88] Appearing alongside articles depicting other morals offenses, including "pederasty," this coverage represented Algerian men as criminal and perversely sexualized.[89] The illustrated popular press likewise highlighted how Kabyle women were abused by mercenary family members. A 1902 article in the newly created *La Revue nord-africaine illustrée* described how they were treated like property, "given over in marriage, or more exactly sold, before even reaching the age of puberty. It is truly a sale

86. Besson, "Étude comparative sur la constitution de la famille," 284. And, *La législation civile de l'Algérie*, 92–93. Maine's work was translated into French in 1874; see Maine, *L'ancien droit considéré dans ses rapports avec l'histoire de la société primitive*. On Maine's importance in shaping colonial family law see Kennedy, "Savigny's Family/Patrimony Distinction"; Mantena, *Alibis of Empire*; Stephens, *Governing Islam*.

87. Wahl, *L'Algérie*, 195.

88. *Journal des tribunaux algériens*, May 7, 1899. On the high rates of acquittal see Vandier, *Histoire de la Cour d'Alger*, 40.

89. The *Journal des tribunaux algériens* frequently reported on trials of husbands for indecent assault. See, for example, case summaries on April 19, 1891; March 9, 1892; May 17, 1893; July 26, 1896; May 9, 1897; May 7, 1899; July 14, 1901; and January 29, 1902. The *Revue algérienne* also covered some of these trials: El Aïb ben Aïssa v. Min. pub., Con. Perm. d'Alger (February 12, 1891), *RA*, pt. 2, 1891, 197–201; Cour d'assises d'Alger (June 24, 1895), *RA*, pt. 2, 1895, 398. On forensic evidence and sexual crime see Kocher, *De la criminalité chez les Arabes*, 188–208; Gouriou, "Le sexe des indigènes"; Ghabrial, " Traumas and Truths of the Body."

that these parents conduct, with the sole aim and desire being to sell this living merchandise for the highest price."[90] These accounts of Algerian men's endemic rapaciousness and sexual criminality underwrote renewed calls for reform, despite the "protected" character of personal status law.

Fantasies of Imperial Rescue

Stories of women's suffering, both real and fictional, also found their way into the metropolitan press. In the fall of 1891, the major metropolitan daily *Le Temps* featured a model of the genre by novelist Élie Berthet. In this racy feuilleton, *L'amour au desert*, Julien Desrosiers, an explorer "born in the heart of France," sets off on an adventure to the "most barbarous country of North Africa."[91] He fulfills his dream of becoming the first "European" to set foot in a remote region of the Sahara, inhabited only by nomadic tribes, including the particularly belli-cose Oulad-Delim. Having acquired a thorough knowledge of the Qur'an, Julien hopes to pass as Muslim despite his fair features. He overcomes the tribesmen's initial skepticism in part by convincing Eliazize, the young and beautiful daugh-ter of a notable, of his religious devotion. Although she is only twelve years old, he is able to judge that she has already become a woman, "thanks to the thin blue cotton garment that left a portion of her bosom open to view." A recurrent cliché in the story, this image of her hidden "treasures" enacted contemporary erotic fantasies of visual appropriation.[92]

In passing himself off as Abd-el-Malek, Julien seeks more than a stolen glance. After the two fall in love, he asks her father for her hand in marriage. Once they agree on a dowry price, Julien sets off in order to obtain the necessary riches (the equivalent of forty camels). A complicated set of events intervenes, and he returns to France. Soon tiring of his facile existence in the metropole, he finds himself inexorably drawn back to his desert love, only to learn that Eliazize's father has now promised her instead to Abdallah, Julien's "mortal enemy." "Abd-el-Malek" protests, arguing that according to Qur'anic law, they were already married. Once it is known that Julien was, in fact, Christian, the couple realize that their future together is in danger. Julian nonetheless hopes that "wisdom and

---

90. Louis Calmeilles, "La femme Kabyle," *La Revue nord-africaine illustrée* 1, no. 10 (1902): 317–20. See also Maxime Massoni, "Fatima la répudiée," *La Revue nord-africaine illustreé* 3, no. 12 (1904): 427–31.

91. Berthet, "L'amour au désert," *Le Temps* (October 9, 1891, and after).

92. Alloula, *Colonial Harem.*

justice" will prevail. But Eliazize knows better, explaining that the couple "cannot have any confidence in their justice." She begs Julien "not to throw her into the arms of the accursed Abdallah," and he solemnly promises to stay by her side. A fanatical crowd, made up of warriors and tribeswomen, urge Eliazize to leave her infidel beloved. Refusing, she shouts back at Abdallah that "Abd-el-Malek is my husband—whether or not he is Christian, I love him as much as I hate you." When Abdallah curses Eliazize, Julian shoots his revolver at the man and "blows his brains out," at which point the crowd attacks the star-crossed lovers. When it is all over, their "bloody cadavers" are laid out on the desert rocks. The novella ends with Eliazize's father claiming, over their dead bodies, his "right" to the inheritance of "Abd-el-Malek." In the story, Julian's desires are celebrated as noble, while "Muslim law" appears a pretext for obscenity, violence, and greed.

Berthet's horrible romance in the desert offers an extraordinary condensation of colonial cliché: a white man dies trying to save a brown woman, who desires a European man and is victimized for it. The story reprises that of the venal Algerian father arranging his daughter's marriage, but with a telling twist. In this version, Julien occupies two apparently contradictory positions: he poses as a Muslim husband of a "child bride" *and* bears the promise of "French" justice to reform the *droit de djebr*. Eliazize's desire for him makes the seemingly impossible—and hence fantasmatic—combination possible. What is more, her love sanctions Julien's murderous violence against his illegitimate rival. In this erotic twist on Spivak's famous formulation, the agency of the woman's desire justifies Julien's purportedly chivalrous action. The apparent failure of his mission does not interrupt the fantasy. It allows for a perpetual projection of eroticized rescue into the future.

Berthet's novella exemplifies how, in the colonial legal imaginary, stories of the Algerian woman's conjugal desires were intertwined with fantasies of French justice. These dreams of romantic rescue traversed legal fiction and fact. Just after *Le Temps* serialized Berthet's story, a parallel tale of disrupted marital bliss unfolded in the pages of the same newspaper. In 1891, a judge separated Fatima bent Ali, a young Kabyle woman from Mekla, near Tizi-Ouzou, from her husband, Haud ou Brahim, and "returned" her to another man, Tahar ou Rhamoun. The young woman's tragic fate—legally torn from her beloved and thrown into the arms of a voracious predator—erupted into a minor scandal.[93]

Ironically, in this case it was a French magistrate who issued this customary law ruling. He accepted Rahmoun's claim that Fatima had been promised

---

93. See *Le Temps*, January 27 and February 28, 1892.

to him by her father. Like many in his position, he had a limited knowledge of the local community and thus applied the description of customary law in Hanoteau and Letourneux's volume literally.[94] As recounted across the Algerian and metropolitan press, the case placed the French magistrate in a compromising position: he had to choose between civilized French law and an indecent indigenous law. Fatima's lawyer reportedly drew out this irony in the course of the trial: "Who would dare throw this woman back into the barbarity of slavery? No, not a French tribunal!" he pleaded.[95] In making a French judge appear barbarous, Fatima's case confused the cultural and sexual categories that undergirded the organization of Algerian civil law status. It rendered explicit the contradictions that Algeria's at once plural and hierarchal legal order produced and contained.

Fatima and Haud were, however, exceptional litigants. Educated in and employed by French schools, they appeared to be models of Kabyle assimilation. Contemporary observers decried their subjection to obsolete Kabyle custom, and by a French magistrate, no less. One of the couple's most vocal advocates was Pierre Foncin, a founder of the Alliance française, school inspector, and devoted proponent of the *mission civilisatrice*. He condemned the French tribunal's "savage justice" in no uncertain terms: "What is the meaning of a judgment that takes a woman away from a husband who loves her to throw her into the arms of a legal abductor? Is it really the duty of French judges to recall *indigènes* to the strict observation of brutal and barbarous customs, when those *indigènes* have themselves abandoned them"?[96] Joining Foncin in this denunciation was theater critic Francisque Sarcey, who depicted Fatima's tragedy in suitably melodramatic tones: "Our entire being is revolted in horror by the mere idea that, on the order of a French judge, a young woman can be torn, by French magistrates, from the man who legally wed her out of love, to have her dragged into the bed of another man who paid for her with money down." Were the decision to be upheld, proclaimed Sarcey, "there remains only one thing for Fatima to do: it is to arm herself with a revolver and, if she can, to blow out the brains of the man who uses

---

94. Hanoteau and Letourneux, *La Kabylie et les coutumes kabyles*, 2:212–20. For a contemporary account of the predicament, written by a *juge de paix* from Kenchala, see Gentil, "Administration de la justice musulmane," 346–47.

95. Francisque Sarcey, "Chronique," *Le XIXᵉ siècle*, February 12, 1892.

96. Pierre Foncin, "Fatima et la politique française en Algérie," *La revue bleue* 49, no. 6 (February 6, 1892): 182–84; "Le cas de Fatima," *La revue bleue* 49, no. 6 (March 5, 1892): 319; Clarisse Coignet, "L'Algérie et le gouvernement des indigènes," *La revue bleue* 49, no. 25 (June 18, 1892): 807–12; Alfred Rambaud, "L'enseignement primaire chez les indigènes musulmans d'Algérie notamment dans la Grande-Kabylie," *Revue pédagogique* 20, no. 2 (1892): 111–33.

such violence."[97] The resonances between Sarcey's dramatic call to arms and the brutal ending of *L'amour au désert* are striking. In both cases, the legal violation of women's marital desires sanctioned an exceptional, punitive violence against indigenous men.

Fortunately for Fatima, recourse to force proved unnecessary. Foncin and Sarcey's incendiary pieces spurred an avalanche of press reports that embellished the story in order to better denounce the decision. No major journal, in the metropole or Algeria, neglected the sensational story.[98] These accounts revealed the contradictions and compromises entailed by putting French magistrates in charge of local law. Journalists hotly debated what kind of reforms should be put in place, including proposals to ban child marriage. Because the story coincided with the work of major parliamentary commissions on Algerian reform, the stakes of these discussions were high. Some newspapers defended the judge's decision as legal, because it was in keeping with native custom—which demonstrated, in their view, the *indigène*'s ineradicable difference and alien character.[99] Meanwhile, those who denounced the decision often viewed it as a source of French shame. The *Petit Parisien* proclaimed in its editorial column: "How can we reconcile respect for Arab Law with the ideas of morality, with the principles of civilization, that it is France's mission to make triumph?"[100] Several journalists cited English legislation banning sati as a model for the French to follow.[101] The case was remarkable not only for the attention it garnered, but for the dissonant opinions it revealed. The satirical *Charivari Oranais* published several articles

---

97. Francisque Sarcey, "Chronique," *Le XIXe siècle*, January 20, 1892. Critical responses to this "Parisian" intervention into Algerian matters included C. Allan, "La justice à la Française," *La Vigie algérienne*, January 29, 1892; V. de Cottens, "Choses d'Alger et de partout: Tue-le!," *La Vigie algérienne*, February 2, 1892.

98. For the metropolitan press see Jean Frollo, "Un mariage Algérien," *Le Petit Parisien*, January 29, 1892; "Fatima la Kabyle," *L'Attaque*, February 23, 1892; *La Croix*, February 25, 1892; Léon Millet, "Justice algérienne," *La Justice*, February 25, 1892; "La belle Fatima," *La Lanterne*, March 1, 1892; "Le mariage de Fatima," *La Presse*, March 4, 1892.

99. See, for example, Jules Dietz, *Journal des débats*, January 26, 1892, 1; Aumerat, "La monitrice Fatima," February 13, 1892; Aumerat, "Toujours la monitrice," *La Dépêche algérienne*, February 21, 1893; Émile de Samie, "L'affaire Fatima," *L'Indépendant de Mascara*, February 14, 1892.

100. Jean Frollo, "Un mariage Algérien," *Le Petit Parisien*, January 29, 1892; "Un mariage algérien," *Moniteur de l'Algérie*, February 6, 1892; Charles Marchal, "À propos de Fatima," *Le Petit colon*, February 16, 1892; Marchal, "Le cas de Fatima," *Le Petit colon*, February 17, 1892; Marchal, "Un conte de la Mère-L'Oie," *Le Petit colon*, February 18, 1892; Marchal, "Le droit musulman sur les mariages," *Le Petit colon*, February 20, 1892; Marchal, "Conte de Grand'Papa," *Le Petit colon*, February 26, 1892; Marchal, "Dernier mot," *Le Petit colon*, February 29, 1892.

101. Lissagaray, "Fatima, la Kabyle," *La Bataille*, January 26, 1892, 1; Paul de Cassagnac, "Une femme vendue," *L'autorité*, January 31, 1892; Senex, "À propos de Fatima la Kabyle," *La Dépêche algérienne*, February 3, 1892.

mocking the uproar in the Parisian and Algerian press, as well as the apparent hypocrisy of having a "civilized" French judge enforce "barbarous" Muslim law.[102] Aided in part by Charles Jeanmaire, the reformist head of the Académie d'Alger, the local education administration, the couple eventually won out. The Tribunal of Tizi-Ouzou overturned the *juge de paix*'s initial decision. Ruling on a technicality rather than moral principle, it claimed that Fatima's union with the pretender was invalid because it had not followed to the letter the model of a Kabyle marriage ceremony outlined by Hanoteau and Letourneux.[103] The decision, while it preserved the happy Kabyle couple's marriage, did not establish an overarching rule, "inspired from the principles of universal morality."[104] Indeed, the proceduralism reinscribed rather than remedied a literalist approach to *qanouns*. The court's ruling drew widespread criticism, as journalists again denounced how it was demeaning to French magistrates.[105]

This heated controversy resulted in calls to codify Muslim and customary law, most notably by the head of the Law Faculty of Algiers, Robert Estoublon. In an article published in the *Revue algérienne et tunisenne de jurisprudence*, he held that it was on "the terrain of natural law and morality that our efforts should constantly work to reconcile [*rapprocher*] these two legislations." In his view, Muslim law "should not be made responsible for the injustices and the abuses of power for which it has frequently served as a cover." Official proposals in favor of codification cited this article on "Muslim and Kabyle Marriage," both when Senator Alexandre Isaac (Guadeloupe) launched a call for codification in 1895 and again when the endeavor was actually taken up in earnest in 1905 with respect to Muslim law.[106]

---

102. Momus, "Le cas de Madame Fatima," *Le Charivari oranais*, February 21, 1892; "Le cas de Fatma, jugé par Phalène," *Le Charivari oranais*, February 28, 1892.

103. Ali Ibahouten v. Tahar ou Rhamoun, Tribunal de Tizi-Ouzou (February 26, 1892) in *RA*, pt. 2, 1892, 76–80.

104. Robert Estoublon, "Mariages musulmans et kabyles," *RA*, pt. 1, 1892, 86.

105. E. Morinaud, "Editorial," *Le Républicain de Constantine*, March 3, 1892; "Lettre d'un musulman," *Le Républicain de Constantine*, March 4, 1892; E. Morinaud, "Au panier!," *Le Républicain de Constantine*, March 7, 1892; A. Algiéri, "Justice musulmane," *Moniteur de l'Algérie*, March 4, 1892; Aumerat, "À propos du droit musulman," *La Dépêche algérienne*, March 5, 1892. See as well "Revue de la presse algérienne," *La Vigie algérienne*, March 3, 1892. These discussions of the honor and dignity of French magistrates resonate with Mrinalini Sinha's discussion of the Ilbert Bill in India; see Sinha, *Colonial Masculinity*.

106. Estoublon, *RA*, 1892, 90–91. The jurist and journalist Charles Marchal issued a similar proclamation in "Nécessité de codifier les lois musulmanes en Algérie," *Le Petit colon*, February 22, 1892. Isaac cited Estoublon's article verbatim in his senatorial report, Alexandre Isaac, "Justice française et musulmane; Police et sécurité," *JO*, Doc. Parl., Sénat, February 28, 1895, annexe 36, 218–19. Estoublon's article continues to be cited in recent accounts; see Bontems, "Les tentatives de codification du droit musulman," 118.

French feminist Hubertine Auclert joined in this generalized condemnation. Auclert learned of the case while living in Algeria with her husband, Antonin Levrier, who was a *juge de paix* in Frenda (Oran Province). Her account focused less on Fatima's "perfect love" than on the fate of other "ordinary victims who might be eloquent and supplicating, but whose desperate voices move neither the public nor the [French] judges."[107] In denouncing the legal treatment of Fatima's case, Auclert both deployed and reoriented colonialist clichés about "child marriage." More specifically, she turned the logic of colonial rescue against itself by accusing "l'homme [the French man]" and his law with "tolerating this crime, because of his solidarity with those who take advantage of it." Rather than drawing a distinction between French and Muslim law (and French and Muslim men) Auclert emphasized a patriarchal complicity between them.[108]

French colonial jurists meanwhile promoted Muslim and Kabyle marriage reform as the only way to reconcile French and "indigenous" law. Their attention to the question coincided with the flurry of parliamentary activity on Algeria that had drawn metropolitan attention to Fatima's case in the first place. The Senate's "Commission of XVIII" conducted an exploratory mission to Algeria in 1891. Presided over by former minister of education and then senator Jules Ferry, it brought ongoing conflicts over indigenous legal, political, and social reform onto the national stage.[109] In his budgetary report before the Chamber in 1891, Deputy Auguste Burdeau also called attention to questions about Algerian law and justice with respect to both persons and property. Skeptical of thoroughgoing "assimilation," Burdeau endorsed relative accommodation instead. He both defended the punitive *indigénat* and recommended measures to reduce local dissatisfaction with French justice in the wake of the 1886 and 1889 judicial reforms. While avowing ongoing challenges to the separation of religious and civil doctrine in Algeria, he endorsed the power of the secular state. Islam would, in his view, have to "adapt to our essential ideas of the religious neutrality of the State, the moral equality of the sexes, the incessant progress of human reason and civilization."[110] To this end, the prosecution of "non-nubile" marriage would be an effective state tactic "to impress minds [*frapperaient les esprits*] and proclaim the subordination of religious prescriptions to superior principles." By criminalizing

---

107. Auclert, *Les femmes arabes en Algérie*, 46–47. On the ambivalences of Auclert's text see Clancy-Smith, "La Femme Arabe"; Eichner, "La citoyenne in the World"; J. W. Scott, *Only Paradoxes*; Lehning, *To Be a Citizen*.

108. Auclert, *Les femmes arabes en Algérie*, 49.

109. Pensa, *L'Algérie*.

110. Burdeau, *L'Algérie en 1891*, 214.

these marriages, the French state could assert its secular power and the moral (rather than political) equality between men and women.[111] For Burdeau, in other words, the regulation of "child marriage" was a powerful mechanism of colonial government.

Sovereignty and Sexual Consent

Algerian magistrates endorsed this view of secular state power in their calls for marriage reform. Their concerns about "prepubescent marriage" spurred Governor-General Jules Cambon to issue a January 24, 1896, circular on the declaration of marriage and divorce of "*indigènes musulmans.*" The new directive reminded prefects that failures to register marriages or divorces was subject to prosecution under the *indigénat*.[112] But in the eyes of many, the existing law remained inadequate. The following year, in the pages of the *Revue algérienne*, Louis-Auguste Eyssautier, a lawyer at the Court of Algiers and specialist of colonial Muslim law, issued yet another plea for reform. Like many jurists and journalists before him, he condemned how marriage and market logics were confused in Muslim and customary law: "The right of the father leads to worst abuses; marriage becomes a traffic, a sale; the dowry, of which the father could take a part, is a sale price." Only "the personal consent of the spouses" could put a stop to the abuse. The sanctity of this principle separating personhood from property, in turn, justified the "right of France to abolish a law or custom which is contrary to public order and social interest."[113] Consensual marriage thus came to symbolize French legal supremacy and sovereignty.

In order to better police child marriage, Eyssautier recommended changes to the 1882 law on civil registry: imposing a minimum marriage age of fifteen for women and eighteen for men and obliging women to appear in person at the registry. He had high hopes for what it would achieve for the French state and for Algerian women. In his estimation, the reform would "prevent the gravest abuses, the most shameful assaults; it would assure the repression of those which continue to be committed; and it would return necessary dignity to native

---

111. Ibid., 222.

112. "Circulaire du Gouverneur Général relative aux déclarations de mariage et de divorce des indigènes musulmans et à l'application des peines de l'indigénat en cette matière, 24 janvier 1896," in Estoublon and Lefébure, *Code de l'Algérie*, 2:15. And follow-up by the *procureur général*, February 1, 1896, 16.

113. Louis-Auguste Eyssautier, "Projet de loi sur le mariage indigène," 100. Eyssautier also cited an 1895 circular issued by the prefect of Alger, dated October 8, 1895.

marriages and would place the native civil registry on the firmest ground."[114] Underwritten by moral horror, Eyssautier's proposal aimed to enhance the reliability of the state registry of Algerian persons.

At the opening session of the Court of Algiers in 1898, child protection again served to justify proposed limits on Muslim and customary law. In his inaugural speech on the *droit de djebr* and "prepubescent marriage," Assistant Prosecutor Alphonse Étienne cataloged recent trials and reformist ideas. Changes to the civil registry alongside the required presence of qadis at marriage ceremonies would, he claimed, guarantee that "Muslim marriage would no longer be a form of legal abduction [*un rapt juridique*], because it would unite free wills in a free union." His concluding remarks underscored what was at stake in calling attention to "these abuses of parental authority, these lamentable unions of children, these odious assaults," namely the imposition of limits on Muslim and customary law. In other words, "under the pretext of respecting the personal status of our subjects, let's not legally authorize indecent assault and the rape of children."[115] Moral outrage enhanced these jurists' arguments about the sexual excess of the personal status.

Charles Barbet, an assistant prosecutor in Sidi Bel Abbès and occasional travel writer, expressed similar sentiments in an article he penned for the *Revue algérienne*. His emotionally charged essay detailed the "deplorable consequences, the intolerable abuses which result from the exercise of this exorbitant right of matrimonial constraint, granted fathers by Qur'anic legislation and recognized as legitimate by our legislation, which is overly respectful of the traditions and barbarous customs of Muslim *indigènes*."[116] For Barbet the recognition of these marriages by "our legislation" was scandalous. In taking exception to indigenous exceptionality, he concluded that only those laws should be respected that "were not in formal contradiction to the intangible, imprescriptible, and sacred principles of justice, liberty, and morality, which more and more dominate our epoch."[117] Depicting legal difference in viscerally and affectively laden terms, Barbet understood the French Civil Code to be a timeless bearer of universal principles. His focus on "child marriage" cast indigenous personal status—and existing French colonial law—as morally objectionable and sexually perverse.

---

114. Ibid., 102.

115. Étienne, "Le droit de 'djebr' et le mariage des impubères."

116. Barbet, "La femme musulmane en Algérie," *RA*, pt. 1, 1903, 169. For some of Barbet's Algerian "impressions," in particular an account of a "Kabyle wedding" of a fifteen-year-old girl and a sixty-year-old man, see Barbet, *Au pays des burnous*, 245–53.

117. Barbet, "La femme musulmane en Algérie," 177.

Despite these repeated calls for reform, legislative and administrative measures remained stalled. Practical as well as legal obstacles to implementing the civil registry persisted, given the endlessly complex, uneven, and expensive bureaucratic procedures involved.[118] Jurists' lurid accounts of marital consent trials nonetheless did establish an understanding of indigenous legal difference in visceral moral and physical terms. Like polygamy, marital coercion came to instantiate the embodied difference of personal status. French colonial jurists, politicians, and journalists continually invoked it in order to condemn Muslim and customary law as a source of scandal.[119] In doing so, they also reproduced romanticized fantasies of legal rescue.

As reactions to the Fatima case demonstrated, settler advocates interested in Algerian autonomy dismissed the ambitious proposals of metropolitan reformers. They focused instead on the political preservation of the purity of French citizenship—and French law. In the process, the newly defined legal domain of Muslim personal status came to represent an abhorrent legal exception that confirmed French sovereignty and the exclusive dignity of the citizen.

The contours of this logic became visible when, beginning in the late 1880s, several deputies and senators issued proposals in favor of extending political rights to "Muslim" subjects, even while their personal status (including the "right" to polygamy and the *droit de djebr*) was maintained. In making a case for *political* (as opposed to civil legal) assimilation, metropolitan officials downplayed differences in marriage law. As Senator Isaac explained in his 1893 proposal: "It would not be impossible, after having set aside religious prescriptions maintained strictly within the domain of personal status, to set aside a local legislation, that would only represent, with respect to metropolitan legislation, differences of detail that are justified by a diversity of needs." Because, as Isaac noted, most aspects of French law *already* applied to Algerian natives, he claimed it was "an error to say that Algerian Muslims are not submitted to French law." Their legal status was, in fact, no less exceptional than that of the settlers themselves, who likewise benefited from special legal dispensations.[120]

By contrast, skeptical colonial jurists insisted that the sexual privileges of Muslim personal status rendered it incompatible with French civil law and

---

118. The confusions and abuses of the registry when it came to marriage were numerous and extensive; see Saïd ben Achour, "Des actes de l'état-civil reçus par les adjoints indigènes et de leurs irrégularités," *Le Moniteur des justices de paix d'Algérie* 1 (1886): 46–47; Kateb, *Européens, "indigènes" et juifs*, 114–15.

119. This logic resembles the "repugnancy principle" as it operated in British colonial regulation of customary law in Africa. On its productive function see Mamdani, *Citizen and Subject*, 63.

120. Proposition de loi par M. Isaac, *JO*, Doc. Parl., Sénat, annexe 134, April 4, 1893, 287. Isaac referred to both the "old colonies" and French India as examples.

citizenship. They evidently had a professional as well as political stake in pre-serving "Muslim" personal law, in (almost) all of its cultural, religious, and sexual difference. With the transition to civilian rule after 1870, jurists' own legal status was enhanced by their expanded jurisdiction over Muslim and customary law matters and the specialization of legal expertise that accompanied the creation of a law faculty in Algiers in 1879.[121] They affirmed, as did Emmanuel Besson in his prize-winning legal thesis, that "there should not be, on French soil, citizens with contradictory rights. We cannot accept the idea that a French man, just because he is of the Arab or Kabyle race, should be permitted to legally marry four women or sell his prepubescent daughter. That would truly degrade [avilir] the title of French citizen"[122] This indexing of the honor of citizenship to the purported (sexual) purity of French civil law condemned Muslims to a state of legal and political exception.

Conflicts over the droit de djebr and mariage impubère further worked to elaborate this expertise and legal oversight. As one former lawyer at the Court of Algiers, Adrien Leclerc, explained at an international conference on colo-nial sociology in 1900, marital coercion required continual regulation precisely because Muslim "mœurs and customs" could not be altered: "there is nonethe-less, one right which should be regulated. It is the droit de djebr, which sometimes has results that are absolutely contrary to the demands of humanity and civili-zation."[123] This ongoing regulation of Muslim men's sexual privilege shored up French legal sovereignty by aligning it with universalist principle.

Over the course of Algerian colonization, the legal regulation of the droit de djebr served as a node of colonial governance: it symbolized the military's "moral" conquest in the 1850s; it asserted French judicial authority over Muslim law in the 1860s; it underwrote efforts to transform property law and institute the civil registry in the 1870s and 1880s; and it offered a moral justification for the excep-tional treatment of the indigène in political, criminal, and civil law. French jurists' accounts of the seemingly timeless fantasy of the patriarchy and perversity of Muslim law were thus firmly anchored in concrete contexts of colonial policy. Integral to the legal imaginary of colonial Algeria, this regulatory imperative had specific political, social, and psychic effects. This chapter shows how the conflicts

---

121. Vatin, "Exotisme et rationalité"; "Science juridique et institution coloniale"; Blévis, "Juristes et légistes au service de l'état colonial" and "Une université française en terre coloniale"; Auzary-Schmaltz, "La magistrature coloniale."

122. Besson, La législation civile de l'Algérie, 340.

123. Leclerc, "Des indigènes musulmans d'Algérie," 114. And his "De la condition de la femme musulmane."

over the *droit de djebr* established "Muslim personal status" not as an exception to law, but as an exception *within* law.[124] As sites of intense affective investment, marriage trials worked to expand the purview of French law, rather than establishing a zone beyond it. Not least, they made a fantasy of women's marital desire into an index of legal civilization and personhood, while making girls and women into subjects of colonial state regulation.

By focusing attention on marital consent, this legal fantasy interpellated Algerian women as legal subjects and, implicitly, as subjects of desire, into the domain of French colonial law. Access to French courts indeed allowed women (and their families) to renegotiate the terms of undesirable unions. These trials over marital constraint hinged on—and were hitched to—the expression of women's conjugal desire (or its refusal). These cases thus granted Algerian women a very specific legal personhood, at once constituting and circumscribing their agency. In tactically appealing to French tribunals, women were asked to speak about their marital desires. This appropriation of women's legal strategies thus also underwrote colonial Algerian law, its animating fantasies and telling repressions.

---

124. On colonial law and the "state of exception" see Hussain, *Jurisprudence of Emergency*; Benton, *Search for Sovereignty*, chap. 6; Spieler, *Empire and Underworld*; Saada, "Law in the Time of Catastrophe."

5

SPECIAL *MŒURS* AND MILITARY EXCEPTIONS

In 1891, a heated conflict between two officers in the Algerian spahis (native-recruited light cavalry), second-class *médecin* Major Samuel Abraham Boyer and squadron head Captain Albert Jean Marie Joseph Bouïs, spiraled out of control. The officers' quarrel over petty criminality, pederasty, and personal honor threatened military hierarchy and authority, especially once their respective charges of dishonor spilled beyond the barracks and into the colonial garrison town of Médéa's public square. Exceeding their superiors' best efforts to contain it, the scandal called the army's hierarchy into question. Competing models of legality and masculinity, professional honor and dignity, clashed as the case played out across military and civil jurisdictions as well as the colonial public sphere.

The dispute between Bouïs and Boyer exacerbated a host of wider social and political tensions in Médéa and beyond: within the military, between military officials and colonial settlers, and between the town's European, Muslim, and Jewish inhabitants.[1] The "Scandal of Médéa" exemplifies how these conflicts took embodied and legal form at a moment when the colony and the nation were scandal prone. From Panama to Dreyfus, politicians and a flourishing popular press capitalized on politically charged revelations of corruption.[2] Algeria's volatile political scene presented a particularly extreme case of this proliferation of "affairs," as local administrators and metropolitan officials used accusations of malfeasance to influence politics at a local and national level.[3]

The publicity garnered by "child marriage" cases took part in this broader culture of colonial scandal. As we saw in the last chapter, sentimental narratives

---

1. For a contemporary account of intercommunal tensions in the town, especially surrounding local elections, see Pensa, *L'Algérie*, 222–24. See also accounts in *Le Petit Alger*, July 3, 1892, and July 10, 1892.
2. Forth, *Dreyfus Affair*; Harris, *Dreyfus: Politics, Emotion*.
3. Guignard, *L'abus de pouvoir*.

denouncing the *droit de djebr* pathologized the perversity of Muslim and customary law. By giving extensive coverage to the voices and bodies of young female litigants, the legal and popular press contributed to a broader effort to both indict and regulate colonial law. In this chapter, I focus on a different colonial sexual scandal: accusations of sodomy in a unit of the native cavalry. In this case, it was not Muslim law, but military law that was put on trial as a distinct and deviant jurisdiction that transgressed the norms of civilian law and rule.

The army doctor Boyer's accusations linked military corruption to charges of sexual indecency. His intimations to higher-ups that Captain Bouïs had sexually abused his native orderlies provoked official consternation. Clearly concerned about the army's image, Boyer's superiors ultimately inverted the charge of "inversion": they turned it back against the doctor. Rather than drawing out witness testimony, the military investigation silenced it. As a result, the officers' military personnel dossiers do not clearly reveal what happened between Captain Bouïs and his aides. What they do clarify is how military officials saw the doctor's public disclosures to be an even greater threat than the indecent acts themselves.

Boyer's charges did not provoke sympathy for Bouïs's young victims. In contrast to the testimony of girls in *droit de djebr* cases, that of youths in this case was mocked and marginalized. Boyer's potent charge of pederasty at once revealed and unsettled the sexual and racial hierarchy on which military order depended. The military archive worked to contain this challenge, becoming a site of official obfuscation.[4] It served as a legal and psychic defense against threats to the army's juridical as well as sexual and racial integrity. For critics of the army's special *mœurs* and laws, by contrast, this defense represented the military's own implicitly racial and sexual corruption.

The Story of the Spahis

Created in 1834, the Algerian spahis were based on the Ottoman cavalry (*sipahi*) that had existed under the dey. Over the course of the following decade, three regiments were formed in the cities of Algiers, Oran, and Constantine under the command of General Joseph "Jusuf" Valentini. Their flamboyant uniforms—a

---

4. Arondekar, *For the Record*, 41.

red cape or "burnous," turban, and flowing blue pants—quickly became iconic, spurring exotic fashion trends in the metropole.[5] By the 1850s, Governor-General Randon organized the troops into villages or *smalas* in order to guard the territorial limits of the Tell. Drawn from prominent Algerian families, the cavalrymen were granted land close by to accommodate their family members and herds, as a powerful way to promote loyalty, especially since colonial officials believed that garrison service was "profoundly antipathetic" to native soldiers. The military colonization scheme thus sought to combine strategic as well as agricultural aims.[6] While ideally conceived as "model farms," this organization soon spurred conflicts with recently arrived European settlers, who viewed land grants to Algerians as a waste of resources.[7] In the 1860s, the army attempted to scale back the size of the *smalas* by recruiting bachelors rather than notables with large family entourages. The efforts were widely considered a failure, turning up, according to one inspecting officer of the First Regiment of Alger, "drunkards" and "pederasts."[8]

Once civilian settler power was established in 1870, the fantasy of military colonization was systematically dismantled, especially after the insurrection of soldiers from *smalas* located on the Tunisian border in Tarf, Bou Hadjar, and Aïn-Guettar on January 20, 1871. The revolt, set off by the soldiers' refusal to fight in the Franco-Prussian War, contributed to the wider Moqrani Rebellion the following March. According to Orphis Léon Lallemand, the general who had first issued the order, the spahis refused to leave their families behind. As he explained to President Gambetta on January 24, 1871, "The Spahis of Souk-Arhas refused to march. They said that they had enlisted only to serve in Algeria. They have wives and children. And had never served in other wars." He noted that, by contrast, "the squadron of bachelors from Constantine did not pose the least difficulty."[9]

Instead of the sedentary family regime of the *smala*, settler critics promoted mobile units of bachelors.[10] The settlers' principal motivation was to gain access to the lands that had been set aside for the spahis and their families. As a result, an 1874 law reorganized the corps by opening new mobile divisions to unmarried

---

5. Thoral, "Sartorial Orientalism."
6. Xavier Yacono, "La colonisation militaire," 353.
7. Duval, *Réflexions sur la politique de l'empereur en Algérie*, 80; Lunel, *La question algérienne*, 105–6.
8. Yacono, "La colonisation militaire," 377.
9. Telegram cited in Déposition of Crémieux, Rapport De la Sicotière, vol. 1 (1875), 251.
10. Simon, *Algérie. Les spahis et les smalas*, 10.

as well as married men.[11] Even under the new regime, settler interests exerted political pressure on the military authorities and installations that remained in the Tell, including in Médéa. Settlers were no less critical of the degraded moral and sexual condition of garrison life than they had been of the inefficiency and insubordination of the *smalas*. One contemporary travel writer could find little redeeming to say about the garrison town: "This city, with its walls, its barracks, its hospitals, feels like a prison, a bastille, a penal colony." Arriving on a Sunday morning, during the hour of Mass, he detected a strong odor, "not of incense, but of absinthe."[12] The Bouïs-Boyer Affair erupted in this sordid milieu.

The Scandal

In July 1891, town police surprised Captain Bouïs in his hotel room with Mohammed Soumati, a local youth who was thought to be fifteen years of age. The incident of *flagrant délit* occurred after rumors about Bouïs had circulated around Médéa for several months. Across the Algerian press, journalists intimated a complicated backstory in the affair, which, by pitting the police against a military officer, staged a jurisdictional and sexual conflict between local settlers and the army. Earlier that spring, Boyer and a lieutenant serving under Bouïs, Albert Rocas, jointly accused the captain of sexual indiscretion with his orderlies. While the military initially tried to keep the matter in house, Bouïs's arrest brought the morals charge into the town square and civilian courts, garnering precisely the public scrutiny that the army hierarchy sought to avoid. In a synthetic report to the Ministry of War, General Joseph Arthur Dufaure du Bessol, the commander of the Algerian Nineteenth Army Division, attempted to account for this unruly state of affairs.

Archived in the army doctor's personnel file (and notably not in the captain's), the division commander's report insisted that conflict had originated in personal enmity, rather than professional misconduct. Bessol claimed that the dispute between the officers had in fact arisen during a *"partie de campagne"* at which Bouïs, Boyer, Rocas, and their wives were present. Before the event, the atmosphere at the headquarters of the cavalry unit had been "calm." The regiment was largely spread out across the Algerian territory, between Médéa and

---

11. Décret portant sur la réorganisation des régiments de spahis, January 6, 1874, *Dalloz, Jurisprudence générale* (1874), pt. 4, 56.

12. Desprez, *Voyage à Oran*, 71–72.

an outpost in a Saharan oasis, El Goléa, far to the south. Médéa itself was an isolated provincial town (the rail line would arrive the following year), situated in a major wine-producing region. Given their remove, the few men in charge of the unit had to, in Bessol's words, "make do with one another" on "outings where individualities with such different *mœurs* and conduct mixed together."[13] Portraying the conflict as an aberrant and unfortunate clash of personalities, Bessol tried to contain its significance in order to preserve the regiment's honor.

Bessol's account intimated the boredom and violence, narcissism and pettiness that suffused everyday life in the colonial garrison town.[14] His psychological analysis of the characters deployed the kind of "affective knowledge" that Ann Stoler has identified as "at the core of colonial rationality."[15] The report worked retrospectively to make sense of events that initially confounded the unit's military and racial hierarchy.

Bessol's report underscored a considerable social and moral contrast between the Boyer and Bouïs ménages. The former was "very unified, honorable with respect both to morality and money"—thanks, it seems, to the good match that Boyer had made to an heiress from Sedan in 1887.[16] Boyer's own background was humble. His father, a schoolteacher from the small city of Thiers in the Auvergne, named him for a Protestant evangelist, Abraham Charbonney, who served as a witness on his birth registry in 1850.[17] After graduating third in his class at Val de Grâce, the prestigious Parisian academy of military medicine, Boyer was on a fast track of career advancement. Before taking up a post in the Zouaves in 1888, he had served in the campaign in Tunisia in 1881 and for over a year in the occupation of Tonkin in 1887.[18] By 1890, his superiors recommended him for promotion to first class *médecin-major*, as well as the Legion of Honor.[19]

---

13. Notes remises par M. le Général du Bessol, October 16, 1892. See also Livret matricule, Boyer, Samuel Abraham, dossier Boyer, Service Historique de la Défense (hereafter SHD) 10Yf 671. Contemporary statistics estimated the number of "European" inhabitants, who principally worked as civil servants, to be 1,373 out of a total population of 15,242. Cortes, *Monographie de la commune de Médéa*, 55.

14. On the monotony of colonial administration see Auerbach, "Imperial Boredom."

15. Stoler, *Along the Archival Grain*, 98–99.

16. Notes remises par M. Général du Bessol, October 16, 1892. See also Livret matricule, Boyer, Samuel Abraham, dossier Boyer. On Bessol's wife see Min. of War, Rapport sur une demand de permission de mariage, January 10, 1887, dossier Boyer.

17. Acte de naissance de Boyer, Samuel Abraham (May 21, 1850), État civil, Mairie de Thiers, dossier Boyer. On Abraham Charbonney's work see Charbonney, "Auvergne, Alpes maritimes."

18. Livret matricule, Boyer, Samuel Abraham, dossier Boyer.

19. Inspection générale de 1889, 1890, 1891, Feuille de notes concernant M. Boyer and Feuille technique, dossier Boyer.

While Boyer "had a certain professional merit," Bessol judged his nature to be "nervous, worried, and indecisive," and hence vulnerable to being "absolutely dominated by his wife, a neurotic *bas bleu* [bluestocking] who was perhaps a little hysterical." On paper, Boyer was a model of medical men's heroism in French imperial expansion. In person, however, he did not conform to the norms of martial masculinity and sociability. He did not, according to Bessol, have "any serious friendships, but rather the banal sympathy that is born of indifference."[20] No charismatic figure of empire, he did exemplify a certain moral and meritocratic ideal.[21] That ideal quickly unraveled in his confrontation with Bouïs.

Bouïs was an entirely different sort. Boyer's rank equivalent, he was nine years older, but had little to show for it. His personnel file, in contrast to Boyer's, contained early signs of trouble. Born in 1841 in the Languedoc region, he began his career in the Second Regiment of Hussards in 1859, where he achieved the rank of lieutenant in 1875.[22] His advancement stalled when he ran into serious money problems. An 1880 request for his suspension made his defects clear: "Bouïs, who is a mediocre officer and fairly bad serviceman, has always been inclined to spend money far beyond his means."[23] Heavily in debt, he withheld pay from soldiers under his command and engaged in other shady dealings. He did not return to full activity until 1883, when he had managed to pay off his creditors. His transfer to the post as captain in the First Regiment of the spahis seems to have been designed to prevent him from causing more trouble. This return to service coincided with his marriage to a wealthy widow, an arrangement that his superiors looked at askance, given her dubious morality. Although "a widow and charming," she was, as Bouïs's superiors discovered, "in a perilous situation."[24] According to Bessol, the couple's relationship was an "arrangement between two beings who each had some failings in their past." Bouïs brought arms and debts, while she had what was "left of a small fortune that had been wasted," and "opulent and gaudy charms."[25] In short, they spelled trouble. While Boyer was in Algeria to advance his career, Bouïs's transfer there symbolized personal and professional failure.

---

20. Notes remises par M. Général du Bessol, October 16, 1892, Livret matricule, Boyer, Samuel Abraham, dossier Boyer.

21. On imperial charisma see Berenson, *Heroes of Empire*.

22. Livret matricule, dossier Bouïs, SHD 5Yf 70970.

23. Bessol to Min. of War, August 18, 1880, dossier Bouïs.

24. Proposition d'autoriser M. le lieutenant Bouïs à épouser Mme. Vve. Richon, Rapport fait au Ministre, April 1, 1884, dossier Bouïs. Lucie Malinet's dowry had an estimated value of close to 80,000 francs.

25. Notes remises par M. Général du Bessol, October, 16, 1892, dossier Boyer.

The third player in the drama was Lieutenant Rocas, who served unhappily under Bouïs's orders. As Bessol noted, both Rocas and his wife were born in Algeria and had landed interests in the area, as well as important social connections. Rocas had gone to school with local journalists and literary figures, which explains the explosive treatment of the scandal in regional newspapers. According to Bessol, it was Rocas who first recruited Boyer to take his side. While he managed to extricate himself from the affair by professing profound regret for his disorderly behavior, Rocas "continued with his work behind the scenes [son travail occulte]" and took into his confidence "people from the locality, known to be very hostile to the army."[26] His initial instigating role was, however, soon overtaken by Boyer's furious campaign against Bouïs.

It is unclear what exactly happened at the picnic. In its aftermath, Bouïs reportedly changed how he ran his squadron. He had previously led the unit rather lackadaisically, "perhaps on account of his past." After the outing, he became harsher and more controlling. Switching his "attitude of camaraderie for that of the Chef," he became "positively villainous." Resentment-filled, Rocas roped Boyer into the argument. As a second-class médecin-major, Boyer was technically Bouïs's equal in rank. Given their radically different comportments and styles of masculinity, it is unsurprising that this ambivalent hierarchical equivalence fueled the ensuing conflict.[27] While the captain's character appeared morally suspect, Boyer and Rocas's machinations against him clearly threatened military order. Their mismanagement of the situation reflected poorly on the military hierarchy, which used its bureaucratic and juridical procedures to cover up the incidents. Boyer, by contrast, did everything in his power to publicize the scandal.

The regiment's commanding officers, squadron head Vicomte Henri de La Panouse and Lieutenant Colonel Maurice Jean de Vergennes, took Boyer's actions as an affront to their own authority and honor. At one critical point, La Panouse punished Boyer with fifteen days of confinement to his quarters [arrêts simples] because he had supposedly performed an "ironic salute" on horseback and in uniform in "the view of the public which was spread out at a sidewalk café."[28] Boyer denied the charge, claiming that La Panouse, who was seated at a table reading a newspaper, could not have seen him give a salute.[29] In response,

---

26. Dossier Rocas, SHD 8Yf 4824. And Notes remises par M. Général du Bessol, October 16, 1892, dossier Boyer.

27. Notes remises par M. Général du Bessol, October 16, 1892, dossier Boyer.

28. La Panouse, Note de service, July 25, 1891, dossier Boyer. Reprinted in Boyer, Affaire Bouïs contre Boyer, Official Correspondence, 1.

29. Boyer to Bonnefous, Provisional Commander of the subdivision of Médéa, July 26, 1891, dossier Boyer.

Boyer received an even harsher sentence: thirty days of confinement [*arrêts de rigueur*]. For La Panouse and Vergennes, Boyer's insolence violated codes of military hierarchy and honor.

In their view, Boyer's comportment was difficult to comprehend. According to Vergennes, Boyer, while "a good doctor," had been "dragged into an affair against a Captain of the Regiment—which didn't concern him—by a stubbornness, which was inexplicable for a man of honor. . . . Ignoring the opinions of his *chefs*, rebelling against all punishments, even assuming an arrogant attitude, he pursued a path of complete indiscipline."[30] Boyer's publicly visible insubordination disturbed the officers, whose trail of correspondence struggled to make sense of his unpredictable behavior.

Vergennes sought assistance from the cavalry commander for the Division of Alger. He expressed hope that Boyer would "return, with calm, to a healthy understanding of the situation." Worried by July that Boyer's "sentiments" would not improve, he suggested that "keeping Boyer in the garrison of Médéa could lead to very serious incidents."[31] A July 28, 1891, telegram from Algiers sent to ministerial officials urged a rapid intervention.[32] The concerns were warranted, but Paris did not act quickly enough. Three days later, the town police found Bouïs in his hotel room with Mohammed Soumati.

Archiving Transgressions

The dossiers of Boyer, Bouïs, and Rocas were designed as instruments of military administration. Constructed by specific bureaucratic aims, army personnel files usually tracked career achievement, evaluated promise and promotion, and determined pension levels at retirement. La Panouse and Vergennes, the commanding officers in the affair, have tellingly thin ones: a few folders containing dispensations to marry, yearly inspections, an orderly progression of transfers, promotions, and honors.[33] By contrast, the thick dossiers of Bouïs, Boyer, and Rocas document the army hierarchy's struggle to comprehend and contain the bizarre actions and reactions that led these officers' careers off-track. The folders are swollen by their individual efforts to influence ministerial decisions in letters

---

30. Vergennes, Compte rendu d'une punition infligée, July 25, 1891, dossier Boyer.
31. Vergennes to Cavalry Commander, July 25, 1891, dossier Boyer.
32. Min. of War, Telegram, July 28, 1891, dossier Boyer.
33. See SHD 5Ye 7343 Vergennes, Maurice Jean de, Lieutenant, Cavalrie, April 9, 1900, rayé; and SHD 6Yf 17,781 Lapanouse, Henry Charles Alexandre, Col., 4ᵉ Spahis, April 22, 1901, 6000.

addressed to officials in Paris, personal entreaties by their wives, and multiple libel suits and countersuits. In Boyer's case, a voluminous series of self-published pamphlets and press articles protested against his unjust treatment at the hands of his superiors. Frustrated by an inability to gain a fair hearing, Boyer started to publicize his accusations of Bouïs's "special *mœurs*" and then began to attack the "pederastic" corruption of the army itself.

The charge of same-sex vice lay at the core of Boyer's case against Bouïs and, eventually, his assault on the army as a whole. The accusations were part of a contemporary arsenal of political denunciation. In an era of greater journalistic freedom fueling a new mass press, newspapers played up the allusive possibilities of sodomy, describing incidents with winking circumlocutions and double entendres. This rhetoric formally echoed the association of "special *mœurs*" or "pederasty" with closed institutions, such as the church and the army or the police.[34] Accusations of a failure to prosecute men's same-sex vice presented the institutions as riddled with hidden depravity. Louis Fiaux, a contemporary critic of state-regulated prostitution, used pederasts' apparent legal immunity as evidence of just such corruption in the Paris vice squad. It was, in his view, a "scandal that, despite everything, taints the whole corporation, which must be avoided at all cost. Priests, missionaries, former African officers, certain socialites who are more or less visible in circles and on the boulevards, are rarely brought before the courts."[35] As Fiaux's comments indicate, officers who served in Africa were thought to have a particular penchant for same-sex vice.

Playing on this link between "special *mœurs*" and legal exceptionality, Boyer's charges drew on widespread suppositions about pederasty's prevalence in the army in Algeria, especially in its notorious disciplinary battalions.[36] Since 1864, the army had sent soldiers convicted of "immoral acts" to the Bataillons d'Afrique as punishment, which in turn produced anxiety about their corrupting effects on the system of military punishment itself. The problem was seen to be severe enough that by 1888, the minister of war Charles de Freycinet decided that in order to prevent the "contact of depraved individuals with good subjects,"

---

34. Consider, for example, the infamous case of the Catholic politician Comte Eugène de Germiny, who was arrested in a public urinal in 1877; see Gury, *L'honneur musical d'un capitaine homosexuel*, and *L'honneur perdu d'un politicien homosexuel*; Verhoeven, *Sexual Crime, Religion and Masculinity*.

35. Fiaux, *La police des moeurs en France*, 135–36.

36. The criminal anthropologist Alexandre Lacassagne had helped establish this connection. Lacassagne, *Dictionnaire encyclopédique des sciences médicales*, 22, s.v. Pédérastie, 245. See also Artigues, "Étude sur le recrutement et l'hygiène morale de l'armée," *Le Spectateur militaire*, no. 154 (1864): 123–46; Raffalovich, *Uranisme et unisexualité*, 114–16.

they would be assigned to different units.[37] Sexual deviance pervaded official and popular accounts of disciplinary companies in Algeria, as memorably captured by the dystopian depictions of Georges Darien's novel *Biribi*.[38] In 1890, several scandalous antimilitarist tracts reinforced this view of the army hierarchy as corrupt because sexually degenerate.[39]

While the spahis were reputed to be a noble unit, they too were haunted by the reputation of same-sex vice. The novelist Guy de Maupassant's 1884 Algerian travel notes recount a story that, in certain respects, prefigured the Bouïs affair. In the tale, a young Arab cavalryman, who was "very handsome, intelligent, and with a fine figure," becomes the orderly of a French officer and soon gains an honorable reputation among his peers for being the officer's "wife." Maupassant's story was intended to mock the normality of "unnatural love" among Algerians.[40] The satire nonetheless rendered the relations as conceivable, albeit in the distorted form of a joke. Such stories contributed to the metropolitan imaginary of Algerian soldiers and reinforced concerns about colonial infection of the metropole. Citing a sodomy scandal that exploded in the barracks of Châlons-sur-Marne at the same time as the Bouïs-Boyer affair, the criminal anthropologist Armand Corre worried that these "foyers of contamination have now spread to the metropole."[41]

Boyer's accusations drew on these ideas of colonial military degeneracy. By publicizing Bouïs's purported transgressions, however, Boyer violated military deontology and law. In the eyes of his superiors, his was, in the end, the greater crime. His stubborn drive to publicize Bouïs's acts appeared more dishonorable and dangerous to his commanders than the unproven acts themselves. For this same reason, the personnel dossiers do not reveal a hidden homosexual truth about Bouïs. They allow doubt to linger over what exactly happened in Médéa.

The army's professional and political concerns—and the personnel files that were their material support—at once incited and disavowed the uncertain scandal around which the political and professional conflict turned. Reading these files "along the archival grain" reveals how the military hierarchy at once

---

37. War Minister (Freycinet) to Commandant le 8ᵉ Corps d'Armée (Bourges), "Mesures à prendre à l'avenir à l'égard des militaires convaincus d'actes de pédérastie, August 22, 1888," in Cabinet du ministre, Correspondance générale, SHD 5N 5.

38. Kalifa, *Biribi*, 242–63. Several scandals relating to "military novels" that denounced the army hierarchy as corrupt and vice ridden had exploded in 1890. See Darien, *Biribi—discipline militaire*; Descaves, *Sous-Offs*. See also Aldrich, *Colonialism and homosexuality*.

39. Hamon, *Psychologie du militaire professionnel*, 158–62; Gohier, *L'armée contre la nation*, 54–56.

40. Maupassant, *Au soleil*, 88–89. See also Taraud, "Virility in the Colonial Context."

41. Corre, *L'ethnographie criminelle*, 13. See also Hamon, *La France sociale et politique*, 653.

produced and obscured knowledge about the affair.[42] While apparently seeking to discern what happened, the files avoid stating a truth. Relying on euphemism and equivocation, they represent Bouïs's guilt as unresolved and irrelevant. The amassed documentation instead "proved" that the accusations against the spahi captain were impossible to substantiate. By contrast, Boyer's voluminous file of press articles and vitriol-filled pamphlets gave ample evidence of his lack of military discipline as well as his apparent dishonor. Rather than definitively demonstrating Bouïs's perversion, Boyer's archival accumulation displayed his own deviance from a martial norm.

Don't Ask, Don't Tell

The dossiers do give a clear sense of incidents that occurred in the spring and summer of 1891 as the scandal unfolded. The official record begins on March 6, 1891, when Boyer reported to La Panouse about the poor quality and quantity of meat that was being served to soldiers in Bouïs's squadron.[43] On that occasion and in Bouïs's presence, Boyer made a rather ambiguous comment—"several words containing serious insinuations"—according to a subsequent report.[44] Boyer's statement was indeed equivocal in its allusion to what he would not say "because it would go too far." When asked to explain the statement, Boyer refused, calling instead for an official inquiry into Bouïs's actions. Bouïs promptly challenged Boyer to a duel, but the doctor refused to fight.[45] The affair dragged on, as "they negotiated, exchanged letters for two or three weeks," without resolving the *différend*, much to Bouïs's frustration.[46] Boyer, meanwhile, kept a careful record of the correspondence and urged his interlocutors to do the same. He was intentionally building an archive that he hoped would vindicate him.

But no official report was forthcoming, at least as far as Boyer knew. Perhaps hoping to avoid a duel, he once again made an allusive statement to La Panouse. When called on to respond in an official communication, Boyer contended

---

42. Stoler, *Along the Archival Grain*, 53.

43. Such accusations had contemporary symbolic and political resonance. They were, for example, at the heart of the Marquis de Morès's and Édouard Drumont's antisemitic diatribes in exactly these same years; see Kauffmann, "L'affaire de la 'viande à soldats.'"

44. Min. of War to Military Governor of Paris, November 26, 1894, dossier Boyer. The document explains Boyer's convocation before the Conseil de région in November 1894.

45. See the exchange of letters collected in Boyer, *Affaire Bouïs contre Boyer*, Correspondance particulière, 8–13, Correspondance officielle, 68–75.

46. Min. of War to Military Governor of Paris, November 26, 1894, dossier Boyer.

that the meaning of his statement was clear, that the men in Bouïs's squadron were "given insufficient and rotten food."[47] The commander reiterated his order "to send to the *Chef de corps* the complete, precise, and probing explanation demanded by the Head of the Regiment."[48] According to both Bouïs and La Panouse, Boyer had said at once too little and too much. When he refused to be more forthcoming, La Panouse confined him to his quarters for thirty days.[49] In the intervening weeks, Vergennes took over as head of the regiment, and the conflict between Bouïs and Boyer continued to brew.

Lieutenant Rocas also offered up unsolicited information on Bouïs ("insinuations of a serious nature"), and he, too, was punished.[50] His remarks were judged out of order because they had been "neither solicited, nor authorized." When ordered to "state facts and justify his statement," Rocas demurred, accepting to do so only on the brigadier general's orders.[51] His superiors did not reward his candor; instead, he was sent south to Laghouat. In addition to this punitive transfer, his annual evaluation from 1891 noted that he had been removed from the promotion and the Legion of Honor lists. According to the general inspection, Rocas was a fairly good officer, but he had "recently compromised his situation by denouncing his commanding captain by means unbefitting an officer and which cannot be excused by the real faults [*les torts réels*] of Captain Bouïs."[52] In other words, no matter how true the accusations (the content of which remained unspecified), Rocas's unsolicited denunciation had betrayed professional honor.

Boyer later claimed that the command in Médéa had engaged in a cover-up by eliminating a crucial witness and severely mistreating Rocas. While Rocas resented the reassignment, General Bessol dismissed Boyer's assertion, claiming that "many officers view it as an advantage to be sent south."[53] The transfer had an apparently negative effect on Rocas's health. Although he had lived in Algeria all his life, Rocas was sent to Vichy for a cure several months after arriving in

---

47. Boyer to La Panouse, no. 26, March 16, 1891, in Boyer, *Affaire Bouïs contre Boyer*, 70.

48. La Panouse to Boyer, no. 13, March 17, 1891, ibid.

49. The punishment was then lifted six days later (subsequent reports determined the punishment to be unjustified). Supplément au Rapport du 19 Juin 1891, August 14, 1891, dossier Boyer.

50. Feuillet de personnel, March 10, 1891, dossier Rocas.

51. Note pour le cabinet du Ministre, Min. of War (Cavalry), August 21, 1909, dossier Rocas. For a copy of Rocas's report (in Boyer's hand and accompanied by a letter from Boyer addressed to the Min. of War, May 24, 1891) see Rocas to M. Général de Lavigne, March 12, 1891, dossier Boyer.

52. Notes de l'Inspecteur général, Rocas, Albert, Inspection générale de 1891, and Vergennes to General Inspection, June 10, 1891, both in dossier Rocas.

53. Notes remises par M. Général du Bessol, October 16, 1892, dossier Boyer. See Rocas to Letellier, reprinted in pamphlet "Documents," dossier Boyer.

Laghouat.[54] In 1892, commanding officer Vergennes noted that his "health was severely compromised by the Algerian climate."[55] In order to move back up, both hierarchically and geographically, Rocas would have to prove himself once again worthy of his superiors' trust.

By contrast, Boyer was not sent away immediately, much to General Bessol's frustration. Bouïs also remained in town, even though the army put him into early retirement. The official explanation for this action was vague. His evaluation in 1891 noted his "robust" constitution but also described his character as "weak," his morality as "bad," and his judgment as "unsound"—as tending to "deviate from the right path [*devié de la voie droite*]." According to Vergennes, the decision was made after "an inquiry established less than honorable activities on his part, in the administration of the squadron and in his private life."[56] The details dredged up by that inquiry are nowhere to be found in his file.

While his professional reputation was compromised, Bouïs refused to let Boyer's implied accusations stand. Once relieved of his official duties, he sought a reckoning with his adversary. Given Bouïs's "good military qualities," we can surmise why Boyer wanted to avoid an armed confrontation.[57] For the doctor, their conflict could only be resolved by an official inquiry, not a private duel. Bouïs refused Boyer's jurisdictional argument. Intent on seeking reparation and with time on his hands, he stalked Boyer, who was avoiding him. He managed to catch Boyer in public, in front of his house, right next to the Hotel de Ville.[58] Finally, on May 10, at nine in the morning, as Boyer was returning from his rounds at the military hospital, "Captain Bouïs passed from words to acts. When M. Boyer was in uniform, he publicly insulted [*outragea*] him; slapped him in the middle of the street; called him 'Diafoirus' and coward; and spat in his face. When Boyer only responded with 'You would never do this in public,' Bouïs dragged him into the cabaret next door and repeated the same assaults on him in front of witnesses."[59] By publicly humiliating Boyer, Bouïs hoped to transform the affair into a matter of personal honor and thus force him to duel.

In his explanation to Vergennes, Boyer noted that because the initial insult had taken place only in front of "Arabs, who tried to get away," Boyer and Bouïs

54. Feuillet de personnel, 1891, 2ᵉ semestre, dossier Rocas. On the role of spas in French colonial service see Jennings, *Curing the Colonizers*.

55. Rocas, Inspection générale de 1892, dossier Rocas.

56. Bouïs, Inspection générale, 1891, Note de chef de corps [Vergennes], dossier Bouïs.

57. Ibid.

58. Bouïs to Vergennes, May 11, 1891, dossier Bouis.

59. Min. of War to Military Governor of Paris, November 26, 1894, dossier Boyer.

pursued their argument inside a café.[60] It was here that they each found credible witnesses. Their mutual dismissal of "Arab" bystanders is a small but telling indication of the everyday violence of racial hierarchy in the town.

Upon hearing of the incident, Vergennes called a meeting of the regiment's superior officers. He demanded to know if Boyer had responded to Bouïs's public humiliation of him. Boyer once again refused to answer, using his adversary's dishonorable character as an excuse. Condemning this intolerable pusillanimity, Vergennes was categorical in his response to the doctor: "You are unworthy of remaining among us. Leave!" Meanwhile, Boyer's attempt to take the case before the justice of the peace in town went nowhere. Both he and Bouïs were again issued a thirty-day punishment by their superiors.[61] For Vergennes and the other officers, submission to public indignity violated professional as well as personal honor.

A letter from Jules Aron, who was doctor-in-chief for the Nineteenth Army Corps, communicated the gravity of the situation to Bessol. Aron had recently passed through Médéa at the end of April and was witness to the events that, in his words, were of "a nature to nastily spatter [*éclabousser désagréablement*] our uniform." He had since heard of the confrontation between Bouïs and Boyer in front of the Hotel de Ville. While he was not Boyer's superior, Aron had sought to impress him with a sense of professional duty, arguing that "whatever the reasons for the indignity of his adversary," Boyer had placed himself in "an equivocal posture by seeming to hide behind casuistic arguments, dossiers, and *procès verbaux*." The "dignity of his person and his uniform" required him to fight, rather than to shield himself with paper. Refusing to listen, Boyer called again for an official inquiry into Bouïs's immorality, despite the absence of a "corpus delicti."[62] Aron warned that Boyer should be immediately transferred before the situation worsened. Following that advice, Bessol requested that the doctor be returned to France at the end of May "because of the echo that this unfortunate affair has had throughout Algeria."[63]

But Boyer was not transferred. He was instead called to appear before a military commission of inquiry to judge whether his "fault against honor" was serious enough to warrant dismissal. In early June, the cavalry division decided that Boyer, "by tolerating Bouïs's deliberate and stinging insult, had failed to

---

60. Rendu compte des insultes graves faits publiquement par Capitaine Bouïs du 1er spahis au médecin major du régiment, Boyer to Vergennes, May 10, 1891, dossier Boyer.

61. Boyer to Min. of War, May 24, 1891, dossier Boyer.

62. Jules Aron, 19e Corps Armée to Dir. of Cabinet, May 11, 1891, dossier Boyer.

63. Bessol to Min. of War (Confidential), May 27, 1891, dossier Boyer.

uphold his honor, no matter how undignified his aggressor." Bouïs would also be called before a commission of inquiry on account of Boyer's "serious accusations" against him. The appearance was largely pro forma: Bouïs was already in early retirement, so he could not be punished by a discharge.[64] In authorizing the military court, the ministry nonetheless insisted that it be conducted *"with great care"* and in strict conformity to military law, especially with respect to the composition of the record.[65] The ministry literally underscored legal and archival discretion when it came to Bouïs's case.

Suspecting that he would not get a fair hearing from the officers in his regiment, Boyer tried to sidestep the hierarchy by sending letters denouncing Bouïs to officers further up the chain of command, including to the minister of war. He indicated that his direct superiors were unfit to judge him precisely because they, too, were implicated in the affair. His detailed accusations contained the specifics that he had previously declined to discuss with Vergennes and La Panouse.

According to Boyer, Bouïs was "a man whose honorability was disputable and whom one could not decently accept as an adversary in a duel as long as he had not completely exonerated himself of the accusations of brutality, indelicacy, and malfeasance which have been made against him; and furthermore, with regard to *mœurs*, he remains under the suspicion of acts of pederasty, offenses [*attentats*] all the more criminal and even falling under the application of the law (articles 334 and 335 of the Penal Code), because they were committed by this French officer on three Spahis *indigènes* (Saïd ben el Bachir; Chourar; and Mohamed ben Mahmoud) under his orders."[66] These were serious charges indeed. In order to guarantee that the Ministry of War in Paris received his damning reports, Boyer even sent his wife to deliver his letter.[67]

Boyer also called on fellow military doctors to advocate for him. His file contains a sympathetic letter from François Cros, a doctor in Algiers who had been keeping track of the affair for the doctor-in-chief Aron. Cros reported that while Bouïs was generally considered "degenerate" (*un homme taré*) and "riffraff" (*une canaille*), his superiors needed Boyer to be able "to prove what he advanced." Sympathetic to Boyer's claims, Cros urged the direction of the Military Health Service "not to sacrifice the content for a question of form." Like Boyer, he suspected that the regimental commission of inquiry would not get to the bottom

---

64. Bessol to Min. of War, June 6, 1891, and Min. of War to Bessol, June 13, 1891, dossier Boyer.

65. Min. of War to Bessol, June 15, 1891, dossier Bouïs. Emphasis in the original.

66. Boyer to Min. of War, July 1, 1891, dossier Boyer. I have been unable to locate the personnel files of these soldiers.

67. Lucie Boyer to Director, Min. of War, June 2, 1891, dossier Boyer.

of the case. He warned them that he "did not think that it would be possible to muffle such a dirty affair." As proof, Cros enclosed one of the first press articles from the *Vigie algérienne* to be devoted to the brewing scandal.[68] The editorial and the many that followed it defended the army doctor's professional honor and integrity. The ministry's marginal note on the clipping indicated official suspicion of the local press campaign. From the military's perspective, it represented "a deviation" from the real stakes of the case.[69]

The public and private entreaties on Boyer's behalf came to naught. The military tribunal condemned Boyer for violations of both discipline and honor, while exonerating Bouïs. The commission, which included both La Panouse and Vergennes, unanimously recommended that Boyer be dismissed (*mis en réforme*). Bessol pled for leniency because he viewed the refusal to duel to be questionable grounds for dismissal. For Bessol, dueling was "forbidden by French legislation." He thought that a temporary suspension would be more fitting. Time off would allow the doctor to "reestablish calm in his spirit, which had seemed to be imbalanced for some time."[70] Bessol's more lenient recommendations ultimately won out. But Boyer was not prepared to let the matter rest. In his view, the army had an inverted conception of honor and dignity. He would stop at little to set the record straight.

To Duel or Not to Duel

This case reflected the broader jurisdictional problem posed by the military duel. From the press in Algeria to the parliament in Paris, discussions turned around the question of whether Boyer could be found guilty of refusing to duel. Could Boyer's commanding officers order him to fight Bouïs? Bessol worried that obliging Boyer to duel was tantamount to forcing him to commit a crime.

Despite Bessol's claim to the contrary, dueling was not forbidden as a distinct crime in postrevolutionary French law. While considered an act of lèse-majesté, and hence an encroachment on sovereign power under the ancien régime, dueling was no longer a separate crime after the Revolution. Under the common law established by the 1810 Penal Code, it was criminal only in cases of personal injury or death. Jurisprudence on the subject was inconsistent and convictions

---

68. Cros to Aron, July 7, 1891, dossier Boyer.
69. C. Allan, "Informations algériennes," *Vigie algérienne*, July 2, 1891, and marginal notes, dossier Boyer.
70. Bessol to Min. of War, no. 119 (Confidential), July 16, 1891, dossier Boyer.

by no means assured.[71] Legislators who sought to remedy this legal lacuna often pointed out that "the duel, in itself, is not punishable."[72] In the military, which continued throughout the nineteenth century to dishonorably discharge soldiers for refusing to duel, prosecutions were rare. One forensic doctor explained in 1890 that dueling remained appropriate, especially in the army, for those cases in which "the law is impotent to combat attacks on individual honor."[73] For many contemporaries, it was necessary to maintain the duel's legality as an honorable supplement to the written law.

For Bessol, forcing Boyer to duel nonetheless carried a risk of eventual prosecution. As he later explained, "It was impossible to send an officer before a Commission of Inquiry for being in conformity with the law of his country; and, if following the command's order, the duel had an unfortunate outcome, they [the command] could be pursued in court by the injured party."[74] The minister of war Freycinet had implicitly recognized this tension in a July 5, 1889, circular, which recommended the use of less lethal arms.[75] Doing so nonetheless affirmed the duel's legality in military jurisprudence. The question remained unresolved, and subsequent efforts to pass a "special law" on dueling ultimately failed.[76]

As many observers noted, the problem lay in perceived differences between the distinctive case of the duel and more straightforward crimes like murder. The exceptional circumstances of the duel, they held, called for an exceptional law. One jurist summed up the problem as follows: "The special nature of the crime [dueling], its particular aspect, the favor accorded it by opinion, and the difficulties that we have noted in applying the common law of the Penal Code to it, all demonstrate the evidence of a special ill, for which a special remedy is needed."[77] For advocates of such legislation, Boyer's case illustrated why the particular harm of the military duel required a specific cure.

Deputy Gustave Paul Cluseret, a socialist with a long military career, raised the matter before parliament in 1892. A pronounced antisemite and later

71. Guillet, *La mort en face*.

72. See "Rapport fait au nom de la commission chargée d'examiner la proposition de loi de M. Herold tendant à la répression du duel," *JO*, Sénat, Doc. Parl., February 1, 1883, annexe 30, 28.

73. Teissier, *Du Duel*, 8. Also, Nye, *Masculinity and Male Codes of Honor*, 132.

74. Notes remises par M. Général de Bessol, October 16, 1892, dossier Boyer.

75. The circular is reprinted in Croabbon, *La science du point d'honneur*, 442. For an approving account of the circular, "Chronique de la quinzaine," *Le Spectateur militaire* 46, no. 216 (August 1, 1889): 284–86.

76. See, for example, Mgr. Freppel, "Dépot d'une proposition de loi," *JO*, Chambre, Session ordinaire 1888, July 17, 1888, 2101–2. And "Proposition de loi contre le duel, présenté par M. Cluseret," *JO*, Chambre, Doc. Parl., December 3, 1889, 263–64.

77. Andriveau, *De la répression pénale du duel*, 231.

anti-Dreyfusard, Cluseret provoked "consternation" (*bruit*) in the Chamber when he invoked the army doctor and the "captain and squadron commander denounced for misappropriation of supplies and pederasty" to make his case. Cluseret questioned the perversity of military authorities who had ordered the reputable Boyer to fight a man of dubious morality. In his view, it was a conflict between the force of the law and that of military discipline: "Isn't the law more important than discipline?" he queried. The only solution to this apparent conflict was a "special law."[78] At this time, Jewish army officers, viciously under attack by Édouard Drumont's *La libre parole*, defended their honor in duels. Just a few weeks before the debate, the Marquis de Morès had killed Captain Armand Mayer in one such contest. When Cluseret denounced the duel as contrary to, rather than an affirmation of, the French nation's "moral energy," the deputy Camille Dreyfus (who would later challenge Drumont himself to a duel) characterized Cluseret's pronouncements as "odious."[79] For Cluseret, by contrast, a duel could not bestow dignity on an undignified man. He claimed that, because pederasts (like Jews) were unworthy opponents, it was wrong of the army to command Boyer to fight.

Motivated by his fierce antisemitism and a racialized conception of the nation, Cluseret sought to regulate the contours of military honor and French citizenship. In 1895, he cosponsored a proposition to declare recently naturalized French (especially Jews) ineligible for army service *and* to forbid colonial officers and administrators from marrying foreigners.[80] In 1897, Cluseret's antisemitism also found expression in an "arabophilic" proposal, co-signed with the former Boulangist deputy Henri Michelin. Their exceptional proposition would have extended citizenship to Algerian Muslims, who maintained their Muslim "personal status," in a bid to counter the political power of naturalized Algerian Jews.[81] Together, Cluseret's legislative proposals shared a certain logic. They were special laws that targeted what were in his view exceptional threats to France's military and moral fiber. They illustrate a broader political and military context in which the Bouïs-Boyer affair exploded and why it provoked such a heated response.

---

78. "Discussion sur la prise en considération de la proposition de loi de M. Cluseret contre le duel," *JO*, Chambre, July 2, 1892, 1012–13.

79. Ibid., 1012. On dueling, masculinity, and antisemitism before and during the Dreyfus Affair see Forth, *Dreyfus Affair*; Nye, *Masculinity and Male Codes of Honor*.

80. "Proposition de loi," *JO*, Chambre, Doc. Parl., Session ordinaire, January 8, 1895, annexe 1130, 18.

81. "Proposition de loi," *JO*, Chambre. Doc. Parl., Session ordinaire, Séance 16 Janvier 1897, annexe 2203, 134. For a critical account see "Les musulmans et les israélites algériens," *Archives israélites* 58, no. 27 (July 8, 1897). On the politics of anti-Jewish "arabophilia" see Ageron, *Les Algériens musulmans*, 1:600–604.

Sociologist Gabriel Tarde, for example, found that Boyer's case epitomized contemporary legal and social malaise. Like Cluseret, he found it "monstrous" that duels could be "authorized, and sometimes ordered, by military authorities."[82] Dueling, in his view, illustrated the atavistic social dynamics of "imitation," especially in compact and closed institutions such as the military. The military's sexual homogeneity and hierarchy created a context in which, "whether good or bad, everything is contagious and exaggerated."[83] For the sociologist, Boyer's absurd condemnation by his superiors exemplified underlying contradictions between the laws of military discipline and enlightened laws of reason and progress. According to Tarde, the former needed to be aligned with the latter.[84]

The question of the military duel's legality highlighted tensions between republican law and morality and a purportedly perverse military justice that covered over crime by exonerating Bouïs and condemning Boyer. The army's judgment seemed to be twisted. Or at least, this is what Boyer and his advocates, with the aid of the local press, led external observers to believe. The blind injustice of military procedure seemed all the more glaring when the local police in Médéa claimed to catch Bouïs in *flagrant délit*.

Caught Out

Several weeks after the two commissions of inquiry, on August 3, General Bessol informed the ministry by telegram that Bouïs had been the subject of a police report for "acts of pederasty." The details of the story were sordid. A local journal, *Le petit médéen*, reported on the *fait divers* immediately. On the night of August 1, police agents "surprised captain B . . . of the 1er Spahis sleeping with a so-called Mohammed S . . . , age 15 years, in a hotel room in Médéa. When they heard knocking on the door, Captain B . . . made the young Arab jump out the window. But the agent Marin, posted to this spot, caught him in a complete state of nudity."[85] Bouïs was immediately arrested and taken to the police station, where he was held overnight. In reporting on the case, the paper tried to shield itself from the accusation that it was insulting the army. It asserted that, rather than tainting the corps as a whole, it was serving military honor. In a republican army in which "everyone is a soldier," the editorial claimed, "it is good that

---

82. Tarde, *Études pénales et sociales*, 43.
83. Ibid., 41.
84. Ibid., 53.
85. "Une vilaine histoire," *Le Petit médéen*, August 6, 1891.

[a soldier's] fault be rendered public, because that publicity exonerates all his colleagues." In other words, the army "no longer had to force itself to hide, to keep secret the villainous acts of one depraved individual: everything takes place out in the open now."[86] Following the lead of *Le Petit médéen*, other journals similarly proclaimed that "indiscretion is sometimes the duty of the journalist." For *Le Petit Alger*, "it is necessary to signal the exceptions" in order to controvert the belief that "the indignity of one should cast doubt on the honorability of all."[87] Predictably, neither the high command in Paris nor the officers on the ground in Médéa embraced this view of publicity as purification. In their eyes, these reports clearly sullied the army's honor.

The spahi command could not simply ignore the affair either. Its parallel investigation, conducted by La Panouse, set out to establish "the culpability of Captain Bouïs, based on the facts furnished by the police in its report, information, and witness testimony, with respect to the acts of pederasty that took place on the 2nd of August and in their preludes in the days before." La Panouse claimed that he had "expected to find culpability." In the end, however, he stated that "it was not possible for the most discriminating spirit to discover the truth, to find anything that could move beyond the most complete doubt as to M. Bouïs's culpability."[88] According to the military report, in other words, no definitive evidence with respect to Bouïs's acts could be found.

The actual police report was much less equivocal. Filed by the civilian police commissioner on August 2, it contained the testimony of the two local police agents, Marin and Torre, who had apprehended Bouïs and the youth, Mohammed Soumati. Soumati's account of events evidently met with Bouïs's forceful denials. According to the commissioner, the police had put Bouïs under surveillance after receiving complaints that he had recently made "propositions against nature to several youths." The agents Marin and Torre claimed to have witnessed Bouïs entering a bathhouse with Soumati and their exiting together, with Soumati following Bouïs to his hotel. They knocked on Bouïs's door, which he took five minutes to open. At that same moment, the naked Soumati landed in the arms of officer Marin, who was expectantly waiting on the ground below. Soumati, described here as "about 16 years old," confirmed the agents' story: after leaving the bath, Bouïs requested that Soumati accompany him to his room. The two of them "lay down naked in the same bed." According to Soumati, Bouïs "took my hand, placed it between his legs, and asked me to caress him." Upon hearing the

---

86. "À propos d'un scandale," *Le Petit médéen*, August 6, 1891.
87. Jaïnos, "Le cas du Docteur Boyer," *Le Petit Alger*, August 26, 1891.
88. La Panouse to Colonel Commandant (Médéa), August 4, 1891, dossier Bouïs.

knock, Bouïs took him by the arm and forced him out the window, throwing his clothing afterward. Bouïs predictably denied the accusations. In his deposition and in a long supplementary letter, he elaborated a detailed disavowal. Pitting his word against that of the two agents and Soumati, the police report cast those claims in doubt.[89] For La Panouse and other military officials, the equal treatment of the youth's testimony contributed to the police officials' affront against the army. They refused to recognize that Bouïs's testimony could be invalidated by that of his supposed accomplice, an "Arab" youth and supposed prostitute. Their account relied on prevailing representations of Algerians' constitutional criminality and corruption, including their penchants for same-sex vice.[90]

La Panouse's inquiry attacked the police report's veracity. Following Bouïs, he privileged the theory of entrapment. The witness testimony collected by the army suggested that the material traces found by the police (the unmade bed; a shirt of Soumati's left behind) were planted. Perhaps most importantly, the military investigation lined up witnesses to attack Soumati's credibility. A prominent Jewish merchant, a certain Abraham Caroby, claimed that he had overheard Soumati in conversation "with several Arabs," admitting that the police had pressured him to participate in the sting.[91] Henri Manny, a clerk with a local messaging service, made the same claim.[92] Another clerk, Abdelkader Khourab, depicted Soumati as untrustworthy: "publicly known for prostitution," he was a "child abandoned to all vices, who often has problems with the police."[93] The military investigation focused on refuting the youth's claims and justified La Panouse's dismissal of his testimony. Placing Soumati on trial, he depicted Bouïs as the injured party in the affair.[94]

The army pursued this line of argument up the chain of command. When Bessol forwarded to the ministry a copy of the army's inquiry alongside that of the police, he endorsed Bouïs's claim to be a legal victim: "It emerges from the reading of the different pieces of the dossier that M. Bouïs was the victim of genuine entrapment [un guet-apens], followed by a violation of domicile, and illegal arrest, facts on the basis of which the officer has filed a case before the appeals court of Algiers."[95] Bouïs and the commanding officers claimed that the local police's action was illegal and suspect, because tainted by complicity

---

89. Commissaire de police de Médéa / Affaire Bouïs, August 2, 1891, dossier Bouïs.

90. Adolph Kocher, De la criminalité chez les Arabes, 169–72. Also, Gouriou, "Le sexe des indigènes."

91. Statement signed by Abraham Caroby, August 4, 1891, dossier Bouïs.

92. Statement signed by Henri Manny, August 4, 1891, dossier Bouïs.

93. Statement dictated by Abdelkader Khourab, dossier Bouïs.

94. Report, la Panouse to Colonel Commandant of Médéa, August 4, 1891, dossier Bouïs.

95. Bessol to Cavalry Direction, August 7, 1891, dossier Bouïs.

with corrupt and corruptible "Arab" youths. Effectively bracketing the question of Bouïs's culpability, they sought to discredit the police. In this account, Bouïs appeared not as a dishonorable soldier, but as a rights-bearing citizen, whose private domicile (even if located in a dodgy hotel) had been illegally violated.

Bouïs's personal reputation clearly suffered after the arrest, but it was not enough to vindicate Boyer in the eyes of his superiors. Even after the local press gave ample coverage to the incident in the hotel room, ministerial officials refused to reopen Boyer's case.[96] He continued his campaign to reestablish his professional honor with even greater tenacity and conviction. Beyond distributing information and evidence to the press, he published a pamphlet that reproduced his archive of the affair in the hope that the righteousness of his cause would be widely recognized. In the years that followed, he would publish two more such pamphlets.[97] After failing before the military court, he sought out the jurisdiction of public opinion. The *Vigie algérienne* regularly called for a reversal of his punishment.[98] These efforts again backfired. They only worked to antagonize army officials in Algeria and back in Paris. In the eyes of his superiors, these pamphlets, which reproduced official and unofficial correspondence, provided evidence of his "faults against discipline."[99] They would not be his last.

Private Right and Public Dishonor

Bouïs was not content to leave the situation as it stood either. In the fall of 1891, he turned to the civilian justice system to pursue his case against the police agents Torre and Marin for "violation of domicile" and "illegal arrest." He hoped that their indictment would clear his name. The public prosecutor pursued the complaint on the state's behalf (notably with the army's encouragement), while Bouïs fought for civil damages. But the press coverage, likely fueled by Boyer and Rocas's efforts, only gave more publicity to the charges. It was, in other words, along this avenue that Boyer pursued "justice."

An article from *Le Petit Alger* illustrates how sexual innuendo and insult pervaded these reports. The journal mocked Bouïs's effort to "remake his virginity" by appealing to civilian courts. Its unsparing coverage focused on his animalistic

---

96. See especially C. Allen, "L'affaire du 1ᵉʳ Spahis," *La Vigie algérienne*, August 22, 1891.

97. Boyer, *Affaire Bouïs contre Boyer*. See also *Médecine Militaire—Scandales de Médéa*; *Médecine Militaire—Les Scandales de Médéa, Mars 1891–Janvier 1895*.

98. Vergennes to Poizat, September 17, 1891, dossier Boyer. And article in *La Vigie algérienne*, September 16, 1891.

99. Bessol to Min. of War (Confidential), September 24, 1891, dossier Boyer.

perversity: "All the witnesses proved beyond a doubt that Bouïs gave himself over to ignoble practices; that he spent nights, until four in the morning, in the stables seeking to catch little natives, foaming at the mouth and tormented by his rut, bestial and against nature."[100] Bouïs became a target of humiliating animus among a notable segment of the Algerian settler press and in several Boulangist, metropolitan journals. In the process, they used the affair to attack Freycinet as inapt to head the Ministry of War.[101]

Despite this manifest press hostility, Bouïs ironically had the privacy protections of civilian law on his side. The local police agents had no official warrant for his arrest and no sufficient cause to force entry into his room. The prosecutor, Joseph Durieu de Leyritz, while refusing to comment on whether Bouïs was "worthy of esteem or deserving of disdain [*digne d'estime ou mérite le mépris*]," proclaimed that the policeman had indeed committed "an attack on individual liberty." He underscored that the liberal principle of privacy did not provide "a certificate of good morals [*bonnes mœurs*]." From a legal standpoint, however, a "violation of domicile" had indeed taken place. Simple presumption was not enough to justify the police action, and Bouïs had not committed a crime because "there was no public indecency, because the doors and windows were closed. And there was no indecent assault because Soumati gave himself over willingly. Nor was there indecent assault against a minor, because that crime requires the victim to be aged less than thirteen, while Soumati is fifteen."[102] For the prosecutor, the two agents deserved to be imprisoned for violating Bouïs's rights.

The prosecutor's speech pursued a double strategy: it publicly announced Bouïs's sexual conduct, while defending his legal right to privacy. Unsurprisingly, Bouïs's adversaries picked up on the statement's implications, publicizing the prosecutor's speech as ample evidence of Bouïs's dishonor, if not of his legal crime. In their view, the evidence from Bouïs's civil case called attention to an original miscarriage of (military) justice against Boyer. The press, fellow military doctors, and Boyer himself wondered how, given such public discrediting of the captain's character, the military could continue to hold its official line.

Boyer's vindication finally seemed certain when the Appeals Court of Algiers acquitted the police agents Marin and Torre of any wrongdoing. After detailing

---

100. "L'Affaire Bouïs," *Le Petit Alger*, October 14, 1891.

101. See articles in Henri Rochefort's *Intransigeant*, "Les scandales de Médéah," November 27, 1891; "À propos des scandales de Médéah," December 4, 1891. According to Boyer's pamphlet, the notorious antisemite and future anti-Dreyfusard André de Boisandré published an article denouncing Bouïs in *Le Pilori*, February 7, 1892.

102. Text of the prosecutor's speech in *Le Petit Alger*, October 14, 1891.

the incident as outlined in the police agents' testimony, the court held that "while somewhat regrettable that an excess of zeal led them to penetrate in this way, in the middle of the night, and without a warrant, into the domicile of a citizen, it is just to recognize that they were acting in response to instructions that were formal, if badly defined, and with the conviction that they had a crime or *flagrant délit* to certify [*constater*] and a duty to accomplish."[103] This court decision appeared to incontrovertibly establish the truth of Bouïs's indignity. Newspapers commented extensively on his implicit condemnation.[104] But neither the ruling, nor multiple courts' refusal to condemn journals for libel, convinced ministerial officials to budge. Boyer was told in no uncertain terms to cease and desist. In a personal meeting with Boyer at the War Ministry on January 12, 1892, the director of the Service de Santé, Dujardin-Beaumetz, "formally forbade him from continuing his press campaign and warned him that in case of further disobedience he inevitably exposed himself to further disciplinary measures."[105]

But Boyer did not stop. He sought out one final jurisdiction: a petition to the Senate. The radical Protestant, former pastor, and anticlerical Auguste Dide took up his cause. In addition to denouncing the individual injustice against Boyer, Dide attacked the army's handling of the affair on principle. He summarized the arguments of Boyer's advocates, including those found among military doctors who had risen to their colleague's defense: "They think that, in muffling such affairs, as has been done, and in transforming them into personal questions in order to save the honor of the army, debate can be hidden in the shadow of a special justice [*justice spéciale*]. Sacrifices are made to strange prejudices of caste and a false solidarity, 'for keeping Bouïs in the ranks of our army, would concentrate all that is most criminal in the country.'"[106] Dide implicitly connected these "strange prejudices of caste" with the Bouïs's pederastic crime and framed the arbitrary operations of the military's "special justice" as a violation of individual rights and of the general good. Like the Algerian soldiers with whom he was presumed to have had sexual affairs, Bouïs (and the army) appeared here as foreign bodies within the nation, operating according to their own perverse laws.

With a favorable recommendation from the petition committee, the Senate delivered the petition to the Ministry of War. While Boyer found support in the

103. Decision reprinted in *Médecine Militaire—Scandales de Médéa*, 23.

104. "L'Affaire Bouïs," *Le Radical Algérien*, January 25, 1892; "L'affaire Bouïs," *La Vigie algérienne*, January 16, 18, 19, 24, and 25, 1892. For a limited defense of Bouïs see *La Lanterne Médéenne*.

105. See Convocation by Dujardin-Beaumetz, January 8, 1892, Minutes of meeting in Min. of War, 7th Direction, January 12, 1892, dossier Boyer.

106. Dide, *Sénat, Feuilletons*, no. 34, March 3, 1892, 25.

press, the ministry once again met the plea with silence.[107] Ministerial officials were as stubborn as Boyer. They refused to accept the evidence on which the charges were based. In a report preparing Boyer's definitive expulsion from the army, Dujardin-Beaumetz dismissed the Senate's findings as irrelevant: "The Senator wrote his report without noting a single one of the documents sent by the Ministry of War, whose dossier was in complete disagreement with Senator Dide's conclusions." As far as the ministry was concerned, there was no cover-up and no injustice, because "the personal cowardice of Major Boyer was the sole reason for the disciplinary measures taken against him."[108] Boyer's myriad efforts to reclaim his professional honor established only one thing in the eyes of the ministry: that he was no longer suitable for army service. As Dujardin-Beaumetz summarized, "We gave him the time to resume more honorable conduct; but he has only become more engaged in his indiscipline."[109] On January 31, 1895, President Félix Faure authorized the order that expelled Boyer from the army for "serious violations against discipline."[110] Boyer's appeal of the decision before the administrative high court, the Conseil d'État, predictably failed. In his last pamphlet on the "Scandals of Médéa," Boyer referred to the decision as the "Triumph of Sodom."[111]

Obscure Bodies

The final document filed away in Boyer's dossier is a report, written in Boyer's hand, on the "affaire des mœurs" in the spahi unit. Undated, it details Bouïs's alleged crimes and his relationship to two men in particular, Saïd ben el Bachir and Mohamed ben Mahmoud. According to the account, in the month following the outbreak of the scandal in the regiment, the two men under Bouïs's command, an orderly and a soldier, were punished with imprisonment. Once they were released, their names were removed from the rolls [rayé des controles] of the regiment and purposefully effaced from the official record. According to the report, General Gustave Laveuve visited Médéa on April 21, 1891, in order to conduct the annual general inspection. During his tour of the prison, Boyer urged the general to "proceed with an inquiry" of the two men, despite Commander

---

107. "Une pétition," Le Radical, March 31, 1892; "Le Major Boyer," Le Petit Parisien, April 6, 1892.
108. Dujardin-Beaumetz to Minister, September 21, 1894, dossier Boyer.
109. Ibid.
110. Min. of War, report to President, January 31, 1895, dossier Boyer.
111. Médecine Militaire—Les Scandales de Médéa, Mars 1891–Janvier 1895, 53.

Vergennes's protestations. The general declined, responding that "if it is true that the entire regiment has passed over them, they must be extremely tired." Boyer expressed regret: "You are missing out in not seeing them, General, they are *two documents*." In response, the general simply "smiled and moved on."[112]

Boyer's report recorded the general inspection's literal refusal to see the two material witnesses, men with whom Bouïs engaged in "acts against nature." Their imprisonment and official erasure illustrate the regiment's containment strategy. According to the anecdote, Laveuve already knew, but did not want to see the evidence they might provide of Bouïs's acts, which Boyer sought to reveal as material proof of Bouïs's crimes. The men who had apparently served the penchants of their hierarchical superiors were grounds not for an inquiry, but for a joke. In refusing to see them, the general revealed official uninterest in archiving their testimony. On one level, the quip indicates that the imprisoned men were unremarkable, as the sexually passive and racially degraded objects of superior officers' licit, if immoral, sexual pleasure. On another level, the general's turning a blind eye to their presence was a form of scotomization, a denial that literally refused to see their bodies. For Boyer, the general's dismissive joke and smile nonetheless left a trace of displaced recognition, which is why he mentioned it in the report. It is evidence of how these two attitudes coexisted and hence why they came into conflict in the affair. The military hierarchy's response both acknowledged and disavowed the acts whose de-virilizing public revelation threatened the honor and reputation not just of Bouïs, but of the regiment as a whole. The commanding officers knew very well. But they preferred to look away.

In the affair, dueling conceptions of masculine honor were linked to a growing debate over the legitimacy of an exceptional structure of military law that the army jealously sought to preserve. By at once seeing and not seeing, the official response to this emasculating threat of public dishonor took the form of fetishistic disavowal. As Freud suggested in his brief essay on the subject, the panicked reactions of "grown men" to threats to the sovereign legitimacy of "throne and altar" resemble the infantile response to the revelation of castration and its denial.[113] The Bouïs-Boyer affair illustrates how authorities turned their attention to substitute objects in order to displace the delegitimating threat. The archive indicates the material dynamics of this displacement both in the military's system of punishment and in its filing of personnel dossiers. In this case,

---

112. "Affaire Mœurs," dossier Boyer. The scene is also recounted in a letter sent by Rocas on April 22, 1891, to Alfred Letellier, deputy from Alger, denouncing his own mistreatment. Reprinted in Boyer's pamphlet, "Documents," 5, dossier Boyer.

113. Freud, "Fetishism (1927)," 215.

the blockages created by bureaucratic paperwork served as a political and psychic defense, preserving the integrity of military law and honor from encroachment by civilian and settler concerns.[114]

Major Boyer also imagined archiving as a form of defense. With a counter-cache of documents, he sought to set the record straight. Even as he launched a vitriolic assault on his superiors, he seemed to believe that this archive could restore his honor and integrity. What he failed to register is how these efforts represented an intolerable institutional challenge rather than a corrective to the military's legal procedure. While sent to the Ministry of War to incriminate Bouïs, Boyer's voluminous documents were instead filed in his own dossier. There, they became evidence of what ministerial officials saw as Boyer's perverse, because dishonorable, undisciplined, and ultimately de-virilizing, penchant toward public disclosure.

The Ministry of War indeed preserved the hundreds of pages of paper that Boyer forwarded to it over four years. This selective classification of documents, gathered in his personnel dossier, became a bureaucratic marker of the military's control over evidentiary truth. It thus became a kind of fetish, a bureaucratic "fig leaf" that obscured Bouïs's acts, even as it avowed them. This equivocal cover served instead to indict Boyer. By papering over threats to its sexual and racial order from within and without, the army in its archive preserved a fantasy of integral military masculinity, even as vocal critics worked to unsettle its exceptional authority and power.

This scandal in the spahis, in focusing on the contest between Bouïs and Boyer, also occluded the Algerian youth and soldiers that stood at its center. There is no record of statements by Saïd ben el Bachir or Mohamed ben Mahmoud. Although the transcription of Mohammed Soumati's police deposition was filed in Bouïs's dossier, the military's reports actively worked to dismiss its veracity and significance. Officials preferred to look the other way. This archive evidences a systematic and psychic production of that silence.[115]

The military hierarchy worked to maintain sovereign control over its archive as an extension and expression of its legal power. Its bureaucratic strategy was perhaps summed up best by the minister's instructions to Bouïs's commanding

---

114. On the contemporary fetishism of the archive see Smith, *Gender of History*, 124–27. On the psychic mechanisms of bureaucracy see Kafka, *Demon of Writing*.

115. On the historiographical as well as archival elision of male youth see Pande, "'Listen to the Child.'"

officers, advising them to take "*great care*" in constructing his record.[116] This insistence on archival discretion clarifies why Boyer's feverish filing was one of his many perceived faults. A rich archive of this affair exists in part because of Boyer's exceptional and, in the eyes of his superiors, ultimately indecent graphomania. His public actions, more than Bouïs's private sexual proclivities, were the greater menace and proof of his lack of masculine military control.

A psychoanalytic account of the fantasy of archival control as a response to perceived threats also helps to locate the Bouïs-Boyer affair historically. The case exploded at a moment of hierarchical and jurisdictional uncertainty for the spahi regiment in Médéa, for the army in Algeria, and, as the Dreyfus Affair would soon reveal, for the army in the Third Republic as a whole. This seemingly singular case made manifest how racialized sexual fantasies conditioned disputes over law and sovereignty in Algeria and beyond it. While this contest was between military and civil justice, rather than the Civil Code and native laws, it, too, shows how competing conceptions of legal personhood were structured by race and sex. For civilian critics, the military exemplified the sexual danger of special *mœurs* and special laws.

Like the social tensions that erupted at the officers' *partie de campagne*, there is much about this scandal that was born of local circumstances. The dispute clearly arose out of an Algerian context that continued to produce conflicts between military and civilian jurisdictions even after the transfer to civilian rule. But the spahi scandal was not just a symptom of colonial exceptionalism. It is difficult not to read its history alongside the struggle between military and civilian justice in the much more famous case of Alfred Dreyfus.

Urbain Gohier, the virulently antimilitarist pamphleteer (and antisemite) drew this very comparison at the height of the Dreyfus Affair. Writing in *L'Aurore*, which had published Zola's *J'accuse* earlier that year, Gohier penned an article on the army's "special *mœurs*" that attacked the military for protecting Bouïs's corruption, while unfairly blaming Boyer and Rocas. Noting "abundant similarities" in the affairs, he suggested that between "the honest Boyer and the infamous Bouïs, the military leaders did not hesitate any more than between the honest Picquart and the Uhlan Esterhazy." In other words, in both cases, military justice shielded immoral traitors like Bouïs and Commandant Ferdinand Walsin Esterhazy—the latter had actually committed the crimes for which Dreyfus was condemned—rather than avowing the corruption brought to light by truth

---

116. Min. of War (2nd direction, Kermartin) to Bessol, June 15, 1891, dossier Bouïs. Emphasis in the original.

tellers like Boyer and Colonel Georges Picquart. Citing Senator Dide's petition in defense of Boyer, Gohier condemned how, in the shadow of its "special justice," the army had repeatedly sacrificed honest men to the "strange prejudices of caste and false solidarity."[117] The account, republished in his screed against military power, *L'armée contre la nation*, provided further evidence that the military and its law were "the concentration of all that was most criminal in the country."[118]

For Boyer and many of his Algerian and metropolitan defenders, this attack on the military's special law coincided with a racialized and sexualized conception of the nation and its civil law. From this perspective, military law, like Muslim law, appeared as deviant and foreign. In their eyes, French citizenship— and masculinity—needed to be protected from corruption by perverse justice and *mœurs*.

---

117. Dide, Sénat, *Feuilletons*, no. 34, March 3, 1892, 25.

118. Urbain Gohier, "Mœurs spéciales," *L'Aurore*, June 10, 1898. And Gohier, *L'armée contre la nation*, 58.

6

CONVERSION, MIXED MARRIAGE, AND THE CORPOREALIZATION OF LAW

According to the Algerian demographer and politician René Ricoux, the failure of population mixing or "fusion" between "*indigènes*" and "Europeans" in colonial Algeria was not merely the result of religious and legal difference. Their sexual incompatibility had, he claimed, a physiological basis: "Two causes that are more powerful [*autrement puissantes*] than the difference of religions can explain the small amount of interbreeding [*croisements*] with *indigènes*, and allow us to predict that they will not become more frequent: they are *syphilis* and *sodomy*." For Ricoux, a doctor at the civil hospital in Philippeville, these "endemo-constitutional vices" explained past resistance to fusion and rendered any future reconciliation between the populations "an unrealizable utopia." This corporealized conception of Algerian sexual perversity made "Franco-Muslim" mixing unfeasible and unwise as a strategy of colonization. Published in the wake of the advent of civilian rule, Ricoux's 1880 demographic study gave a scientific ground to arguments for "European" settlement.[1]

The biological basis of Ricoux's claim did double work. It explained not only why Franco-Algerian unions were undesirable, but also why Arabs and Kabyles would eventually perish as a result of their own habits and vices. In sum, concluded Ricoux, "the French people have no interest in compromising their native qualities, their moral superiority, in mixing with these corrupt races whose blood is polluted [*vicié*]."[2] By contrast, "European" mixing, optimally

---

1. Ricoux and Bertillon, *La démographie figurée de l'Algérie*, 258–59, emphasis in the original. On "Arab syphilis" see Amster, "Syphilitic Arab?"
2. Ricoux and Bertillon, *La démographie figurée de l'Algérie*, 262.

between French men and "Southern" or Latin women, promised to physically and politically solidify French rule in Algeria. It would produce vigorous French offspring while also "disaggregating" communities of Italian, Spanish, and Maltese settlers.[3] Over the next several decades, demographers from Victor Demontès to Henri de Peyerimhoff to Félix Dessoliers reinforced these presumptions about the inevitable failures of "Franco-Muslim" as opposed to "European" fusion.[4]

While Ricoux bracketed the question of religion, not all commentators on the "mixed marriage" question did. This chapter explores how "the Muslim" came to be viewed as imbued with perverse physicality. As I show, the colonial legal construction of Muslim "personal status" and its differences from a secular Civil Code elaborated a corporealized conception of Islam. The legal status of French citizens, "European" nationals, and Algerian colonial subjects or *indigènes* increasingly took on bodily attributes and qualities. In focusing on the legal quandaries posed by conversion and "mixed marriage," jurists detailed a conception of Muslimness that wed together faith and family law, religion and sex. Their focus on the implications of mixed marriage framed Muslim law as a threat to the presumptive dignity and integrity of the Civil Code. In this way, colonial jurists and administrators linked the corporealizing assumptions elaborated by racist demographers to law.

Official reports ceaselessly underscored that mixed marriages with Muslims were exceedingly rare. Based exclusively on the civil registry, the *Annuaire statistique de France* for 1876 recorded, for example, eleven marriages between European men and Muslim women and four between Muslim men and European women. In 1880, there were five and six total marriages, respectively.[5] Officials used these numbers to dismiss the viability of "Franco-Muslim" mixing as a strategy of colonization. They nonetheless continued to worry about the legal questions these marriages posed. In this chapter, I show how these legal arguments contributed to an increasingly corporealized conception of the difference between "Europeans" and Algerians.

---

3. On disaggregation see Dain, *Étude sur la naturalisation des étrangers*.

4. Dessoliers, *De la fusion des races européennes*; Demontès, *Le peuple algérien*; Peyerimhoff de Fontenelle, *Enquête sur les résultats de la colonisation officielle*. On demography and European settlement see Andersen, *Regeneration through Empire*.

5. Ministère du Commerce, *Annuaire statistique*, 6:653.

Corporealizing Codes

As we have seen, Algerian colonial jurists came to see Muslim men as stubbornly attached to their personal status because it accorded them patriarchal sexual privileges such as polygamy, repudiation, and forced marriage. The 1873 Warnier Law that territorialized French property law had set aside this new domain of "family law" as a distinct jurisdiction.[6] Land transactions in selected areas were made subject to French civil law, while marriage, divorce, and inheritance "as matters of the freedom of conscience, of religion, of the intimate life of families" were to be regulated by Muslim and customary law.[7]

While the Warnier Law was unevenly applied across Algerian territory, the distinction that it drew between a territorialized property law and personal status soon became a fixture of legal reasoning and political argument about Muslim Algerians. It structured the laws reorganizing the judicial system in 1886 and 1889 and nascent debates about extending political rights to Algerians. In colonial legal discourse, personal status condensed and confused religious attachment and patriarchal sexual rights.

The supposed "institutions" of polygamy, child marriage, divorce, and repudiation thus became metonyms for Muslims' conflation of religious and civil law. They exemplified an implicitly embodied connection between sex, religion, and legal status. Charles Roussel, who had been a magistrate in Algeria in the 1860s, would thus claim in 1875, "Because their religious status is confounded with their civil status, naturalization [*naturalisation*] touches their faith in modifying their civil status. Polygamy, divorce, and repudiation, which it eliminates, are fundamental institutions in Islam, the abandonment of which implies a certain heresy."[8] These clichés structured arguments about Algerians' resistance to full legal assimilation. The prominent specialist of international private law André Weiss similarly viewed naturalization in terms of the loss of men's sexual rights: "for him no more divorce by mutual consent or simple repudiation, no more polygamy."[9] Jurist Albert Hugues described code switching in analogous terms: "If, in becoming a citizen, the Muslim remains in control [*maître*] of his religion

---

6. On "family law" as a novel legal domain see Halley and Rittich, "Critical Directions in Comparative Family Law"; Halley, "What Is Family Law?"

7. Rapport Warnier, "Loi relative à l'établissement et à la conservation de la propriété en Algérie," July 26, 1873, in Estoublon and Lefébure, *Code de l'Algérie*, 1:400.

8. Roussel, "La naturalisation des étrangers en Algérie," 914.

9. A. Weiss, *Traité théorique et pratique de droit international privé*, 1:399.

[*culte*], it is on condition that he free himself [*se dégager*] from those conse-quences which French law condemns, such as polygamy, repudiation, wife pur-chase, paternal constraint. It is, however, these rights that are cherished in the heart of every believer."[10] According to this at once racializing and secularizing logic, the Algerian man's embodied investment in Muslim law made legal assimi-lation impossible. In studying mixed marriage, jurists imagined and explored this (im)possibility.

As much existing literature shows, concerns about interracial sex, concubi-nage, and mixed-race children were crucial nodes of colonial governmentality. Social policy and policing of these relationships elaborated complex hierarchies of race, class, and gender in both colonial and metropolitan contexts.[11] The juridical conflicts associated with mixed marriage demonstrate how colonial jurists increasingly represented Muslim law, while nominally based on a religious rather than racial difference, as intimately linked to bodies.[12]

The mixed-marriage question thus sheds light on the colonial history of secularism and the legal production of a secular European as well as Muslim body and sex. In these Algerian cases, administrators and jurists elaborated fantasies of Muslim law as bound to men's sexual rights and women's sexual degradation by polygamy, repudiation, and child marriage. They projected those fantasies onto the bodies of Muslim persons, while casting French civil law as integral and dignified, especially in its treatment of women. In the pro-cess, Muslim personal status and French civil status each assumed an embodied meaning, combining and confusing racial, religious, and sexual difference. This chapter illuminates an apparent paradox: how the legal rhetoric of secularism and religious freedom shaped a corporealized conception of Muslim personal law and sex.[13]

---

10. Hugues, *La nationalité française chez les musulmans de l'Algérie*, 194.

11. Stoler, *Carnal Knowledge and Imperial Power*; Saada, *Empire's Children*; Ghosh, *Sex and the Family in Colonial India*; Levine, *Prostitution, Race, and Politics*; Bland, "White Women and Men of Colour" and "British Eugenics and 'Race Crossing.'" On mixed marriage in other colonial contexts see Tabili, "Empire Is the Enemy of Love"; Ray, *Crossing the Color Line*; Savage, "More Than One Mrs. Mir Anwaruddin"; N. Chatterjee, "Religious Change" and "English Law, Brahmo Marriage."

12. In her important study of the *métis* as a French colonial social and legal problem, Saada sug-gests that questions about "mixed" children were virtually absent in Algeria because religion rather than race structured social and legal hierarchies. While Saada notes persistent concerns with mixed marriage, she does not explore why it became an intense focus of juridical interest and jurisprudential debate, despite its seeming rarity. See Saada, *Empire's Children*, 25–30.

13. J. W. Scott, *Sex and Secularism*, and *Politics of the Veil*; Mahmood, *Religious Difference in a Secular Age*; Fernando, "Intimacy Surveilled." See also Van der Veer, *Imperial Encounters*; Warner, VanAntwerpen, and Calhoun, *Varieties of Secularism*.

Conversion, Marriage, and the Secularization of Religious Law

As a religious jurisdiction *internal* to the French state's system of secular law, Muslim personal status set aside marriage, divorce, and inheritance as matters to be adjudicated by state-appointed Muslim jurists.[14] The religious basis of Muslim personal status was nonetheless ambiguous. It could not be acquired, and it could only be abandoned according to the procedures outlined in the 1865 *sénatus-consulte*. Persons were born into Muslim personal status by virtue of the fact that they had "indigenous" ancestors. While religious sensibility served as its purported ground, the status was, in fact, based on and limited by "blood ties" of filiation to former inhabitants of the Regency of Algiers. In this sense, it was a *jus sanguinis* with a religious name. Religious conversion alone (i.e., without recourse to official "naturalization") did not alter Muslim legal status. Inversely, converts to Islam did not acquire Muslim personal status. Conversion thus remained a matter of private personal faith, not public law. As a secular state matter, legal status was thus distinguished from individual belief.[15]

Because neither individuals nor clerical authorities could alter personal status, converts to Christianity remained legally Muslim. (Some jurists would hence argue that a more accurate description in this case was *"indigène catholique."*)[16] Christian converts to Islam likewise kept their French or other European nation's civil status. Muslim personal status was at once "ethno-political" *and* implicitly religious, in part because secular public law claimed independence from what it designated as religious matters.[17] In other words, the de facto ethnicization of Muslim status was a partial effect of French civil law's claim to secularity.[18] The ambiguity of Muslim personal status—as at once religious and not—actually made it an effective node of Algerian colonial government.[19] As I show in this

---

14. Christelow, *Muslim Law Courts*. On contemporary anxieties about canon law courts see C. C. Ford, *Divided Houses*, chap. 3.

15. Larcher, "Des effets juridiques du changement de religion"; Bonnichon, *La conversion au christianisme de l'indigène musulman algérien*. Shepard, *Invention of Decolonization*, 34–35. For the comparable case of British India, where Christian converts also remained under "Hindu law," see Viswanathan, *Outside the Fold*, chap. 3. See also N. Chatterjee, "Religious Change."

16. Larcher, "Des effets juridiques du changement de religion," 12.

17. Weil, *Qu'est-ce qu'un Français?*, 235. Weil highlights the "ethno-political" construction but does not draw the link to claims about the secularity of French law.

18. For parallel discussions of Jewish racialization see Brown, *Regulating Aversion*; Markell, *Bound by Recognition*.

19. On ambiguity as a mechanism of secular power see Agrama, *Questioning Secularism*.

chapter, legal accounts of Islamic faith as implacably bound to a gendered juridical organization of sex and kinship consolidated this ethnicized understanding of personal status. Because it lacked a national territorial referent, that status became anchored in Muslim bodies and affects instead.

In contrast to conversion, marriage had profound effects on personal status, especially for women. A French woman's marriage to a foreigner altered her nationality. Article 12 of the Civil Code established that a foreign woman who married a French man became French, while article 19 determined that "a French woman who marries a foreigner follows the condition of her husband."[20] Up until a 1927 reform, the Civil Code privileged the "legal unity" within the conjugal family.[21] This model of marriage entailed both a specific legal construction of conjugality (as distinct from extended kinship) *and* a related subordination of married women to their husbands' law.

By the end of the nineteenth century, new divorce laws, rising rates of immigration and emigration, concerns about demography, and the development of organized feminism put new pressures on the principle of conjugal legal unity. Jurists and feminists debated married women's relationship to nationality at international private law conferences, feminist congresses, and in proposals for new civil codes and nationality laws. Some small reforms in 1889 helped widows and divorcées regain French nationality and protected women who did not gain nationality by marriage. Otherwise, the principle of marital unity based on patriarchal prerogative remained in place. In one of the many dissertations devoted to the topic at the end of the nineteenth century, Albert Cauwès highlighted how legal uniformity in marriage was wedded to sovereignty. As he explained, "Marital power is an essential factor in the principle of nationalities: the state must, in itself, assure unity everywhere." In his view, "the power that it attributes to the husband to modify the original nationality of his wife by marriage" was a "translation" of the state's power.[22] The conjugal family both constituted and expressed this coincidence between sovereign and marital authority.

Colonial mixed marriages raised pointed questions about this patriarchal principle, testing the unity of law within both the family and the state. The problems could be seen, to use Cauwès's language, as "translations" of one another. More specifically, such marriages made the lacunae and contradictions of colonial legal pluralism visible. Jurists, politicians, and administrators continually

---

20. On the history of this principle see Heuer, *Family and the Nation*, 131–32.

21. On the 1927 law see Camiscioli, *Reproducing the French Race*.

22. Cauwès, *Des rapports du mariage avec la nationalité*, 3. See also Gruffy, *De l'unité de nationalité dans la famille*; Garcin, *Du changement de nationalité entre époux*.

grappled with how to assign legal status to the husbands, wives, and children whose kinship relations were governed by conflicting codes: What was the nationality of a Spanish woman who married a man with Muslim status? What would happen to a woman with French civil status who converted in order to marry a man with Muslim status? Would she legally follow her husband's status to become Muslim? And what legal status would be assigned to their children?

At the beginning of colonization, administrators and jurists improvised answers to these questions. By the end of the nineteenth century, they devised fixed rules with which to manage them. As often as not their "fixes" created new problems in turn. By juxtaposing conflicts over the course of the nineteenth century, we grasp the import and extent of this shift.

Early Questions

On November 22, 1833, the civil intendant of Algiers wrote to the minister of war with an urgent question. He wondered whether Mohammed ben Kertilon, a soldier in the Zouaves, should be allowed to marry an Italian Catholic woman, Marie Maurice. Based on conditions that she set, ben Kertilon agreed to convert and marry before a French civil official. In his confidential letter, the civil intendant Genty de Bussy expressed concern that the marriage could be perceived as proselytism: "Might one not see in this lone event a tendency toward the propagation of our religious doctrines? Might it not shock the susceptibility of the *Maures*?" Concerned about provoking a negative emotional reaction, he warned that "the most intense passions are in play." Looking ahead, he thought that the issue would likely recur "in a wholly different manner" when Frenchmen and Europeans sought to marry *Mauresques*. To effectively govern these feelings, he urged, "we must prepare in advance." In a marginal note, the minister agreed, suggesting that the question was "very serious and deserving of political consideration."[23]

Because ministerial officials sought to protect both religious freedom and local religious sensibilities, the specific legal solution to this sensitive affair remained unclear. The case was forwarded to legal adviser Charles Paravey, who, as we saw in chapter 1, had experience with the complex legal situation on the ground after drawing up an influential report on Algeria's judicial organization in 1832. Now working at the Ministry of War, he explained why outlawing mixed

---

23. Genty to Min. of War, November 22, 1833 (Confidential), AN BB30/624.

marriages was unreasonable—and illegal. While the government "might, up to a certain point, be interested in not allowing this cause of irritation and disturbance to multiply," Paravey thought that it was "absolutely impossible to refuse a Muslim the right to marry a Catholic in converting to her religion." In banning the marriage, the government would be seen as "intolerant and arbitrary."[24] The minister agreed, noting that "as long as both parties were in conformity with the law," no further action could be taken.[25] The ministry instructed Genty that the marriage could proceed. But it also underscored the importance of limiting future conversions, as part of its broader strategy of religious government. The minister's confidential letter to Genty outlined the policy, which in taking local sensibilities seriously also subordinated Christian religious interests to state concerns. "Foreign missionaries residing in Africa by agreement of French authorities, like the French priests who are supported by state funds," had to understand that the government could not "tolerate any system of proselytism which would be contrary to the mutual understanding [*bonne intelligence*] that it is important to maintain between all the classes of the population."[26]

This affair predated the official commitment to colonization and subsequent juridical organization in 1834. It nonetheless indicates a prevailing circumscription regarding "mixed marriages" at the outset of colonization. Official discourse framed the question as politically sensitive on account of the presumptive religious "susceptibility" of Algerian Muslims. In that ben Kertilon's conversion was considered a matter of private conscience separate from civil law, the marriage itself appeared to be unproblematic and hence beyond the purview of administrative interference.

Notwithstanding this commitment to religious freedom, ministerial authorities could have raised questions about the legal effect of the contract on Marie Maurice's nationality. They did not. The answers to these questions were, however, far from settled, as a case that appeared before the Tribunal of First Instance of Algiers in 1836 soon showed. This trial featured prominent members of a local elite family. Drawing on international private law principles, the court decided that a French woman would be subject to the Muslim legal status of her husband, even if the marriage did not make her into a native Algerian. When the case was

---

24. Paravey, Report to Minister, December 8, 1833, AN BB30/624.

25. Min. of War, Note pour le Conseil des Ministres, AN BB30/624.

26. Min. of War to Genty, December 13, 1833 (Confidential), AN BB30/624. For contemporary accounts of this policy of limitation from the perspective of those who advocated for conversion as a strategy of colonization see *De la conversion des musulmans au christianisme*; Godard, *La nouvelle Église d'Afrique*, 48; Also see Curtis, *Civilizing Habits*; Francis, "Civilizing Settlers"; Schley, "Tyranny of Tolerance."

taken up on appeal, the court confirmed that while she could not become an *indigène* by marriage, she and her child would be subject to "Muslim law."[27]

The case involved Si Hamdan ben Abderaman Bourkaïeb, an Algerian notable who had worked with the French after the capitulation in 1830. Bourkaïeb was hastily appointed to the position of "agha of the Arabs" on July 8, 1830, but soon fell into disgrace with French authorities. Twice exiled to Paris, he married the daughter of a French consul, Josephine Zabel, even though he already had two wives. Ailing, he returned with Josephine to his residence in Algiers, after which he soon died, leaving behind a considerable fortune.[28] He and Josephine had one son, whose personal and financial trusteeship was the fundamental question at issue in the trial. Before his death, Bourkaïeb had, in a document drawn up before a qadi, named his nephew Mustapha, not Josephine, as administrator of his son Ismaël's inheritance. Because a French official had performed their marriage in Paris, Josephine claimed that French law should govern their marital regime and its effects on the person and fortune of her son. The court considered whether Bourkaïeb's acceptance of the French forum represented an abjuration of the "rights that he holds based on his birth and the capitulation of 1830."[29] Would the French forum determine the law's content as well?

The first court's reasoning drew on international law or *jus gentium*—namely, that according to the principle of *lex fori*, "the form of a contract is determined by the place in which it occurs." The Tribunal of First Instance thus found that Bourkaïeb could contract marriage before French authorities (as no qadis could be found Paris) while maintaining his own civil law status. As a Muslim, he contracted under "Moorish law," which permitted marriages between Muslim men and Christian women. The court also decided that because "a woman follows the condition of her husband," his widow would likewise be subject to this law. She remained Catholic, but the marriage and its effects would be regulated by her husband's law. The initial decision explained that, "according to French law [i.e., article 19 of the Civil Code], because she became the wife of a Muslim, she must be governed by 'Moorish law,' at least relative to the effects of

27. Droit-Tribunaux, *Revue africaine*, no. 6 (October 1837): 113; Dame Hamdan Bourkaïeb v. Mustapha ben Ahmed ben el Adgi Sehid, Tribunal supérieur d'Alger (June 20, 1836), in Estoublon, *Jurisprudence algérienne*, vol. 1 (1836), 15–17.

28. Pellissier de Reynaud, *Annales algériennes*, 2:381–82.

29. Droit-Tribunaux, *Revue africaine*, no. 6 (October 1837): 108. Dame Hamdan Bourkaïeb v. Mustapha ben Ahmed ben el Adgi Sehid, in Estoublon, *Jurisprudence algérienne*, vol. 1 (1836), 15–17. The extent of the family's wealth is indicated in the inventory of his possessions, which included an important collection of jewels. See Eudel, *L'orféverie algérienne et tunisienne*, 321–22.

her marriage." The court had little patience for Josephine's attempt to reclaim French legal status. Indeed, it met her demand with outright disdain, noting her consent to the marriage in the first place. In its view, "she engaged in advance to submit" to that law, "in uniting her destiny to that of a man who she knew benefited from civil rights different from her own."[30] Her status as widow and mother did not sway the decision. While the court granted Josephine custody over Ismaïl's young person, it upheld Mustapha's authority as administrator of his possessions.

Josephine appealed, but she made no further headway in securing French civil status for the marriage. The court did, however, use the occasion to clarify its effects: "One cannot conclude from this marriage that it had the effect of rendering the dame Zabel indigenous to the territory of Alger, as the first judge seems to have established in his first judgment, since the quality of *indigène* can only belong to a person who was born in this territory." In other words, the court placed a legal limit on "local" status: one had to be born an *indigène*; one could never become one. The Superior Tribunal of Algiers nonetheless affirmed that "women follow the condition of their husbands." Zabel's marriage to Hamdan Bourkaïeb and its effects were "Muslim."[31]

This early decision is remarkable from the perspective of subsequent juris-prudence. By the last third of the nineteenth century, jurists and politicians actively worked to protect the French legal status embodied by "European" women and occasionally by Algerian women who had been "naturalized." They upheld the precedence of French civil law over a subordinate and exceptional Muslim law. Unsurprisingly, they castigated the Tribunal of Algiers's early find-ing in the Bourkaïeb case.[32] What had made legal and political sense at the outset of colonization was later dismissed as an idiosyncratic error in juridical thinking, a misplaced analogy. Later mixed-marriage cases instead appealed to "European" women's status in order to affirm the hierarchical distinction between "French" and "Muslim" law. By contrast, Josephine Zabel's case preserved the Civil Code patriarchal principle: a wife had to follow the law of her husband, even when he and his law were "Muslim."

---

30. Droit-Tribunaux, *Revue africaine*, no. 6 (October 1837): 113.

31. Dame Hamdan Bourkaïeb v. Mustapha ben Ahmed ben el Adgi Sehid, in Estoublon, *Jurispru-dence algérienne*, vol. 1 (1836), 15–17.

32. Clavel, "Mariage contracté devant l'officer de l'état civil français," 1003; Larcher, "Des effets du mariage d'une femme indigène," 214. See also E. Norès, "Essai de codification," *RA*, 1905, pt. 1, 46.

Categorical Confusion

The civil registry carries occasional traces of marriages between Algerian men and "French" and "European" women in the decades that followed. In 1849, the military interpreter Hassan ben Mohammed obtained permission to marry Julie Frédéric, who had been born in the department of Orne. Her parents, who now lived in Guelma, gave their consent. In Miliana in 1854, Ehmed ben Hadji, a merchant from the Mzab, married Elizabeth Rivoire, a sixteen-year-old minor who had been born in Lyon. Her father had died, but her mother gave her consent. In 1855, Jean-Baptiste Haoussin (Emhamed Ben Haoussin) married a twenty-two-year-old Swiss woman, Marie Borgéat, in Koléa. The name "Jean-Baptiste" indicated the husband's prior conversion.[33]

The civil registry gave no indication of the official concern provoked by Jean-Baptiste's conversion by the bishop of Algiers, Louis-Antoine-Augustin Pavy. Born in Blidah, Emhamed Ben Haoussin lost his parents while he was still a minor. At age seventeen, he sought out the governor-general's help in an inheritance dispute. His employer at the time, settler publicist Louis de Baudicour, requested that the government extend French legal protection to him by naming a family council (*conseil de famille*) to act in his interest, thus sidestepping a local qadi. The *juge de paix* in Blidah refused to honor the request. In his eyes, Haoussin remained an "*indigène*," his conversion to Catholicism notwithstanding.[34]

The question was particularly sensitive, given a context of political tumult following the Revolution of 1848 in France. The interim governor-general, Aimable Pélissier, consulted with the chief prosecutor of Algiers, Achille Marrast. The brother of the prominent journalist and republican politician Armand Marrast, Achille was known to have anticlerical tendencies. He had been implicated in controversies provoked by the campaign of the republican newspaper *L'Atlas* against Bishop Pavy's charitable works focused on orphans.[35] Haoussin's protector and employer, Baudicour, by contrast, endorsed Catholic charity as a tactic of colonization.[36]

---

33. ANOM État Civil, Algérie.

34. Baudicour to Gov. Gen., "Fonds du Procureur Général: Correspondance (Abjuration d'un jeune musulman)," March 16, 1850, ANOM ALG/GGA/1T/2.

35. Félix Klein, "Le Prédecesseur du Cardinal Lavigerie: La question Arabe en Algérie," *Le Correspondant*, June 25, 1902, 1154–67. Pavy, *La Nouvelle Église d'Afrique*, 487–514; *Notice sur M. Joseph Girard*; Émerit, "Le problème de la conversion des musulmans."

36. Baudicour, *La guerre et le gouvernement de l'Algérie*, 591–96. Also, "Des orphelinats des Jésuites en Algérie," *L'Ami de la religion*, July 5, 1851, 49–52.

In pondering Haoussin's fate, Marrast considered how religious conversion should impact his legal status: "Should a change in religion also have for an effect to submit the Muslim—now Christian—to the requirements of French law with respect to his civil status and the administration of his fortune and belongings? If he is a minor and an orphan, who should be his trustee?"[37] Marrast ultimately concurred with the *juge de paix*'s original decision that Haoussin remained an *indigène*. In doing so, he notably appealed to the principle of paternal authority, even though the minor's father was dead. He wondered: "What would I say to the Muslim father who might come to me reclaiming the aid of my authority to make his minor son, his child, return to the house from which he was led away or which he deserted? Could I uphold that this child had had recourse to baptism and that from now on, he has ceased to be Muslim and even to belong to him?" For the prosecutor, a clerical assault on "paternal authority" [*la puissance paternelle*] was illegal and politically dangerous. In contemplating the case, Marrast identified with an imagined Muslim father, deprived of his natural rights by the devious and deviant actions of the Catholic Church.[38]

According to Marrast, lending legal effects to the minor's conversion would subject "the Arab family" to "all the ruses and moral violence of religious antagonism." In his view, French law needed to protect the father's religion and authority from a proselytism that targeted minors. Secularism underwrote this legal protection, because "French legislation attaches no civil effect to religious abjuration, especially on the part of a minor who becomes Catholic." In other words, religious law addressed the "*for intérieur*" alone, which is to say the "soul" and "purely spiritual things." Civil status, by contrast, was governed by secular law.[39]

The justice minister, Eugène Rouher, and the governor-general ultimately circumvented these broader legal and political issues. Rouher suggested that a "tutor" could be named to protect the minor's inheritance without effecting a change in his civil legal status, effectively separating his property from his personal status. While the *conseil de famille* would manage Jean-Baptiste's belongings, its oversight would not "assimilate" the "foreign minor to French status."[40]

---

37. "Abjuration d'un jeune musulman," undated, ANOM ALG/GGA/1T/2.

38. On the liberal defense of paternal authority against clerical influence see C. C. Ford, *Divided Houses*, 39.

39. In another controversial and related case the following year, Marrast supported the right of a deacon in Bône to marry, despite the church's opposition. He claimed in that case as well that matters of religious faith were beyond the purview of civil law. See Pavy, *La Nouvelle Église d'Afrique*, 529–31.

40. Min. of Justice to Procureur, May 13, 1850, ANOM ALG/GGA/1T/2.

This improvisational solution skillfully sidestepped confusing questions of status, thus downplaying the case's potential legal as well as political significance. Haoussin's subsequent marriage to Marie Borgéat notably did not appear to give rise to further legal disputes.

Mixed-marriage cases did nonetheless assume heightened significance for jurists and legislators in later decades. These concerns emerged in tandem with the legal delineation of "Muslim personal status." According to the civil registry, officially recorded mixed marriage increased moderately in the 1860s and 1870s. Based on the names and family histories included in the marriage acts, there were at least twenty-five in the 1860s, fifty-nine in the 1870s, and seventy-one in the 1880s, up from eight between 1839 and 1849 and fifteen in the 1850s.[41] While these numbers remained low, jurists' concern about the unions increased considerably, especially in the wake of the 1865 *sénatus-consulte* and 1873 Warnier Law. The presumptive rarity of such romances spurred both legal and novelistic imaginations, as jurists worked to distinguish French and European from "Muslim" law. The relative infrequency of the marriages contributed to their legal and symbolic significance. More specifically, the imagined fate of French and European women in these marriages came to embody what jurists saw as a grave conflict of law.

The Power of Small Numbers

One famous case of mixed marriage was that of Aurélie Tijānī, née Picard. As depicted in later biographies of the "princess of sands," its singular circumstances were worthy of a novel. In 1870, Aurélie, the daughter of a gendarme who had served in Algeria, met Ahmed al-Tijānī, the powerful and wealthy head of the Tijaniya Islamic confraternity, which had long-standing political links to French colonial authorities.[42] The couple met in Bordeaux, where Ahmed was in exile from political turbulence around his home in Aïn Mahdi. Aurélie accepted Ahmed's marriage proposal and the prospect of an adventurous life in the Algerian South. She moved to the desert town, where she developed a measure of political influence in the Tijaniya and among French colonial authorities. With her husband, she worked to expand French influence in the Sahara. When

---

41. This was no doubt an effect of increased migration of "European" women. Statistics compiled from ANOM État Civil, Algérie.

42. For a colonial account see Coppolani and Depont, *Les confréries religieuses musulmanes*, 496–31.

Ahmed died in 1897, she married his brother. By the end of her life, she became a colonial heroine of sorts, garnering public recognition and praise, including being named a chevalier of the Legion of Honor.[43] At French Algeria's centenary in 1930, Louis Bertrand, the lead spokesperson for the "Algerianist" literary school, praised her civilizing achievements: "She knows how to understand seminomadic Muslim souls, and while always distinguishing the profound differences separating her from these men, she does not give up on exercising her influence, an influence that is discreet, persevering, and ultimately triumphant, because it is accompanied by so much generosity."[44] In addition to her colonial political work, Picard's marriage to al-Tijānī left a legacy in the domain of colonial law, influencing the proceedings of Algerian marriage law in the last decades of the century.

While their union was retrospectively celebrated, Picard and al-Tijānī's marriage plans initially provoked resistance on the part of French authorities. In order to be legal, the union had to be contracted under French civil, not Muslim, law. In their case, this was impossible, because al-Tijānī already had two other wives, making the union invalid according to the Civil Code. Aware of the law and apparently unwilling to displease French authorities, the qadi of Algiers refused to officiate. Tijānī and Picard's appeal before the Court of Algiers ended in failure.[45] Their "marriage," eventually overseen by an imam and blessed by Cardinal Lavigerie, went unrecognized by French authorities. The case did not, however, indicate a blanket rejection of "mixed marriage," as Claude Liauzu has suggested.[46] Other "mixed" unions officiated at the *mairie* and recorded in the civil registry that same year did not produce similar legal wrangling, including those between Belkassem ben Sedira, a candy seller, and Marie Nava; between Kaddour ben Larby, a teacher at the *école normale*, and Marie Fernando; between Abdallah ben Messaoud el Maadi, an army medic, and Jeanne Lacavo; and between Ali ben Saïd, a lieutenant in the spahis, and Jeanne Nadal.[47] What Picard's marriage did provide was a unique occasion to outline the hierarchal relation between civil and Muslim law at the moment of Algeria's transfer to civilian rule.

---

43. Augustin Bertrand, "Madame Aurélie," *Annales Africaines* 43, no. 13 (July 1, 1931): 196. See also Trumbull, *Empire of Facts*, 116–25; Hart, *Two Ladies of Colonial Algeria*; Friang, *Femmes fin de siècle.*

44. Bassenne and Bertrand, *Aurélie Tedjani, "princesse des Sables."*

45. Tedjani v. Demoiselle Picard, Cour d'appel d'Alger (October 24, 1871), in Estoublon, *Jurisprudence algérienne*, vol. 4 (1871), 25.

46. Liauzu, *Passeurs de rives*, 22.

47. ANOM État Civil, Algérie.

Named governor-general in March 1871, Admiral Louis Henri de Gueydon implemented civilian rule by eliminating many of the administrative structures of the Second Empire's "Arab Kingdom."[48] Fusionist fantasies of Franco-Muslim marriage were another facet of the previous regime that settler advocates had long sought to dismantle. The author of the 1873 property reform, Auguste Warnier, had, for example, attacked Saint-Simonian convert Ismayl Urbain's politics and policies with less than veiled assaults on his marriage to a Muslim woman.[49] Drawing on this political-legal critique of mixed marriage, Gueydon firmly opposed the prospect of Picard's "Muslim" marriage.

In June 1871, Gueydon assembled a commission of legal, military, and religious advisers to study "diverse questions of legislation." While promising that "no attack would be made on the religious law of Muslims," he urged the elimination of "the differences that exist between French law and Muslim law in civil matters."[50] The proposition elicited a skeptical response from Ahmed Boukandoura, a Muslim adviser [assesseur] at the Court of Algiers. According to Boukandoura, it "was not possible to establish a division between Muslim civil law and Muslim religious law, given that everything that concerns religious interests, but also social, civil, and commercial interests, as well as conventional and criminal matters, is found in the two books [i.e., the Qur'an and Sunna] that make up Muslim law and legislation." For Boukandoura, in other words, the civil/religious distinction made no sense from the perspective of Islamic jurisprudence. Above the Muslim jurist's strong objections, Gueydon insisted that "the Muslim Code seemed to him legally susceptible to modifications."[51] Unsurprisingly, real estate questions were paramount, as Gueydon sought to make "the obstacles that stand in the way of property transactions disappear."[52]

As discussions surrounding a proposed "Algerian Code" continued in July, the commission's Algerian members voiced their collective opposition, proclaiming, "We do not want any innovation to be introduced into our legislation."

---

48. See, for example, the creation of the "commune mixte," Mussard, "Réinventer la commune?"
49. Warnier, L'Algérie devant l'empereur, 156. In addition to this implicit attack on Urbain, Warnier cited the "arabophile" pamphlet recommending the legitimate union between "Europeans and indigènes." L'Algérie et la lettre de l'empereur, 69. On Urbain's marriage see Michel Levallois, "Le 'mariage arabe' d'Ismaÿl Urbain." The fantasy of fusion as a strategy of domination was common in the first decades of colonization; see Beaumont, De la consolidation de la puissance française, 37; Pontier, Souvenirs de l'Algérie, 64.
50. La commission instituée pour étudier diverses questions de législation, Procès-verbal, June 22, 1871, ANOM GGA/3/E4 (18MIOM/71).
51. Procès-verbal, June 22, 1871, ANOM GGA/3/E4.
52. Procès-verbal, June 29, 1871, ANOM GGA/3/E4.

Against these objections, the governor-general contended that while the commission would pursue reforms, no changes would be made to "personal status, which no one has the intention of harming [*porter atteinte*]."[53] While Muslim jurists on the commission clearly disagreed with these claims, Gueydon persisted in his promise to defend the novel legal entity of "Muslim personal status." He asserted that "personal status forms in Muslim law a homogeneous whole that cannot be touched without upsetting the economy of the law, unless there is a significant public interest." Following this logic, he rejected several other members' proposals to reform marriage age and divorce.[54] At the end of the July meeting, a unanimous vote approved his motion that "no innovations would be made in the personal status of Muslims, from the point of view of marriage, filiation, and divorce."[55]

In the wake of these meetings and the Picard-Tijānī case, Gueydon addressed a November 1871 circular on "mixed marriage" to Algeria's new prefects, mayors, and qadis. Presenting Picard's marriage as symptomatic of broader conflicts between European and Muslim law, his text denounced the "anomalies caused by undefined legal relations between two populations, European and *indigène*, each having, one and the other, their own personal status and real property status." He targeted both the "impossibility of property transactions" and the purportedly "more serious inconveniences" in matters of personal status. This punctual intervention was a quick and convenient way to score political points. As he explained, "while waiting for the radical solutions that will soon be submitted to the National Assembly [i.e., what would become the 1873 Warnier Law], the existing state of legislation already poses, notably regarding mixed marriages, certain obstacles to what I will call the abuse of Muslim law."[56]

Gueydon's circular drew on an opinion issued by the justice minister that proclaimed "the application of Muslim law cannot be allowed to compromise public order." This "public order" principle preserving the integrity of the Civil Code stood as a necessary limit to Muslim law jurisdiction, especially in cases of marriage. The Picard-Tijānī union thus helped to clarify French public policy at the moment that "Muslim personal status" was legally distinguished from real property law. As Gueydon's circular explained, "In no case can a mixed marriage be celebrated according to Muslim law, without the production of a marriage act certifying that

---

53. Procès-verbal, July 13, 1871, ANOM GGA/3/E4.
54. Ibid.
55. Ibid.
56. Circular, November 3, 1871, *BOGGA* 11 (1871): 558–59.

a civil marriage has taken place before a French official."[57] Because Picard was a French citizen, she could only be married according to French civil law.

In this case and those that followed in its wake, Picard's French law status trumped that of her prospective husband, even though the reverse rule had applied in international private law. This gender inversion came to distinguish colonial law from international conflicts of law. In the 1836 Bourkaïeb case, the French statute did not prevail, even though that marriage had been performed before a French civil officer. The husband's "Moorish law" remained predominant when French legal sovereignty was still uncertain at the outset of colonization. By the end of the century, jurists asserted the Civil Code's ascendency over a subordinate and exceptional Muslim law. In an ironic reversal and denegation of the Code's own patriarchal principles of marital unity, colonial jurists argued that "European" women needed to be protected from the patriarchal excesses of Muslim law.[58] The sexual integrity and dignity of the European woman thus came to embody the sovereignty and secularity of the Civil Code.

Properties, Persons, Personal Properties

As Gueydon had pledged, the law designed to eliminate conflicts between French and Muslim law—what would become the Warnier Law—was presented before the National Assembly in January 1872. While promising, as the later law did, not to infringe on "personal status or the rules of succession among *indigènes*," this version also addressed mixed unions: "In the case of mixed marriage, French laws, both civil and penal [*répressives*], will regulate marriage, for the forms and conditions of its celebration and for its effects, as much for the spouses as for the children."[59] As Minister of the Interior Casimir Périer explained to parliament, "It is impossible to admit that [Muslim laws] might regulate contracts where French, or other European colonists intervene as parties, especially when the effects of the contract as derived from Muslim law contradict [*sont en opposition*

---

57. Ibid. See also the note of approval, *L'Akhbar*, November 5, 1871, and the subsequent discussions of "mixed marriage" and "public order" in Gov. Gen. to Min. of Int., December 5, 1871, "Projet de loi sur la propriété en Algérie et les contrats entre Indigènes et Européens," in ANOM GGA 3E92. Gueydon addressed international legal principles in his circular on the status of "Algerian Muslims'" personal status abroad (in Egypt) and their right to divorce. Circular, "Mariage et divorce des indigènes algériens en Égypte," December 30, 1871, *BOGGA* 11 (1871): 558–59. Also, ANOM F80 1725.

58. See also Renucci, "Confrontation entre droit français et droits indigènes."

59. *JO*, Assemblée, January 29, 1872, annexe 861, 123.

avec] the best established principles of our public law." The same French public law principles were supposed to apply to both property and to marriage contracts. "One cannot understand," continued Périer, that "on French soil, a French woman who marries a Muslim might be exposed to divorce, as can happen today, nor that a French woman might marry a Muslim engaged in a prior union, even with her fully voluntary consent." The proposed law would also guarantee that a French woman's children would not be excluded from "Muslim" inheritance. It was, in other words, designed to "make French law prevail over [*prédominer*] Muslim law."[60]

In his report to the Assembly, however, Warnier urged deputies to remove all these references to mixed marriage, whose existence he sought to render unthinkable for French women. In his view, "Marriages between French women and Muslims are extremely rare, and it is understandable; the Christian woman, who has preserved her sense of dignity, will never submit to a marriage, whether monogamous or polygamous, which reduces her to the status of a thing." He further worried that any explicit discussion of marriage in the property reform bill would confuse issues, precisely because "among Muslims, too many consider women to be property."[61] According to this Orientalist trope, Muslim marriage supposedly differed from French marriage because it made women into property. On Warnier's advice, the final version of the law contained no reference to mixed marriage and thereby affirmed the "dignity" and superiority of French law by distinguishing market contracts from marital ones.[62]

As Warnier's comments indicate, the presumptive rarity of Muslim-European marriages shored up arguments about the superiority of French civil law. Starting in 1878, yearly listings on Algeria in the *Statistique générale de la France* publicized these small numbers.[63] Listed in the single digits, unions between "*Européens et musulmanes*" and "*Musulmans et Européennes*" paled in significance beside the hundreds listed between French and foreigners, and the thousands contracted between French nationals or foreigners among themselves. These small numbers were supposed to prove European women's dignity.

---

60. Ibid., 121–22.

61. Warnier, "Rapport sur le projet de loi relatif à l'établissement et à la conservation de la propriété en Algérie," in Estoublon and Lefébure, *Code de l'Algérie*, 1:402.

62. On this distinction as foundational to "family law exceptionalism" see Halley, "What Is Family Law?," 31.

63. See Ministère du Commerce, *Annuaire statistique de la France*. The earlier serial publication, *Tableau de la situation des établissements français dans l'Algérie (1838–1866)*, did not have an equivalent statistic. It listed marriages between "French" and between "French and foreigners." *Indigènes* were treated separately. On the organization of the new statistical service in Algeria see Kateb, *Européens, "indigènes" et juifs*, 103.

TABLE 1 / Official marriage statistics for Algeria, 1875–1887

MARRIAGES	1875	1876	1877	1878	1879	1880	1881	1882	1883	1884	1885	1886	1887
French men and French women	1,235	1,178	1,168	1,256	2,249	1,378	1,385	1,407	1,470	1,442	1,474	1,482	1,500
Foreign men and foreign women	795	919	879	1,019	996	1,1417	1,200	1,173	1,188	1,170	1,206	1,153	1,248
French men and foreign women	299	335	290	308	311	329	332	360	367	400	393	407	450
Foreign men and French women	102	106	122	107	125	123	143	137	126	140	160	123	140
European men and Muslim women	4	11	2	9	4	5	12	6	7	5	*	4	1
Muslim men and European women	1	4	6	9	5	6	3	14	9	9	12	5	3

Source: Compiled based on tables published in Ministère du Commerce. *Annuaire statistique de la France*, vols. 1–13 (Paris: Imprimerie nationale, 1878–1890).

Exactly how the census arrived at these numbers is unclear. As Kamel Kateb has demonstrated, even those demographers who played a crucial role in the development of the Algerian statistics bureau, such as Ricoux, raised questions about their reliability.[64] The so-called European *état-civil* does contain traces of French civil marriages contracted between Muslims and Europeans that were not necessarily recorded as such in the published statistics. Official counting was no doubt uneven and inconsistent, especially since civil marriage made religious affiliation irrelevant. The registries do sometimes indicate the partners' legal status as, for example, "*indigène et française.*" In the registry of Mustapha from 1872, the marriage between Jeanne Nadal and a daily laborer named Ali ben Saïd has the word *indigène* scribbled in the margin. Subsequent mixed marriages in Mustapha contain no such denotation. In 1874, the unions between Louis Gaspard and Lahalli bent Ahmed (*dite* Marie Josephine), an orphan from Saint-Cyprien-des-Attafs (El Attaf); between Antoine Dubois, a locksmith, and Josephine Marie Aicha bent Mohammed, a nurse, in 1875; and between Kaddour ben Allouah, a driver, and Marie Josephine Raibaldi in 1876 have no marginal commentary. As their names suggest, the first two unions involved women who had most likely been converted at Cardinal Lavigerie's orphanage in Saint-Cyprien and that of the Sisters of Saint Vincent in Mustapha.[65] According to the civil registry, the number of parentless girls who married Europeans rose sharply in the 1870s and 1880s in part as a result of the cholera epidemic and famine that struck in 1866–1868. Some of these women's registrar entries mention their parents' death as a result of the famine.[66] They technically maintained "Muslim" legal status, even when then married Europeans.[67] How the marriages were categorized on the census, if at all, is unclear.[68]

---

64. Kateb, *Européens, "indigènes" et juifs*, 107.

65. Mustapha, Marriage, Ali ben Saïd and Jeanne Nadal, Marriage, Mustapha, 1872; Louis Gaspard and Lahalli bent Ahmed, Marriage, Mustapha, 1874; Antoine Dubois and Josephine Marie Aïcha bent Mohammed, Marriage, Mustapha, 1875; Kaddour ben Allouah and Marie Josephine Raibaldi, Marriage, Mustapha, 1876, all in ANOM État Civil, Algérie.

66. For example, Dieu, Charles Alphonse, and Amélie Saala bent Kaddour, Marriage, Maison Carrée, 1881. She was born in 1860, and her parents died "of cholera or famine" in 1867 or 1868. Similar marriages can be found throughout the 1880s in the État civil of Misserghin, the site of another orphanage. See Paulin, Claude Joseph, and Thérèse Fathma ben Adda bel Aredj, Marriage, Sidi Bel Abbès, 1885. ANOM État Civil, Algérie.

67. On Algerian orphanages see Turin, "Enfants trouvés, colonisation et utopie." On orphans, conversion, and intermarriage see Taithe, "Algerian Orphans and Colonial Christianity," 254; McDougall, *History of Algeria*, 150–51. On the famine see Taithe, "La famine de 1866–1868." On orphanages and religious difference in Algeria see Saada, *Empire's Children*, 29.

68. In contrast to those from Mustapha, a marriage registration from Dely Ibrahim in 1877 describes Aïcha bent Ahmed ben Youssef *dite* Eva, who married Joseph Paul, as the daughter of "*indigènes musulmans.*" The town was the site of a Protestant orphanage, and its director, Maurice Chevally, and the Protestant pastor of Algiers, Frédéric Müller, both served as witnesses. It is impossible to know if this union was one of the two marriages between "*Européen et musulmane*" officially listed for the year 1877. See "Algérie—Tableau 2: Mouvement de la population—3 Mariages," *Annuaire statistique de la France* 6 (1883): 569.

Not all mixed marriages were between orphans, however. The registries of Algiers, Constantine, Bône (Annaba), and Philippeville (Skikda) list dozens of unions between seamstresses and shop employees, day laborers, café waiters, and servants. Less frequently, they feature army officers, interpreters, and property holders. Parents often attended these civil ceremonies. And, as was required by the Civil Code for men under thirty years of age and women under twenty-five, they gave their approval. When the marriages were between minors, parents authorized the unions; in their absence, they sent statements of assent. This was the case, for example, for the marriage between Sadok ben Hadj Mohamed Aloui ben Larbi and Marie Gaudier in Philippeville in 1881. The registrar listed Sadok as "*indigène*," even though he was born in the Regency of Tunis and hence legally a foreigner. Other entries in the city's registry note nationality such as Anglo-Maltese, Italian, or Spanish, but Sadok was instead categorized as a colonial subject. Was his marriage one of the three between "*Musulman et Européenne*" officially counted for 1881?[69]

Other notations of spousal origin sometimes appear. In Oran in 1878, the register indicated that both Mohamed ben Munez (a translator who married a Spanish woman, Maria de Jesus Catherineau Garcia) and Aoued Ould Ahmed ben Abdallah (who married Maria Ascencion Martinez) were of "Arab origin." Several years later, no such indication appears on the act of Mohamed ben Abderrahman, who also married a Spanish woman, Antonia Ramona Juana Artero.[70] Was this marriage classified on the census as one contracted between "*Français et étrangère*," based on his and her nationality? Or was it between "*Musulman et Européenne*"? Was it enumerated at all?

Labeling in the marriage registry was occasional and far from uniform. It reflected an unstable relationship between religion, ethnicity, and nationality in the minds and actions of officials who worked to form "Muslim" and "European" into statistical and legal realities. The annual production of demographic tables, as well as the scientific studies and public policy that were based on them, called attention to these marriages, in part because of, rather than despite, their small

---

69. Sadok ben Hadj Aloui ben Larbi and Marie Gaudier, Marriage, Philippeville, 1881. "Algérie—Tableau 2: Mouvement de la population—3 Mariages," *Annuaire statistique de la France* 9 (1886): 653. See also subsequent notations in the État civil of Philippeville: Moussa ben El Taïeb ben Ahmed El Meslaoui and Ryder, Anna Maria (*Indigène et suisse*), 1885; Hadj Mohamed ben Moustafah ben Satouf and Martin, Jeanne Marie Pauline (*Indigène et française*), 1887; Mammi ben Mahmoud ben Mamoun and Clément, Caroline Thomasa (*Indigène et espagnole*), 1890, in Marriage, Philippeville. By contrast, the marriage of Mohamed ben Saïd and Catherineau, Marie Berthe Catherine, is listed as "*Français*," presumably because Mohamed, a military interpreter, had been naturalized by decree earlier that year: Marriage, Philippeville, 1898, ANOM État Civil, Algérie.

70. See Mohamed ben Munez and Maria de Jesus Catherineau Garcia, Marriage, Oran, 1878; Aoued Ould Ahmed ben Abdallah and Maria Ascencion Martinez, Marriage, Oran, 1878; Mohamed ben Abderrahman and Antonia Ramona Juana Artero, Marriage, Oran, 1885, ANOM État Civil, Algérie.

numbers. In contrast to Aurélie Picard's exotic and romantic marriage to Ahmed al-Tijānī, these unions occurred between modest characters. Despite this banality, statistical and legal accounts nonetheless presented them as exceptions to the endogamy of European settlement, marriage, and law.

Invalid Acts

Unaddressed by formal legislation, instances of conflicting marriage codes continued to come before French courts. Among them was the case of a twenty-six-year-old Corsican-born woman, Émilie Danési, who married an Algerian Muslim in 1878. It stands out because the litigant who brought the case to trial was not a disgruntled family member, but the state itself, acting in the name of the public order of French law.

At issue was the legitimacy of Danési's "Muslim law" marriage to Ismaël ben Boursali following her sworn "abjuration" of Christianity and embrace of Islam before the Hanefi qadi of Algiers. Using her newly adopted name, Mimi bent Abdallah registered her marriage contract with Boursali on August 25, 1878. The public prosecutor, Jean Baptiste Fourcade, brought the case before the Muslim Chamber of the Appeals Court of Algiers in order to annul both acts. He declared that her conversion and marriage were "contrary to public order" and "illegal assaults on the personal status of citizens."[71] So grave was the offense that they had to be invalidated. The state stepped in to protect the French personal status that she embodied, overruling her stated wishes to the contrary.[72]

As with the Picard marriage, the Muslim Chamber threw the case out on the basis of jurisdiction. Despite Danési's religious conversion, her French nationality and citizenship required her to appear before a French civil court, rather than the forum that had been set aside to hear Muslim law cases and litigants. The case passed to the Tribunal of First Instance. It too denied its competency to judge Danési's conversion, "which only had the effect of changing her religion and not her nationality." The court decided that it had no jurisdiction over a purely "religious" act: "from no point of view can courts interfere with or recognize an act of this nature, which depends solely on the conscience of those who submit to

---

71. Proc. Gén. v. Boursali et Émilie Danési, Cour d'appel d'Alger–Ch. Musulm. (October 28, 1878), *BJA* 3, no. 50 (January 16, 1879): 24–29.

72. On "public order" as a mechanism of state sovereignty and governmentality see Agrama, *Questioning Secularism*; Mahmood, *Religious Difference in a Secular Age*.

it."[73] As a question of individual conscience, her conversion was beyond the consideration of civil law.

The marriage act was, however, fully in the domain of secular French law and hence subject to public concern and policing. Danési's marriage act was found to be "radically null and void" because "the personal status reserved for Muslim *indigènes* of Algeria can never apply to a person who does not have the quality of *indigène*."[74] Extending beyond the inner life of conscience, marriage altered legal personality, especially for women. Matters of spirit were on one side, personal law on the other. The court's decision affirmed a principle that soon became axiomatic: that French and "European" women could never assume Muslim law status, even by marriage. As the adamantly secular colonial jurist Émile Larcher explained in the case of foreign women, "A European woman, in marrying a Muslim *indigène*, becomes, not an *indigène*, but a French citizen: her personal status is governed by French law, not Muslim law."[75] Up until 1927, the Civil Code subordinated married women to their husbands' "foreign" law. In Algeria, by contrast, a woman's civil law status took precedence over that of her Muslim husband, even as she acquired "his" French nationality in the marriage. She thus personified the French Civil Code's superiority. This "protective" gesture was also disciplinary. In the Danési case, it set the terms according to which a Corsican migrant could marry a Muslim man.

The Appeals Court of Algiers occasionally went to extraordinarily lengths to secure the Civil Code's precedence in marriage and filiation. The elaborate arguments and legal fictions used to do so could be seen, for example, in a 1903 case about the nationality of two orphaned minor children, Belkacem and Khadidja. They were the son and daughter of Mustapha ben Mohamed Mazouni and a Spanish woman, Teresa Aragonès, who had converted to Islam and married Mazouni "in conformity with Muslim practice [*habitudes*]."[76] As in the Danési case, their marriage was invalid under French civil law. This became an issue after their death, when a creditor disputed the right of Larbi Fekar to act as the children's guardian. Fekar, who had married Khadidja in 1902, had an affective,

---

73. Min. Pub. v. Émilie Danési et Ismael ben Mohamed Boursali, Tribunal d'Alger (January 4, 1879), *BJA* 3, no. 50 (January 16, 1879): 31.

74. Min. Pub. v. Émilie Danési, *BJA* 3, no. 50 (January 16, 1879): 32. The public prosecutor who pleaded the case, M. Valette, would subsequently argue in favor of the abolition of Muslim personal status *tout court*: Valette, *Un projet de loi sur la réorganisation de l'Algérie*.

75. Larcher, "Des effets du mariage d'une femme indigène," 212n11. For a strong statement of Larcher's commitment to the "secularization" of Algerian law see "Des effets juridiques du changement de religion." Reprinted in *RA*, 1910.

76. Larbi Fekkar (époux) v. Onedieu, Cour d'appel d'Alger (February 13, 1903), *RA*, 1904, pt. 2, 145.

financial, and ideological investment in the case.[77] After training at the *école normale* of Bouzaréah, he taught in Oran and founded a short-lived dual-language newspaper, *El Misbah*, which advocated for Algerian assimilation.[78]

While the French creditor claimed that the children's status was Muslim, the court determined that Belkacem and Khadidja were not, despite their mother's conversion and "Muslim" marriage. Because Teresa Aragonès was of European origin, her legal status, and hence that of her children, had to be French. As the decision explained, "a foreign woman who marries a French man follows the condition of her husband; a European woman who marries an *indigène algérien*, who is therefore French, becomes a French woman." In other words, "because she cannot acquire Muslim personal status, she thus assumes French personal status." Aragonès's religious conversion was irrelevant, because, as previous cases had made clear, "religious acts could not have civil effects."[79] But how could the court recognize the "Muslim marriage" of Teresa and Mustapha, since it was not performed before French civil officials and was hence void?

It did so by granting the marriage a "putative" status. Using this legal fiction, which had its origins in canon law, the court treated their "Muslim marriage" *as if* it were valid, because they had acted in good faith. Its putative effect did not make Teresa "Muslim," but it did retrospectively make her French for the purposes of determining her children's nationality. (The 1901 death registry listed her own nationality as Spanish.)[80] While bracketing her religion, the court decided on her conjugal good faith. Going further, it determined that, because a French mother's illegitimate children had French nationality and citizenship, the same should hold for Belkacem and Khadidja, "even if they practice Islam."[81] According to the court, illegitimate children should not be given better treatment (i.e., French status) than Belkacem and Khadidja, whose parents' marriage had been in "good faith."

In the *Revue algérienne et tunisienne de jurisprudence*, a Paris-based specialist in private international law, Armand Lainé, denounced the judges' ruling for following their "intimate sentiments" about the superiority of French legal status. While granting Aragonès's French nationality, Lainé disputed the judges' claim that her children should be granted the retrospective civil status of their mother. In Lainé's interpretation, because these children's father was indeed known, the patriarchal assumptions of *jus sanguinis* prevailed, making them "Muslim."[82]

77. Fakkar, Marriage, Oran, 1902, ANOM État Civil, Algérie.
78. Ihaddaden, *Histoire de la presse indigène*, 169. And Hamet, *Les Musulmans français*, 206.
79. Fekkar v. Onedieu, *RA*, 1904, pt. 2, 146.
80. Aragonès, Teresa, Death, Oran, 1901, ANOM État Civil, Algérie.
81. Fekkar v. Onedieu, *RA*, 1904, pt. 2, 147.
82. Lainé, note, Fekkar v. Onedieu, *RA*, 1904, pt. 2, 142.

By making Belkacem and Khadidja French, the court overturned cherished assumptions and established principles that linked legitimacy, personal status, and patriarchy.[83] For the next several decades, jurists equivocated on this point, wary as they were of how the Fekar case undermined "the idea of the man's predominance in the domestic group."[84] As Lainé's note hinted, the judges' thinking may have been clouded by sentiment in claiming the children as *French* even though their father was a Muslim *indigène* and their mother a Spanish convert to Islam. These fine legal points were perhaps ancillary to the financial considerations motivating Larbi and Khadidja Fekar to bring their appeal, but they nonetheless resonated with the assimilationist program of Fekar's journal. According to the decision, the "Muslim" children were legally French. This finding nonetheless upheld an embodied distinction between "European" and "Muslim" in the deceased person of Aragonès in order to confer that condition onto her children.

Teresa Aragonès's "Frenchness" was an elaborate retroactive legal fiction. While attempting to fix her legal identity and that of her children, the decision demonstrates how unstable the categories of "Muslim" and "French" could be. As contemporary commentators noted, it was no small irony that a canon law carryover, enshrined in articles 201 and 202 of the Civil Code, could grant legitimacy to Muslim marriages. For Portalis, the secularized canonical principle of "putative marriage" tempered the potential excesses of "positive law" by aligning it with natural law. As he explained, this protection affirmed a "natural principle" that "the essence of marriage consists in the faith that spouses give one another."[85] By granting legal effects to an invalid contract, putative marriage preserved conjugal morality in secular civil law.

The flexibility of putativity was particularly useful in Algeria, with its overlapping legal codes and mobile multinational population. It served to protect unsuspecting partners who might be unaware that those with French or "European" civil status could marry only before a French registrar. In some cases, it was even used to grant legal effects to a Muslim divorce. As the jurist Larcher wryly commented in his account of the case, "The doctors of the canon, in constructing the theory of putative marriage, would never have guessed that it would be used to facilitate divorce!"[86]

---

83. This scenario reverses the situations of concubinage and the resulting question of the *métis* in Indochina; see Saada, *Empire's Children.*

84. Meylan, *Les mariages mixtes en Afrique du Nord*, 185–86.

85. Portalis, *Discours, rapports et travaux*, 38. See also Pilastre, *Du mariage putatif*; Couchené, *Du mariage putatif et de ses effets.*

86. Ben Daoud v. Dame Ben Daoud, Cour d'appel d'Alger (November 2, 1905), *RA*, 1906, pt. 2, 70.

By offering creative solutions to Algerian conflicts of law, putativity was also manipulated by canny litigants. For example, in 1874, the court granted putative status to a "Muslim" marriage between Youssef ben Haffiz and Meriem bent Moulaï, a Spanish woman convert. In the case, bent Moulaï sought to claim inheritance for herself and her son Boumedien after her husband's death. Other members of the Haffiz family, including an uncle and a half brother, wanted to disqualify her—and her marriage—because of her "European" status. In order to guarantee her "Muslim" inheritance rights the court granted her marriage putative status.[87]

That finding opened a new terrain of legal dispute between Boumedien Haffiz and his children. After marrying a fifteen-year-old Spanish woman, Jeanne Caroline Mascaro, Boumedien had three daughters (Marie Charlotte, Jeanne Caroline, and Henriette Mériem) in the town of Mustapha.[88] Several years later, the family moved to Morocco. Upon Mascaro's death, the daughters, who had all married "Europeans," wanted their mother's inheritance to be settled by French law, which presumed the community of property. They claimed that because Haffiz was French, albeit an *indigène*, and because his marriage had been recorded in the "European" registry, the Civil Code's inheritance rules should apply. Haffiz, by contrast, claimed the separation of marital property under Muslim law. Citing the 1874 decision regarding his mother's putative marriage, he sought to claim Muslim legal status for himself.

The tribunal in Casablanca agreed with him. As a graduate of the École d'Alger in Pharmacy who had been interviewed by the 1892 Senatorial Commission, Haffiz no doubt had a firm sense of the procedures and legal arguments that would hold sway before newly appointed French judges in Morocco.[89] The Moroccan court found that "the European woman who marries a Muslim *indigène* should follow the condition of her husband."[90] The family's prior history of overlaying inheritance disputes with contests over personal status surely informed the case, as did the new Moroccan protectorate's structure of Muslim tribunals, which were reserved exclusively for Moroccans.

Algerian colonial jurists disputed their Moroccan colleagues' judgment. Jurist Émile Larcher penned a response to the case in what had now become

---

87. Ismael ben Haffiz et autres v. Veuve Youssef ben Haffiz, Cour d'appel d'Alger–Ch. Musulm (April 14, 1874), in Estoublon, *Jurisprudence algérienne*, vol. 4 (1874): 26–29.

88. Haffiz, Boumedien Youssef, and Macaro, Jeanne Caroline, Marriage, Mustapha, 1883. The registry mentions Mascaro's nationality but does not specify Haffiz's status. Also, Birth, Mustapha, 1884; 1886; 1897, ANOM État Civil, Algérie.

89. Ageron, *Les Algériens musulmans*, 1:520n4.

90. Époux Fulla et autres v. Hafiz, Tribunal de Casablanca (April 27, 1914), *RA*, 1916, pt. 2, 90.

the *Revue algérienne, tunisienne, et marocaine de jurisprudence*, which he edited. The new Moroccan tribunal seemed unaware of the policy established in the Picard/Tijānī case and Gueydon's subsequent circular on "mixed marriage." It broke as well with the jurisprudence in the Danési and Fekar cases. Reiterating the crucial distinction between Algerian "Muslim personal status" and nationality, Larcher aimed to set the colonial record straight. As he explained, in marrying Boumedien, Jeanne Mascaro became French, without ever becoming "Muslim." To underscore this point, Larcher noted that Mascaro was also *Christian*. His explanation thus elided religion, ethnicity, and nationality despite his best effort to uphold legal distinctions between them: "As a Christian, she at no point became Muslim. Indeed, no more than she became an *indigène*." The trial's resolution was, he urged, "completely inaccurate." In sum, it was "a complete mistake to apply Muslim law to a French women, who is of European origin, not a Muslim."[91] The assumption underlying this assertion was that Muslimness was incompatible with being Christian—and hence also with being French.

By correcting jurisprudence in cases such as this, the *Revue algérienne* served both a practical and ideological role. As editor, Larcher viewed juridical commentary as a crucial colonial legal supplement, which worked "to reconstruct an edifice whose plan was never drawn up or to erect a monument whose own architect has not yet traced its principal lines."[92] The architecture was, in this sense, an always unfinished fantasmatic projection. As jurists sought to fill in gaps in order to make it whole, new problems and questions arose, as the story of the Haffiz family's "putative marriage" makes clear.

The question of how to manage mixed marriage and conflicts of law thus remained a persistent spur to these jurists' legal imaginations. In numerous tracts and dissertations, they criticized the effects of mixed marriage on "French" or "European" women and considered how a husband's "naturalization" might impact his Muslim wife. Their questions proliferated: Should a wife be assumed to consent to his decision, or should she be allowed to maintain her "Muslim status"? What should be privileged, the "unity of law" within the family or the wife's individual will? Imagining the Muslim wife's legal position in these situations allowed jurists to ponder the parameters of Algerians' naturalization and implicitly the relationship between "French" and "Muslim" law.

---

91. Note Larcher, Fulla v. Hafiz, *RA*, 1916, pt. 2, 92.
92. Larcher, "L'université d'Alger," 21; Renucci, "La Revue algérienne, tunisienne et marocaine."

Naturalization and Conjugal Conflicts of Law

In 1883, a former military translator and future "Young Algerian," Ahmed ben Brihmat, took French citizenship in the midst of a dispute with his wife, Fifi bent Hamoud ben Turkia. By changing legal status, he wanted to move their trial from the Muslim judiciary to a French court. Brihmat feared that he would not get a fair hearing before his father-in-law, the Maliki qadi in Algiers. Would his new citizenship force his wife to give up the protections afforded her by Muslim law? Or would he remain bound by Muslim law for conjugal matters despite his altered status? For the minster of justice, who weighed in on the case, "the solution concerns the situation of Algerians to the greatest extent [*au plus haut point*]." The Cour de cassation concurred, deciding that Brihmat, as a citizen, should no longer appear before a Muslim judge.[93]

The high court's ruling did not explicitly address the subsequent effect of Brihmat's naturalization on his wife. According to the commentary offered by Jules Jacquey, a member of the Law Faculty of Algiers, the question distilled "the conflicts between the French law applicable to *indigènes* who are French citizens and the Muslim law applicable to *indigènes* who are not French citizens."[94] Of course, those *indigènes* who became French citizens were no longer legally *indigène*. Jacquey's comment clearly indicates semantic slippages in the term. In his view, allowing Brihmat's naturalization to have a retroactive effect on the couple's marriage was a violation of the Civil Code. The court's finding and Jacquey's commentary demonstrate how the individualized model of naturalization adopted by the *sénatus-consulte* of 1865 had a confusing effect on the legal status of families. Governor-General Tirman sought to address the issue in a circular to Algerian prefects in 1884. Following instructions from the justice minister, he announced that "the personal status of native Muslim women should follow necessarily that of their husbands."[95] According to this directive, wives were to be automatically naturalized along with their husbands, but courts did not always follow the instruction. Jurists, in turn, hypothesized about resulting conjugal conflicts of law and how to resolve them.

These discussions coincided with a legislative reform in the 1880s that gave renewed scrutiny to the links between marriage, filiation, and nationality. In the

---

93. Fifi bent Hamoud ben Turkia v. Ahmed ben Brihmat, Cour de cassation (June 15, 1885), *RA*, 1885, pt. 2, 309.

94. Note Jacquey *RA*, 1885, pt. 2, 310. See also Jacquey, *De l'application des lois françaises*.

95. "Circulaire relative à la naturalisation des femmes indigènes algériennes dont les maris indigènes sollicitent la naturalisation française," June 24, 1884, in Estoublon and Lefébure, *Code de l'Algérie*, 1:638.

run-up to the adoption of a new nationality law in 1889, jurists and politicians debated whether a husband's naturalization should be purely personal or have "collective" effects on his family. While eager to promote "the unity of law" within the family, representatives wondered whether the "collective" principle violated wives' and adult children's consent. In 1884, the Conseil d'État endorsed the "collective" solution. In his report before the Senate on behalf of the Conseil in 1886, Camille Sée thus advocated for "unity within the family." In his view, "the woman who mixes her fate with that of her husband has to follow the nationality of her husband."[96] In debates surrounding nationality law reform, this position, which evidently negated married women's independent will, faced some resistance. In his report to the Chamber in 1887, Deputy Antonin Dubost (Isère) held that "it would be an exaggeration of the rights of marital power and paternal power to declare that the naturalization of a husband and father should automatically naturalize a wife and adult children."[97] In the law's final version in 1889, wives were granted autonomy, while minor children were naturalized alongside their fathers. Wives had the option to change their status at the same time as their husbands, but were not forced to do so.[98] As André Weiss explained in his commentary, "The natural submission of a wife to her husband does not go so far as to completely annihilate her will."[99] Or, at least that was the assumption with respect to French women and foreign women who might become French.

By naturalizing thousands of "European" foreigners, this 1889 nationality law had a dramatic effect on the Algerian population. Increasing the size of the French national population and "disaggregating" communities of foreign settlers, it applied a new logic of *jus soli* to children born in Algeria to foreign parents.[100] Algerians with Muslim personal status, as French subjects rather than foreign nationals, were excluded from the law's application. As a result, the effect of a Muslim husband's "naturalization" on his wife and children continued to be debated in juridical treatises and occasionally settled in court. Would jurists assume or annihilate the Muslim woman's will?

---

96. Rapport Camille Sée, Rapport, *JO*, Sénat, November 13, 1886, 1183. See also Gruffy, *De l'unité de nationalité dans la famille*, 33–34; Delecaille, *De la naturalisation en droit civil*, 156–57.

97. *JO*, Doc. Parl., Chambre, annexe 2083, November 7, 1887. See Gruffy, *De l'unité de nationalité dans la famille*, 77. For an early discussion that advocated for the unity of legislation in the family see Foelix, "Des effets de la naturalisation."

98. Le Sueur and Dreyfus, *La nationalité (droit interne)*, 85.

99. A. Weiss, *Manuel de droit international privé*, 46. See also Bickart, *De la naturalisation*, 111–17.

100. Ageron, *Les Algériens musulmans*, 1:349; Kateb, *Européens, "indigènes" et juifs*, 188. Many contemporaries remained skeptical of its ability to effectively convert "foreigner" into French; see Olier, "Les résultats de la législation sur la nationalité en Algérie."

Louis Hamel, a bureaucrat in the governor-general's office, devoted several long articles in the *Revue algérienne* to the question of how Algerians' naturalization impacted their own legal status and that of their families.[101] He imagined a host of scenarios in which conflicts might arise. What should happen when an already married man was naturalized, but his wife was not? What would happen to children who had already been born? Those who were not yet born? These hypotheses, taken up by subsequent jurists, were occasions to showcase the supposedly profound differences between French and Muslim law.

Basing his argument on an analogy with the 1889 law, Hamel claimed that Algerian naturalization should remain purely individual. Disputing the positions adopted by the minister of justice and the Conseil d'État, he held that "nothing in Muslim legislation nor in French legislation allows us to pretend that the naturalization obtained by a native husband should be imposed for good or for bad on the wife." He notably questioned whether she should be forced to give up the advantages that Muslim law held for her when, "exceptionally, French law is less liberal toward the married woman than Muslim law." He thus argued forcefully in favor of maintaining Muslim law for wives rather than rendering them "incapacitated like the married woman in French law."[102] The specialist in international private law André Weiss agreed. He disputed presumptions that the "*femme indigène*" lives "in the strictest dependence on her husband and can have no other will but his."[103] In his view, wives and children would retain their Muslim law—and its clear advantages—when a husband became a full citizen.

Other jurists disagreed, however, claiming that the persistence of two different statutes within a marriage represented "a triumph of Muslim law" and hence "an abdication of our sovereignty."[104] In his thesis on Algerian conflicts of law, Léon Dunoyer proclaimed that it was "inadmissible that preeminence does not belong to French law. Because the conciliation between the two laws is impossible, because the two spouses and their family must be ruled by one and the same law, the wife of the naturalized Muslim and the children born of that marriage before naturalization should be treated, from that day on, as truly French, entirely submitted to French legislation."[105] In Dunoyer's assimilationist program, Algerian conflicts of law were transitory, "an anomaly destined to disappear," unlike international ones, which represented durable conflicts between

101. Hamel, "De la naturalisation des indigènes musulmans" (1886).
102. Hamel, "De la naturalisation des indigènes musulmans" (1890), 24–25.
103. A. Weiss, *Traité théorique et pratique de droit international privé*, 1:400.
104. Dunoyer, *Étude sur le conflit des lois special à l'Algérie*, 207.
105. Ibid., 208.

sovereign states.[106] By endorsing the "unity of legislation" in the Algerian family, he promoted the unity of Algerian legislation *tout court*. Following this argument, Emmanuel Besson, a government tax official, also insisted on the "unity of legislation." He dismissed the significance of Muslim women's relatively advantageous marital property regime, insisting instead that "the Muslim woman does not have, in principle, free disposal of her person."[107] Because Muslim personal status was an exception to French territorial law, he believed it "natural that, in this conflict, French law should have the last word."[108]

Other advocates of the "collective" solution explicitly linked French legal sovereignty to patriarchy. In his thesis, Albert Hugues firmly rejected Hamel and Weiss's "individualist" model, refusing to allow a husband's naturalization to become "a source of infinite conflicts and tensions, whose existence could only hurt the authority of the husband and father and the good order of the familial association."[109] In his view, the "supreme divergences" between Muslim and French law "in particular in matters of family status" made the risk of conflict particularly great. It was "in the interest of French domination" to limit this cause of "serious and frequent difficulties."[110] Larcher adopted a similar position. In his *Traité élémentaire de legislation algérienne*, first published in 1903, and in subsequent critical commentaries, Larcher embraced the patriarchal principle, declaring that "a single law is necessary: that of the head of the family imposes itself, which is to say French law."[111] There is evident irony in these pronouncements that criticized Muslim legal patriarchy, from the right to polygamy to forced marriage, in order to defend *French* legal patriarchy. These advocates had no qualms defending the erasure of the Muslim wife's legal personhood, and indeed her distinct property rights, in order to uphold the patriarchal "unity" of French law.

These theoretical discussions had a broader political context: a series of proposals in the late 1880s and 1890s to extend citizenship rights to Algerians in exchange for their military conscription. Set forth by leftist deputies, these were among the first propositions to offer Muslims political rights, while maintaining their personal status. Motivated in some cases by antisemitism, authors drew parallels with the "collective naturalization" of Jews, who they claimed were part of the same "family." In contrast to the Crémieux Decree, their proposals

---

106. Ibid., 232.
107. Besson, *La législation civile de l'Algérie*, 103.
108. Ibid., 79.
109. Hugues, *La nationalité française chez les musulmans de l'Algérie*, 179.
110. Ibid., 186.
111. Larcher, *Traité élémentaire* (1903), 2:191.

would maintain Algerians' Muslim and customary "family law." Deputies Henri Michelin (Seine) and Alfred Gaulier (Seine) explained in their project how "the rules of the Civil Code notably regarding marriage and the organization of the family cannot be imposed on Muslims."[112] While approved by a commission in 1888, the plan was not pursued. Subsequent proposals for extending political rights to Algerians over the next decade made analogous arguments.[113] When Michelin and Deputy Gustave Paul Cluseret (Var) resurrected the proposal in 1897, they explicitly dismissed the significance of divorce and polygamy as obstacles to Algerians' citizenship.[114]

Their argument drew on the pamphlet by the assimilationist doctor Taïeb Ould Morsly, a member of the Municipal Council of Constantine, who endorsed Senator Isaac's proposal to extend political rights to Algerians while maintaining their personal status. In his *Contribution à la question indigène en Algérie*, Morsly argued that what stood in the way of assimilation was systematic property seizure, heavy taxation, restricted Muslim law jurisdiction, and the *indigénat*, not "polygamy and divorce, seen for all ages, as the greatest abominations of the Muslim religion." Morsly professed to personally admire "single households" (*ménages uniques*), but also explained the historical and practical reasons for which the Qur'an authorized polygamy. He also highlighted the glaring double standard of French sexual morality, which banned polygamy but authorized men's extra-conjugal sex. In his view, legal polygamy was more ethical than its "hidden" French counterpart: "On careful reflection, because the flesh is weak, is it not better to have two legitimate wives than to have one legal ménage and two or three irregular ones? The only difference between the avowed polygamy of Muslims and the hidden polygamy of others is the legality of one and the illegality of the other."[115] For Michelin and Cluseret, this passage clarified why the conferral of political rights (and the duty of military conscription) should not require the abolition of the "personality of laws."

---

112. Michelin and Gaulier, "Proposition de loi ayant pour objet de conférer les droits de citoyens français aux musulmans indigènes des départements algériens," *JO*, Doc. Parl., Chambre, annexe 1846, June 16, 1887, 197.

113. Proposition Albert Martineau, "Proposition de loi portant naturalisation progressive des indigènes de l'Algérie," *JO*, Doc. Parl., Chambre, annexe 857, July 27, 1890, 1625; Senator Isaac, "Proposition de loi portant modification du système de représentation des indigènes algériens," *JO*, Sénat, annexe 134, April 4, 1893; Gaston Bazile, "Proposition de loi portant naturalisation des indigènes anciens militaires," *JO*, Sénat, annexe 1667, December 11, 1895.

114. Henri Michelin and Gustave Paul Cluseret, "Proposition de loi ayant pour objet de conférer les droits de citoyen français aux musulmans indigènes des départements algériens," *JO*, Doc. Parl., Chambre, annexe 2203, January 15, 1897, 135.

115. Morsly, *Contribution à la question indigène*, 59.

Colonial jurists and politicians met these propositions with nearly uniform resistance, drawing on discussions of mixed marriage to make their case. The threatening prospect of political inclusion found expression in anxieties over the sexual degradation and defilement of citizenship by Muslim status. In direct reaction to the Michelin and Gaulier proposal, the jurist Besson proclaimed: "We cannot accept the idea that a Frenchman, based on the sole fact that he is Arab or Kabyle, could legally marry four wives or sell his prepubescent girl. To do so would really debase [avilir] the title of French citizen."[116] In his 1894 report on the Algerian budget, Deputy Pourquéry de Boisserin (Vaucluse) cited Besson to argue against Algerians' political representation at either the parliamentary or local level. He, too, made family-law conflict the principal stumbling block, arguing that Algerians "want to maintain their personal status, especially with respect to the constitution of the family from the point of view of matrimony and inheritance." While Michelin and Gaulier claimed that the rarity of polygamy and the 1884 French legalization of divorce had reduced the prospect of such conflicts, Pourquéry insisted on the sexual difference of Muslim personal status. In his view, the "exorbitant" right of repudiation meant that their "monogamy . . . has more than a point in common with polygamy."[117]

Debates about Algerians' accession to local representation likewise cast Algerian naturalization as a sexual rather than as a political problem. The Conseil supérieur resisted Ali Cherif's proposal to allow selected "indigènes serviteurs," who either worked in government or served in the military, to vote in local elections. J.-F. Bouvagnet urged that, to gain political representation, they had to "accept our responsibilities, which is to say that they come entirely toward us, in getting naturalized, and in bending themselves in this way to the exigencies entailed by the quality of Frenchness [les exigences entraînées par la qualité de Français]."[118] In these and other statements, consent to the sexual discipline of citizenship became a precondition of political participation.[119] Such discussions reified personal status as a distinct legal object and sexual stumbling block to political equality. Algerian men's attachment to Muslim personal law was imagined as the expression of their stubborn bodies, not their political wills.

Conscription, not polygamy, was a significant reason why Algerian men (alongside European settlers) might resist naturalization, as a 1902 case heard

---

116. Besson, La législation civile de l'Algérie, 340.
117. Pourquéry de Boisserin, Rapport du Budget 1895, JO, Chambre, Doc. Parl., July 28, 1894, annexe 906, 624.
118. Conseil supérieur de Gouvernement, Procès-Verbaux, January 1897, 578.
119. On republican sexual discipline see Surkis, Sexing the Citizen.

by the Cour de cassation in 1904 made clear. In this dispute, the child of a mixed marriage, Sekfali Braham ben Tahar, appealed a 1902 decision that asserted his citizenship and eligibility for conscription.[120] While Sekfali's parents were both Algerian, his legal status was mixed, because his father had been naturalized in 1869, while his mother had remained "Muslim." Born in 1870, ben Tahar claimed that he was not a full citizen and hence ineligible for military service. In response to the case, the high court clarified the effects of naturalization on wives as well as sons. Following the "individualist" thesis, it found that "the effects of the admission solicited by the husband alone do not extend to the wife." To protect patriarchal filiation (and Tahar's military obligation), the court nonetheless held that the child would "follow the condition of the father."[121] This decision paradoxically made a man into a full citizen against his will, while claiming to protect the wife's consent. In its wake, the governor-general addressed a circular to prefects affirming that "the Muslim wife does not benefit from naturalization," although the option was extended to them.[122] With the adoption of this individualized model, conflicts of law within families would inevitably persist.

Meanwhile, subsequent debates about conscription and political reform continued to reify and corporealize personal status. In response to ongoing population concerns and mounting international tensions, military policy makers proposed turning to Algerian recruitment in order to raise troop levels, especially once a 1905 law reduced citizens' military service from three years to two. These discussions were haunted by the French military's perceived decline in manpower and by questions of how conscription related to citizenship. The proposals, especially one by Minister of War Adolphe Messimy, provoked considerable resistance. Deputies from Algeria's departments fiercely opposed the recruitment of "Muslim" Algerians, because they worried that it would reopen the question of naturalization and political rights.[123]

"Young Algerian" members of the French educated elite and their metropolitan sympathizers grasped this as an opportune moment in which to pursue reform. One liberal journal, the *Revue indigène*, published legal opinions on the question of extending political rights to Algerians while preserving their "personal status." While several prominent international jurists endorsed the measure, the specialist of colonial law Arthur Girault rejected it, citing the dangers of

---

120. Sekfali Tahar v. Préfet de Constantine, Cour d'Alger (May 13, 1902), *RA*, 1905, pt. 2, 133.

121. Sekfali Braham ben Tahar v. l'État, Cour de cassation (October 26, 1904), *RA*, 1904, pt. 2, 12.

122. "Circulaire du Gouverneur Général relative à la naturalisation des femmes musulmanes," December 14, 1904, in Estoublon and Lefébure, *Code de l'Algérie*, 2:109.

123. Ageron, *Les Algériens musulmans*, 2:1056–78.

family law conflict and the disruption of conjugal unity, among other concerns. Referencing Larcher, whose assimilationist vision he shared, Girault explained: "The naturalized *indigène* is not an isolated being without relations to those surrounding him [*ses semblables*]. He doubtless has a family. What will become of his wife and his children? If his wife and children remain subjects as before, the unity of the family will be ruptured. If one decides that the wife and children should follow the head of the family's condition, it will confer French nationality on persons who are in no way prepared for it and who it does not fit in any way."[124] In order to avoid such conflict, Girault wanted to limit naturalization, by making it a response to individual demands, rather than a blanket extension. Rather than giving citizenship away, he thought that the French should "play hard-to-get" (*faisant les difficiles*). Imagining French citizenship as an object of desire, he proclaimed that "whoever wants to please must know how to use *coquetterie*."[125] In this fantasy, the eroticized body of French citizenship would seduce Muslim men to give up their attachment to personal status. It was a potentially risky strategy, however. Both during and after the First World War, colonial and military officials worried that relations between North Africans and French women would become much less exceptional.[126] Those unions and their legal effects would hence remain a persistent object of official concern.

Despite their apparent statistical insignificance, cases of mixed marriage incited considerable colonial juridical inquiry as synedoches of the conflict between a secular Civil Code and Algerian Muslim law. Present from the outset of colonization, these questions became more pointed with the condensation of Muslim personal status as a legal shorthand for family, sex, and confessional sentiment. Cleaved from a universal and universalizable French law of property transaction, Muslim personal status (including Kabyle customary law) signified the particularized "quality" of the *indigène* and his patriarchal sexual rights. Matrimony was its ground (i.e., "marriage, divorce, and inheritance" defined its jurisdiction) and its limit, since indigenous status was not transferable by marriage. In court decisions, legislative reports, and legal treatises, French jurists and politicians construed Muslim religiosity, legality, and kinship as intertwined and intimately bound to the embodied Muslim person.

---

124. "La naturalisation des musulmans dans leur statut: Opinion de M. Arthur Giraud [*sic*]," *La Revue indigène* 6 (July–August 1911): 427.

125. Ibid., 428. On Girault see El Mechat, "Sur les *Principes de colonisation* d'Arthur Girault (1895)"; Saada, "Penser le fait colonial."

126. Lapradelle and Morand, "Du mariage en France des marocains et des indigènes musulmans d'Algérie."

This story resonates with other accounts of deep social ambivalence about ethno-religious mixing in colonial societies. In focusing on juridical developments, we see how the secular status and sovereignty of French civil law gave form to a corporealized religio-legal personhood for Muslims and implicitly for French and European subjects as well. While forum-shopping litigants could and did manipulate these unstable categories, the elaboration of embodied differences between French civil and Muslim law nonetheless had persistently discriminatory political and social effects.

From the outset of colonization, mixed marriages remained legally protected by principles of religious freedom. Conversion, as a pure matter of private conscience, was beyond the domain of secular law. But the legal effects of mixed marriage were a subject of public concern. At a crucial moment of political and legal transition in the 1870s, the cases of Aurélie Picard and Émilie Danési reveal how this secular logic, dividing private conscience from public law, outlined the contours not only of Muslim persons, but that of "French" and "European" persons as well. Indeed, protecting the integrity of *French* personal status from the implicitly sexual incursions of Muslim law such as repudiation and polygamy became a crucial question of "public order" and hence of the sovereignty of French civil law. Inverting the conjugal logic of legal unity that governed international law, French women's civil status took precedence over their husbands' Muslim status. French woman became bearers of abstract claims about French law's sovereign dignity, while Muslim men's legal status was particularized. In a revealing twist on the paradoxes of postrevolutionary French citizenship, women embodied the universality of French personal status.[127]

It is not the least irony of the Danési story that the court intervened in order to annul her consensual marriage. As we saw in chapter 4, jurists invoked "public order" to protect Muslim women's consensual conjugality in cases of the father's right to force their marriage (*djebr*). In trials of French and European women, by contrast, the state dismissed women's consent (and conscience) in order to uphold the integrity of French law. This mixed-marriage jurisprudence corporealized both Muslim *and* French personal status, endowing them with embodied meaning and material effects.

---

127. J. W. Scott, *Only Paradoxes*.

7

THE SEXUAL POLITICS OF LEGAL REFORM

Legal treatments of mixed marriage created a corporeal distinction between secular civil law and Muslim personal status. Muslim law was, nonetheless, also French and had been since 1834. The ambivalent location of Muslim law within the body of French law continued to raise pointed questions about Algerians' standing as civil and political subjects. By the beginning of the twentieth century, these quandaries prompted new efforts at reform. Colonial jurists spearheaded a project to codify Muslim law in 1905, while young Algerian intellectuals and their metropolitan allies sought, beginning in 1908, to extend political rights to Algerian men in exchange for military service. In this chapter, I analyze how ideas about Muslim law's sexual difference from the Civil Code played a central role in these debates. The discussions turned around concerns that we have traced throughout this book: forced marriage and polygamy. They illuminate how men's sexual rights and imagined sexual pleasures continued to shape the idea and practice of Algerian colonial law into the twentieth century.

Previous chapters have shown how fantasies of Muslim pleasure structured the colonial relationship between French and Muslim law. Colonial clichés of child marriage and polygamy condensed imagined ideas of Muslim men's excessive rights. Cast as foreign privileges that were intolerable in French civil law, these clichés evoked both fascination and repulsion. They worked in tandem at the turn of the century to simultaneously stimulate and stymie legal reform.

From the perspective of colonial jurists, Muslim men's sexually different personal status explained and sustained their political and social exclusion. I suggest that this inside/outside construction of Muslim law in French law had a related psychic dimension. It relied on a fantasy of Muslim men's access to forms of sexual pleasure that were denied to French male citizens. Jurists and politicians displayed ambivalence toward this excluded excess. In their accounts, legal and sexual discipline were constitutive of the superiority—and masculinity—of French citizenship and law. Their statements and writing nonetheless indicate how they simultaneously rejected and coveted the sexual rights that they attributed to Muslim men.

This apparently contradictory attitude can be illuminated by Lacanian accounts of the psychic effects of social law. These suggest how the seemingly universal structures of law ("the Symbolic") are never fully universal or fixed: they always produce threatening residues that do not conform to hegemonic prescriptions. Apparently unrecognizable, these "extimate" transgressive remainders are at once feared and desired, foreign and familiar, as an unruly surplus that is simultaneously inside and outside the legal subject. Extimacy, as Jacques-Alain Miller notes, is thus "not the contrary of intimacy." It instead describes how "the intimate is Other—like a foreign body, a parasite."[1] This "alien" kernel remains paradoxically fundamental, because, as Mladen Dolar explains, "this non-integration is constitutive for the subject, although it may appear as its limit, reduction, or failure."[2] Understanding the sexual privileges of Muslim men's personal status as extimate projections helps to explain how they became so affectively as well as politically charged.

In protracted discussions of Algerians' legal and political status, journalists, politicians, and magistrates fixated on sex, cynically deploying stereotypes to restrict Algerian Muslims' legal and political rights. I elucidate why these charges were so tenacious and effective. I suggest how, taking displaced form, disavowed desires and pleasures expressed themselves through such fascination with Algerian men's imagined difference and deviant pleasure. As Miller suggests, extimate jealousy animates such racist fantasies, including resentment of "our Islamic neighbor" that is "founded on what one imagines about the Other's *jouissance* [enjoyment]."[3] Such hostility evidently fueled politicians' charges that Muslim men were inapt to exercise citizens' rights. A 1914 speech made by Paul Cuttoli, a deputy from Constantine, displays the rhetorical and affective excess underlying such arguments. Citing jurist Émile Larcher, Cuttoli insisted that Algerians' degraded bodies and morals disqualified them from citizenship: "The man is bestial. He shares with oriental peoples the practice of sodomy. He doesn't respect children. Repeated

---

1. Miller, "Extimacy," 76.
2. Dolar, "Beyond interpellation," 80.
3. Miller, "Extimacy," 79. In Lacanian terminology, "it is in its relation to *jouissance* that the Other is really Other." In his account of extimacy, Lacan suggests how the biblical proscription on coveting the neighbor's wife contains within it a fantasy of the neighbor's forbidden sexual pleasure. Lacan, *Seminar VII*, 236–37. See also Seshadri, *Desiring Whiteness*, 58–60.

circulars have forbidden the celebration of marriages with prepubescent wives, and despite that, the practice remains frequent. Women are unfaithful and there are entire tribes that continue to live off prostitution." The adoption of French civil law, Cuttoli insisted, "disturbs natives in their divorce and polygamy."[4] An extimate kernel was at the heart of these claims. They illustrate how politicians' and jurists' articulation of the legal and sexual norm of French citizenship—and masculinity—came to rely on the imagined excesses of Muslim deviance and pleasure.

In this chapter, I elaborate on how these arguments against Muslim men's sexual excess coalesced and how French-educated Algerian intellectuals, the so-called Young Algerians, critically responded to them.[5] In pursuing their own reformist agenda, this assimilationist elite answered attacks on the supposed sexual rights preserved in Muslim family law. In newly founded newspapers, metropolitan journals, public and political speeches, these intellectuals offered a powerful critique of the status of Muslim law in French law. Foregrounding the denials on which politicians and jurists' insistent claims about Muslim difference were based, they revealed the colonial repressions in French law. The young Tlemceni lawyer Taleb Abdesselem exemplified this critical stance. His life and writing pointed to the mutual imbrication of French and Muslim law in order to expose their extimate relation.

Portrait of a Young Algerian

Taleb Abdesselem was well positioned to dislodge the Orientalist legal fantasies of colonial jurists. Highly educated and from a prominent family, he studied at the Medersa Supérieur in Tlemcen and eventually received degrees from the Faculties of Letters and Law in Algiers. In 1912, he received a law doctorate in Paris with a timely thesis on the "financial organization of the Moroccan empire." His early writing attacked Orientalist accounts of Eastern decadence and Muslim fanaticism, which in his view served as a pretext "to intervene in the internal

---

4. Paul Cuttoli in *JO*, Débats, Chambre, January 27, 1914, 250. For the original citation see Larcher, *Traité élémentaire*, 1:83.

5. On the Young Algerians see Fromage, "L'expérience des 'Jeunes Algériens' et l'émergence du militantisme moderne"; Merad, "Islam et nationalisme arabe en Algérie"; Ageron, "Le mouvement 'Jeune-Algérien'"; Smati, *Les élites algériennes sous la colonisation*; McDougall, *History of Algeria*; Aissaoui, "Politics, Identity and Temporality."

LES BEAUX FILMS

L'Agonie de Jérusalem

Tandis que son père et sa mère, — le premier, Marc Verdier, ancien professeur à l'École des Hautes-Études, fervent catholique, l'autre, la vieille Oladame Verdier, paralysée depuis de longues années, — se sont retirés à Jérusalem où ils habitent une pittoresque maison sur le haut du Mont des Oliviers, Jean-Louis Verdier qui fait, loin des siens, ses études à Paris, s'est depuis longtemps laissé entraîner dans la compagnie de gens douteux qui l'ont rapidement gagné aux rêves creux, aux dangereuses utopies anarchistes, et il est ainsi devenu, sous le nom de guerre de « Sirius », un des leaders du mouvement révolutionnaire. Cette transformation s'est opérée à l'insu de ses parents, à l'insu aussi de sa petite amie d'enfance, Alice Leroy, orpheline élevée dans un couvent de Jérusalem, pour laquelle il réalise tous les espoirs de jeune fille.

Des grèves, des révoltes sont fomentées dans le monde entier par le parti anarchiste et, de Paris, Jean-Louis entrevoie de sa main à Larsac qui travaille à Jérusalem l'ordre de faire sauter le barrage que la Société pour l'Électrification de la Palestine a momentanément fait construire le long du Jourdain. Ce Larsac, individu sans scrupules, enveloppés épais dans un milieu oriental à demi sauvage, est un militant qui a la haine de la société. Il prendra aussitôt ses dispositions pour exécuter l'ordre qui lui vient de Paris. Il a, d'ailleurs, fait la connaissance d'Alice Leroy dont le charme et surtout la fortune l'ont séduit.

Un jour, au cours d'une promenade, il rencontre Alice Leroy que son oncle Septime accompagnait. Ce dernier, collectionneur enragé, ne se déplace jamais sans s'encombrer d'un attirail aussi pittoresque qu'hétéroclite. Armé d'une énorme loupe, toujours prêt à courir après tout ce qui court ou ce qui vole, il n'hésite pas ce jour-là à laisser Alice pour s'emparer d'un insecte rare qui manquait à sa collection. Il ne s'était pas aperçu que Larsac les suivait. Ce dernier, malhabile, brutal, se rend aussitôt odieux à la jeune fille qui le repousse. Or, Larsac est parvenu à établir que « Sirius », chef anarchiste, et Jean-Louis Verdier, fils du vieux catholique Marc Verdier, ne sont qu'une seule et même personne. Aussi, pour se venger d'Alice qui l'a éconduit, il dévoile par des procédés anonymes la nouvelle redoutable aux parents bouleversés de Jean-Louis.

Atterré par cet abaissement d'une vie d'honneur et de probité, le vieux Marc Verdier se rend à Paris et ne parvient à rencontrer son fils que dans un meeting d'anarchiste organisé par le parti et où il doit prendre la parole. Et c'est le cœur broyé que Marc entend son fils — son fils dont il avait lui-même surveillé les premières études ! — lancer à l'assistance : « Le droit du père sur l'enfant est arbitraire ! » N'y tenant plus, Marc, de sa place répond : « L'orateur vient-il son père et sa mère ? ». Et la discussion se poursuit, âpre, violente, entre le père et le fils qui ignore l'identité de son contradicteur, et la salle plus honteuse à chaque minute. Jean-Louis, surexcité par cette intervention, invite son adversaire à descendre à la tribune. Et c'est pour Marc Verdier le douloureux calvaire de traverser la foule tour à tour enthousiaste ou hostile, pour retrouver devant son fils échoué là, l'esprit faussé par les théories les plus subversives.

L'intervention de Marc au sein même de la harangue provoque de vifs incidents et une violente bagarre se produit au cours de laquelle le jeune homme, pour défendre son père qu'un individu vient de gifler devant lui, est frappé de plusieurs coups sur la nuque. Relevé évanoui, Jean-Louis est transporté à la clinique par Marc Verdier à qui, quelques jours après, le médecin annonce la fatale nouvelle : le jeune homme est devenu aveugle ! Alors, ayant perdu tout goût de la vie, Jean-Louis se laisse ramener à Jérusalem par son père effondré de chagrin.

Et c'est le retour dans la maison endeuillée. En arrivant, Jean-Louis tend désespérément les bras vers sa mère qu'il ne voit plus... sa mère qui ne peut aller à lui, clouée dans son fauteuil par la paralysie ! Tout comme lorsqu'il était enfant, le jeune homme tombe aux genoux de Madame Verdier, cherchant là son ultime consolation. Alors commence le calvaire des pauvres gens autour de Jean-Louis, muré dans la nuit intérieure, fermé à tout, refusant de s'intéresser à rien et ne tendre recommandance. La jeune fille ne peut retenir ses larmes et pleure, mais Madame Verdier lui en demande courageusement la raison : « Je pleure, répond-elle, mais c'est de joie... MAMAN !!! »

se représenter mentalement et avec force une certaine qu'on lui déverait et lui donner le désir intense de le voir. Mais que trouver, susceptible de réveiller l'attention de Jean-Louis dans cette ville qui agonise sous la malédiction des siècles ?

C'est alors qu'une étrange intervention donne à Alice l'idée de faire revivre à Jean-Louis sur les lieux mêmes où elle se déroula, « la plus belle histoire du monde », l'histoire du Christ. Et par Bethléem, Nazareth, Thabériade, Jéricho, par le désert de Galilée, parmi les paysages auxquels s'attachent de prodigieux souvenirs, les deux jeunes gens retrouvent pas à pas, l'un le goût à la vie, l'autre l'espoir de voir tomber le masque de mutisme et d'impassible froideur. Alice, lentement, progressivement, suggestionne l'aveugle qui, un jour, est pris du désir lancinant de « voir » ce qu'on lui décrit.

Pendant ce temps, Larsac qui a reconnu en Jean-Louis le maître qui a commandé la destruction du barrage le retrouve un jour au cours d'une promenade qui lui rappelle ses doctrines de haine et de destruction. Mais Alice est là qui veille sur le malade, sur ses yeux clos et sur son âme ; aux doctrines envenimées de Larsac elle répond par des paroles d'apaisement et quand, ivre de rage de la voir empêcher autour de jeune homme il crie à celui qui fut « Sirius » : « Reviens venir les iniquités et les injustices ! », elle répond avec douceur : « Aime-tous ! tu es mes tu es frères ! ». Jean-Louis, haletant, s'est rapproché d'Alice et, lentement, attiré le jeune fille auprès de lui, Larsac, vaincu par la bonté s'éloigne en proférant des paroles de haine. De plus en plus hanté du désir de « voir » ce que lui décrit Alice, Jean-Louis demande un jour qu'elle le conduise au Gethsémani, là où cet, lieu l'agonie du Christ ployé sous le poids écrasant des péchés des hommes, assiste au baiser du Judas, à l'arrestation de l'Homme-Dieu, et, dans une tension suprême de toutes ses facultés, la suggestion s'opère ; IL VOIT.

Égaré dans Jérusalem où le conduit une exaltation bien compréhensible, voici qu'il se trouve — aujourd'hui Vendredi-Saint — sur le chemin de la Procession qui monte la Voie Dolorosa ; depuis qu'il suive par le Christ. Flévreux, hallucine, Jean-Louis s'imagine alors, tandis que la Procession débouche à ses yeux, que c'est le cortège du Christ qui monte au Calvaire. Et comme le centurion, devant la cinquième station, fait signe en face de lui à Simon de Cyrène d'aider Jésus défaillant, c'est le jeune homme qui s'approche et, sous les yeux éperdus de la Divine Victime, saisit la Croix et la porte sur le Golgotha. Mais ce n'est qu'un rêve éveillé. La Procession passe et Jean-Louis vaincu prend place parmi la foule, celle d'une mystique et fervente exaltation.

Pour Larsac, sonne le châtiment. Tandis qu'il s'apprête à exécuter l'ordre jadis envoyé par Sirius, il se tend le crâne dans la Vallée de Josaphat et meurt, tandis qu'à ses yeux, voilés de sang, s'évoque la scène tragique et formidable du Jugement Dernier qui, selon le Prophète, doit avoir lieu là.

Et c'est le retour dans la maison du Mont des Oliviers. Lorsque Jean-Louis se dirige vers sa mère aux pieds de laquelle il tombe à genoux, c'est parent une tendre reconnaissance. La jeune fille ne peut retenir ses larmes et pleure, mais Madame Verdier lui en demande courageusement la raison : « Je pleure, répond-elle, mais c'est de joie... MAMAN !!! »

Mᵉ Taleb Abdesselem

Parmi les personnalités algériennes promues dans l'Ordre national de la Légion d'honneur nous relevons le nom de Mᵉ Taleb Abdesselem, docteur en droit, avocat, conseiller municipal et conseiller général de Tlemcen, vice-président du Conseil général d'Oran.

Mᵉ Taleb appartient à une des plus vieilles et des plus honorables familles de Tlemcen. Son grand-père, ancien cadi du Méchouar de cette ville, a été un des principaux signataires du traité conclu en 1836 avec le maréchal Clauzel.

De tous temps, la famille Taleb s'est distinguée par son dévouement à la France. Aujourd'hui encore, l'aîné des quatre frères de Mᵉ Taleb, ancien professeur du droit musulman, commandeur de

Ça et Là

L'âge de la corne.

Il s'agit, bien entendu, d'archéologie. A propos de Glozel, un journal suisse, le « Paysan Vaudois », rappelait, ces jours-ci, que naguère un artisan neuchâtelois employait ses loisirs d'hiver à travailler et graver des cornes de cerf, trouvées dans les dépôts lacustres.

Puis il les enterrait sur les bords du lac de Neufchâtel.

Quelques années après, il les exhumait, pour le plus grand émerveillement des savants spécialistes.

Au point que l'on parla d'un « Age de la Corne » et que des galeries archéologiques suisses et allemandes s'enorgueillirent de posséder les sensationnelles trouvailles de l'astucieux Helvète.

Le métier problématique.

Vous avez tous vu, trôlant aux terrasses des cafés, les « sidis » portant sur le dos tous leurs magasins : quelques tapis galeux, des chaînes de montre ou tué et des bretelles de valet de ferme.

Vous pouvez les suivre.

Des clients goguenards marchandent, ces clients apparaissent dans la Mecque, chevalier de la Légion d'honneur, est cadi à Orléansville. Enfin, le quatrième frère de Mᵉ Taleb, ancien élève du Lycée d'Oran, a obtenu en 1913 la croix de guerre avec palmes sur le front d'Orient comme maréchal-des-logis à la Division marocaine et a été cité à l'Ordre de l'Armée.

Cinq autres membres de la famille Taleb ont été, pendant la grande guerre,

la Légion d'honneur, est Mufthi à Sidi-bel-Abbès. Le second, ancien représentant du Gouvernement français auprès du Sultan du Hedjaz, officier de la Légion d'honneur, est cadi dans cette dernière ville, la troisième qui a été également chargé pendant la guerre d'une délicate mission à la Mecque, chevalier de la Légion d'honneur, est cadi à Orléansville...

soldats, dont un a été mortellement blessé.

Au cours de cette guerre, Mᵉ Taleb a été affecté au 5ᵉ Spahis et à l'État-Major de la 10ᵉ région. Il a été démobilisé comme officier interprète du service des renseignements au Maroc.

Ancien élève des Médersas de Tlemcen et d'Alger, et de nos Facultés de Droit d'Alger et de Paris, Mᵉ Taleb a complété ses études littéraires à la Faculté des Lettres de Rennes.

Mᵉ Taleb est auteur d'un ouvrage sur l'organisation financière de l'Empire marocain (thèse qui a été retenue en 1911 avec la mention très bien par le Jury de la Faculté de Droit de Paris) et d'une brochure publiée en 1920, intitulée « Les Ambitions algériennes ». Il est un autre collaborateur de différentes revues et journaux de la Métropole et de l'Algérie. Une des conférences qu'il a eu l'occasion de faire aux étudiants et aux étudiantes de l'Université de Rennes sur l'Islam et l'Europe a été reproduite intégralement par l'Ouest-Éclair de Bretagne, dans son numéro du 8 février 1918.

M. Taleb Abdesselem.

ment, serre en étiquettant marchandise et repart, désabusé.

Cependant ces clients ont fait manger. Il faut dormir. Il faut vivre.

De quoi peuvent bien vivre les « sidis » ambulants, et quel mystérieux trafic dissimule leur improductif et illusoire commerce ?

affairs of the Orient in the name of protecting Christians."[6] He saw the lesser treatment of Muslims by Western powers as evidence of intolerance. The legal status of Muslims in Algeria exemplified that discrimination. Abdesselem thus decried the "pitiful" subordination of the Algerian Muslim who "is struck with a sort of *capitis deminutio* and does not have the honor of being considered as a citizen; he is only a subject."[7]

Refusing this position of subjecthood for himself, Abdesselem petitioned for citizenship and went on to serve in the First World War as a military translator. After 1918, he launched a political career as municipal councilman in Tlemcen and eventually became a representative in the Algerian budgetary assembly, the *délégations financières*.[8] Like other Young Algerians, he mobilized his wartime service to critique the persistent legal exclusion of Muslims from political rights. In his view, that marginalization was hypocritical, given that Muslim law was French law. He made the point forcefully in an article on personal status published in the journal *L'Europe nouvelle*, in which he explained all the ways in which Algerians were indeed legally French. He thus queried his presumptively "European" interlocutors: "Don't Muslims conform to elements of the Civil Code? Isn't what is regulated by Muslim personal status sanctioned by a French law, regulated by a decree (from 1886 to 1889) and executed by a functionary (qadi) named by the French government? Don't courts of the first instance hear appeals of qadi court judgments? In obeying these decisions, don't Muslims follow a French law?"[9]

Abdesselem had an acutely personal as well as political sense of this contradiction. After the war, he became embroiled in a dramatic family conflict over his marriage to Fatima Bouali, a sixteen-year-old from a prominent Tlemceni family. The passionate contest over their marriage would be settled by a decision of the Cour de cassation in 1923. The case clearly illustrated how Muslim law's technical imbrication in French civil and procedural law had affectively charged as well as material effects. It made manifest the deeply felt ways in which personal status was politicized after the war, for French jurists and Algerian families alike.

Consternation over the union originated with Fatima Bouali's family. While Fatima's mother and maternal grandfather lent the union support, her half brother and legal executor Ahmed mobilized legal and, eventually, extralegal

---

6. Abdesselem, *L'organisation financière de l'Empire marocain*, 31.
7. Ibid., 33.
8. On the *délégations* see Bouveresse, *Un parlement colonial*, vol. 1.
9. Abdesselem, "Le statut personnel des français musulmans."

means in order to prevent it. While property interests were clearly in play, the legal arguments of the case focused on Fatima's marital consent, when she took her brother to court in order to override his opposition. He claimed that their deceased father had promised Fatima to her cousin Abdallah in just exercise of his "right to force [*djebr*]." According to court documents, Ahmed's contestation originated in the "grave complications entailed for his family by his sister's marriage to a Muslim who had become French and who was now submitted to French law."[10] Because Abdesselem was a French citizen, this was a legally mixed union that required Fatima to assume her husband's civil status. Her brothers worried that the new legal status would impact her (and hence their) property rights, effectively abolishing them.[11]

The qadi of Tlemcen became Fatima's guardian (*walī*) after her father's death. While charged with protecting her interests, he sided with her brother and refused to assent to the marriage. Judging Ahmed's opposition to be "purely abusive and vexatious," the French tribunal authorized the union instead. It reduced the multiple personal and financial conflicts at play to the question of Fatima's "formal will to marry [*s'unir*] Taleb Abdesselem." It held that Fatima "clearly declared that she intended to marry Taleb Abdesselem only," as evidenced by her appearance alone before the magistrates. Her "will to contract the marriage" was, the court confirmed, "formal and without contest."[12] Ahmed's claim was judged legally irrelevant because only fathers, not brothers, could exercise marital constraint. When this route failed, her cousin Abdallah raised new objections based on a marital agreement notarized by the qadi of Tlemcen. Despite the new evidence, the Appeals Court upheld the lower court's findings, affirming that because "Fatima was more than sixteen years old, and was both nubile and an orphan [i.e., fatherless], she could not be married without her consent, in conformity with Muslim law."[13] In authorizing the union, the court also granted her French civil status.

---

10. Bouali Ahmed ben Salah v. Bouali Fatima bent Salah, Cour d'Alger (May 6, 1920), *RA*, 1921, pt. 2, 52. Indeed, the ruling of the Appeals Court of Algiers highlighted the fact that her brother's opposition was "in reality inspired by the sole fact that the future husband is a French citizen" (55). See also Charnay, *La vie musulmane en Algérie*, 260–63. Also, Meylan, *Les mariages mixtes en Afrique du Nord*, 83. This story speaks to how and why "Muslim personal status" became a touchstone for the ʿulamaʾ movement and Algerian nationalism in the 1930s. On how the colonial legal invention was "colonized" by Islamic reformism as essential to Algerian "personality" see McDougall, *History and the Culture of Nationalism in Algeria*, 86–96.

11. See also Abdesselem, "À propos des mariages musulmans en Algérie."

12. Bouali Ahmed ben Salah v. Bouali Fatima bent Salah, Cour d'Alger (May 6, 1920), *RA*, 1921, pt. 2, 54.

13. Ibid., 59.

Out of apparent desperation, Ahmed and Abdallah attempted to assassinate Abdesselem on August 13, 1920. Remarkably, the young lawyer survived, despite being shot in the head. Pitting two prominent local families against one another, the affair created considerable consternation in Tlemcen. Leading Young Algerian press organs such as *Ikdam* lent Abdesselem their support, celebrating his return to health and politics in 1921.[14] When the Cour de cassation moved the criminal trial from Tlemcen to Algiers in 1922 for security reasons, Algerian and metropolitan dailies began to report on what came to be called the "Drama of Tlemcen."

Like Abdesselem, Abdallah had several advanced degrees. After graduating from the Tlemcen medersa, he was certified to work as a medical auxiliary in Sebdou, a commune close by. From there he had traveled to Tlemcen, sought out Abdesselem in town, and, gun ready, lay in wait (apparently hiding behind a tree). His motivation seemed to be calculated financial interest, although one settler newspaper also described "the hatred of the Muslim against one of his race who, in becoming naturalized, became a *roumi* [Christian/European]." Abdallah claimed to have acted spontaneously out of amorous passion, contending that it was "out of jealousy, that a superior force had taken hold of his arm."[15] The Bouali family's reaction to Abdesselem seemed to reflect an extimate hatred: a violent jealousy of Fatima's person and property. Her brother Ahmed had reportedly told her, "I could not tolerate that a stranger might be your husband and participate in our patrimony." The prosecution believed that Ahmed had corralled Abdallah into committing the crime. The two accomplices were ultimately convicted to five years of prison for a "simple murder" attempt (i.e., voluntary, but not premeditated) as well as a fine of 15,000 francs in damages to be paid to Abdesselem.[16]

Both sides paid for prominent legal counsel. Ahmed and Abdallah hired a politician, Rodolphe Rey, who was a *délegué financier* and *conseiller général*. While opposed to Muslim "tradition" when it came to property matters, Rey defended Ahmed and Abdallah's personal status. For Rey, the assimilationist Abdesselem was a far greater political threat than Fatima's traditionalist kin. Writing in the *Le Journal des débats*, he excused the Bouali family's exercise of patriarchal privilege and defended Abdallah: "From childhood she had been solemnly promised to him by her father who used in advance of his death the consecrated right of

14. See, for example, "À travers l'Algérie—Cherchell: En l'honneur de Taleb Abdesselem," *L'Ikdam*, January 28, 1921; "À travers l'Algérie—Tlemcen: Taleb Abdesselam," *L'Ikdam*, April 15, 1921.

15. "Le Drame de Tlemcen," *L'Écho d'Alger*, March 4, 1922. Also, March 5, March 7, March 8, 1922. See also *Le Temps*, March 9, 1922; *Le Petit Journal*, March 8, 1922.

16. "Le Drame de Tlemcen," *L'Écho d'Alger*, March 7, 1922.

'*djebr*' or paternal constraint." He presented Abdesselem as a troublesome inter-loper "whose ambitious political calculations would destroy Abdallah's happi-ness." In the defense attorney's account, Abdallah, far from being the aggressor, was the victim of the "Young Turk's" calculations, while Fatima was his "passive, entirely dominated" pawn.[17]

In a lengthy response, Abdesselem claimed the mantle of French patriotism, noting his wartime service as well as that of three brothers, several cousins, and nephews.[18] Underscoring the legality of his union, he paraphrased the decision of the Appeals Court of Algiers in their favor: Fatima "had the right to choose her husband and she could pronounce her choice in full liberty." In his view, Fatima's brother and cousin had manipulated the case in order to stir up political oppo-sition to him, pronouncing "sermons in small mosques against voting for me, the 'Roumi' (the abjurer/Christian/*renégat*)."[19] The Bouali family's efforts were unsuccessful: Abdesselem won reelection to the Conseil municipal and Conseil général. While he continued his political career, the Bouali family pursued its appeal.

Suspicion of French civil law did not prevent Ahmed and Abdallah from bringing the case before the highest French court in order to contest its civil jurisdiction over Fatima. In this sense, they upheld Muslim law as part of the sys-tem of French law. In their view, because Fatima was Muslim, only a qadi could determine the validity of her marriage to Abdallah. Indeed, the 1889 decree on judicial organization had guaranteed indigenous law jurisdiction for matters of "personal status," inheritance, and those land transactions not encompassed by the 1873 Warnier Law.[20] The court had to decide whether the Appeals Court of Algiers had overstepped its jurisdiction by allowing Fatima and Abdesselem's marriage to proceed. The counselor Paul Auguste Fabry rejected the Bouali's argument, urging that it was "inadmissible" to subordinate a civil tribunal to an "exceptional jurisdiction" (i.e., the qadi of Tlemcen). The Cour de cassation ultimately agreed, holding that "in Algeria, the qadi constitutes with respect to Muslim *indigènes*, an exceptional jurisdiction whose competency ceases as soon

---

17. R.R., "Lettre d'Algérie," *Journal des débats*, April 13, 1922. For Rey's discussion of Muslim property law see *Délégations financières algériennes*, 1904, 281. Bouveresse, *Un parlement colonial*, 1. On the perpetual suspicion of Young Algerians see Smati, *Les élites algériennes sous la colonisation*, 238.

18. "À propos des mariages musulmans," *Journal des débats*, June 1, 1922. See also "Les haines obscures," *L'Afrique du nord illustrée*, February 18, 1922, 8–9; March 4, 1922, 7.

19. Abdesselam, "À propos des mariages musulmans en Algérie."

20. "Décret relative à l'organisation de la justice musulmane en Algérie, 17 avril 1889," in Estou-blon and Lefébure, *Code de l'Algérie*, 1:859.

as French law applied."[21] Fabry presented the inadmissibility of Muslim law in distinctly impassioned terms; the decision described Fatima's promised marriage to Abdallah as tantamount to sexual violation. She "could no longer be forced by a legal decision to give herself over [se livrer] to a man that she rejects [repousse] as a husband and who tried to kill the spouse that she had chosen, the father of her child."[22] The defense upheld both Abdesselem and Fatima's rights: "the right of a French citizen to freely choose his spouse" and "the right of a Muslim woman to acquire French nationality by marrying a French man."[23] Their marital freedom illustrated the superiority—and, indeed, desirability—of French civil law.

For the Cour de cassation, the legal stakes were clear: Muslim jurisdictions should not trump civil ones, even though both were, in fact, French law. In the case of this mixed marriage, Fatima's "right" to marry personified this principle, legitimating the subordination of Algerian Muslim law. This line of legal argument evidently obscured the patriarchal logic of what French law compelled in article 12 of the Civil Code: that women assume their husbands' French civil status. The court focused instead on the extimate patriarchy of Muslim law and Fatima's marital choice.

In his plea for Fatima, Fabry urged the court to "end the long intrigues that aimed, without the least legal motive, to prevent a Muslim woman from becoming French as a result of her marriage." The Cour de cassation concurred, proclaiming that "the exercise of this right conferred by French law on the femme indigène cannot depend on Muslim jurisdiction."[24] From its vantage, the core question in the case was Fatima's desire to be married in (and to) French law. If French civil law was a guardian and, indeed, desirable object of women's marital choice, Muslim law appeared, by contrast, as a repository of illegitimate patriarchal privilege.

While Abdesselem succeeded in his marriage case, his political efforts would be stymied by these same arguments. When he proposed to the Conseil général of Oran in 1920 that "Muslim French" be allowed to select parliamentary representatives, Counselor Germain Sabatier forcefully rejected the plea. Sabatier, a lawyer and longtime mayor of Tlemcen, had long used legal arguments to resist "assimilationism," describing in a previous work how "the Muslim family is different from the French family in every way." In his view, the "characteristic

21. Bouali Abdallah v. époux Abdesselam ould Benouda ben Taieb et autres, Cour de cassation (July 18, 1923), RA, 1924, pt. 2, 247.
22. Ibid., 244.
23. Ibid., 246.
24. Ibid., 247–48.

divergences in the organization of the family, alongside religious antagonism, sufficiently demonstrate that it remains chimerical to dream of assimilation."[25] Sabatier made nearly identical arguments in response to Abdesselem's proposal, and cruelly used evidence from Abdesselem's case against him, lamenting the case of "a young girl of seventeen who had been refused the right to marry following her heart." Sabatier asked his fellow council members, "Would you allow natives who have maintained polygamy, who protested when it was a question of abolition of the *droit de djebr*, of matrimonial constraint, to collaborate on the making of laws that organize the French family"? For Sabatier, it was unthinkable that "the sons of the French Revolution, which affirmed the equality of the sexes," could allow "these men to impose on us a regime that we do not want."[26] This condemnation of Muslim patriarchy evidently obscured both the past and present-day gender inequalities in French civil and political law.

Abdesselem understood the obfuscation. While he secured his marriage in French civil court, he also argued forcefully against the fantasy of Muslim patriarchy on which the court's decision, drawn out in Sabatier's arguments, was based. Schooled in both legal traditions, he promoted a more nuanced account of the relationship between Muslim and French civil law. In a 1918 speech, "Islam and the Allied Cause," Abdesselem illustrated his critical awareness of reigning Orientalist accounts of Muslim men's sexual rights. Appearing before a local student association in Rennes, where he was stationed, he urged his listeners not to "imagine that Muslim men marry as many women as they please, submitting them to a life of martyrdom or repudiating them at will."[27] In order to refute distorted accounts of "the Muslim woman," he highlighted how Qur'anic principles made women's status "equal to that of man, in granting her the power to dispose of property as she wishes and allowing her to appear in court on her own behalf." He used the argument to answer disingenuous claims about French women's superior status:

> I will allow myself to recall that no legislation in Europe yet grants this right to women, despite all the appearances of liberalism that animates these laws. French women, like their sisters, are struck, under any property regime, with the "*capitis deminutio*" and are, for all their acts, de-

---

25. G. Sabatier, *Études sur les réformes algériennes*, 35–36.

26. "La représentation des indigènes au Parlement," *Progrès d'Orléansville*, October 5, 1922.

27. Reprinted in "Une conférence sur les musulmans," *L'Ouest-Éclair*, February 8, 1918. The speech was occasionally republished in the French-language indigenous press. See, for example, *L'Ikdam*, July 26, 1919; *L'Union (El Tihad): Journal Républicain d'Union Franco-Musulman*, August 18, 1928.

pendent on their husbands. Neither their grace, nor their charm, nor the lively intelligence that is their gift, has helped them to obtain—like Muslims—civil equality in order to obtain the political equality about which they dream.[28]

Pointing to the political limits of what Joan Scott has described as "French seduction theory," Abdesselem made clear that French women had no advantages over Muslim women when it came either to matters of property or political rights.[29] In highlighting French women's legal subordination, Abdesselem noted their ironic resemblance to Algerian men.

Abdesselem was, however, critical of polygamy. He acknowledged the Qur'anic acceptance of the practice, while highlighting "the harsh prescriptions added by the law itself, which make this tolerance impossible." Like many of his contemporaries, he claimed that the normative injunction to absolutely equitable treatment of multiple wives made it unethical in practice. What is more, he asserted that "legendary 'harems' no longer exist, at least in North Africa, except in the more or less novelistic [romanesque] fantasies of poets and tourists."[30] In his view, the preoccupation with polygamy was principally an extimate projection of heated European imaginations. His speeches and writings instead aimed to "dissipate the prejudices that exist against us," so that Muslim French subjects could gain their "droit de cité."

Skeptical responses to Abdesselem's speech illustrate the extent of this prejudice and its persistent fascination with Muslim men's sexual privileges. One letter writer highlighted the "moving calls of distress that are sometimes heard by French women who become Muslim wives and even by Muslim women whose eyes have been opened and have become conscious of their condition."[31] Another questioned Abdesselem's ability to act as "an impartial psychologist of the feminine condition" and reiterated clichéd images of the harem as a "golden prison."[32]

---

28. "Une conférence sur les musulmans," L'Ouest-Éclair, February 8, 1918. Married women's civil incapacity would be reformed in 1938, but contemporary feminists remained disappointed by the limits of that law.

29. "French Seduction Theory," in J. W. Scott, Fantasy of Feminist History.

30. "Une conférence sur les musulmans," L'Ouest-Éclair, February 8, 1918. His position on the question resembled that of contemporary Egyptian reformers such as Qasim Amin and Mohammed 'Abduh. For a contemporary account of 'Abduh's position see Aksékli Ahmed Hamdi, "L'islamisme et la polygamie," Revue du monde musulman, vols. 26 and 27, 1914. See also Haj, Reconfiguring Islamic Tradition; Esmeir, "At Once Human and Not Human."

31. E.N., "À propos d'une conférence sur les Musulmans," L'Ouest-Éclair, February 9, 1918.

32. L.-M. Enfrey, "Réponse à une conférence sur les musulmans," L'Ouest-Éclair, March 4, 1918.

Young Algerians like Abdesselem commented on these conscious and unconscious contemporary fantasies about Muslim sex precisely because they recognized their political power. More specifically, they understood that French officials' fixation on marital constraint and polygamy were symptoms of French legal disavowal. As Abdesselem later explained, "In order to clear away [*dégager*] their responsibility for this state of affairs, Europeans pretend that their distance from Muslims is caused by the latter's religion and the idea that they have of woman and marriage. But this is a tendentious argument [*procès de tendance*]." "Enslaved to their old habits," the French maintained an extimate idea of "Muslim law" in order "to satisfy their prejudice."[33]

As Abdesselem's own marriage trial showed, arguments that French law freed Muslim women from patriarchal constraint maintained legal force, despite his own and others' efforts to challenge those claims.

Codifying Difference

As we saw in chapter 4, proposals to reform Muslim personal status began to take shape at the end of the nineteenth century in controversies over the *droit de djebr*.[34] Colonial jurists regularly called for reform in the name of girls' and women's liberation from a patriarchal Muslim law. Casting prepubescent marriage (which they equated with sexual consummation) as a violation of both children and law, their accounts focused on the moral horror of rape. They linked legal progress to proper child development, while representing Muslim law as unnatural and backward. This extimate, sexualized horror sustained an evolutionary legal logic that structured arguments about codification reform.[35]

While colonial jurists cited contemporary projects in Egypt and Tunisia when devising their new Algerian codes, their reforms had French jurists in mind. A judge in Constantine, Edmond Norès, tellingly conceded that his 1903 draft code had "nothing 'Muslim' about it." As he explained, it "is purely artificial, but it has this very serious practical advantage of recalling to the reader a familiar classification thus facilitating consultation."[36] Combining sources from the Qur'an

---

33. Taleb Abdesselem, "Le statut personnel des français musulmans."

34. Estoublon, "Mariages musulmans et kabyles."

35. On "moralized sexual horror" as the inversion of the developmental futurity of the child see Edelman, *No Future*, 105. On narratives of progress and reproductive development see Pursley, "Stage of Adolescence."

36. Edmond Norès, "Essai de codification du droit musulman algérien," *RA*, 1903, pt. 1, 11.

and handbooks of *fiqh* with metropolitan legislation, the text, which followed the structure of the French Civil Code, was designed for jurists who applied "Algerian Muslim law" but had virtually no knowledge of Islamic jurisprudence.

Influenced by Norès's text, the *colon* section of the *délégations financières* voted on a project to codify Muslim law in 1904.[37] Their colonial state fantasy of codification sought "a veritable code, with simple, easily interpreted rules and precise articles."[38] It aimed, in particular, at "simplifying property questions."[39] In response, Governor-General Charles Jonnart created a commission to survey the opinions of experts and officials, including prefects, *medersa* directors, judges and lawyers, qadis, and *juges de paix*. Its initial work cataloged responses to the proposed reform, reported on the findings, and outlined "Book One" of the Personal Status section, which, following the Civil Code, was devoted to marriage.[40] While the *délégations* had focused on property, the commission began with marriage reform.

The prefects of the departments of Alger, Constantine, and Oran treated codification as a police measure to promote transparency, facilitate the surveillance of Muslim justices, and, as the prefect of Oran noted, "make the application of Muslim law easier for young magistrates who come from the Metropole and are unfamiliar with the subtleties of interpreting the Qur'an."[41] Some jurists, like Paul de Lalagade, a public prosecutor from Mascara, underscored the need to align French and Muslim law, calling for the elimination of conflicts related to women and children's rights. For Lalagade, "The rules related to inheritance, testimonial proof, and those concerning marriage, the age of puberty, women's consent, should all be categorically repealed where they contradict our law and institutions. In a code written and promulgated by France, one must not find principles that are so clearly opposed to the fundamental rules of the rights of man and such restrictions of individual liberty."[42] This strong claim for the ethical as well as political import of the reform was featured in the commission's summary report, which highlighted the need to eliminate Muslim law's

37. Bouveresse, *Un parlement colonial*, 1:759.

38. *Délégations financières algériennes*, March 8, 1904, 204. For a critical account of colonial projects of codifying Muslim law see Hallaq, *Sharīʿa*. For a reframing of the problem of codification as principally one of state power see Emon, "Codification and Islamic Law."

39. Sabatier, *Délégations financières algériennes*, March 14, 1905, 28.

40. Gouvernement général de l'Algérie, *Projet de codification du droit musulman*, vols. 1–3. The project would in total comprise nine volumes, which also included proposals to reform rules of inheritance and *habous* as well as real estate.

41. Ibid., 1:31–36.

42. Ibid., 1:61–62.

"antiquated and inhuman institutions."[43] This moralizing injunction focused on Muslim law's extimate sexual difference.

Muslim magistrates were, meanwhile, wary of the proposed changes and the broader project to transform their jurist-centered law into a form of positive law. They contended that Khalil ibn Ishâq's *Mukhtasar*, a fourteenth-century reference handbook of the Maliki rite, was a more than adequate compendium. As a group of qadis and their deputies (*bachadels*) from Batna pointed out, French ignorance, not textual inexactitude, was the true source of colonial jurists' confusion. Affirming their own expertise, they explained that "Muslim law" was "very clear and very precise for anyone who knows the jurisprudence, in particular, those qadis charged with ruling on cases between Muslims."[44] Muslim jurists' reactions were nonetheless split between allegiance to an administration on which their jobs depended and bids for jurisdictional autonomy. Striking something of a balance, the qadis of Algiers confirmed that it would be good "to end fluctuations in Muslim jurisprudence and to fix it according to uniform rules," but endorsed following Khalil or his later interpreter, Cheikh Edderdir, rather than an entirely new code.[45] In the end, of the eighty-seven Muslim jurists who responded, forty-two were in favor, forty-three opposed.[46] Despite these divided opinions, law faculty professor Marcel Morand, who was overseeing the codification project, called for "modernization."[47]

Morand's project was influenced by the Orientalist scholar and inspector general of medersas, Octave Houdas, who argued that because Khalil's text was not sacred, it could easily be reordered along the lines of the Civil Code. Pursuing the project would, he claimed, help to cleave religious principles from the dictates of a secular civil law.[48] For Houdas, the recent evolution of the "Muslim family" had already demonstrated such modernizing and secularizing transformation. Muslims' contact with—and indeed destitution by—Europeans had induced polygamy's decline. And, in his view, because "impoverishment had introduced monogamy in a generalized way into *mœurs*, it should, without difficulty, be

---

43. Gouvernement général de l'Algérie, *Projet de codification du droit musulman*, 2:27.

44. "Lettre des Qadis de Batna et de Baali et des Bach-Adels des Acheches et de Belezma à M. le Procureur de la République de Batna, July 11, 1904," in Gouvernement général de l'Algérie, *Projet de codification du droit musulman*, 1:164.

45. Ibid., 1:85–86.

46. "Résumé des avis," in Gouvernement général de l'Algérie, *Projet de codification du droit musulman*, 2:2. For the ambivalent position of official Muslim jurists see Christelow, *Muslim Law Courts*.

47. Arabi, "Orienting the Gaze"; Renucci, "La doctrine coloniale en République."

48. Gouvernement général de l'Algérie, *Projet de codification du droit musulman*, 1:21–2.

made obligatory in civil law, without religion really suffering."[49] This secularizing vision informed the drafting of the code.[50]

Morand's own account of Algerian society and law also followed an evolutionary framework that borrowed from ethnographer Charles Letourneau and the British colonial jurist Henry Sumner Maine. Morand claimed that what he called "the Muslim family" had "undergone, in a manner of speaking, neither modification, nor transformation." By contrast, the modern family was supposedly marked by an evolution and implicit spiritualization, becoming "more and more concentrated, folded in on itself" over time and increasingly "animated by a purely internal life."[51] For Morand, Muslims remained "fundamentally attached to the old idea of sexual inequality as well as their crude conception of marriage," which explained why their "family law" had not evolved. Treating marriage as a sale and "fundamentally polygamous," it was based on patriarchal prerogatives that had, he claimed, been written out of modern French family law.[52] Morand's juxtaposition effectively effaced French women's subordinate legal and political status, claiming that among "modern people," women had gained rights equal to men "in one of the most important acts in life, marriage" and "in the family."[53]

These arguments underwrote Morand's claim that the "Muslim family" would evolve as a result of external, and implicitly French, influence. He pointed to Egyptian and Turkish projects of codification as proof of such contemporary transformations. In fact, the French Civil Code was a formative model for Muhammed Qadri's unofficial code of Egyptian "personal status" law, which was first published in 1875 for use by the Mixed Courts. In the echo chamber of Morand's argument, this Egyptian compendium became a legitimating reference for "Algerian Muslim law."[54]

Casting "the family" as a universal category filled with particular content, Morand's analysis made invidious comparisons between Muslim family law and

---

49. Houdas, L'Islamisme, 278.

50. Résumé des avis, in Gouvernement général de l'Algérie, Projet de codification du droit musulman, 2:5. Amar, "Projet de codification du droit musulman." See also Mahieddin, "Le droit musulman et l'école de droit d'Alger."

51. Morand, La famille musulmane, 7. For Letourneau's discussion of "la polygamie arabe" see Letourneau, L'évolution du mariage et de la famille, 173–84. For an earlier account see Chevillotte, De la famille musulmane en Algérie. On Maine and colonial legal thought see Mantena, Alibis of Empire.

52. Morand, La famille musulmane, 75.

53. Ibid., 74–75.

54. Morand, Avant-projet du Code, 6–7; Arabi, "Orienting the Gaze"; Bontems, "Les tentatives de codification du droit musulman." On the influence of Algerian colonial efforts to systematize Muslim "personal law" in Egypt see Cuno, Modernizing Marriage, 161–66; Wood, Islamic Legal Revival, 107–16.

the Civil Code possible.[55] While he fixated on *family law* difference, he strongly opposed the codification of Muslim real estate law (*statut réel*), because "doing so would give those laws a fixed and durable character that it is undesirable to see them acquire."[56] Morand believed that property law, unlike family law, should remain dynamic and mobile, and hence uncodified. By contrast, because the "Muslim family" had been static, codification would, paradoxically, serve to modernize it.

Adopting the plan of the Civil Code, the commission first turned to marital capacity and consent. Handily citing the already existing Egyptian Code elaborated by Qadri, Morand encouraged the adoption of Hanafi school principles on marital constraint and consent.[57] The first seven proposed articles established "puberty" and "manifest consent" as requirements, fixing puberty to chronological age: eighteen for men, fifteen for women. Referencing articles 51 and 53 of the Egyptian Code, article 5 affirmed "there is no marriage without the consent of future partners."[58] Departing from Maliki principles, there was no explicit provision for fathers to oversee the unions of their prepubescent daughters, although article 7 established that "legal representatives" would "complete" consent for those not yet twenty-one. Formally and ideologically, the proposed code foregrounded women's marital consent.

These provisions received pointed criticism from many qadis, who claimed that the text departed from orthodox jurisprudence. Quite a few asserted that "the marriage of prepubescents is admitted by all four orthodox rites."[59] An extensive commentary by the qadi of Tlemcen underscored the Maliki rite's provision for a father's authority over virgins, no matter their age.[60] The qadi of Médéa warned reformers to be wary of the sensational trials reprinted in the colonial press. "You should not," he wrote, "allow yourself to be moved because you have learned of certain young girls who have addressed the courts, declaring that they do not accept the husband chosen by their father." In his view, these

---

55. On the politics of colonial comparison see Stoler, *Haunted by Empire*. On the "family" and comparative family law see Halley and Rittich, "Critical Directions in Comparative Family Law." On the effects of reimagining shariʿa in the framework of comparative, positive law see Esmeir, *Juridical Humanity*, 50.

56. Gouvernement général de l'Algérie, *Projet de codification du droit musulman*, 1:31.

57. Ousamma Arabi also notes the focus on marital consent; see Arabi, "Orienting the Gaze," 63.

58. Gouvernement général de l'Algérie, *Projet de codification du droit musulman*, 2:5–7. For the references to the Egyptian Code see ibid., 64. See also Qadrī Bāšā, *Droit musulman. Du statut personnel et des successions d'après le rite hanafite*, 18–20. Also, Cuno, *Modernizing Marriage*, 175.

59. Gouvernement général de l'Algérie, *Projet de codification du droit musulman*, 3:45.

60. "Relevé des observations," ibid., 3:48.

girls were "profoundly ignorant" and could not be trusted to know their own interests.[61] Fueling contestation over the very issues that it sought to fix, this official survey made marital age and agency into a litmus test for the authenticity, acceptability, and modernity of the reformed code.

The commission ultimately ignored the Muslim jurists' critical responses. It did, however, revise article 7's provisions for parental assent upward, in order to conform not to Muslim law, but to *French* law. A recent natalist reform of the Civil Code had reduced marital majority to age twenty-one (from twenty-five for women, and thirty for men), while maintaining parents' rights of marital consent.[62] Despite this recent restriction of French parental authority, magistrates were shocked by the liberality of the proposed Muslim Code. In their view, the negligible role allotted to legal guardians by the project was "excessive in comparison to French law." They worried over the dangerous consequences of girls' liberty: "The Arab girl, absolutely subject to paternal authority, will accede at fifteen, if she is free to dispose of her property, to the most complete freedom, a freedom that is refused to the young French girl."[63] In order to scale back that freedom, they modified the article, extending legal guardians a right to consent to marriages up to age twenty-five. The discussion clearly demonstrated how French jurists remained attached to the patriarchal assumptions inscribed within their own legal code, even as they denounced the purported excesses of Muslim law.

Some Muslim jurists heralded the reform as salutary. For example, Aboubekr Abdesselem ben Choaïb, a student of the Algiers law faculty and professor at the medersa of Tlemcen, defended the proposed code in the *Revue du monde musulman*. Ben Choaïb's views fit the vision of evolving Muslim modernity prominent in the journal, founded under the auspices of Alfred Le Chatelier, the new chair in Muslim sociology at the Collège de France.[64] An author of diverse texts on the philosophy of Muslim law, Islamic jurisprudential argument, and ethnographic studies of customary law, ben Choaïb defended the project's orthodoxy, basing his argument not only on Qur'anic reference, but also on analogy (*qiås*) and independent legal reasoning (*ijtihad*).[65]

---

61. Ibid., 3:53.

62. "Loi du 21 Juin 1907, modifiant plusieurs dispositions légales relatives au mariage," in *JO*, Lois et décrets, June 25, 1907, 4397–98.

63. Gouvernement général de l'Algérie, *Projet de codification du droit musulman*, 3:55.

64. On the *Revue du monde musulman* see Burke, "France and the Classical Sociology of Islam"; Bayly, "Racial Readings of Empire."

65. On the role of *ijtihad* in contemporary Islamic legal reform see Peters, "Idjtihad and Taqlid in 18th and 19th Century Islam"; Hallaq, "Was the Gate of Ijtihad Closed?"

Because matters of marriage and sex emerged as an important index of the proposed code's authenticity, Ben Choaïb answered fellow Muslim jurists' concerns. He suggested that, in imposing age limits, "the members of the commission have only done their duty in putting a stop to these precocious unions that have had such unspeakable results." In his view, the commission's text was "in conformity not only with equality" but also with "the ideas of the Muslim legislator himself."[66]

While some Muslim jurists like Ben Choaïb praised the project, some prominent French jurists rejected it. The most notable was Émile Larcher, Morand's law school colleague and editor of the *Revue algérienne et tunisienne de jurisprudence*. In stark contrast to Morand, Larcher claimed that codification would exacerbate legal conflict and halt rather than promote jurisprudential evolution. Close to colonial legal pedagogical and publishing institutions, Larcher also criticized the excesses and irregularities of Algerian law. A member of the association for the Progressive Assimilation of Algeria to France, he condemned the legal anomalies, or what he referred to as "*bizarreries*," of French rule in Algeria, including the excesses of its exceptional penal law.[67] In his view, the danger of codification lay in creating "another obstacle to the evolution of natives toward our civilization."[68] He used marital compulsion as a case in point: "With codification, will we maintain all the institutions of Muslim law, notably the *droit de djebr*, the marriage of prepubescents? If yes, isn't there a disadvantage to consecrating these institutions? If not, won't we be attacking the *sénatus-consulte* which guarantees the natives' personal status?" From Larcher's assimilationist standpoint, codification risked making Muslim law more resistant to change.[69]

Answering Larcher's criticisms directly, Morand explained that marital constraint could not "have a place in a code written by a European power."[70] Further, he did not believe that codification would make Muslim law more inflexible, precisely because he viewed codification as a force for modernization. Appealing to the precedents set by the Egyptian and Ottoman codes, he claimed in his preliminary report that "it is in Turkey and in Egypt, which is to say in two Muslim

---

66. Ben Choaïb, "La codification du droit musulman," 454–55.

67. Larcher, *L'énigme*. And Renucci, "La doctrine coloniale en République."

68. Séance of June 14, 1905, in Société d'études politiques et sociales, "Assimilation progressive de l'Algérie à la France," 130. The statement was cited in the codification survey, Gouvernement général de l'Algérie, *Projet de codification du droit musulman*, 1:113.

69. Émile Larcher, "Bibliographie 'Projet de codification,'" *RA*, 1907, pt. 1, 124.

70. Marcel Morand, "Le Sénatus-consulte du 14 juillet 1865 et l'application de la loi musulmane aux indigènes de l'Algérie," *RA*, 1907, pt. 1, 126.

countries and under the order of Muslim sovereigns . . . that the first attempts at codifying Muslim law have been made."[71] Morand's gesture here reversed logics of colonial mimicry: he claimed to be imitating Egyptian and Ottoman modernization, in order to prove that a code "written by a European power" had Islamic authenticity. He used these examples to underwrite an "Algerian Muslim law" for the French imperial state.

Morand's code was published as a "preparatory project" in 1916, although its status remained uncertain. Governor-General Jonnart tried to adopt it by decree in 1909. But the project met with resistance. In a letter to President Georges Clemenceau, the liberal deputy of the Haute-Marne, Albin Rozet, questioned the code's legality and, like Larcher, worried that it "pour[ed] into a rigid mold the still uncertain and controversial rules of custom."[72] A decade later, Jonnart relaunched the proposal. His explanatory letter emphasized that "marriage is one of the institutions that, in the practice of Muslim legislation in Algeria, gives rise to the worst abuses." Noting how Morand's code fixed marriage age and consent, Jonnart declared it to be "a notable improvement in the juridical condition of the weakest of the Muslim Algerian population."[73] This and subsequent efforts at adoption again ran up against marital consent as an obstacle.[74] The Morand Code nonetheless functioned *as if* it were official. As one author noted, this "rejuvenated, vivified, and modernized" code became, by 1920, the "bedtime reading of Algerian jurisdictions."[75]

The *droit de djebr* remained, in French eyes, an excessive patriarchal prerogative that civilized law had supposedly overcome; its reform underwrote the proposed code's legitimacy. Colonial jurists elaborated an evolutionary narrative of Algerian legal reform in which uncodified Muslim law appeared to be at once backward and unnatural because of its improper management of the girl child's sexual development. By fixating on the imagined excess of child marriage, colonial jurists displaced their own ongoing investment in patriarchal control over women's personhood and property onto an extimate fantasy of Muslim law.

---

71. Morand, *Avant-projet du Code*, 6.

72. Rozet to Pres. du Conseil, July 15, 1909, in Droit musulman / Codification / Justice Ministry, in AN 19950167/10.

73. Gov. Gen. to Garde des Sceaux, "Codification du Droit Musulman," July 22, 1919, in Droit musulman / Codification / Justice Ministry, in AN 19950167/10.

74. See the critical article by Jean Mélia, "Respectons l'Islam," *Ikdam*, November 6, 1919. Also, Bel, "La codification du droit musulman en Algérie." See also the subsequent inquiry in ANOM 17 H 17.

75. "Vingt ans de politique algérienne: Le départ de M. Luciani," *Revue du monde musulman*, no. 40–41 (1920): 5.

Personal Status, Polygamy, and Political Reform

While the outbreak of war in Europe stalled Morand's codification project, it spurred the efforts at political reform launched by Young Algerians and their allies to link their political demands to conscription. In the previous decade, reform-ist advocates' early initiatives had faced considerable opposition. When Deputy Adolphe Messimy (Seine) first proposed to open military service to Algerians in 1907, settler politicians in parliament met the idea with virulent disapproval. Traditionalist members of the "Arab sections" of Algerian local government also voiced opposition, claiming that their Muslim legal status shielded them from conscription. Some Algerians penned petitions and protested in towns, includ-ing Rovigo, Arba, and Touka, which in turn further fueled settler opposition.[76] By contrast, assimilationist lawyers and jurists such as Ben Ali Fekar and Ahmed Bouderba supported the measure on condition that it would give way to legal and political reform. They organized local meetings, published articles in jour-nals such as *Rachidi* (The Guide), and met with Georges Clemenceau in the fall of 1908 to plead their case.[77] These demands worried settler politicians and their supporters. One journalist from Orléansville explained that an excess of "senti-mentalism" would lead the parliament to "impose on our Muslim subjects the political rights that would make them pass from the condition of subject to that of citizen."[78] The recruitment of Algerian soldiers further represented a political and martial threat to French masculinity, pointing to the deficiency of French troop numbers and a perceived decline in French men.

Articles in the popular as well as the colonial juridical press evinced responses that mixed sexual jealousy with moral horror. Marcel Savoyant, who would go on to receive his law doctorate in Algiers, exemplified this extimate reaction. He castigated Algerians' libidinal investment in their law: "Our subjects have the exceptional freedom to practice polygamy, to buy or sell their wives and daugh-ters, to marry before puberty or nubility, to exercise marital constraint, to divorce freely [*par consentement mutuel*]." The sexual benefits of their Muslim rights explained their refusal of civil and political assimilation. They were, that is, "too attached to maintaining their personal status to prefer the quality of French citi-zenship."[79] Given how such exceptional sexual privileges were denied to French

---

76. See, for example, *Le Progrès de Orléansville*, October 1, 1908; "La conscription des indigènes," *Le Progrès de Mascara*, October 31, 1908.

77. Ageron, *Les Algériens musulmans*, 2:1064–65; Meynier, *L'Algérie révélée*, 89–96.

78. Paul d'Atys, "Fusil et Bulletin de Vote," *Le Progrès*, January 2, 1908.

79. Marcel Savoyant, "La conscription des indigènes," *Le Courrier de Tlemcen*, October 16, 1908.

men, granting Algerian Muslim men political rights was unthinkable. Doing so would be, for Savoyant, an inversion of colonial legal, social, and sexual hierarchy.

Critics used charges against Algerian men's sexual privilege to question the Young Algerians' motives. In efforts to cast doubt on their patriotism, opponents represented the assimilationist elite as scheming and disingenuous (as we have seen in the case of Taleb Abdesselem). Camille Brunel, a former government land surveyor and author of an influential work on the 1901 Margueritte Revolt, mobilized these claims against Messimy's conscription plan. Speaking to the French Colonial League, he presented "the Arab" as "our moral antipode," including "from a physical point of view." He suggested that "more than ever attached to their traditions," the "literate" elite was no exception. Brunel thus cautioned that when they spoke of assimilation, it "really means our absorption." These political anxieties were suffused with sexual jealousy and resentment, as Brunel's extimate reflections on mixed marriage made clear: "We can immediately see the consequences: the Muslims who approach us—and especially the urban ones—hasten to take our girls, while refusing us their own; they continue to visit our houses, while forbidding us to enter their foyer: in this way, they place us, Frenchmen of origin, in a position of moral and social inferiority, while waiting to absorb us. In believing that we are granting equality, haven't we pronounced our own destitution [*déchéance*]?"[80] Brunel's fantasy of reverse colonization resonates with the pervasive anxieties that, as we saw in chapter 6, had long preoccupied colonial jurists. His comments make the political and psychic resonance of those legal concerns clear: Muslim men's presumptive sexual privileges, including over French women, were both enviable and degrading to French men.

New pressures on the French army due to the Moroccan crisis in 1911 led to a February 3, 1912, decree that established obligatory military service for Algerians. Seizing on this opportunity, a delegation of Young Algerians met with President Raymond Poincaré to demand, in exchange, "a serious and sufficient political representation in the Assemblies of Algeria and the Metropole."[81] While the government made several concessions, including the exemption of veterans from the *indigénat* and repressive tribunals, the question of Algerian men's access to political rights remained unresolved. Throughout, the specter of the "polygamous citizen" haunted these discussions.

---

80. Camille Brunel, "À propos du service obligatoire des indigènes Algériens," *Le Courrier de Tlemcen*, July 17, 1908. Also published in "Le service militaire obligatoire pour les indigènes en Algérie," 148–54. The statements resonate with the analysis in Fanon, "Algeria Unveiled."

81. *L'Islam*, July 23, 1912. Also, Bouveresse, *Un parlement colonial*, 1:842–43.

In an effort to answer these fears, assimilationist reformers sought to clarify that polygamy was more a tolerated practice than a legal "right." Army translator Ismaël Hamet endorsed "the elasticity of Islamic law." Expressing optimism regarding Algerians' evolution, he suggested that polygamy was destined to fade away along with the "social and economic necessities" that had given rise to it.[82] Polygamy had declined since the late nineteenth century, not least because of the economic and social devastation wrought by colonization. According to official statistics, only 6.4 percent of a population of about five million Algerians lived in polygamous households in 1911.[83] But these feeble statistics did nothing to counter the symbolic weight that jurists and politicians gave Muslim Algerian men's "right" to have up to four wives.

Some jurists already accepted the idea of the polygamous citizen, as long as he remained at a territorial and psychic distance from the metropole. In response to a 1912 survey on naturalization by the *Revue indigène*, Robert Doucet and Numa Léal wondered "how it could disturb us if, in Algeria or in Tunisia, a French Muslim (*Français-Musulman*) continues to marry one or several wives."[84] Bordeaux jurist Charles de Boeck likewise assented to the prospect of "polygamous French citizens" if they were "separated from the Metropole by the Mediterranean."[85] While presuming an underlying sexual conflict between French civil and Muslim law, these advocates territorialized it by placing Algeria and Algerians at a distant remove.

Algerian legal treatises and press organs were less emotionally detached. They refused to have as their neighbors full citizens with different sexual rights. In response to the *Revue indigène*'s survey, the law faculty graduate and Cour d'Alger lawyer Amédée Rinderhagen exclaimed: "Can one conceive of a polygamous French citizen who has the right to repudiate his wife on a whim and demand from her a ransom to give her back her freedom?"[86] In a legal dissertation on Algerian conscription, Achille Sèbe likewise argued, citing the parliamentary discussion of the 1865 *sénatus-consulte*, that it was unthinkable in a "democratic regime" that "what is permitted for some be forbidden to others."[87]

82. Hamet, "La naturalisation des indigènes algériens," 383–84.

83. Kateb, "Polygamie et répudiation." See also Ministère du Commerce, *Annuaire statistique*, 1906, 335.

84. "Position de la Question: Au point de vue juridique," *La Revue indigène* 6, no. 63–64 (July–August 1911): 420.

85. Charles de Boeck, *La Revue indigène* 6, no. 63–64 (July–August 1911): 451.

86. Amédée Rinderhagen, "La naturalisation des indigènes dans le statut musulman," *L'Écho d'Alger*, July 7, 1912.

87. Sèbe, *La conscription des indigènes d'Algérie*, 80–81.

In the projective identification of these critics, the virtues of citizenship paled in comparison to the sexual privileges of personal status. "These natives," wrote Deputy Émile Broussais (Alger), "refuse naturalization in order to keep their personal status—which maintains for them polygamy and the enslavement of women."[88] For adversaries of Algerian political rights, the polygamous citizen inspired jealousy and horror.

Liberty, Equality, Polygamy?

During the course of the war, as Algerian soldiers were being conscripted, liberal politicians elaborated several different projects extending citizenship to a limited number of "qualified" Algerians. In one proposition, Deputies Georges Boussenot and Ernest Outrey suggested that the wives of polygamous men could be given "putative" status under French civil law.[89] Georges Clemenceau and Georges Leygues, who headed the foreign affairs commissions in the Senate and Chamber, endorsed the initiatives. In a letter addressed to President Aristide Briand published on January 1, 1916, in Le Temps, they praised North African soldiers for their "loyalty and profound attachment to France." In recognition of this service, they called for the "admission of indigènes to a new regime of naturalization that does not entail a renunciation of personal status."[90] The political effects of these propositions would be significant, as some 173,000 Algerians served in the military during the course of the war.[91]

Their call spurred Algerian politicians into action. A commission convened by Governor-General Charles Lutaud and headed by none other than Marcel Morand drafted a response calling for all proposed legislation to be suspended until the end of the hostilities. Claims about the patriarchy of personal status featured prominently in their arguments against the law. As Morand explained, if the Algerian did not forgo his "personal status," it "is especially because he

88. Émile Broussais, "L'Esprit Algérien," L'Écho d'Alger, December 28, 1912. See also Broussais's letter in Le Temps, December 27, 1912.

89. Georges Boussenot and Ernest Outrey, "Proposition de loi ayant pour objet de régler les conditions d'accession des indigènes civils et militaires de l'Algérie, des colonies et protectorat à la qualité de citoyen français," JO, Chambre, annexe 1034, June 24, 1915, 5–6. And Albin Rozet, Georges Leygues, Henri Doizy, Lucien Millevoye, "Proposition de loi ayant pour objet de faciliter aux militaires et anciens militaires indigènes originaires de l'Algérie, de la Tunisie et du Maroc à l'accession à la qualité de citoyen français," JO, Chambre, annexe 820, April 1, 1915.

90. Georges Clemenceau and Georges Leygues, "Les réformes algériennes," Le Temps, January 1, 1916.

91. McDougall, History of Algeria, 136.

does not want to abdicate his male superiority, and to impose upon himself a sacrifice, which, for him, is a genuine destitution [*déchéance*]."[92] Like other colonial politicians and journalists, he bluntly equated Muslim personal status with a masculine sexual privilege, whose sacrifice he imagined as a de-virilizing loss. His report thus answered Clemenceau and Leygues's proposal by maligning the Algerians who were the intended beneficiaries. Citing jurisprudence on the *droit de djebr*, Morand emphasized how "shocking it would be to allow a French citizen to maintain a personal status that authorizes him to force his prepubescent daughter to marry."[93] As depicted here, personal status entailed patriarchal rights that Algerian men refused to give up and that "full" French citizens were denied.

In order to enact a postwar reform, these divergent positions needed to be sorted out. Socialist deputy Marius Moutet (Rhône) surveyed the options and elaborated a project for the Chamber's Commission on External Affairs. His program extended full political rights to a limited number of "elite" Algerians, including veterans, and expanded local electoral rights to a wider segment of the male population. In its original formulation, Moutet's proposal allowed for the "exceptional" admission of those who did not "renounce" their personal status, which entailed "polygamy" and "the absolute right of a father over his children." In doing so, it sought a compromise between both sides.[94] Discussion of these provisions continued in the fall of 1917, when the proposal passed to the Interministerial Commission on Muslim Affairs and then the Conseil supérieur de l'Algérie in the spring of 1918. Throughout, polygamy played an outsize role in the debates both for and against reform.[95]

Moutet also presented the proposal to the Ligue des droits de l'homme. Addressing its annual Congress in 1917, he called for the "true representation of natives in the metropole." Aware of the controversy that his proposal would elicit, he warned the audience that opponents would no doubt deride his project for authorizing "polygamous deputies."[96] No stranger to this debate, Deputy Blaise Diagne, elected from the Four Communes of Senegal in 1914, weighed in on the

---

92. Morand, *Contribution à l'étude des réformes*, 22. Speaking vehemently against the Viollette Bill on March 21, 1935, Senator Paul Cuttoli reprised this exact passage. *JO*, Sénat, March 21, 1935, 357. Also cited in Jeanne Bowlan, "Polygamists Need Not Apply," 117.

93. Morand, *Contribution à l'étude des réformes*, 18. See also Conseil supérieur de l'Algérie, *Procès-verbaux*, Séance June 30, 1916, 116–17.

94. Rapport Moutet, *JO*, Doc. Parl., Chambre, annexe 4383 (March 1, 1918), 348. For an overview see Ageron, *Les Algériens musulmans*, 2: 1205–8.

95. See Bowlan, "Polygamists Need Not Apply," and Fogarty, *Race and War in France*, 252–57.

96. Ligue des droits de l'homme, "Le Congrès de 1917—Les droits politiques des Indigènes en Algérie," 74.

question as well. He had recently taken advantage of wartime to develop legislation that granted military recruits from the Four Communes and their descendants recognition as citizens without regard to their personal status.[97] A precedent for advocates of Algerian political reform, Diagne's measure provoked considerable resistance from colonial jurists on similar grounds. For Pierre Dareste, the founder of the leading French journal of colonial law, polygamy emblematized how the Muslim law of these "new citizens" from Senegal was "diametrically opposed to the Civil Code."[98] In now lending his support to Algerian political reform, Diagne marshaled a witty response at the Ligue assembly: he pointed out how the French army actually needed Muslim men to make up for their own diminished forces and low birthrate. Echoing Charles Mangin's claims in *La Force noire*, he provocatively proclaimed: "Don't you think that it is a service, a happy chance for France to have possessions with polygamous populations?"[99]

In her speech to the Ligue on the subject, feminist journalist Séverine also overturned assumptions about Muslim Algerians' political and sexual difference. Her address highlighted instead what Algerians and women shared: political marginalization despite their wartime sacrifices. For Séverine, women's and Algerians' suffrage rights were linked, because "all inequalities are connected." She presented jurists' focus on Algerians' polygamy as diversionary both politically and psychically, observing that "if we look around ourselves well, it might be possible to detect a certain Occidental phariseeism: the thing is practiced, but the word is denied [*la pratique de la chose, le refus du mot*]."[100] In other words, for Séverine, a literalist interpretation of the Civil Code that presented the French citizen as monogamous in contrast to the presumptively polygamous Algerian obscured sexual inequality in French society, including persistent legal protections on men's sexual license. Denying its existence "at home," jurists and politicians projected patriarchy onto Muslim men in order to justify their political exclusion. Séverine's brief statement distilled the double denegation at work in the politicization of polygamy. Obscured by the language of law, the unnamed "thing" continued in practice. It was avowed only by symptomatic negation: the refusal of full citizenship to Muslim Algerians who had maintained this "right."

---

97. "Loi du 29 septembre 1916," *JO*, Lois et décrets, October 1, 1916, 8667–68. Also, Conklin, *Mission to Civilize*, 155; Mann, *Native Sons*, 69–70; Fogarty, *Race and War in France*, 239–40.

98. Pierre Dareste, "Les nouveaux citoyens français (loi du 29 septembre 1916)," *Receuil de législation et jurisprudence coloniales*, 2, 8. For Dareste the religious basis of "Muslim law" presented an essential conflict with the "laïcité" of the Civil Code. Cited in Saada, *Empire's Children*, 104.

99. Ligue des droits de l'homme, "Le Congrès de 1917—Les droits politiques des Indigènes en Algérie," 91–2. Also, Mangin, *La force noire*, 285.

100. "Le Congrès de 1917—Les droits politiques des Indigènes en Algérie," 93.

In their interventions before the Ligue, Diagne and Séverine slyly pointed to the affective denials and displacements at work in contemporary debates about Algerians' polygamy and political rights. They showed how the imperative to renounce polygamy "in name, if not in practice" obscured sexual privileges and gendered exclusions that endured in French political and civil law. Contrary to jurists' claims, that law did not instantiate universalism, nor did it extend equality to all citizens. Unrepresented in the "Symbolic" language of the Civil Code, the unnamed "thing" of polygamy persisted, but was only expressed in a displaced and apparently unfamiliar form.[101] "Muslim" polygamy exhibited the sexual difference that was maintained in French codes as if it were foreign. In this sense, it was extimate to French law.

The question of whether polygamy was compatible with citizenship remained at the heart of the debate over Algerian political reform. Moutet's voluminous report discussed the question at length, answering the multiple objections raised by Governor-General Lutaud and Morand on personal status and citizenship. In Moutet's view, polygamy furnished "the strongest objection to naturalization in status." He nonetheless argued that personal status could be reconciled with political rights and marshaled a host of arguments in support of this position. Using statistics to support his claims, he urged that polygamy was always "limited and exceptional," ultimately destined to disappear. While avowing that "Muslim personal status goes against our sense of moral conceptions, of our juridical notion of public order," he did not consider that status and the polygamy that it permitted "a definitive obstacle to the concession of political rights or the quality of citizen."[102] For Moutet, refusal of such rights was hypocritical, as it was for Abdesselem, precisely because polygamy was *already* part of French law: "this supposedly immoral custom is already legal; the legislator is not unaware of it— and what is more our judges must apply it every time it comes before their tribunals." Moutet also expressed a certain moral skepticism toward French claims to superiority: "Can we seriously ask whether, based on our conceptions, our monogamous societies are more moral than polygamous societies? Is there less adultery, are there fewer illegitimate children [*enfants naturels*], less prostitution, fewer sex crimes [*attentats criminels aux mœurs*]?"[103] Adopting a relativist stance, his proposed law ultimately required candidates to submit to French civil law, but only for the *future* (articles 11 and 12). Men who already had multiple wives would remain married to them, and their children would remain legitimate.

---

101. On the uncanny representation of the "thing" see Lacan, *Seminar VII*, 71.
102. Rapport Moutet, *JO*, Doc. Parl., Chambre, annexe 4383 (March 1, 1918), 330.
103. Ibid., 332–33.

Provisions for polygamous citizens provoked a vigorous response from the Algerian Conseil supérieur de gouvernement. The secretary-general of the Conseil declared it "unacceptable that polygamy, which is considered contrary to public order and is even qualified as a crime in penal law, could be tolerated among *indigènes* who are French citizens under the pretext of respect for their vested right [*droit acquis*]."[104] Pointing to potential conflicts of law, the director of indigenous affairs Dominique Luciani feigned concern for women: "In the family of the French citizen who has remained polygamous, what will be the situation of women?"[105] Governor-General Jonnart concurred, asserting that there was a need for "a line of demarcation between the two legislations; it is best to establish it at the moment that natives ask to be admitted to the quality of French citizen."[106] As he explained in his final version of the project, "It is hard to admit that there might be polygamous citizens given that French law forbids polygamy."[107] The Conseil and the governor-general sought to restrict not just polygamy but more substantive rights, such as expanded political representation and the elimination of repressive tribunals. In the course of the debate, polygamy served to symbolically demarcate the two laws and hence the two populations.

A month later, representatives in the *délégations financières* displayed equally violent reactions. As Émile Morinaud explained in his report to the *non-colon* section, "it would be enough for *indigènes* to assemble their family according to Muslim law before naturalization in order to maintain the benefits of their personal status when they become French." "French Algeria" would, he urged, not be "fooled" (*ne sera pas dupe*) by articles that allowed the new citizen's family to remain under personal status law.[108] Defending a revised version of the law, indigenous affairs director Luciani stressed that any Algerian who became a citizen "will notably renounce polygamy, and as a result, there will be equality of rights and duties between him and all French citizens."[109] Faced with such opposition from Algerian politicians, it was ultimately this iteration that was adopted as the so-called Jonnart Law on February 4, 1919. The symbolic and practical victory of this exclusive vision of Frenchness featured prominently in

---

104. "Projet de loi fixant les conditions d'accession des indigènes à la qualité de citoyen français," Délibérations du Conseil du Gouvernement, Extraits des procès-verbaux, April 5, 1918, 38–39, in AN 19950167/2.

105. "Projet de loi," Délibérations, in AN 19950167/2.

106. "Projet de loi," Délibérations, 43, in AN 19950167/2.

107. Gov. Gen. to Pres. du Conseil, "Envoi d'un projet de loi," April 19, 1918, 7, in AN 19950167/2.

108. Morinaud, *Délégations financières algériennes*, May 29, 1918, Section *non-colons*, 249. Duret in his report to the Section *colons* reproduced Morinaud's motion, *Délégations financières algériennes*, June 22, 1918, Section *colons*, 580. For an overview see Bouveresse, *Un parlement colonial*, 1:174–79.

109. Luciani, *Délégations financières algériennes*, May 29, 1918, Section *non-colons*, 259.

the second article, which required that all those who asked for citizenship had to be "monogamous or a bachelor."[110]

Population and Polygamy

The Jonnart Law's restrictive framework marked the foreclosure of the political possibilities created by the war. Loaded down in the end with cumbersome administrative requirements, it resulted in few new citizens (some 1,204 successful applications between 1919 and 1930).[111] The law did, however, extend the franchise for Algerians without citizenship in municipal council and mayoral elections, as well as for the Conseil général and *délégations financières*.[112] For the reform's most virulent critics, however, the law conceded too much. A regular columnist for the *Écho d'Alger*, Fernand Ancey, who was president of the Union of Algerian Tobacco Farmers and vice president of the Confederation of Agriculture, demonstrated how fears of the polygamous citizen's demographic and political threat persisted. Ancey claimed that because "Muslim" marriages were infrequently registered, Algerians could claim citizenship, while "continuing to live maritally as they do now." He predicted that the French element in Algeria would "disappear, engulfed by the primitive race, or forced away [*refoulée*]."[113] Ancey likewise denounced prepubescent marriage as evidence of Algerian criminality, as "the male spouse's lubricity, the father's desire for wealth, incite them to violate the law . . . and even other things." For Ancey, these libidinous traits evidently rendered Algerians' political assimilation "impossible."[114]

Such cliché-filled commentary was, as we have seen, in many ways unremarkable. The response that it drew, not only in letters to the editor, but also in an increasingly visible and vibrant liberal Algerian press, was, however, new.[115] In the wake of the war, Young Algerians founded new French-language publications to advocate for their positions, while escaping the heavier censorship that was imposed on Arabic-language publications. The most prominent, *Ikdam* (Courage) was close to the newly influential and charismatic politician Emir

---

110. "Loi du 4 Fevrier 1919 sur l'accession des indigènes de l'Algérie aux droits politiques," *JO*, Lois et décrets, February 6, 1919, 1358–59.

111. Weil, "Le statut des musulmans en Algérie coloniale," 106.

112. McDougall, *History of Algeria*, 152.

113. Fernand Ancey, "La question indigène: Électeurs et éligible," *L'Écho d'Alger*, February 16, 1919.

114. Fernand Ancey, "La question indigène: Le statut personnel," *L'Écho d'Alger*, March 16, 1919.

115. See letter by Ioulalen Arezki in *L'Écho d'Alger*, February 26, 1919.

Khaled, grandson of the hero of Algerian resistance, Abd el Kader. In addition to operating as a political organ for the francophone Algerian elite, the paper spoke to a "French" readership, including in the colonial administration.[116] From its first issues in 1919, the journal responded to what one contributor called Ancey's "long hateful diatribe." M. Kherroubi refuted the accusations by asserting that personal status was indeed French law: "The personal status of *indigènes* is regulated by laws, decrees, and *arrêtés*. In matters of marriage, divorce, and inheritance, by the Muslim Code. This Muslim Code has been sanctioned by laws; it has become the French Code for Algeria."[117] As he made clear, Muslim law was not just legitimate, it was legitimately French. According to Oukali Sadi, a wounded veteran, Ancey's column, with its focus on Muslim sex and marriage, displayed an outdated settler mentality. He dismissively denounced Ancey as "a little potentate of the very old school who must have been in a profound sleep from August 2, 1914, until today."[118] Reversing tropes of Orientalist backwardness, Sadi's settler slumbered in a historical time lag of petty tyranny, while young Algerians now represented modernity.

Bringing our story full circle, *Ikdam* chose to republish Taleb Abdesselem's 1918 "Islam and the Allied Cause" speech in the context of this debate. As we saw at the beginning of the chapter, Abdesselem explicitly rejected outdated fantasies about polygamy as an obstacle to Muslim Algerians' "*droit de cité*." Asserting Algerians' sexual modernity, he noted that "today a French Muslim blushes at the idea of having two wives."[119] Abdesselem's powerful intervention was not, however, the paper's last word on the prospects of the polygamous citizen.

A multipart article, "On Polygamy," by A. D. de Beaumont offered a remarkable rejoinder to what Beaumont referred to as Abdesselem's "false modesty" on the subject. The prominently placed series was hyperbolic and satirical, but like a good joke it expressed a kernel of unconscious truth. In answer to Abdesselem, it claimed that "Christians of Europe do not blush at all in possessing several women/wives [*femmes*], and in France, those who are known to have much success with the fair sex, far from being singled out, are the object of laudatory admiration that is traced with envy." "No," Beaumont continued, "Christians, neither in Europe, nor elsewhere, do not blush at having several women/wives.

---

116. Dunwoodie, *Francophone Writing in Transition*, 56. See also Meynier, *L'émir Khaled*, 271; Ihaddaden, *Histoire de la presse indigène*; Asseraf, "Foreign News in Colonial Algeria, 1881–1940."

117. M. Kherroubi, "J'ai souri," *Ikdam*, April 5, 1919.

118. Oukali Sadi, "Réflexions d'un poilu," *Ikdam*, April 5, 1919. See also the responses in *Ikdam*, March 29, 1919.

119. Taleb Abdesselem, "Une conférence sur les Musulmans," *Ikdam*, July 26, 1919.

Only they don't admit it [*ne les avouent pas*]. For there is a lot of hypocrisy in human nature and Christians are not exempt, despite their pretention to superiority." In his view, the perverse and dangerous effects of "Christian pseudo-monogamy," including abortions, infanticide, and depopulation, made French sexual mores not only dishonest, but deadly.[120] What is more, the legalization of paternity searches in 1912 had now opened the way for the legal recognition of this "de facto polygamy."[121] Given "French law's idea of matrimony" he could not explain "our legislator's horror of polygamy . . . among other people [*chez les autres*]."[122]

Beaumont's subsequent articles ironically elaborated on natalist themes by illuminating the mortal implications of France's fake monogamy: "Our conception of monogamy aggravates a falling natality, facing us with this very real danger, O Frenchmen, of being submerged by more prolific races and especially the race that we think we have just vanquished."[123] He underscored that it was "strange" to "refuse the sons of Islam full entry into the French city under the tacit pretext that they can marry several women," while "our civilization, supposedly edified and consolidated by the mortar of monogamy, practices, in fact, but hypocritically, a fatal polygamy."[124] Mocking clichés of the sexual civilizing mission, Beaumont represented France's pseudomonogamy as a source not of advancement, but of decline.

Beaumont's articles humorously suggested how polygamy could be a fantasmatic solution to grave population decline, the erosion of French masculinity, and the dangers of an excess of unmarried women.[125] In Algeria, anxieties about the size and growth of the "French" population were particularly acute, exacerbated by declining migration rates and birthrates, as well as the increased sense of the political threat posed by the native Muslim population. In the decade following the war, associations such as the Ligues des familles nombreuses of Algeria actively promoted measures to politically and materially support large

---

120. A. D. de Beaumont, "De la polygamie," *Ikdam*, August 16, 1919. Subsequent articles appeared on August 23, September 20, October 30, and November 6, 1919. He also wrote regularly for *Islam* before the war.

121. A. D. de Beaumont, "De la polygamie," *Ikdam*, September 20, 1919. On the *recherche de paternité* see Fuchs, *Contested Paternity*. The law did not apply in the colonies: Saada, *Empire's Children*; Pedersen, "'Special Customs.'"

122. A. D. de Beaumont, "De la polygamie," *Ikdam*, August 16, 1919.

123. A. D. de Beaumont, "De la polygamie," *Ikdam*, September 20, 1919.

124. Ibid.

125. On how the postwar imagination of polygamy was linked to fears of single women and population concerns see M. L. Roberts, *Civilization without Sexes*, 155.

"European," as opposed to native Algerian, families.[126] The fantasy of polygamy could be seen as a distorting mirror of these more familiar natalist strategies. An article in the *Annales africaines* in 1916 made the argument explicitly, proclaiming, "We only have to have recourse to ourselves, our own human resources . . . in instituting polygamy!"[127] In 1923, the scabrous pamphleteer Georges Anquetil's *La Maîtresse légitime* likewise suggested how polygamy could solve France's gender and population ills.[128] And a cartoon in a risqué humor magazine, *Le journal amusant*, pursued the theme in its satire of polygamy's potential to save France's population—and men—from the gender crisis precipitated by the war. As depicted by Max Radiguet, the legalization of polygamy could overcome sterility and lesbianism, give all women a "right to legitimate conjugal joys," and grant French men access to the pleasures of a colonial harem. It would also repopulate France.[129] Similar to Beaumont's column, the cartoon registered how polygamy was desired and disavowed. What made it funny was, as the debate about Algerians' access to citizenship made clear, how polygamy appeared as an extimate fantasy of French men.

For opponents of reform, Algerians needed to sacrifice the sexual *jouissance* of personal status in order to accede to the abstract *jouissance* of citizenship. I have suggested how these arguments were based on projective identification, in which jurists and politicians denounced the exorbitant sexual rights of personal status as incompatible with citizenship because they granted unfair advantages to Algerian men. These assertions were suffused with affective and erotic investments. They displayed recurrent resentment and jealousy, as well as fears of French de-virilization. The relationship between French and Muslim law was not, however, a relationship of pure opposition, given how French fantasies and desires regularly disavowed the sexual privilege and inequality that persisted in French civil and political law. Understanding how "Muslim law" was extimate to "French law" helps clarify the visceral intensity of French charges against Algerian men at the very moment that the latter began to claim a measure of political equality. It also explains how and why those charges were vulnerable to both mockery and critique.

---

126. Barthelet, "Natalité et peuplement en Afrique du Nord." Also, Andersen, *Regeneration through Empire*, 215–16.

127. C. Mairin, "Après la guerre: Repopulation," *Annales africaines*, May 1, 1916, 103. See also "Les vieilles filles," *Annales africaines*, March 1, 1917. Also, the account of a campaign in favor of polygamy in *L'Union républicaine* of Philippeville, in *Annales africaines*, July 15, 1917, 169.

128. Anquetil, *La maîtresse légitime*.

129. Radiguet, "Polygamie," *Le Journal amusant*, April 7, 1923.

FIGURE 10 / Max Radiguet, *La Polygamie*, from *Le Journal amusant*, April 7, 1923, 11. Bibliothèque nationale de France.

In their publications and their pronouncements, Young Algerians and their allies called attention to these affectively laden legal arguments. In asserting that Muslim law *was* French law, they critically recast understandings of these sexually demarcated legislations. Intellectuals such as Taleb Abdesselem pointed to how Muslim personal status was a French legal construct, while working to undo "novelistic" sexual fantasies about it. These critiques also indicated how denial structured claims about French law's sexual superiority by pointing to ongoing restrictions on married women's property, their exclusion from citizenship, and the persistence of "polygamy" in extramarital practice.

That which was supposedly most different about "Muslim law" appeared in such accounts as unsettlingly familiar, as critics of French "pseudomonogamy" made clear. The apparent irony of the 1919 Jonnart Law's strictures on monogamy was all the more apparent in France's widely perceived postwar population crisis, with its deficit of young French men and a surfeit of single women. The fantasy of polygamy as a parodic population panacea tellingly emerged at precisely the moment that monogamy became a condition of full citizenship. By criticizing French fantasies of Muslim law, young Algerians simultaneously asserted their own modernity. They suggested how jurists, politicians, and (as we will see in the next chapter) novelists were tethered to a colonial past anchored by such fantasies. In calling attention to this historical and legal disjuncture, they sought to shift the place of Muslim law in French law from a structuring *extimité* to a future-oriented *droit de cité*.

8

COLONIAL LITERATURE AND CUSTOMARY LAW

In 1907, a young woman named Thamil'la stood before a judge of the Appeals Court in Tizi-Ouzou, a sub-prefecture in the heart of Grand Kabylie. She was in a state of "insurrection" and refused to return to her conjugal domicile and husband. Thamil'la had taken refuge at her parents' house, where she had just given birth to a daughter. After removing her veil so that she could be identified and speaking through a translator, she insisted that she "did not want to return to her husband." Her spouse, Akli, also present in the courtroom, implored her, recalling their happy existence in the nearby port city of Dellys. She looked at him searchingly and began to cry, while clutching her newborn child. One of the judges, speaking to her directly in Berber, urged: "Go. Return to your husband and bring him your child. . . . You have the right, the duty, and the freedom!" Thamil'la quietly insisted that she would not go. The judge was obliged "to ratify the will that she has thus expressed against all expectation and to rule according to the exigencies of Kabyle *qanouns*, as excessive as they might seem."[1] Here again was a French magistrate bound by law to enforce a judgment with which he profoundly disagreed. The judge thought that Thamil'la's supposed "insurrection" was in fact orchestrated by the greedy machinations of her father. By extracting payment from her husband before returning her to Akli's home and bed, he would be able to "eat twice from his daughter." The judge's intuition was correct. Once Thamil'la's father obtained his money, he indeed released her, and she returned home to her husband.

This case of a cynical and self-interested patriarch standing in the way of a young woman's marital bliss recalls others that we have encountered in the course of this book. The French judge had the girl's best interest at heart, but custom, as preserved by Algerian colonial law, stood in the way of his chivalric intentions.[2] He had no choice but to enforce this objectionable law.

---

1. Duchêne, *Thamil'la* (1907), 32.
2. On "chivalrous" judges see Sharafi, "Semi-autonomous Judge in Colonial India."

Thamil'la's case did not appear in the *Revue algérienne et tunisienne de jurisprudence* or, for that matter, any other colonial legal digest. Originally published in *L'Illustration*, the trial was a scene in a novel by colonial magistrate Ferdinand Duchêne. A longer, and even more tragic, serialized version of the "turtledove" story appeared in the biweekly *Les Annales africaines* in 1914. In that later rendering, Thamil'la returned to her husband only to be eventually repudiated, remarried to an old man, to be once again repudiated and ultimately reduced to prostitution. In the end, she is put out of her misery when she dies mad in an asylum. This image of the suffering Algerian woman was legible to contemporary readers—as it is now to us. If I have initially recounted the case *as if* it were an actual trial, it is to underscore how sentimentalism pervaded both fiction and jurisprudence in colonial Algeria. The artifice of such stereotypes, as Lauren Berlant suggests, is paradoxically what makes them so effective. Bridging realism and fantasy, the readily recognizable cliché links individual cases to apparently universal feelings in order to bind together their readers. In this chapter, I suggest how the "sentimental fiction" of imperial reform, as Laura Wexler has suggested, extended beyond a literary genre. The feelings that it elicited, for example in Duchêne's novels, animated colonial projects that often subjugated the very populations that those projects promised to protect.[3]

Sentimental and eroticized depictions of characters such as Thamil'la spurred colonial legal reform in Algeria, including new efforts in the interwar period to alter Kabyle "customary law." Duchêne's fictions make discernible how colonial juridical argument drew on feeling, rendering palpable how legal narratives relied on literary tropes and techniques. This connection between law and literature was explicit in the case of Duchêne. In addition to writing novels, he worked in Kabylie as a magistrate for over twenty years.

Reformist Sentiments

Duchêne encountered the places and people that spurred his literary imagination in the course of his long Algerian legal career. Born near Limoges in the Haute-Vienne in 1868, he moved to Algeria in 1895 after tiring of his life as a provincial

---

3. Berlant, *Female Complaint*, 36. Also, Berlant, "Subject of True Feeling." Laura Wexler analyzes the parallel "sentimental fiction" of projects of Indian schooling in the late nineteenth-century United States: see Wexler, *Tender Violence*, 105.

lawyer.[4] The move helped him to advance. After winning the inaugural Grand Prix Littéraire de l'Algérie in 1921, he became one of the most influential writers and jurists in Algeria, shaping not just public opinion but also "native affairs" policy. Working as a government expert, he publicized the Kabyle woman's plight and sought to reform it.

Duchêne was not the only literary magistrate in Algeria. Other contemporary jurists, such as Charles Barbet, Marie-Louis-Raymond Vaissié, and Maxime Massoni, also drew on judicial expertise to publish sensational and sentimentalized accounts of suffering Algerian women. They often focused on Kabyle women from the regions to which they were assigned.[5] The Kabylie region itself constituted a separate jurisdiction, overseen by French *juges de paix* since 1874; its customary law, because it was unwritten, was particularly challenging to administer. Technically assisted by *assesseurs kabyles*, French judges often relied on Hanoteau and Letourneux's 1873 compendium of *qanouns* in formulating their judgments.

Presumed to be distinct from Qur'anic law, these *qanouns* were unaffected by earlier reform efforts focused on Muslim law. A separate campaign around them coalesced in the 1920s, when Duchêne, alongside law faculty doyen Marcel Morand and several representatives of the Kabyle section of the *délégations financières*, spearheaded this effort. These reformers began to fixate on Kabyle women's plight just as thousands of Kabyle men left to work in the metropole after the First World War.[6]

Pursuing this cause, Duchêne located himself within a long tradition of sentimental novels. Hoping that his book would provoke "great emotion," he wanted it to be, "for Berber women, what *Uncle Tom's Cabin* was for slaves."[7] His novel indeed bore resemblances to Stowe's abolitionist ur-text, which famously opposed the immoral "masculine" state law of slavery to higher principles of moral and religious law.[8] Duchêne's *Thamil'la* similarly mobilized moral feeling

4. See Henri Casanova, "Ferdinand Duchêne: Romancier Algérien," *Nouvelles littéraires*, February 21, 1925.

5. The competency of French *juges de paix* in the jurisdictions of Tizi-Ouzou and Bougie were fixed by the decree of April 29, 1874.

6. Slimani-Direche, *Histoire de l'émigration kabyle en France*.

7. See Henri Casanova, "Ferdinand Duchêne: Romancier Algérien," *Nouvelles Littéraires*, February 21, 1925. Duchêne was not alone in making the connection; an earlier review drew the same analogy: see Guillon, "Thamil'la," *L'Attakadoum*, December 15, 1923. The novel was notably translated into English by American missionaries: see Duchêne, *Thamilla*, "*The Turtle-Dove.*"

8. On sentiment and law in Stowe see Brophy, "Harriet Beecher Stowe's Critique of Slave Law." There are also notable parallels with anti-Mormon novels that focused on polygamy: see Gordon, "Our National Hearthstone," 334–35.

against the apparent inhumanity of a customary law that had been "preserved" (but, as we have seen, also produced) by the colonial state.

Duchêne's fantasy of rescue exhibited moralized horror at the Kabyle woman's sexual degradation. By stimulating powerful feelings, he sought to spur the transformation of customary law, which, without fixed statutes, had no stable textual ground. But this hoped-for reform also raised epistemological and political problems that emblematized the legally ambivalent status of Algerian subjects. With no structure of political representation, it was difficult to say who actually represented Kabyle custom and who could authorize its reform. To answer this political quandary, the colonial administration called on Duchêne's legal and novelistic imagination.[9] Drawing on a long sentimentalist genealogy, Duchêne and other jurists' writings elicited ambivalent emotions about the very colonial subjects whose plights they made palpable.[10] His cliché-ridden novels notably gained public currency just as debates about Algerians' access to political rights intensified. Thought to appeal to a female readership, these sentimental fictions simultaneously obscured the political exclusion that French women actually shared with Algerians.

Not all readers were seduced by Duchêne's touching tales. On the one hand, contemporary "Algerianist" writers who valorized *pied noir* virility dismissed Duchêne's fixation on Algerian women's misery as decadent and feminizing. On the other, Young Algerians criticized his clichéd stories of the suffering Kabyle woman for reinforcing their legal and political exclusion. In response, these intellectuals elaborated what can be seen as a *counter*-sentimental project that both reflected and reflected on sentimentalism's imperial power.[11]

Fantasies of Rescue

Kabylie's distinct juridical organization had its origins in official reactions to the 1871 Moqrani Rebellion. As a punitive response, the French imposed new *juges de paix* in the region in order to assert control over a population that long had a

---

9. On affect and the production and regulation of customary law see Povinelli, "State of Shame." On storytelling and the colonial crafting of "customary law" see Reichman, "Undignified Details." On sentiment and unwritten law see Hartog, "Lawyering, Husbands' Rights, and 'the Unwritten Law.'"

10. Festa, *Sentimental Figures of Empire*, 4. On the genealogy of sentimentality as perpetually unfinished see Berlant, *Female Complaint*.

11. Fromage, "L'expérience des 'Jeunes Algériens'"; Merad, "Islam et nationalisme arabe en Algérie"; Ageron, "Le mouvement 'Jeune-Algérien.'" On counter-sentimentality see Berlant, *Female Complaint*.

reputation for fierce independence. The distinct and supposedly "secular" status of local *qanouns* informed how colonial administrators conceived Kabyle difference. Their presumptive secularism led republican reformers and Catholic missionaries to view the mountainous region as a promising challenge.[12] Reformers assumed that women were key to these missionary efforts. As one administrator explained, "It is not by the head that one should try to assimilate and transform a people: it is by the humble and suffering, which is to say, in Kabylie, by women."[13]

Magistrates who were named to the region as *juges de paix*, including Camille Sabatier in Tizi-Ouzou in the 1880s and Gaston Ricci in Fort National (Larbaâ Nath Irathen) in the 1890s, spearheaded these efforts by presenting Kabyle women's degradation as a shining promise for civilizing reform. A proponent of the "Kabyle myth," Sabatier drew a distinction between Arab and Kabyle on the basis of law. Under French influence, he hoped that "the old Qanouns will everywhere be softened, and the Kabyle woman, so intelligent, so laborious, and so gifted, will certainly cease to be an object of pity."[14] Ricci, a *juge de paix* in Fort National (and eventual Algerian deputy in the National Assembly), worked to modify Kabyle custom through jurisprudence.[15] In a famous case from 1899, he permitted a woman, Hamama bent Mohamed, to divorce her husband after she refused to return to her conjugal domicile. While her husband, Bouzid Mohamed ben Abdelaziz, claimed that the divorce violated the custom fixed by law in 1874, Ricci appealed to principles of "public order." Asserting the prerogative of the French magistrate, he proclaimed that "the French judge always maintains the ability to give, in certain cases, preference to French law," thus releasing judges from "the obligation of remaining enslaved to sometimes barbarous and monstrous customs."[16]

Sexual horror played a crucial role in Ricci's account of these monstrous customs. His decision in this divorce case foregrounded Hamama's embodied sexual suffering, as "she could not tolerate the intimate relations to which her husband forced her to submit." A forensic pathologist buttressed the argument, finding

---

12. Lorcin, *Imperial Identities*; Slimani-Direche, *Chrétiens de Kabylie*.

13. H. Dubouloz, "Contribution à l'oeuvre de Madame Attanoux," *La Revue nord africaine* 1 (1902): 602.

14. C. Sabatier, "Étude sur la femme kabyle," 68–69. On Sabatier and the "Kabyle myth" see Lorcin, *Imperial Identities*, 158–63.

15. Marcel Morand suggested how subsequent jurisprudence was informed by Ricci's 1899 ruling: see *RA*, 1922, pt. 2, 82, note Morand. And, Maurice Olivant, "La femme kabyle," *Les Annales africaines* 37, no. 4 (December 4, 1925): 1.

16. Hamama bent Mohamed v. Bouzid Mohamed ben Abdelaziz, Justice de Paix de Fort National (January 11, 1899), *RA*, 1899, pt. 2, 520–21. For a related discussion of Hamama's case see Ghabrial, "Traumas and Truths of the Body," 295–96.

that "there exists a real disproportion between the genital organs of the husband and those of the wife." For Ricci, these "serious motives sufficiently explain why the young woman feels a kind of horror for her husband and formally refuses to return to him." In a state of "insurrection," as it was termed, Hamama could not remarry unless Bouzid Mohamed released her. Asserting French legal supremacy, Ricci liberated her from the bond, making her "free" to marry again.[17] Focused on visceral pain and disgust, Ricci drew on this sentimental supplement to bolster his argument about the superiority of French law. These affectively charged accounts of custom were points of departure, not only for jurists' legal decisions, but also for their "literature."

Marie Louis Raymond Vaissié, a *juge de paix* in Fedj M'zala and Ténès, wrote novels of "Kabyle" *mœurs* under the pen name Raymond Marival. An associate of the cross-dressing travel and fiction writer Isabelle Eberhardt, Vaissié had none of her literary gifts. He did have a talent, however, for recycling clichés about Kabyle custom, including in his 1901 novel *Chair d'ambre* (Amber flesh). It told the story of a young peasant girl, Taous, who was "thin, delicate, small, with flesh of amber and sunshine" and the "prettiness of a small savage animal."[18] After falling in love with the young Tahar, Taous learns that she has already been promised to Abderrahman, who had paid dower money to her father in advance. Upon discovering that Taous is no longer a virgin, Abderrahman sends her back to her parents. Pregnant, she is subject to the village elders' judgment, based on the local *qanouns*. They condemn her to death by stoning. The journal *Mercure de France*'s review of the story described Taous's fate in the language of religious sentiment and devotion, commending Marival for testifying to her suffering: "Dying a martyr, she fell victim to ferocious prejudices; no one will burn a candle before her alter of brutal stones, but Raymond Marival, author of her grace, should be glorified among all men of letters for the delicious creation of a virgin mother, so naïvely culpable."[19]

These themes of love, sacrifice, and sacrificed love recur in Marival's follow-up novel, *Le Çof*, about a young *juge de paix* named André Miral who comes to Algeria from the metropole on the eve of the Margueritte revolt. Miral's naïve hopes of colonial progress distinguish him from the prejudiced settlers whom he encounters in the fictional Kabyle village of Gravelotte. He soon falls for the

17. Ibid. For another case where Ricci employed a similar logic and jurisprudential strategy see Areski ben Rabah v. Laah Kaci, Justice de Paix de Fort National (June 16, 1902), *RA*, pt. 2, 263–66.

18. Marival, *Chair d'ambre*, 92.

19. "Chair d'Ambre," *Mercure de France* 38, no. 138 (June 1901): 749–50.

young Miassa, "in whom he sensed the Muslim woman's qualities of abandon and tenderness[;] he little by little transferred the sympathies filling his heart to the entire race."[20] André draws closer to Miassa, lending her works of Orientalist fantasy by Pierre Loti after her family no longer permits her to attend school. When André realizes that he has fallen in love, he is stunned by the revelation: "For a long time, love for Miassa was in him, nestled like a timid bird, and he alone did not know. This love smoldered, like a fire under ashes. With an indiscreet blow, the flame had just suddenly leapt forth." His affection surges forth as the belated recognition of an unconscious feeling that eroticized the compliant qualities of the woman he hopes to save. He embraces her abandon and tenderness, as well as the "sweet and docile soul that shone in the depth of her eyes and reached the edge of her lips, as limpid and as pure as a stream of water." The scene is set for romantic fusion when André declares his love: "Miassa, I have come to you as a supplicant and as a liberator. I offer you, with my soul, keys that open to the unknown, the wide free air from which you were severed. Would you like for me to guide you on the route?"[21] Leading her to liberty, André was always ahead.

The events of the Margueritte revolt and a feud between rival tribes intervene to disrupt this dream. André leaves for France, and when he returns, Miassa has been "sacrificed" by her father, promised to the head of the rival tribe as a gesture of peace. She "no longer held out hope, but her wound continued to bleed." The novel ends with André's last fleeting glimpse of his now sequestered love: "André choked. He long cried for the one he loved and who would no longer know the free caress of the sun."[22] As in *Chair d'ambre*, the pathos of *Le Çof* is produced by the sacrifice of amorous desires to patriarchal Kabyle custom. The judge's first repressed and then avowed fantasy of rescue is interrupted in the final scene by the resented Kabyle law. The novel as a whole offers insight into how, in its colonial legal imaginary, seeming failure, rather than undermining the fantasy of rescue, preserves the eroticized victim as an object of desire. In her perpetual suffering, Miassa forever remains a "sweet and docile soul."

The *Revue nord africaine* regularly featured similar stories of spoiled innocence and female sacrifice. Maxime Massoni, a *juge de paix* from Michelet (Aïn El Hammam), penned a typical tale, *Fatima, la repudiée*, about a young but infertile wife whose husband unilaterally divorces her. Forced to leave at night, she flees in a delirious state. Swallowed up by a river of melting snow, she meets a lonely

---

20. Marival, *Le Çof*, 90. The novel initially appeared in serial form in *Mercure de France*. On Margueritte see Phéline, *L'aube d'une révolution*.

21. Marival, *Le Çof*, 164, 76.

22. Ibid., 251, 55.

demise: "Fatima is now but a cadaver carried away by the torrent." This pathos-filled ending was an ideal platform for the jurist's appeal. Mobilizing the pain of Fatima's fictional suffering, he drew on the sentimental tropes of abolitionism to propose reforms to customary law: "From woman to slave there is only a step. Custom does not allow women to demand divorce: in response to the husband's right of oppression only the right to escape corresponds." In publicizing his salvationist fantasy of the Kabyle woman, Massoni hoped to "raise her moral level in the family, and in order to do so, make her the equal of the spouse, give her the same rights and notably the right to demand divorce when she believes that she has sufficient motive." He declared these to be necessary goals of a new "fortunately [heureusement] undertaken humanitarian and social project."[23] This short story allowed Massoni to assume the reassuring role of liberator.

Duchêne's Thamil'la, especially the revised version, embraced this same fantasy. In a new conclusion, he described his encounter with the "svelte and fine" girl in his town and in the agonizing trial he oversaw. In a direct address to his deceased heroine, he avowed an excess of wrenching emotion in the face of apparent juridical impotence: "An immense pity welled up in me, a desperation as well to find myself watching you go by, to be able to do nothing, nothing, me a Christian for you a Muslim." He claimed to have been haunted by the scene: "Later, your image came back to me, obsessing me." The novella ends with a tragic apostrophe to his departed at her grave: "Sleep, rest in peace, Thamil'la, the well named, little sweet and frail turtledove of Kabyle country, poor child who only knew to do three things in your short life: love, cry, and die."[24] Like the fictional works of other literary magistrates, Duchêne's eroticized fantasy of rescue was sustained in and by its perpetual failure. Similar to the grave he visits, his story memorialized the pathetic figure of the "sweet and frail turtledove."

In Duchêne's case, literary success advanced his career, as his Ministry of Justice personnel dossier makes clear. After arriving in Algeria in 1895, he was assigned a typical position for a young magistrate, an assistant justice of the peace or "suppléant de juge de paix rétribué" in Dellys. In 1905, Governor-General Jonnart recommended his promotion to a full judgeship, explaining that "Duchêne is an enlightened magistrate and, at the same time, a very distinguished writer. I am particularly interested in him."[25] Following the recommendation, Duchêne was named as a judge in Guelma a year later and eventually assumed positions as

---

23. Massoni, "Fatima la répudiée," 430–31. See also Louis Calmeilles, "La femme kabyle," La Revue nord africaine 1 (1902): 316–20.

24. Ferdinand Duchêne, "Thamilla," Les Annales africaines, June 26, 1914, 319.

25. Gov. Gen. to Garde des Sceaux, January 7, 1905, in AN BB/6 (II)/829 Duchêne.

an investigating magistrate in Tlemcen and Blidah.[26] In 1917, Deputies Eugène Étienne (Oran) and Gaston Thomson (Constantine) endorsed him to become a prosecuting attorney at the Tribunal of Constantine.[27] The failure of that effort, according to Governor-General Charles Lutaud, caused "painful disappointment among prominent Algerians."[28] Under pressure from these politicians, the ministry relented, appointing Duchêne president of the Tribunal of Tizi-Ouzou in June 1917. Acknowledging the role of literature in his professional success, the *Annales algériennes* encouraged him to publish another "masterpiece of painful sensibility and which is a follow-up [*pendant*] to the so dramatic and yet so truthful story of the unfortunate little Kabyle."[29] Further promotions—and novels—followed. Jonnart requested another transfer for Duchêne, this time to the post of vice president of the Tribunal of Algiers. Praising the writer's talents, he explained that the magistrate devotes "the leisure time left to him by the court to letters."[30] In a follow-up letter, Jonnart highlighted how Duchêne "has studied indigenous milieus in particular" and "knows how to describe them in works of high literary standard, that have been very well liked by the Algerian public and all those who understand the charm of our African France."[31] The strategy was successful: Duchêne was promoted in May 1919. Based in Algiers from that point on, he became a fixture in the social, political, and literary scenes of the capital.

Duchêne's Sentimentalism

Duchêne's success was crowned by the award of the first Grand Prix Littéraire de l'Algérie in 1921. Eminently political, the new literary prize was intended to recognize and publicize the blossoming of Algerian letters. Duchêne happened to be close to the politician who had launched the initiative before the *délégations financières*, Jean-Marie Gustavino, a lawyer and *non-colon* representative from Grand Kabylie.[32] He also had several supporters on the selection committee,

---

26. For an analysis of the career of the colonial magistrate see Renucci, "Le meilleur d'entre nous?"

27. Étienne to Dir. Personnel, Min. of Justice, March 5, 1917; Deputy Gaston Thomson to Min. of Justice, March 10, 1917, AN BB/6 (II)/829 Duchêne.

28. Gov. Gen. to Min. of Justice, April 15, 1917, AN BB/6 (II)/829 Duchêne. "Algerians" referred here to settlers.

29. "Dans la magistrature," *Annales africaines*, July 1, 1917, 150–51.

30. Gov. Gen. to Min. of Justice, March 6, 1919, AN BB/6 (II)/829 Duchêne.

31. Gov. Gen. to Director of Personnel, May 15, 1919, AN BB/6 (II)/829 Duchêne.

32. *Délégations financières algériennes*, Session ordinaire, June 22, 1920, 675.

including Gustavino and Maurice Olivaint, another literary magistrate and lawyer at the Appeals Court of Algiers.[33] Duchêne also had his detractors, especially among supporters of the "Algerianist school," such as Robert Randau and Maximilienne Heller.[34] They spurned Duchêne's hackneyed and lachrymose Orientalism, preferring in their writings to celebrate settlers' Latin virility.[35] The awards committee was initially split between the Algerianist Randau and the sentimentalist Duchêne.[36]

While Duchêne eventually won the prize, controversy over the award persisted. An opinion column in *L'Écho d'Alger* contrasted Duchêne's outmoded "prolongation of contemplative orientalism" with Randau's new virile style, which "affirms itself with force, professes to seize directly in its complexity and in its profound originality the actual life of the colonial province."[37] Algerianist journals such as *Afrique latine* continued to champion Randau, while Duchêne garnered wider appreciation in the metropolitan and local press, which praised his personal and stylistic modesty.[38]

The debate contrasted Duchêne's restraint with Randau's energetic excess. Contemporary critics described how Randau was of the "school of the bulging muscle," providing his readers with "red meat," while Duchêne was "more gracious" and for "vegetarians of literature." Randau's novels featured adventurous, hot-blooded and hot-headed Mediterranean types, like Cassard le Berbère, who "rarely resists his desire, especially when that desire finds itself before a passionate acquiescence."[39] Randau exuded instinctual virility, proclaiming, "I, who have

---

33. Déjeux, "Le Grand Prix Littéraire de l'Algérie."

34. Yvon Evenou-Norvès, "Un grand prix algérien de littérature," *Mercure de France* 148, no. 550 (1921): 255–59. Also, Dunwoodie, *Writing French Algeria*, 135.

35. On Latin virility and the Algerianist school see Lorcin, *Imperial Identities*, chap. 9, and "Women, Gender and Nation in Colonial Novels." On Randau and the Algerianists see Graebner, *History's Place*, chap. 2; Dunwoodie, *Writing French Algeria*, chap. 4; Lanasri, *La littérature algérienne de l'entre-deux-guerres*.

36. Robert Migot, "Le Grand Prix Littéraire Algérien," *L'Afrique du nord illustrée*, December 31, 1921, 2. On the vote see Adam, "Polémiques autour du premier Grand Prix Littéraire de l'Algérie."

37. Essuor d'Erfia, "Robert Randau et le Grand Prix Littéraire Algérien," *L'Écho d'Alger*, March 26 1922.

38. Pierre Edmond, "Autour d'un prix littéraire," *L'Écho d'Alger*, March 28, 1922; "Autour d'un prix littéraire," *L'Écho d'Alger*, March 30, 1922.

39. "Au pas lent des caravanes / Cassard le Berbère," *L'Écho d'Alger*, June 9, 1922. See also Henri de Regnier, "La vie littéraire," *Le Figaro*, January 30, 1922; Ernest Mallebay, "Autour du grand prix littéraire: Les charançons dans le blé," *Annales africaines*, April 6, 1922, 733; "Enquête sur les lettres africaines," *L'Afrique du nord illustrée*, August 17, 1922, 10.

lived my books before writing them, have wanted to only describe men, determined by their needs, their instincts, their head, and their belly."[40]

Randau's detractors condemned his virile vulgarity, praising the prize committee for recognizing Duchêne's more tasteful oeuvre. According to Robert Migot of *L'Afrique du nord illustrée*, Duchêne's novels "seduce the well-read [*lettrés*] and most of the public. With him, no realism and outrageous scenes; a young girl might chance upon one of his books, and find there passionate and ardent passages, but no expression will perturb her. It is an admirable quality in our time of licentiousness, literary and otherwise, a quality that was primordial in the eyes of the jury."[41] According to the *Annales algériennes* and Duchêne's publisher, this sentimental aspect appealed especially to women.

A "beautiful young woman," Madeleine Hocq, who worked in the offices of *Annales algériennes*, was immediately absorbed by Duchêne's manuscript. Reading it in one sitting with "feverish attention," she let out a sob on reaching the end. "Anguished by the profoundly human drama that had entirely penetrated her, conquered by the marvelous talent of the storyteller," she forgot herself. All those who read the story would, according to the critic Ernest Mallebay, "feel their eyes well up with the tears that Madeleine Hocq so abundantly cried." The editors believed that the story of Thamil'la's martyrdom and untimely demise would captivate French women.[42]

Duchêne's writing fulfilled the political ambition of the Grand Prix Littéraire to make Algerian authors more attractive and visible to metropolitan publishers and readers.[43] A major Parisian publisher, Albin Michel, agreed to edit his trilogy and subsequent manuscripts, issuing new volumes at the rate of nearly a book a year for a decade. Explicitly targeting women readers, the publisher seized on sentimentalism as a marketing strategy. An advertisement in *Le Temps* described how after reading "the moving story of a young Kabyle, who, after a delicious love, experiences the worst suffering . . . all women will mix their tears with those of the gentle Thamil'la."[44] A publication notice in *L'Écho d'Alger*

---

40. Cited in Henri de Regnier, "La vie littéraire," *Le Figaro*, January 30, 1922. And "Robert Randau et le Grand Prix Littéraire Algérien," *L'Écho d'Alger*, March 26, 1922. On gender in Randau see Lorcin, "Women, Gender and Nation in Colonial Novels."

41. Robert Migot, "Le Grand Prix Littéraire Algérien," *L'Afrique du nord illustrée*, December 31, 1921, 2.

42. "Enquête sur les lettres africaines," *Annales africaines*, August 17, 1922, 10. Ernest Mallebay retold the story at even greater length when the book-length version was released, in "Thamil'la," *Annales africaines*, March 8, 1923. *Annales* lent considerable support to Duchêne. France Ebra, "Le Grand Prix Littéraire aux *Annales afriaines*," January 19, 1922, 592; Ernest Mallebay, "Intimités," *Annales africaines*, August 10, 1923, 435–36.

43. Lanasri, *La littérature algérienne de l'entre-deux-guerres*, 65–66.

44. Advertisement for *Thamil'la*, *Le Temps*, March 14, 1923.

struck a similar note: "All women will want to read this novel in which emotion predominates and which is, in reality a story in which the author himself was involved."[45] Duchêne's sentimental realism clearly succeeded: the book sold four thousand copies within the first week of its release.[46]

While some critics dismissed this work as facile and formulaic, fellow literary magistrate Charles Barbet, who had likewise "studied, de visu, the mœurs and customs of these Berbers, so attached to their customs," defended Duchêne's "true and sincere painting of Kabyle mœurs" and its broad-based readership.[47] A review in the *Journal des débats* praised the author's courtroom insights: "For those who know how to look with a lucid and penetrating eye, the judge's seat is a marvelous observatory of human passions."[48] Writing in the *Chronique des lettres françaises*, Édouard Maynial praised Duchêne's ability "to make this *Orientale* come alive for our Occidental eyes and souls" and attributed *Thamil'la*'s success to how "the memories of the magistrate fortunately guided the artist's fantasy." This sentimentalism also offered a clear moral: "the protestations of a firm and enlightened conscience against a barbarous law."[49] In stark contrast to the Algerianist school's violence and virility, Duchêne's sentimentalizing fiction embodied a colonial humanism.[50]

By touching French women as well as men, these novels seemed to have a universal appeal that promoted a harmonious understanding of the relationship between France and Algeria. Unlike the Algerianists, who endorsed Algeria's "autonomous dominion" from the metropole, Duchêne sought reconciliation in the name not of "Latin Africa," nor even of "a French Algeria," but of Algeria as "the most beautiful part of France."[51] In his work, the sentimentalized Kabyle woman emblematized why Algeria still needed France and its modern law.

Duchêne also hoped to engage an emerging Kabyle "intellectual elite" who had been trained in French schools.[52] Proclaiming that "times had changed [*le temps a marché*]," he called on them in his preface: "Let's go, *Messieurs, les intellectuals*, let's move forward." As proof that his novel had "already achieved results," he praised the work of Roumane Belkacem, a Kabyle representative in

---

45. "Bibliographie: Thamil'la," *L'Écho d'Alger*, March 12, 1923.

46. "Thamil'la," *Annales africaines*, March 22, 1923. On this new market see Lorcin, *Historicizing Colonial Nostalgia*.

47. Charles Barbet, "À propos d'un roman de M. Ferdinand Duchêne," *La Vie algérienne*, June 7, 1925, 8.

48. "Le Grand Prix Littéraire de l'Algérie," *Journal des débats*, February 2, 1922.

49. "Thamil'la," *Chronique des lettres françaises* 1, no. 3 (May–June 1923): 430.

50. On colonial humanism see Wilder, *French Imperial Nation-State*, 77–78.

51. Ferdinand Duchêne, "France-Algérie: La petite patrie et la grande," *Bulletin de la Société de Géographie d'Alger et de l'Afrique du Nord* 3, no. 103 (1925): 286.

52. Colonna, *Instituteurs algériens*.

the *délégations financières*, who issued a call to reform Kabyle women's status in 1922. According to Duchêne, the appeal solicited a "lively interest and even *moved* the other members of the Assembly."[53] Duchêne's work was indeed effective. Continuing to stir powerful political emotions, it remained for years to come a touchstone in debates about the status of Kabyle women.

Reform Time

Belkacem's report before the *délégations* noted the timeliness of reform, calling directly on the governor-general to alter customary rules excluding women from inheritance. These customs, which developed to maintain intact landholdings and reduce tribal conflict, became crucial to family survival strategy in the context of the colonial assault on indigenous property.[54] Echoing the language of colonial jurists, Belkacem nonetheless described how women had been reduced to the status of "a veritable animal who is sold like merchandise." Clearly familiar with the language of colonial humanism, he proclaimed, "She is a human being, who does not know the laws of humanity." By lending credibility to his own speech, the rhetoric strategically criticized the government for not acting on its own principles. Belkacem also effectively conjured an indigenous political representation that did not yet exist, by suggesting that the officials had been awaiting "the call of those concerned [Kabyles], when they decide to march toward progress" in order to initiate reform.[55]

Belkacem's embrace of legal progress challenged the colonial status quo by emphasizing how times had changed. Kabyle men now left Algeria for employment in France, sometimes for years at a time, leaving wives behind with no legal recourse to divorce. In adopting the cause of "his" women, Belkacem drew on colonial legal tropes of darkness and lightness, barbarity and civilization, in order to claim a new space of political influence. In the face of official inertia, he summoned France to "send a ray of light to illuminate our mountains."[56]

---

53. Duchêne, *Thamil'la*, xiii–iv. Emphasis in the original. And the interview with Henri Casanova, "Ferdinand Duchêne: Romancier algérien," *Nouvelles littéraires*, February 21, 1925.

54. For a recent critical reevaluation of colonial accounts of this history see Djoudi, "L'exhérédation des femmes en Kabylie."

55. Roumane Belkacem, "Communication d'ordre social," *Délégations financières algériennes*, June 22, 1922, 900–901.

56. Ibid., 902. On Kabyle emigration see Slimani-Direche, *Histoire de l'émigration kabyle en France*.

This plea found a rare echo among colonial delegates.[57] Governor-General Théodore Steeg felt obliged to respond to this canny use of colonial humanist sentiment. He greeted the appeal with "lively interest and not without emotion" in order to celebrate how France had managed to "penetrate into their [the Kabyles'] mountains, the warm generous clarity of its genius of light, liberty, justice."[58] More "traditionalist" Kabyle representatives were less keen on reform. Belkacem's fellow Kabyle delegate, Smail Saïd, a wealthy landowner endowed with numerous administrative and honorary titles, urged that any such changes required the approval and endorsement of officially recognized local *djemâa* councils.[59] The divergence of opinion created a challenge for the governor-general of which Kabyle delegate to follow.

Belkacem's reformist program was soon tested by a court case that came before the highest Muslim and customary-law French jurisdiction in November 1922. A *juge de paix* in Michelet ordered Lhocine Mohand Boudjema ben Ali to pay civil damages, in addition to a criminal penalty that he received for beating his wife. Both parties appealed, as the wife, Aït Messaoud Ghenima bent Mohand, wanted more than damages: she wanted a divorce. When the husband was convicted again for "assault and battery," the tribunal of Tizi-Ouzou delcared that it was "impossible to force a spouse, even if she is Kabyle, to submit to an odious union, which is a permanent source of danger to her existence . . . to decide otherwise would be contrary to the most elementary principles of humanity." When the court granted Aït Messaoud a divorce on April 26, 1922, her husband again appealed, arguing that, according to Kabyle custom, she could only enter the state of "insurrection," not divorce. The public prosecutor took the case to the Muslim Chamber of the Appeals Court of Algiers, with the express aim of testing whether "custom is not untouchable and can be revised, under the pressure of public opinion, when it appears overly contrary to natural law." The question placed before the court was whether there had been an "evolution of *mœurs*" in Kabylie.[60]

Belkacem issued his call to the governor-general before the *délégations* in June, which is to say, between the April appeal and the high court's eventual November judgment. It was no doubt cited by Aït Messaoud's counsel in the case, Boudjemâ Ould Aoudia, who was a lawyer from Tizi-Ouzou. Born in 1887,

---

57. Bouveresse, *Un parlement colonial*, 1:765; Bontems, "Coutume kabyle, jurisprudence et statut féminin."

58. Gov. Gen., Procès-verbaux, *Délégations financières algériennes*, June 22, 1922, 903.

59. Smail Saïd, ibid., 903.

60. Prior judgment cited in Proc. Gen., Lhocine Naït Messaoud v. Aït Messaoud Guenima, Cour d'Alger, Chambre de révision (November 18, 1922), *RA*, 1922, pt. 2, 83.

Ould Aoudia had been baptized at the age of eighteen and was naturalized in 1920. Over the course of the next decade, he took up the reformist cause, arguing court cases and publishing articles on Kabyle women's rights, especially in the Catholic journal *L'Effort algérien*.[61] The final decision in Aït Messaoud's favor mentioned Belkacem's appeal, alongside several lower-court decisions granting women divorces. The court embraced arguments about temporal progress, along with the idea that "a new and more humane conception of the rights of woman has appeared in Kabylie."[62]

In a note for the *Revue algérienne*, Marcel Morand highlighted Kabyle social evolution, alongside soaring rhetoric about "justice and considerations of humanity." Citing Belkacem, he endorsed the efforts of "the most enlightened part of the Kabyle population," which he saw as more effective than jurisprudence alone.[63] Claims of Kabyle modernity found an echo, as well, in the *Journal des tribunaux algériens*, which praised the decision as evidence of "an evolution that is very interesting and particularly symptomatic of Kabyle mentality."[64]

But not all of those who read Belkacem's appeal endorsed this reappropriation of civilizational rhetoric. An editorial in *La Voix des humbles*, a journal recently founded by Saïd Faci and Mohand Saïd Lechani, raised pointed questions about the tactic and its potential pitfalls. Their skepticism is notable, given that their primary audience was teachers who, like Belkacem, had trained at the *école normale*. These self-identified agents of indigenous social transformation sought to act as mediators between "French" and "native" society in order facilitate their eventual fusion. According to Lechani's sentimentalized trope, Algeria would become "a French region inhabited by individuals who have the same ideal and are profoundly attached to the same mother who is equally loving to all." Here and elsewhere, Lechani drew a crucial distinction between a contingent, colonial France and an ideal one—between, on the one hand, "the France as seen by the native, with its thousands of harassments" and, on the other, an "ideal France, whose humanitarian principles, genius and glory have placed it at the head of civilization."[65] As Fanny Colonna has suggested, this idealized vision structured these Algerian reformers' self-positioning as an elite. A narrative of colonial modernity as evolving toward its realization authorized their own

61. See, for example, B. Ould Aoudia, "La femme kabyle," *L'Effort algérien*, February 8, 1930.

62. Proc. Gen., Lhocine Naït Messaoud v. Aït Messaoud Guenima, Cour d'Alger–Chambre de révision (November 18, 1922), *RA*, 1922, pt. 2, 85.

63. Note Morand, ibid., 81–82.

64. *Journal des tribunaux algériens*, March 27, 1923, 1.

65. Mohand Saïd Lechani, "Le devoir de l'instituteur en Algérie," *La Voix des humbles* 4, no. 39 (November 1925): 12.

speech.[66] As the editors of *La Voix des humbles* explained, "Any aspiration toward an ideal of greater justice between men cannot displease us."[67]

While sharing this conception of ideal France, the journal's editors were skeptical of Belkacem's recourse to colonial discourse and law. In their view, he risked reinforcing the very prejudices that advocates of assimilation sought to overcome. According to the editors, "It is not in denigrating *les indigènes*, in putting on display and deliberately amplifying the inherent defaults of their race and civilization as some enjoy doing in arabophobe journals, that it will be possible to lead them toward an intelligent observation of modern life and a desire to change those aspects of their *mœurs* that are shocking and backward." Beyond offending fellow Algerians, they sensed that Belkacem's intervention would be reappropriated by the very colonial power it mimicked. In their view, "It is an odd way of understanding our role as *intermediaries* between Europeans and *Indigènes* to publicly and proudly denounce the *mœurs* of our fathers, which are, in many cases, still ours, under the pretext that one is emancipated." They urged instead: "Let us not forget our origin, even once emancipated."[68]

This debate over legal reform staged a broader conflict within the Algerian "intellectual elite." While affirming their own enlightenment, the editors of *La Voix des humbles* worried over their ability to speak on behalf of Kabyles, and Algerians more generally.[69] How could they both claim their elite status *and* maintain a connection to the constituency whose interests they sought to promote? This problem of representativity was also at the heart of the colonial administration's response to Belkacem, as colonial jurists and politicians debated who was authorized to reform Kabyle woman's legal status.

Knowledge and (In)Action

In the wake of Belkacem's appeal and the new jurisprudence on divorce, Governor-General Steeg broached the question of comprehensive reform. In the fall of 1922, he queried the public prosecutor of the Court of Algiers, Eugène Robe, and its president, Gustave Roche. The two magistrates lamented the Kabyle woman's legal condition as, in their words, "her husband's thing,"

---

66. Colonna, *Instituteurs algériens*, 73. McDougall, *History and the Culture of Nationalism in Algeria*, 75.

67. "À propos du Statut de la Femme Indigène," *La Voix des humbles* 1, no. 6 (October 1922): 7.

68. Ibid., 7–8.

69. Saïd Faci, "Le devoir des intellectuels indigènes," *La Voix des humbles* 8, no. 75 (June 1929): 7–10.

but they squarely opposed new legislation, advocating jurisprudential transformation instead. Drawing on the dissertation of Pierre Hacoun-Campredon, a lawyer at the Civil Tribunal of Tizi-Ouzou, Roche explained that "custom can modify custom: it can do so either under the pressure of public opinion or the impetus of jurisprudence." In an argument that combined claims to French sovereignty with those of colonial humanism, he affirmed that France was not obliged to respect "customs which were overly opposed to the elementary principles of humanity."[70]

While paying lip service to humanist principle, Robe, Roche, and Steeg endorsed a largely gradualist approach to "obtain, by a continuous, but prudent and moderate evolution, the progressive adaptation of Kabyle customs to the principles of social and public order that are the essential basis of our civilization." To this end, Steeg forwarded the text of the Court of Algiers's decision on women's right to divorce to magistrates across Kabylie. He also instructed the prefects of Alger and Constantine to inform *juges de paix*, administrators, and local authorities of the new orientation.[71] Robe and Roche remained hesitant about extending the measure too far and cautioned against sending it to "the tribes," because the "question of personal status is extremely delicate and of capital importance." They concluded that the "new conception, as desirable as it might seem, remains at the current hour only one of an elite."[72] For the governor-general and these magistrates, the thoroughgoing reform sought by Belkacem represented a misguided initiative by a select and unrepresentative few.

Belkacem's intervention called attention to a disjuncture between sentimental treatments of Kabyle women's legal status (recall the governor-general's "emotional" response) on the one hand, and gradualist government policy on the other. As in sentimentalist fictions, the governor-general's limited reform proposals vacillated between the urgency *and* impossibility of reform.[73] Indeed, even after the 1922 high court decision and subsequent circular, jurisprudence on divorce remained mixed. One *juge de paix* from Algiers refused to grant a divorce to Fathma Badho in October 1923, despite her testimony that "she would rather die than return to live with the litigant [her husband] who mistreats her like a

70. Prem. Pres. Cour d'Alger [Roche] to Gov. Gen., February 3, 1923, and, Proc. Gen. [Robe] to Gov. Gen., October 17, 1922, and December 28, 1922, both in dossier "Amélioration de la condition de la femme kabyle, 1922–1931," AN 2002495/3 (hereafter dossier "Femme Kabyle"). Roche cited Pierre Hacoun-Campredon, *Étude sur l'évolution des coutumes kabyles.*

71. Gov. Gen. to Proc. Gen. / Prem. Pres., March 2, 1923, and Gov. Gen. to Pref. Alger/Constantine, May 23, 1923, dossier "Femme Kabyle," AN 2002495/3.

72. Prem. Pres. and Proc. Gen. to Gov. Gen, May 2, 1923, dossier "Femme Kabyle," AN 2002495/3.

73. Ageron, *Les algériens musulmans*, 2:877.

slave." While refusing to grant a legal separation, the *juge de paix* reduced what Fathma had to pay her husband to escape her "state of insurrection" and the marriage. Acting in the name of "humanity and morality," the judge hoped to save her from "a life of celibacy" and the risk of "infanticide, abortion, or prostitution," so that she could return to "the natural role in life for which she was created"—which is to say, marriage.[74]

When further reform plans stalled, a Muslim court lawyer (*oukil judiciaire*) and counselor from Fort National, Ameur Tahar, launched a new intiative in the Conseil général d'Alger that called attention to the colonial government's inaction. Similarly to both Duchêne and Belkacem, Tahar based his call for reform on recent historical transformations. In his view, "the Kabyle, educated or not, is in contact with and under European influence, which assaults him from all sides, on his voyages and in Europe; he has improved his moral and material situation and become closer to French laws, whose benefits he understands." Tahar criticized French tribunals for continuing to apply outdated custom to Kabyles, "impos[ing] on them rules which conform, neither to their will, nor to right and equity, taking customary law literally, even though the Kabyle social state had been considerably modified."[75] In his view, it was French judges, not Kabyle subjects, who were behind the times.

According to Tahar, custom needed to be changed because it was now out of step with Algerian subjects' conscripted modernity.[76] More specifically, the postwar context had created new social and legal conditions that made a right to divorce increasingly necessary for Kabyle women who were abandoned by husbands who had traveled to the metropole for war and work. Unmoored from customary kinship and, especially, marital relations, the typical migrant suffered from anomie, "pushed by a desire for a better existence and unfulfilled pleasure [*jouissance inassouvie*], he violates barriers without concerning himself anymore with the being whom he has used as wife and servant, making her life untenable."[77] Claiming access to local knowledge, Kabyle representatives called on the government to act.

Tahar's declaration was well received, including by Counselor Gustavino, who congratulated him and used the occasion to promote his own friend Duchêne's

---

74. Justice de paix d'Alger, October 17, 1923, *Journal des tribunaux algériens*, December 1, 1923.

75. Tahar Ameur, "Révision de la législation kabyle," in Extrait du procès-verbal de la séance du October 19, 1923, Conseil général d'Alger, 1–2, dossier "Femme Kabyle," AN 2002495/3.

76. Asad, "Conscripts of Western Civilization"; D. Scott, *Conscripts of Modernity*.

77. Tahar Ameur, "Révision de la législation kabyle," in Extrait du procès-verbal de la séance du October 19, 1923, Conseil général d'Alger, 4, dossier "Femme Kabyle," in AN 2002495/3.

work: "All those who have read the powerful work of Ferdinand Duchêne, *Thamil'la*, understand that it is abominable to see barbarous *mœurs* perpetuated while the French flag flies over this country." Following a round of hardy applause, Gustavino urged the prefect of Alger to bring the proposed reform to the attention of the governor once it was adopted.[78]

In response, the governor sent yet another round of inquiries to the jurists Roche and Robe, as well as to the prefects of Alger and Constantine. Administrators of communes under customary law jurisdiction were meanwhile asked to answer detailed questionaires about Kabyle women's legal and social position in order to gauge the Kabyle representatives' sociological claims. Roche, the president of the Cour d'Alger, explained what was at stake: "Does the evolution of *mœurs*, the customs that it determines, and the judicial decisions concerning them permit Ameur Tahar's and [Roumane Belkacem's] requests to be met? That is the question."[79]

The extensive inquiry did not yield consistent enough information to justify immediate action. What seemed clear was that jurisprudence alone had not effected significant change.[80] In 1925, Steeg eventually opted to form a commission on how to "ameliorate the condition of the Kabyle Woman." It included magistrates and representatives, including Roche and Robe, administrators and jurists from Tizi-Ouzou and the sub-prefecture of Grand Kabylie, as well as Belkacem and Tahar.[81] Law school doyen Morand was named as its president, while literary magistrate Duchêne also assumed an active role.[82]

The most pressing question before the commission was whether, in the words of Edmond Norès, attorney at the Cour d'Alger, "the reforms would be freely accepted by the indigenous mass." The director of indigenous affairs, Jean Mirante, was especially concerned about "resistances resulting from the particularist spirit of Kabyles."[83] For his part, Duchêne endorsed granting divorce in cases where women were "martyred or abandoned" but thought that the

78. Tahar Ameur, "Révision de la législation kabyle," in Extrait du procès-verbal de la séance du October 19, 1923, Conseil général d'Alger, 6–7, dossier "Femme Kabyle," AN 2002495/3.

79. Prem. Pres. to Gov. Gen., no. 1727, May 28, 1924, dossier "Femme Kabyle," AN 2002495/3.

80. For example, "Commune Mixte de Djurdjura: Au sujet de l'amélioration de la condition de la femme kabyle: Questionnaire," dossier "Femme Kabyle," AN 2002495/3.

81. Gov. Gen. to Proc. Gen. and Prem. Pres. Cour d'appel d'Alger, October 6, 1924, "Rapports, 1924–1926," dossier "Femme Kabyle," AN 2002495/3.

82. Proc. Gen. and Prem. Pres. Cour d'appel d'Alger to Gov. Gen., November 6, 1924, "Rapports, 1924–1926," dossier "Femme Kabyle," AN 2002495/3.

83. "Procès-verbal de la Commission instituée pour rechercher les mesures susceptibles d'améliorer la condition de la femme kabyle," May 12, 1925, 4, 6, dossier "Femme Kabyle," AN 2002495/3. And ANOM 10H. Republished in *Revue des études islamiques*, no. 1 (1927): 47–94.

modification of inheritance rules would meet with "formal opposition."[84] By contrast, Belkacem and Tahar urged that the reform was "ardently desired by the Kabyle masses," not least because "customs have evolved as a result of the war and continue to evolve as a result of the growing exodus of indigenous workers to the Metropole."[85] Other colonial jurists and administrators on the commission nonetheless questioned whether Belkacem and Tahar, as members of an elite, could be trusted to represent the Kabyle masses. Given this divergence of opinion, Morand created a sub-commission to study this sociological problem, with Duchêne at its head

After several months of study, Duchêne presented his findings, making several proposals for reform: fixing an age of marital majority; establishing exceptional provisions for divorce; and granting women limited inheritance rights (of usage or usufruct rather than formal ownership). Responses to Duchêne's propositions varied. Some, like Marcel Malo, the president of the tribunal of Tizi-Ouzou, dismissed Belkacem and Tahar's reformism out of hand: "They make proposal after proposal without being precise about practical means, without mentioning if Kabyle public opinion as a whole, as much as it exists, is asking for this kind of change."[86] In his view, no alterations should be made.[87] Similarly skeptical, Norès feared that Belkacem and Tahar "might be taking their desires for reality." He viewed the commission's sociological project as quixotic, because "Europeans" would have an even greater difficulty establishing a "profound and intimate knowledge of the Kabyle soul."[88]

Despite the reformist pleas in his preface to *Thamil'la*, Duchêne adopted similar caution. Citing Jean Cruet, a contemporary legal sociologist, he insisted that "society remakes law. Law does not remake Society."[89] In other words, legal reform could only follow, not lead social evolution. For Duchêne, recent transformations in Kabyle society justified moderate changes to marriage age, inheritance rights, and divorce. While he denounced custom in his sentimental novels, he worried that "the grand majority of Kabyles" would see further reforms of inheritance, divorce, and the father's right to force "not as elements

---

84. Procès-verbal de la Commission, May 12, 1925, 8, dossier "Femme Kabyle," AN 2002495/3.

85. Procès-verbal de la Commission, May 12, 1925, 4, dossier "Femme Kabyle," AN 2002495/3.

86. Malo to Duchêne, "Note," "Commission pour le relèvement social de la femme kabyle," dossier "Femme Kabyle," AN 2002495/3.

87. Ibid.

88. Edmond Norès to Duchêne, "Commission pour le relèvement social de la femme kabyle," dossier "Femme Kabyle," AN 2002495/3.

89. The statement was an epigraph to Cruet's 1908 work on the sociology of law, *La vie du droit et l'impuissance des lois*. In Procès-verbal de la Commission, January 19, 1926, dossier "Femme Kabyle," AN 2002495/3.

of evolution, but as ferments for a revolution."[90] Duchêne did however plead for girls' "practical instruction," primarily in household arts, as a necessary supplement to law. Education would help transform the Kabyle woman "into a mistress of the house, conscious of her personality and her role, listened to, consulted, no doubt honored. From the thing that she barely was, she will become someone."[91] Duchêne's idea of Kabyle woman's personhood was largely constrained by this domestic ideal.

The commission ultimately endorsed Duchêne's proposal, which was forwarded to the governor-general and the Interministerial Commission on Muslim Affairs. After another round of inquiries, the government decided to proceed with the reform. Morand forwarded the commission's proposals to the governor-general with an outline of a law and decree to enact them; the Interministerial Commission approved them in February 1926. Governor-General Maurice Viollette then launched yet another inquiry, seeking the advice of prefects, sub-prefects, and administrators on how the measures would be received. The sub-prefect of Tizi-Ouzou, Joseph Catalogne, remained doubtful of their success, suggesting that the "practices that we condemn" would continue on as in the past, while the administration remained "impotent" to change them.[92] The prefect of Alger endorsed the reforms, asserting that the "qualified representatives of the Kabyle population from our big assemblies" have "unquestionable value and seem to represent the average opinion of educated and intelligent kabyles who make up in this country a numerous and influential elite."[93] Once the decision was made to proceed, Belkacem and Tahar, as representative of an indigenous expertise, helped to legitimate the reforms.

A project for a decree and law reforming Kabyle marriage and inheritance was ready by the fall of 1927. Justice Minister Louis Barthou's presentation of the proposed legislation read like a précis of Duchêne's fictions. It described how among the inhabitants of Kabylie, "the woman is considered an object of commerce. As a young girl, she is literally sold by her father and elder brother. As a repudiated wife, she remains in debt to her husband [grevé d'hypothèques], who sets her price." Barthou explained that the French administration had to come up with measures to "abrogate the regrettable aspects of these customs."[94] In an

90. Procès-verbal de la Commission, January 19, 1926, dossier "Femme Kabyle," AN 2002495/3.
91. Ibid.
92. Sous-préf. Tizi-Ouzou to Préf. d'Alger, April 20, 1926, dossier "Femme Kabyle," AN 2002495/3.
93. Pref. Alger to Gov. Gen., May 4, 1926, dossier "Femme Kabyle," AN 2002495/3.
94. "Projet de Loi concernant la déclaration des fiançailles et le mariage des Kabyles présenté au nom de Doumergue et Barthou et Sarraut" and "Projet de décret ayant pour objet de réglementer la condition de la femme kabyle," dossier "Femme Kabyle," AN 2002495/3.

effort to limit child marriages, a law mandating marriage registration and fixed legal marriage age at fifteen was adopted on April 2, 1930. A second measure granting Kabyle women a right to divorce and fixing new procedures for their inheritance was adopted on May 19, 1931.[95]

Custom, Conjugality, and the Indigenous Intellectual

Over the course of these policy discussions, the self-described indigenous intellectuals of *La Voix des humbles* regularly weighed in on the question of the *femme indigène*'s status and customary-law reform. Articles—and occasional poems—about women's education and companionate marriage multiplied as the journal expanded its scope beyond the instructors' corporatist concerns. The paper's editors had expressed doubts about Belkacem's reform strategy in 1922. By 1926, their position shifted. An open letter by Ali Satour addressed to the Interministerial Commission made this recalibration clear. He called on its members, including Belkacem, Norès, Hacène, and Cherchali, to overcome the "outmoded custom" that continued to permit "prepubescent marriage," women's disinheritance, and unilateral repudiation. According to Satour, neither the Qur'an nor custom should restrict the "realities of a nascent emancipation." When making his plea, Satour directly addressed himself to men. In his view, reforms held out the promise not just of Algerian women's emancipation, but also Algerian men's: "Will you still close your eyes for a long time to the fact that most indigenous intellectuals are condemned to celibacy because they are unable to meet among their fellow Muslims [*co-religionnaires*], companions who are not only capable of rolling good couscous, but who can think with them, that understand their aspirations, and help them to achieve them with a moral and material life that conforms to their culture and conforms better to this civilization in which men of all races seek a little happiness?"[96] For Satour, legal reform would fulfill a heartfelt aspiration for companionate marriage.

Numerous contributors to the pages of *La Voix des humbles* elaborated on this conjugal ideal of marriage, which they presented as a "communion of ideas

---

95. For a summary of the legislation, including the texts of the laws, see R. Viguier, "La femme kabyle: Quelques remarques sur le décret du Mai 19, 1931," *Revue des études islamiques*, no. 1 (1931): 1–19.

96. Ali Satour, "Questions indigènes: Un courant à remonter: Lettre ouverte à la Commission musulmane au Ministère des Affaires Étrangères," *La Voix des humbles*, June–July 1926, 8.

and sentiments" and not a "drunkenness of the senses."[97] Poems by Ioualalen, a teacher from Petite Kabylie, recounted the indigenous intellectuals' sentimental suffering and hope for an alternative affective future. In "Les deux néants" (the double void) he lamented their fate of "dying without being loved, living alone on earth," while his "Je voudrais une amie" (I would like a friend, I would like a wife) projected the hopeful possibility of a marital future.[98] For these writers, the project of Kabyle women's reform would help men to overcome celibacy and alienation with companionate intimacy. Their normative ideal paralleled Duchêne's domesticated vision of the Kabyle woman's personhood, while marking a difference. Taking increasing distance from the reform's official architect, the editors of La Voix des humbles attacked the jurist-turned-novelist-turned-reformer's claims to authority. In its place, they asserted their own.

In November 1926, Rabah Zenati, one of the journal's founders, denounced Duchêne's pretentions to expert knowledge. He presented the literary magistrate not as a sage jurist, but as a menace: "We believe that it is even dangerous for the future of this country to give credit to Duchêne's ideas, all the more dangerous because he seems to have become an authority in matters of indigenous legislation and has begun to be consulted by public authorities."[99] This antipathy is unsurprising, given how Duchêne's novels, for all their sentimentalism, overtly attacked the assimilationism upheld by the authors and readers of La Voix des humbles.[100] In Kamir: Roman d'une femme arabe, for example, Duchêne mocked the "assimilated" Mohammed, who despite his civilized veneer of "French" taste in clothing and furniture, mistreats his wife. Increasingly jealous, violent, and "anti-French," even though he is the son of a "naturalized father," Mohammed accuses Kamir of committing adultery with a French man. According to the narrator, he thus revealed how "under his elegant jacket [veston à longs revers], the Arab remains an Arab, the male, jealous of his possession and his mastery, constantly jealous, with an obsessive jealousy [jalousie maladive]."[101] Duchêne's repetitions, as in this image of failed assimilation, demonstrated to Zenati that his novels had nothing novel about them ("rien de nouveau dans ses romans").

---

97. Ali Satour, "Aujourd'hui et demain," La Voix des humbles, October 1928, 8. See also Ali Satour, "Extraits d'un lettre," La Voix des humbles, February 1928, 25–26. And M. Mahiout, "Au seuil de la vie," La Voix des humbles, April 1928, 40–41; Antar, "Célibat forcé: Pénibles constatations!," La Voix des humbles, July 1930, 19–20.

98. Ioualalen, "Les deux néants" and "Je voudrais une amie," La Voix des humbles, May 1928, 26.

99. Rabah Zenati, "L'opinion de Ferdinand Duchêne dans Les Barbaresques," La Voix des humbles, November 1926, 4.

100. On their assimilationism see Belmessous, Assimilation and Empire, chap. 8.

101. Duchêne, Kamir, 83.

Duchêne merely "followed in the footsteps of arabophobes and repeats, after them, that nothing can be done with the *indigène*." For the journal, he was a font of colonial clichés, not a reformist visionary.[102]

Against Duchêne's retrograde fictions and reformist claims, the editors of *La Voix des humbles* asserted their own modernity. In doing so, the journal pointed to colonial law rather than native inertia as the source of developmental delay. According to Lechani, while "the Kabyle has clearly entered on the route to progress," his principal obstacle remained the "French judicial mechanism." Condemning the colonial legal system for its torpor, he lamented how "its sluggishness is depressing, especially in such matters where it seeks above all to have respect for the past, even when *Indigènes* themselves denounce it." In his view, indigenous intellectuals understood the modern desires of Kabyle "natives themselves" better than French jurists and administrators. Rather than defending the status quo, he endorsed legislative reform and the eventual "integral application of French law."[103]

These discussions demonstrate how the problem of "native" representation was at the heart of debates over Kabyle women's reform. Colonial administrators and the intellectuals of *La Voix des humbles* worried over a shared problem of how to decide what counted as Kabyle custom and what it should become. In trying to answer this thorny question about legal representation, the paper adopted novel journalistic as well as literary forms, publishing sly and satirical pieces by anonymous or pseudonymous authors alongside straightforward policy analyses and proposals. These ironic interventions drew out the dark side of colonial fantasies of civilization. Alongside Lechani's sober endorsement of customary law reform, the October 1927 edition included a mocking depiction of reformist idealizations of "European" civilization. The title expressed reservations about reforming Kabyle woman's status by answering the call to "move forward" (*en avant*) with a cautious "Stop" (*Halte*). The premise of the article went in the opposite direction from Lechani's reformist optimism, describing how "the war left us with many ills, among others the mania for reform." Mocking reformism as itself a postwar pathology, it played on postwar hygienists' fears of depopulation. The European family, he noted, was far from a model of health: "Forcefully shaken by the call of cities and the egotistical application of the

---

102. Rabah Zenati, "L'opinion de Ferdinand Duchêne dans *Les Barbaresques*," *La Voix des humbles*, November 1926, 8

103. Mohand Saïd Lechani, "L'évolution des coutumes Berbères," *La Voix des humbles*, October 1927, 16. His analysis here was based on Hacoun-Campredon, *Étude sur l'évolution des coutumes kabyles*.

phrase: everyone for him/herself," it was in danger of being undone by the forces of modernity. The article hinted at the perils of unthinking assimilationists, who "in their unreasonable admiration only see the enviable and golden aspects of European society." Meanwhile, the author cautioned, "not everything is so bad for us." He thus advised against reformist mimcry, explaining that "our goal is not servile imitation. We must evolve by making choices, as not everything is perfect in Europe."[104]

The commentary ended with a cautionary note, especially for those who sought out "*la civiliserie*" (i.e., imitative appearance of French civilization) by marrying a French woman. Here as elsewhere, the question of "mixed marriage" emblematized the challenges of assimilationism for the indigenous intellectual. In taking up the question of conjugality, these writers and teachers sought an alternative, indigenous and companionate, form.

The Progress of Mixed Marriage

The question of mixed unions continued to garner attention in the pages of *La Voix des humbles* over the next several years, as indigenous intellectuals reflected on how mixed-marriage plots became fables for the possible pleasures, but also the dangers, of fusionist fantasy. The theme was not new for the indigenous Algerian press. It had been the central theme of Ahmed Bouri's "Muslims and Christian Women," a serial story published in *El Hack* (The Truth) in 1912, and often cited as the first Algerian "novel" in French.[105] An allegory for the desires and disappointments of French colonial modernity, the unfinished story explored failed loves between Algerian men and French women. In the prototypical tale, the spahi Ahmed falls in love with the French woman Marcelle. When her parents refuse to consent, the couple are unable to consummate their marriage. Depicting a failed or impossible union, Bouri's story reflected on the limits of assimilation and the psychic costs of this disillusion. In his revealing fiction, French prejudice, not Algerian backwardness, posed the greatest obstacle to fusion.

---

104. "Salade: L'inévitable femme kabyle et la femme . . . Esthonienne. Notre évolution. En avant . . . halte," *La Voix des humbles*, October 1927, 23, 25.

105. Ahmed Bouri, "Musulmans et chrétiennes," *El Hack*, April 20, 27; May, 4, 18, 25; June 1, 15, 29; July 6, 13, 20, 27; August 3, 10, 17, 24, 1912. On the novella see Hardi, *Le roman algérien de langue française de l'entre-deux-guerres*, 22–23.

A recurrent theme in colonial novels, mixed love and marriage gained even greater currency in the interwar period, when mixed relationships appeared to be on the rise.[106] The large presence of colonial troops and colonial workers on metropolitan soil during the war was thought to increase the likelihood of these marriages. As a measure of precaution, the minister of war issued a circular on June 28, 1918, to commandants in charge of North African workers, urging that "those French women who want to marry a Muslim be carefully informed about the eventualities to which they might be exposed if they proceed with their projects of union."[107] A follow-up study commissioned by Governor-General Jonnart traced the problems raised by "marriages conducted following French law by *indigènes musulmans d'Algérie, non naturalisé Français.*" Jonnart worried that the women's husbands might be engaged in prior marriages or might try to marry again after returning to Algeria. He once again called on the law school dean Morand for advice.[108] According to Morand, the principal "risk" (*inconvénient*) run by the marriages was "the revelation of a previously contracted marriage which has not been dissolved." While the marriage might be granted a "putative status," he believed that the situation would no doubt prove "most painful."[109] Stories of tragic deceptions indeed appeared in *fait divers* in Algerian newspapers. And the *Annales algériennes* worried that "numerous daughters of Eve" would become "addicted to Orientalism and desire to practice the fusion of races with the sons of Islam."[110]

Seizing on this dramatic as well as political potential, interwar colonial novels, including by women, often depicted the tragic consequences of such unions.[111] As Patricia Lorcin has suggested, these literary accounts of

---

106. For the earlier period see "Le rénégat" and "Le soc et l'épée," in Pharaon, *Récits algériens*; Caise, *Teurkia*; Bonnal, *Un amour en Algérie*; Blocqueville, *Stella et Mohammed*; Radiot, *Notre fille de France*; Leblond, *L'Oued*. On the interwar period see Liauzu, "Guerre des Sabines et tabou du métissage"; Lanasri, *La littérature algérienne de l'entre-deux-guerres*, 226.

107. Min. of War to Commanders, "Mariages entre françaises et ouvriers indigènes musulmans," June 28, 1918, ANOM 1AFFPOL/903/1. See also Fogarty, *Race and War in France*.

108. Gov. Gen.—Indigenous Affairs, "Note sur la validité et les effets des mariages contractés suivant la loi française par des indigènes musulmans d'Algérie, non naturalisé Français," ANOM 1AFFPOL/903/1.

109. Morand to Gov. Gen., Septembre 14, 1918, ANOM 1AFFPOL/903/1. This text, alongside a note by Professor Lapradelle on the related question of Moroccan marriages, was published as Lapradelle and Morand, "Du mariage en France des marocains et des indigènes musulmans d'Algérie."

110. *Annales africaines*, September 1, 1918, 105. And *L'Écho d'Alger*, August 19, 1918.

111. See Bugéja, *Séduction orientale*; Faure-Sardet, *Hélia, une française en Algérie*; Lorcin, "Mediating Gender, Mediating Race"; Liauzu, "Guerre des Sabines et tabou du métissage"; Lanasri, *La littérature algérienne de l'entre-deux-guerres*, 107.

romantic fusion were asymmetically structured by gender: while relations between Algerian men and French women were usually condemned, those between French men and Algerian women were condoned and even encouraged.[112] In Yvon de Saint-Gouric's 1923 novel *Mektoub*, a wartime nurse, Simone, makes the mistake of falling in love with an Algerian soldier, Rabah. After they marry and return to Algeria, she realizes her great folly and error in marrying him in order to pursue "terrestrial pleasures": "I loved Rabah and, in order to satisfy my passion, I submitted to the worst brutality, the most odious bestiality; I want to recall them without cease in order to humiliate myself [*me mortifier*] further and to forget that I believed that I could find happiness by his side. No, no, assimilation is impossible."[113] Cliché-ridden novels such as Saint-Gouric's confirmed that sexualized and violently patriarchal Algerians could never become French.[114]

The journalists of *La Voix* actively responded to these representations, decrying how mixed marriage came to represent the failure of assimilation. Annette Godin's *L'erreur de Nedjma* (1923) drew particular ire. In this transparent *roman à thèse*, Nedjma, the daughter of a French army commander and a woman from a prominent Algerian family, is torn between the two cultures, as represented by three suitors, two Algerian brothers, Amar and Ali, and a French lawyer, Pierre. She is strongly attracted to one of the brothers, Ali, a spahi with a French secondary education. Her lapse in judgment is revealed soon enough, when he attempts to rape her. Almost succumbing, she comes to her senses: "I look at the monster, hypnotized by horror. His red eyes fix on me and I think of a tiger before his prey."[115] Realizing her "error" in the end, she chooses her French side and Pierre. While the reviewer for *L'Écho d'Alger* was "very much at ease" with this conclusion, the writers in *La Voix* condemned its clichés.[116] Saïd Faci described Godin's fiction as "in absolute opposition to our aspirations. Whether the author wanted to or not, the novel has an arabophobic tendency, in the manner of Ferdinand Duchêne." Her anti-assimilationist moral was clear: "Why give instruction to

---

112. Lorcin, *Historicizing Colonial Nostalgia*, 78–80.

113. Saint-Gouric, *Mektoub*, 92.

114. Reviews included *Mercure africain*, December 15, 1922; *L'Écho d'Alger*, November 6, 1923; *Annales africaines*, August 10, 1923; *L'Afrique du nord illustré*, August 11, 1923.

115. Godin, *L'Erreur de Nedjma*, 300.

116. Chronique Littéraire, *L'Écho d'Alger*, July 13, 1923. Other reviews included *L'Afrique du nord illustré*, May 26, 1923, 10, and *Annales africaines*, June 14, 1923, 358. Maurice Olivaint praised the novel but raised questions about its underlying thesis in "Causeries d'un Algérois," *Annales africaines*, July 13, 1923, 390–91.

indigènes, if their atavism condemns them to barbarism?" According to Faci, the book had to be read in order to "refute it."[117]

La Voix offered up its own critical mixed-marriage plots in response, including one titled "*L'idéal d'un jeune: Le progrès par le mariage mixte.*" Written by the pseudonymous Candide, the story cast suspicion on the seemingly naïve and even utopian "ideal" of fusion over the course of two generations. It begins with a young Kabyle instructor, Bachir, searching for love after he finishes the *école normale.* He dreams of "a sister soul, an affectionate heart that beats with the same impulses," but remains hesitant about whom to choose. While long nourishing "the sweet thought of marrying a European," he worried that as "a poor wog [*bicot*]," he would never be favored by a European woman. He opts instead for a *co-religionnaire*, who was intelligent but uneducated. In this first generation, the dream of companionate marriage remained "half realized."[118]

Bachir's son Ali revists the same quandary a generation later. After years of studying for the *baccalauréat* and leading a "Europeanized" existence, he too dreams of marrying a French woman. His father, haunted by his own "perpetual incompletion" and "disenchantment," urges him to marry a colleague's daughter instead. But Ali is less willing to compromise than his father. After falling in love with a French student, Eugénie, whose parents do not accept their union, he resists giving up on his French ideal. He resolves instead to marry a metropolitan French woman as the embodiment of "ideal France," in the hope that she won't "know about race prejudice."[119] Ali then considers "sacrificing himself to marry *une indigène*," albeit "*une indigène évoluée.*" Ultimately, he puts off marriage altogether as a dream deferred.

The failures of mixed marriage thus symbolized for writers in *La Voix des humbles* not the incomplete assimilation of Algerians, but the hopeless prejudice of the French. These stories cast critical light on overly optimistic accounts of Franco-Algerian fusion. One article, titled "Forced Celibacy," warned the journal's readers against holding fast to its illusory promise: "instead of finding a goddess," they would end up "only embracing a cloud." From their perspective, the fantasy of mixed marriage would only ever remain a fantasy. Against that misleading fiction, the journal embraced the Algerian woman of the future as their only real hope.[120]

---

117. Saïd Faci, "Bibliographie: L'erreur de Nedjma," *La Voix des humbles*, August–September 1926, 36.

118. Candide, "L'idéal d'un jeune: Le progrès par le mariage mixte," *La Voix des humbles*, November 1928, 16–18. Also, Déjeux, *Image de l'étrangère*, 19–20.

119. Candide, "L'idéal d'un jeune," 7–19.

120. Antar, "Célibat forcé: Pénibles Constatations," *La Voix des humbles*, July 7, 1930, 20.

The Future of an Illusion?

These reflections on mixed marriage and the prospect of Franco-Algerian union took on greater resonance in the context of the politicized celebrations of the 1930 centenary of Algeria's conquest. Reflecting on French Algerian policy at the height of the official festivities, Faci reaffirmed his aspirations for "fusion." He indicted French colonial law for standing in the way of this vision by legally constraining the *indigène*, including in the regulation of mixed marriage.[121] According to the lawyer Aït-Kaci, the centenary nonetheless offered a chance to overcome past discrimination by recognizing Algerians' rights to political representation. Reappropriating the celebration's rhetoric of progress, he castigated the current regime as retrograde: "Is it the fault of *indigènes* that they became French? And is it their fault that they were born Muslim? Can one really not reconcile one with the other so as not to deprive anyone of that little parcel of sovereignty that redounds to each in the midst of fellow nationals? The question has been for a long time resolved in India and Senegal. Should 1930 be behind 1848?"[122] As Kaci explained, the legal contradiction between "French" and "Muslim" was an artifact of the conquest that made Algerians French in the first place. It was thus up to the French to assume political and legal responsibility for that act by recognizing Algerians' belonging as citizens. The failure to do so was, for Kaci, a shameful anachronism and hence a betrayal of France's professed narrative of republican progress.[123]

Writers in *La Voix* further dismantled arguments against Algerian political representation that focused on "family law." As Lechani explained, the "enemies of this reform" ceaselessly spoke "of the violation of the Constitution, of personal status, of polygamy, of the equality of Citizens before the law, of the Muslim religion, of naturalization, and many other things." Rather than being moved by these "grandiloquent expressions," he called for a "cold" and "calm" response. He sought a sober rejoinder to familiar, if fantasmatic, claims about Muslim sex that critics regularly arrayed against Algerians' political rights. For Lechani, these claims clearly functioned as so much ideological cover for settlers' material interests: "It must be stated that the reasons that emanate from the settler milieu [*milieux colons*] only mask, under their political or psychological appearances, sentiments that are uniquely dictated by economic preoccupations." He thus

---

121. Saïd Faci, "La politique française dans ses rapports avec l'évolution des indigènes," *La Voix des humbles*, May 5, 1930, 5.

122. Aït Kaci, "La représentation des indigènes au parlement," *La Voix des humbles*, May 5, 1929, 6.

123. On the Young Algerians' deployment of historical temporality see Aissaoui, "Politics, identity and temporality."

read apparent political and psychic resistances as an extension of brute economic interests.[124]

Directing his sights on colonial novels, Ali Satour nonetheless suggested that representation was more than a mask that could simply be stripped away. He denounced colonial novels, and especially those writers who "attempted to penetrate the native soul," whose "bias, hatred and rancor indoctrinate and falsify the mind." He suggested that their anachronistic perspective remained mired in a fantasy of a past that in fact no longer existed. Colonial writers had to "hurry," he wrote, since "exotic literature is dying, assassinated by the airplane, the caterpillar-car, and Transat hotels." In displacing the epigones of exoticism, Satour sought out a literature that would better represent "greater France."[125]

The events of the centenary nonetheless provoked a "renaissance of orientalism" rather than dissipating it. Commentators in *La Voix* felt compelled to respond.[126] As part of the celebration, Duchêne garnered new awards for his hackneyed work, with two cliché-ridden books—*Ceux d'Algérie* and *Mouna, Cachir et Couscous*—receiving the Centenary Prize alongside Marie Bugéja's reedition of *Nos soeurs musulmanes*.[127] In two long critical articles, *La Voix*'s "Bibliophile" recapitulated Duchêne's drastic failure to represent Algerians. While Duchêne depicted "native society" from "the exterior," Bibliophile sought to "reveal a parcel of its internal photography."[128] This reversal of perspective demonstrated how the failures of assimilation were the result not of native flaws, but of the defects of colonial administration and law. As the author explained, the "special organizations" that hold the Algerian "apart from common law" ultimately "consecrate by maintaining" the "divergences that separate him from the French," confining him to a "regime of exception." That exclusion amplified his investments in religion: "the equality that he misses in his country, he finds in Islam and calls himself 'Muslim.'"[129]

His subsequent criticism focused on Duchêne's depiction of the "Muslim woman" in *Mouna* as particularly problematic. Its clichés of moralized horror

---

124. Mohand Saïd Lechani, "La représentation des indigènes au Parlement," *La Voix des humbles*, June 6, 1929, 5.

125. Ali Satour, "Le roman Algérien," *La Voix des humbles*, June 6, 1929, 13.

126. See the negative review of "Amor Ben Djenoudi" by Marguerite Deval in *La Voix des humbles*, August 8, 1929, 31.

127. "Les lauréats du grand concours littéraire du centenaire de l'Algérie," *Les Annales coloniales*, July 22, 1930, 1. Duchêne, *Ceux d'Algérie*, and *Mouna, Cachir et Couscous*.

128. Bibliophile, "Mouna, Cachir et Couscous: Réflexions d'un lecteur," *La Voix des humbles*, August 8, 1930, 5.

129. Ibid., 6–7.

were all too familiar, as were its obligatory references to multiple wives and concubines allowed under "the serenity of Islamic law."[130] Returning to his eroticized sentimentalism, Duchêne described the Algerian woman's conjugal martyrdom: "Married to a man who generally she meets for the first time the night of the marriage and who immolates her without preparation following the sexual rite—and who presents himself to her, immature [impubère], with a beard that is more salt than pepper . . ."[131] As Bibliophile pointed out, Duchêne's "ideas appear to resemble those of all Europeans who have written about the *femme indigène.*" Rather than demonstrating special insight and expertise, his work revealed nothing more than a catalog of commonplaces. "Imprinted with exaggeration and incomprehension," his writings displayed, according to the critic, a complete failure to "comprehend the true meaning of Kabyle custom." Duchêne, as an "Occidental author," would thus remain a stranger to Kabyle society and unable "to adequately seize its soul."[132] His flawed literary, political, and legal representations illustrated how "a false legend surrounded the *femme indigène.*" Bibliophile called on fellow readers to enact a radical revision: "The erroneous conclusions and commonplaces about her must be corrected."[133] At the centenary's high point, Algerian intellectuals thus seized on the representation of Algerian women as an urgent political, epistemological, and emotional question.

The indigenous intellectuals of *La Voix des humbles* often appear as equivocal actors in the narrative development of Algerian nationalism. Fashioned as a colonial elite by French schooling, they at once internalized and criticized dominant ideologies of "civilization," secularism, modernity, and progress. As Zenati explained in a series of articles titled "These poor indigenous intellectuals," they suffered from deep social, intellectual, and emotional ambivalence. Seen as "suspicious" by their contemporaries, they seemed to be suspended between two worlds, unable to adequately represent either.[134] By the late 1920s, new mass political movements and associations—from the Étoile nord-africaine to the reformist Islam of the 'ulama'—would radicalize the constituency and claims of Algerian politics. From this new vantage, the Young Algerians' assimilationist

---

130. Duchêne, *Mouna, Cachir et Couscous*, 139.
131. Ibid., 178.
132. Bibliophile, "Mouna, Cachir et Couscous: Réflexions d'un Lecteur," 8.
133. Bibliophile, *La Voix des humbles*, September 1930, 9.
134. Rabah Zenati, "Ces pauvres intellectuels indigènes!," *La Voix des humbles*, November 1928, 2; and "Ces pauvres intellectuels indigènes!," December 1928.

aspirations seemed to be little more than a sentimental fantasy that held them in thrall to a compromised colonial political order.[135]

What nationalist teleology obscures is how these intellectuals critically engaged French legal and literary representation. Beyond laying out programs of educational and political reform, indigenous intellectuals called out the sentimental fictions propagated by colonial jurists and politicians. The fantasy life of Algerian colonial law, as condensed in the writings of Duchêne and policy debates over the Kabyle women's status, simultaneously eroticized legal rescue, while lamenting the impossibility of genuine legal reform. This fantasy, arrested in a double bind, was compulsively repeated as a colonial cliché. Writers in *La Voix des humbles* understood and answered these sentimental stories with their own. Their writings understood what made interlinked legal and literary fictions politically powerful.[136]

These *évolué* intellectuals seemed beholden to an illusory idea of France. Caught in a liminal position, they hovered between citizenship and subjection, trapped in an "unfinished dialectic" of dialogue and resistance.[137] A close examination of their work nonetheless shows that they did not just unconsciously repeat those contradictions. Their articles, fictions, and poetry called attention to the sentimental fictions that propped up the insecure foundations of Algerian colonial law. In countering those stories with their own, they made these legal fantasies manifest and revealed the affective life of French colonial law.

---

135. Kaddache, *Histoire du nationalisme algérien*. On the contradictions of the colonial elite see Colonna, *Instituteurs algériens*; Smati, *Les élites algériennes sous la colonisation*. Ferhat Abbas countered this narrative in his "Avertissement au lecteur": see Abbas, *Le Jeune Algérien, 1930*, 26. For a critique of standard histories of Algerian nationalism see McDougall, *History and the Culture of Nationalism in Algeria*.

136. Khelouz, *Le roman algérien des années 1920*.

137. Lanasri, *La littérature algérienne de l'entre-deux-guerres*, 285.

EPILOGUE
Sex and the Centenary

The official volume devoted to the centenary of French Algeria began with an enticing overture: "To celebrate the Centenary of Algeria: does there exist a task that is more seductive, more instructive, more evocative of memories, of emotions, and promises?" Summoning the "smiling beauty" of the country, the event's general commissioner, Gustave Mercier, elaborated on the fantasy that animated the project of French Algeria. Avoiding any reference to the violence of conquest, he called forth an alluring image: a desirable land that had been successfully incorporated into French national territory, and a colonized population that embraced their legal subordination with gratitude, even "love."[1]

Educing emotional attachments between France and Algeria, the centenary elided the brutality of colonization. This mythic fabrication of historical memory followed the lines elaborated in this book. French Algeria relied on a legal and sexual fantasy, but by 1930, that fantasy was increasingly difficult to sustain. As the preceding chapters have demonstrated, the exercise of French sovereignty depended on the legal construction and regulation of both religious and sexual difference. These legally constituted differences structured policies that were elaborated over the course of the nineteenth century, laying hold to Algerian land and disqualifying Muslims from full citizenship. They nullified Muslim land law, while imposing and then naturalizing Muslim personal status under the guise of upholding local law and custom, whose subjugation of women they at once presumed, affirmed, and lamented. This logic of dispossession and exclusion proved radically double-edged. The political subordination of Algerian men depended on authorizing their sexual privileges, including polygamy and child marriage. French juridical fantasies of Algerian men's sexual rights not only gave rise to fears of moral degeneracy, but also incited sexual

---

1. G. Mercier, *Le centenaire de l'Algérie*, 1:9.

resentment. Their erotic fascination with Algerian women sentimentalized female oppression and symbolized French men's legal and sexual frustration. Jealously maintaining their own privileges, many French jurists and politicians denied extending political rights to French women and to Algerians, despite claiming to defend legal equality. By 1930, French feminists and increasingly militant Algerians foregrounded these contradictions in demanding substantive political and legal reform.

In light of this legal and logical bind, the festivities of 1930 represented an ambivalent apogee. The year's events produced revelatory denials at every turn. Military parades, speeches, awards, photograph collections, posters, stamps, congresses, and desert car races romanticized a brutal conquest that official discourse resolutely refused to name. In 1927, the *délégations financières* unanimously approved a project "to commemorate with great splendor the Centenary of the liberatory landing of France in Algeria, and the foundation of its colonizing and peaceful influence on the African side of the Mediterranean."[2] In his justification of the proposed budget for the celebrations, which would ultimately cost 130 million francs, Deputy Gaston Thomson (Constantine) confirmed that "the taking of Algiers is a glorious act, but it is not only that which we want to commemorate. It is [also] the introduction of French civilization in all of North Africa."[3] Governor-General Pierre Bordes hoped that the celebration would have a powerful psychological impact, by creating "everywhere an obsession with Algeria."[4] Invocations of peace and fraternity notwithstanding, the project was a costly exercise of negation, which revealed by denying the violent and covetous desire that had animated French colonization over the course of a century. In retrospect, and from the critical-historical perspective adopted in this book, it appears as a compensatory fantasy that marshaled funds and feelings to secure a status quo that never was and could never be.[5]

The rhetoric of France's civilizing mission publicly held sway, despite mounting political challenges from Young Algerians as well as from new militant movements, including Messali Hadj's Étoile nord-africaine, Abdelhamid Ben Badis's Islamic reformism, and the French Communist Party. Critics at the time highlighted the political hazards involved. Former governor-general and current

---

2. Gustavino in *Délégations financières algériennes*, April 8, 1927, 305.

3. *J.O.*, Débats, Chambre, November 30, 1928, 3092.

4. Edmond Gojon, "Les leçons d'un centenaire," *L'Afrique du nord illustrée*, April 27, 1929, 3.

5. Julien, *Histoire de l'Algérie contemporaine*, 402–11; Henry, "Le centenaire de l'Algérie"; Jansen, "Fête et ordre colonial"; Kaddache, *Histoire du nationalisme algérien*, 223–54.

senator Maurice Viollette, who had been forced from power by opponents of his assimilationist agenda, warned against "wounding the Arab's legitimate pride by making him participate retrospectively in the defeat of his ancestors."[6] According to Jean Mélia, the liberal president of the Ligue en faveur des indigènes musulmans, the centenary would remind Algerians of "how we have taken their native land, recalling to them their defeats with all that they entailed, of massacres, ruins, and humiliations."[7] *Demain*, the Socialist daily in Algiers, denounced the military pomp surrounding the conquest as a "clumsy masquerade" and called instead for an official "Day of Remorse."[8] For Ferhat Abbas, the occasion evinced how "the century which is dying has been a century of tears and blood. And it is particularly we, natives, who have cried, who have bled. We bury it without regret and without joy." Liberals such as Viollette and Mélia and Young Algerians like Abbas kept alive a "timid hope" that political and social reform would more fully integrate Algerians into the French polity.[9] In the decade that followed, they would repeatedly meet with disappointment.

The centenary showcased more than a violent and tragic past. It also marked Muslim Algerians' ongoing legal and social exclusion by bringing into sharp relief their "paradoxical" status as legal French nationals who did not fully participate in national sovereignty. Articles in assimilationist journals such as *L'Union* (El Tihad), *Attakadoum* (Progress), *Le Tribune Indigène*, and *La Voix des humbles* continued to support proposals for "indigenous representation in parliament" launched by the Fédération des élus musulmans in 1927 as well as by Viollette and Mélia. They spoke forcefully against incessant claims that Muslim personal status was incompatible with the exercise of political rights. At the high point of the centenary celebrations, Saïd Faci insisted that while Muslim Algerians had been legally French since 1834 and formally recognized as such by the *sénatus-consulte* of 1865, "the *indigène* is French, but not [*sans l'être*], because he is deprived of political rights: that is his paradoxical situation." Faci's pithy statement underscored how French pretensions to legal sovereignty gave rise to contradictions by simultaneously including and excluding Muslim Algerians. He cited mixed-marriage jurisprudence as proof of this untenable state of affairs. A foreign European woman who married an *indigène* became a French citizen

---

6. Maurice Viollette, "Proposition de loi relative à la célébration du centenaire de la liberation des états barbaresques," in *La Voix des humbles*, December 12, 1928, 13; Cantier, "Les gouverneurs Viollette et Bordes."

7. Mélia, *Le Centenaire de la conquête de l'Algérie*, 21.

8. Albert Truphemis, "Mascarade Balourde," *Demain*, May 3, 1930.

9. Abbas, *Le Jeune Algérien, 1930*, 29.

(albeit a diminished one), while the *indigène* who married her remained legally subordinated. For Faci, the policy "seriously defied logic."[10] It did, however, effectively establish a racial and sexual order in which European women were granted precedence and privileges over Algerian men who were already French.

French political resistance to Muslim Algerians' representation regularly summoned long-standing fantasies of Muslim men's legal privileges. Officially "protected" by the 1865 *sénatus-consulte* and the 1873 Warnier property reform law, Muslim personal status came to be seen by jurists and journalists, politicians as well as novelists, as the embodiment of Algerians' sexual and religious difference. Sexual envy and horror intensified political animus against Algerian men. For instance, the colonial administrator Octave Depont attacked proposals in favor of Algerian representation by rehearsing arguments against these purported privileges, including polygamy, repudiation, and the *droit de djebr*. Alongside familiar condemnations of patriarchal cruelty, Depont revealed the jealous resentment of Muslim pleasure—what I have described as an extimate desire—that aroused these accusations. According to his complaint, "Muslims take the right to marry European women, but it is not reciprocal, because under no pretext can their girls be given over to Christians." Comparing this attitude to that of "prehistoric" men, he decried how the "tribe jealously guards the excess of its feminine element, wanting to keep it exclusively for itself." Depont depicted Muslim Algerians as a primitive horde who kept a surplus of women and sexual pleasures for themselves, hence denying equal enjoyment to French men. Obscuring the violence and violation of colonization, the statement performed a fantasmatic reversal in which Algerians appeared as privileged victors, while French men seemed to be at a loss.[11]

A contemporary caricature in the erotic humor magazine *Le Sourire* portrayed this unsettling inversion. In "The Centenary of Algeria in Montmartre," a stereotypically grotesque Algerian delights in the city's abundant pleasures, as two young scantily clad *parisiennes* attend to him, effectively becoming part of his "harem." The satire mocks the Algerian as illegitimately occupying a position that was desirable for—and an implicit prerogative of—French men (as the illustrated magazine's very existence attests).

Claims that Muslim men possessed a surfeit of pleasure and power by virtue of their family law justified their political exclusion. In hoarding women, they rejected a sexual contract that, as Carole Pateman has argued following Freud,

10. Saïd Faci, "Assimilation," *La Voix des humbles*, May 1930, 5.

11. Depont, *L'Algérie du centenaire*, 373, 118. Depont's fears of miscegenation also underwrote his calls to regulate North African migrants in the metropole. See Rosenberg, *Policing Paris*, 136.

FIGURE 11 / PEM, *Le centenaire à Montmartre*, from *Le Sourire*, 1930. Bibliothèque nationale de France.

grounded men's political equality in the exchange of women.[12] The focus on Muslim personal status made civil legal distinctions between the Algerian and French populations politically, physically, and psychically salient. This assertion of legal and religious difference was anchored by claims about gender and sex. A notorious opinion piece on the centenary by Henry Vidal in *Le Figaro* illustrates this refusal to cede a political and sexual place to Algerian men: "So, we will see them in the Palais Bourbon voting on justice, on marriage and the family, they who have a personal status and who are polygamous, these fanatic believers, in charge of *laïcité*. Crazy!" While claiming to champion republican secularism, Vidal in his defense of French sovereignty linked sexual anxiety to biopolitics. The prospect of representation even by a select few elicited fears of French legal and demographic subjugation. "'The elite,'" he warned, "'belong to a race that grows every day in number. A number—terrible, obsessive word—to whose law we will sooner or later submit."[13] Vidal's commentary demonstrates how sexual insecurity linked French men's concerns about religious difference to a visceral fear of the size of the Algerian population. It makes clear, in other words, how Algerian men's reproductive sexual prowess was at the heart of French men's political concerns.

Young Algerians tried to counter these projective fantasies about their personal status, arguing, as did Ioulalen, a columnist for *La Voix des humbles*, that polygamy was only tolerated, rather than mandated, by Muslim status. Drawing an implicit comparison to French law, he suggested that the tolerance was comprehensible "given man's inconstancy and the prohibition on prostitution and adultery in Islam." For Algerian critics of French prejudice, civil legal difference should not affect political status. As they pointed out, citizens with Muslim status in the four communes in Senegal and in India had long exercised voting rights, as did Alsatians, who also had a "local status."[14] These legal arguments found little traction with politicians and jurists who vehemently opposed granting Algerian Muslims political representation out of deep-seated fears of being sexually and demographically overwhelmed.

Jurists who extolled French colonization instead represented Muslim status as a symbol of French legal tolerance. In his contribution to the centenary volume on law, Dean Marcel Morand summarized France's legal achievements as a

12. Pateman, *Sexual Contract*, 109; J. W. Scott, *Sex and Secularism*, 96–97.

13. Henry Vidal, "Le centenaire de la conquête d'Alger: Aux urnes, citoyens!," *Le Figaro*, March 21, 1930.

14. Ioualalen, "Représentation parlementaire," *La Voix des humbles*, July 7, 1931, 11–14. See also "La polygamie dans l'Islam," *L'Union*, September 1, 15, 1927.

"work of civilization—accomplished by procedures whose legality and morality cannot be contested." He insisted that throughout a century of judicial reforms, France had continued to "respect the religious sentiments of natives."[15] His emphasis on the tolerance for religious feeling obscured the long history of land reform that had, in fact, profoundly transformed Muslim property and encouraged dispossession. As we have seen throughout this book, France's religious "respect" reinforced a presumptive distinction between spiritual and material concerns. In the centenary volume, real estate law was, symptomatically, treated in a separate section. Morand's chronological overview of native institutions, meanwhile, recapitulated the hubristic project of the centenary itself, presenting major material and moral transformations as if they had been moderate and uncontested ameliorations.

In the double discourse of these legal experts, French law had both maintained indigenous law and had a "civilizing" effect on it. Since it required French intervention, the prospect of further family law reform continued to project the "civilizing mission" into the future. A centenary report in the *Revue algérienne, tunisienne et marocaine de législation et jurisprudence* by Georges Henri Bousquet, a professor at the law faculty in Algiers for the next three decades, made the argument explicitly. In his view, the changes wrought to "indigenous family law" over the course of the century had remained overly "modest," leaving its principal differences from French law largely in place. He asserted, on the one hand, that "the indigenous conception of family law is opposed to ours: marriage is a purely carnal union in which the despotism of the husband alone reigns." At the same time, he lamented how, after one hundred years of colonization, a father could be allowed "to sell his young daughter of nine or ten to a lubricious old man, whose only goal is to rape her." This denunciation of Algerian women's subjection to vile and violent patriarchal power justified his rejection of "more or less absurd electoral projects." For Bousquet, Morand's revised Muslim Law Code "would be a much more advantageous gift than the ballot."[16] The modification of Algerian family law appeared here as a substitute for substantive political reform.

The irony of these jurists' critiques of Muslim patriarchy was not lost on contemporary French feminists who continued to fight for women's equality in both public and private law. After all, French women were also "paradoxical"

---

15. Marcel Morand, "Les institutions judiciaires," in Milliot et al., *L'oeuvre législative de la France en Algérie*, 157, 89.

16. Georges-Henri Bousquet, "La législation française et son influence sur le droit de famille indigène," *RA*, 1930, pt. 1, 193, 201. See also Solus, "L'évolution de la condition juridique de la femme indigène."

citizens, without voting rights and subject to their own discriminatory personal status.[17] The centenary offered an occasion to revisit the question of their rights. Rather than drawing parallels between their own subordinated status and that of Algerian men, however, many suffragist activists underscored French women's legal and civilizational superiority. They laid claim, that is, to their embodied legal prestige in order to claim republican political inclusion. Like "imperial feminists" elsewhere, they showcased French women's contributions to the colonial project in order to secure rights for themselves.[18] An issue of *La Française* devoted to the centenary events overtly pursued this strategy. The journal featured statements by two prominent Algerian suffragists, Lucie Richardot and Jeanne Alquier, that negatively compared the status of Algerian men to that of French women. For Richardot it was "sad that the political men representing our nation are thinking of giving the vote to natives of our colony while continuing to refuse political rights to their mothers, their sisters, their wives, and their daughters."[19] Alquier registered her outrage more forcefully, denouncing how "natives, who are only French subjects, which is to say that they renounce our code, our civilization, our ancestors and who are all too often still our enemies . . . can be financial delegates, general councilors, municipal councilors, and vote in the Djemâa." In short, she found it unacceptable that they had "a major share of citizen's rights," while women, "who are submitted to French law, remain nothing for the nation."[20] Several articles on the abject condition of Algerian women appeared alongside these briefs. The journal thus contrasted French women's role in Algeria as colonial aides and exemplars to the moral and legal failings of Algerian men.[21]

The journal's editor, Cécile Brunschvicg, embraced the feminist civilizing mission, undertaking a trip to Algeria in 1931. Touched by the experience, she praised in her reports the influence of literary magistrate Ferdinand Duchêne, who wrote on the subject of Algerian women "with so much emotion."[22] Following the voyage, she proposed addressing the question of Algerian women during the "États Généraux du Féminisme" organized as part of the 1931 Colonial Exposition held in Paris. Among her suggestions, Brunschvicg

---

17. J. W. Scott, *Only Paradoxes*.

18. Lorcin, *Historicizing Colonial Nostalgia*, 129. Also, Kimble, "Emancipation through Secularization"; Boittin, "Feminist Mediations of the Exotic"; Guiard, "Être féministe en contexte colonial"; Andersen, *Regeneration through Empire*.

19. Richardot, "Les indigènes d'Algérie voteront-ils avant nous?," *La Française*, May 17, 1930.

20. "Ce que pense du suffrage des femmes une Française de Constantine," *La Française*, May 17, 1930.

21. Colonel Godchot, "Les femmes indigènes de l'Afrique du Nord," *La Française*, May 17, 1930; Cécile Brunschvig, "La propagande suffragiste en Algérie," *La Française*, May 17, 1930.

22. Cécile Brunschvicg, "Au pays des femmes voilées," *La Française*, February 14, 1931.

imagined "the adaptation of native *mœurs* to our French Code" as one potential solution. Registering the apparent incongruity in this endorsement, she commented ironically: "O Napoleonic Code, how we condemn you in our feminist meetings; but how good, just, and prestigious you seem to us, next to the Arab or Kabyle Code!"[23] In other words, she adopted prevailing arguments about the civilizational superiority of the French Civil Code, even while her newspaper frequently castigated how it subordinated women.

During the "États Généraux" themselves, Jeanne Alquier reported on recent transformations in Algerian women's legal and social condition, upholding the 1930 and 1931 legal reforms to Kabyle women's status as exemplary. Brunschvicg also championed these reforms, again crediting Duchêne's work. Alquier's speech shows how feminist expressions of solidarity with Algerian women also served to target Algerian men's political rights. She urged the feminists at the congress, and implicitly the French government as well, to refuse granting them suffrage: "At this moment, Muslim natives are asking for the vote, they are asking for the same votes as French citizens. We should respond: We cannot give the right to vote to people who rape young girls, to people who have contempt for women, who make them into martyrs."[24] Suffragists used these arguments to explain why French women were more deserving of full voting rights then Algerian men.

They lodged a similar appeal to the senatorial commission presided over by Viollette when he toured Algeria in May 1931. These feminists represented the exclusion of French women from the franchise as a source of "humiliation," given that "new 'French subjects,'" who had "barely achieved our level of civilization," were granted the right to vote.[25] In subscribing to a form of what political theorist Sara Farris has described as "femonationalism," they endorsed the supremacy of French civilization.[26] Seeking the embrace of French law and imperial sovereignty, their claims to full citizenship reproduced the sexual logic of racial prestige that had historically structured Algerian colonial law. They aimed to take advantage of this privilege, rather than denouncing its gendered presumptions.

Another feminist meeting in Constantine in 1932, the Congrès des femmes méditerranéennes, coupled demands for French women's suffrage with legal measures targeting Algerian women (the official adoption of the Code Morand, a mandated marriage age of fifteen years for women, and marital consent), thus

---

23. Cécile Brunschvicg, "La situation des femmes en Algérie," *La Française,* February 28, 1931.

24. *États généraux du féminisme,* 115–16. And Régine Goutalier, "Les États généraux du féminisme à l'Exposition coloniale."

25. "Une commission sénatoriale en Algérie," *La Française,* May 30, 1931.

26. Farris, *In the Name of Women's Rights.*

affirming "the primordial role played by the French Woman in North Africa." The congress concluded with a call to elevate French women's status, proclaiming "the authority of the French Woman would be increased if she possessed the fullness [*la plénitude*] of her civil and political rights." If the "fullness" of French law enhanced the authority of French women, they would, in turn, improve the imperial nation's status, because "France itself has a great interest in augmenting the prestige of its Nationals."[27] In both a symbolic and a numerical sense, women promised to strengthen French sovereignty in North Africa. Increasingly under attack by new political and social movements in Algeria, the colonial fantasy of French law would, according to this argument, be supplemented by French women's political participation.

Algerian observers understandably approached the event with trepidation. An "Open letter to the French Women of the Constantine Congress" published in *La Voix indigène* emphasized that the "egotism of the stronger sex," rather than Qur'anic prescription, was responsible for the subordination of the "Muslim Woman." To reinforce the point that masculine privilege rather than religion was at issue, the author noted how native resistance to "the improvement of women's lot" actually resembled the "French senators" who stood in the way of women's suffrage.[28] In another letter addressed to the organizers and read to the assembled delegates, Mme. Seghir Hacene, the wife of the *caïd* of Sigus, corrected presuppositions about Algerian women as "savage and resistant to all civilization and progress." In her view, the causes of their "atrocious and silent suffering" had "nothing to do with religion, as some people assume." Polygamy was a case in point. From her perspective, men "did not actually grasp or did not want to grasp, the true directives" regarding the practice. Addressed to French feminists, these interventions pointed to patriarchy itself, rather than religious tradition or "Muslim law," as the source of women's subordination.[29] According to an article published in *La Française*, some Algerian men in attendance favored women's suffrage, confirming that "if women voted in France, the situation of the French woman and the Muslim woman would be improved."[30]

---

27. Yvonne-Noel Cunéo, "Le Congrès international des femmes méditerranéennes," *Annales Africaines*, May 1, 1932, 141.

28. "La femme musulmane: Lettre ouverte aux dames Françaises du Congrès de Constantine," *La Voix indigène*, March 10, 1932. Republished as Zenati, "La femme musulmane," *La Française*, April 17, 1932.

29. "Le Congrès des Femmes Méditerranéennes et la femme musulmane," *La Voix indigène*, April 21, 1932. Also, *La Française*, April 17, 1932.

30. Jeanne Bottini-Honot, "Congrès de Constantine: Impression d'un élu musulman," *La Française*, April 17, 1932.

Rather than seeking out such solidarity, many advocates for women's suffrage appealed to civilizational arguments against Muslim men's political rights. They renewed their resistance when proposals to extend suffrage to some twenty thousand "elite" Muslim men were endorsed by the Algerian Muslim Congress in June 1936 and concretized in a bill that Viollette submitted to parliament later that year. Settler politicians such as Senator Pierre Roux-Freissineng (Oran) unsurprisingly denounced the legislation as a "juridical monstrosity," which created "two categories of electors"—one of whom "maintained a status of a religious order" that was contrary to "French civil laws," most notably by authorizing polygamy. In his view, it would be a "death blow to French sovereignty."[31] A survey of critical opinions in *La Française* echoed these statements. Gabrielle Vallé-Genairon declared that adoption of the law would be "a veritable insult to our women [*les femmes de chez nous*]."[32] Denouncing Viollette's measure for upholding "Muslim status," which was the "basis for the enslavement of women," the Comtesse de Brazza intimated that no woman could support the legislation without "dishonoring herself." C. Bouchard likewise condemned Muslim men who wanted to keep their status because "it authorizes polygamy, maintaining the woman in a position of subject vis-à-vis man." Castigating the bill for reinforcing "male domination," she encouraged French women to resist its adoption.[33] These suffragists thus staked their claims to citizenship on a civilizational conception of French women's honor and dignity. Refracting male politicians' extimate fantasies, their defense of French women's privileged status presumed a sexual and racial threat: their political and legal subjection to Algerian Muslim men.

The suffragist journalist Lucienne Jean-Darrouy was one notable exception. Writing in her regular column on women's rights in *L'Écho d'Alger*, Jean-Darrouy objected to the use of distorted representations of Muslim men's sexual privilege to defeat the Viollette law. Without denying "the material and moral poverty of some Muslim and Kabyle women," she urged that "this is not a reason to invent and decry tyrannical *mœurs* that are purely imaginary." Well aware of tenacious colonial clichés, she noted that "it is especially with respect to polygamy that the authors' inventions go too far." As a regular critic of the patriarchal excesses of French law, Jean-Darrouy observed how claims that "all Algerian natives have four wives" were a fantasmatic projection that also served to deny the

31. "Le projet de la loi Viollette sur l'accession des musulmans aux droits politiques," *L'Écho d'Alger*, December 31, 1936.

32. G. Vallé-Genairon, "Le vote des indigènes et les femmes françaises," *La Française*, January 30, 1937.

33. M. L., "Le projet de loi Viollette, confirmera-t-il l'asservissement des musulmanes algériennes?," *La Française*, February 6, 1937.

impoverishment of Algeria's Muslim majority. As she sardonically concluded, "it is not because one is posing as a defender of women that one has the right to create legends."[34] Jean-Darrouy refused to sanction the instrumentalization of feminism to buttress the sexual fantasy of French sovereignty. And she remained wary of suffragists who appeared willing to fuel that fantasy. In her view, the cause of feminists and Algerians alike would be better served by showing how, by denying their privileges and projecting their desires, French men jealously guarded their rights.

As a powerful historical and political fiction, the centenary constructed a progressive idea of French colonial history against an image of Algerian Muslim legal and social backwardness that endures to this day. Settler colonialism conflated Islam and a corporealized conception of Muslim law that supposedly conflicted with the secular (but far from gender-equal) French Civil Code. This erotically charged legal imaginary has endured beyond the end of the legal regime that was French Algeria. Brought into being by the historical exigencies of colonial law, it can be understood in its persistence as a symptom of a historical disavowal or denial.

Algeria's hard-won independence refounded French sovereignty on new terms, while also granting its sexualized imagery a significant postcolonial afterlife in the former metropole. France relinquished its territorial claims and established that Muslim Algerians, who had since become citizens despite their personal status, were no longer French. But even after decolonization and the "forgetting" of French Algeria, a corporealized conception of Muslim law remained, as did the problem of securing French sovereignty over postcolonial migrant populations. Decolonization reconfigured these problems without resolving them, as the enduring preoccupation with the figurative and literal challenges posed by Algerian men to the bodily integrity of French citizenship makes clear.[35]

This recurrent insecurity points to why sexual fantasies about Muslim law have continued to haunt the imaginary of French sovereignty.[36] Present-day debates over the integration of Muslim French citizens, from controversies over head scarves and burqas to fears of violent fundamentalism, display a recurrent public fascination with Muslim men's sexual excess and women's victimization, including on the part of feminists. The ongoing political and legal mobilization

---

34. Lucienne Jean-Darrouy, "Sur les femmes musulmanes," *L'Écho d'Alger*, February 20, 1937. Also, Guiard, "Être féministe en contexte colonial," 144.

35. Shepard, *Invention of Decolonization*, and *Sex, France, and Arab Men*.

36. Surkis, "Hymenal Politics."

of sexualized claims about Muslim men and women continues to justify discriminatory policy, despite politicians' prima facie claims to protect the universalist and egalitarian principles of *laïcité*.[37]

Michel Houellebecq's sensationalist 2015 novel *Submission* offers a striking distillation of the extimate fantasies of Muslim men's sex that continue to operate in the present. Weaving together literature and politics, eroticism and disgust, the work purports to envision France's sovereign and sexual future. In reality, it manifests a deep attachment to an exclusionary fantasy of the French past. Houellebecq's novel imagines a "Muslim Brotherhood" president who comes to power and immediately legalizes polygamy. Male converts rally to the new regime in order to take up young and submissive wives. Initially skeptical, the narrator, an impotent academic, relents in the final pages of the book so that he can access Muslim men's sexual rights by taking his pick of the "pretty, veiled, shy" students who flock to his classes.[38] Polygamy appears in the novel as both a provocation and a panacea. A symptom of a perceived crisis of European (and Christian) civilization and demography, Muslim men's sexual privilege returns as the repressed to prop up France's deficient sovereignty. The novel, like its narrator, displays little interest in documenting or imagining Muslim French existence—past, present, or future. Whether read straight or as a satire, the trope of "Muslim" polygamy is politically and socially stigmatizing, based on debilitating stereotypes of Muslims and women. By lamenting the loss of French potency, Houellebecq's fantasy of France's "Muslim" future inverts the triumphalist image of the centenary of French Algeria. It also indicates how that historical fiction was already haunted by fears of France's sexual and racial decline.

Submission's dalliances with sexual decadence rest on a fantasy with a long French history. The present work documents its emergence and offers tools with which to analyze its recurrence. Rather than confirming an eternal return, these insights into the role of desire and difference in the history of French law demonstrate that exclusionary fantasy of sovereignty can never be secured.

---

37. Souilamas and Macé, *Les féministes et le garçon arabe*; Fassin, "La démocratie sexuelle et le conflit des civilisations"; J. W. Scott, *Politics of the Veil*, and *Sex and Secularism*; Tissot, "Excluding Muslim Women"; Dorlin, "Le grand strip-tease"; Bowen, *Why the French Don't Like Headscarves*; Fernando, "Save the Muslim Woman, Save the Republic"; Selby, "Polygamy in the Parisian Banlieues"; Fredette, "Becoming a Threat"; Farris, *In the Name of Women's Rights*; Vauchez, "Is French Laïcité Still Liberal?"

38. Houellebecq, *Submission*, 238.

BIBLIOGRAPHY

ARCHIVAL SOURCES

Archives nationales, Pierrefitte (AN)

BB/6 (II) Dossiers personnels de magistrats
BB/30/616–624 Algérie. Administration de la Justice. 1831–1870. Organisation judiciaire de la colonie
19950167/1–12 Justice Musulmane
20020495/1–10 Direction des affaires civiles et du sceau. Organisation judiciaire de l'Algérie

Archives Nationales d'Outre-Mer, Aix-en-Provence (ANOM)

Gouvernement Général (GGA)
3/E/4 (18/MIOM/71) Fonds Gueydon, Projets de loi
3/E/92 (18/MIOM/81) Fonds Gueydon, Propriété Indigène
10H Études et notices sur l'Algérie et l'Islam
17H Justice musulmane (1843/1948)
103/I/5 (71/MIOM/504) Bureaux arabes de l'Algérois. Cercle d'Orléansville.
1/T/2 Correspondance—Tribunaux et parquets

Archives ministérielles
F80 475 Rapports des bureaux arabes
F80 1725 Justice musulmane
1AFFPOL 903 1 Direction des Affaires politiques. Algérie et Sahara

Département d'Alger
91/6N Constitution de la propriété indigène par la loi du 26 juillet 1873, 1873–1905
91/8/N/1–3 Service de la propriété indigène. Réclamations des indigènes

Département d'Oran
92/1N/4 Section de propriété—circulaires et décisions
92/2N/77–9 Séquestre et propriété indigène
92/2NN/597–603 Registres concernant l'application de la loi du 26 juillet 1873
État civil de l'Algérie
http://anom.archivesnationales.culture.gouv.fr/caomec2/recherche.
    php?territoire=ALGERIE

Service Historique de la Défense, Vincennes (SHD)

1/H/28–33 Algérie. Correspondance, 1834–35
5/J Justice Militaire—Algérie
5N/5 Cabinet du ministre. Correspondance générale

Dossiers du personnel
10Yf 671 Boyer, Samuel Abraham
5Yf 70970 Bouïs, Albert Jean Marie Joseph
8Yf 4824 Rocas, Albert
5Ye 7343 Vergennes, Maurice Jean de
6Yf 17781 Lapanouse, Henry Charles Alexandre

JOURNALS AND NEWSPAPERS CONSULTED

L'Afrique du nord illustrée
L'Akhbar
Les Annales africaines
Archives parlémentaires
L'Attakadoum (Progress)
Bulletin des Lois
Bulletin judiciaire d'Algérie (*BJA*)
Bulletin officiel du Gouvernement Général de l'Algérie (*BOGGA*)
Le Charivari oranais
Chronique des lettres françaises
Le Courrier de Tlemcen
La Croix
Délégations financières algériennes
La Dépêche algérienne
L'Écho d'Alger
L'Effort algérien
El Hack (The Truth)
L'Europe nouvelle
Le Figaro
La Française
Ikdam (Courage)
L'Indépendant de Mascara
L'Intransigeant
Islam
Le Journal de la jurisprudence de la Cour impériale d'Alger [becomes *Cour d'appel d'Alger et de législation algérienne*] (*Robe*)
Le Journal des débats
Le Journal des tribunaux algériens (*JTA*)
La Lanterne
La Lanterne Médéenne
Le Moniteur de l'Algérie
L'Ouest-Éclair
Le Petit Alger
Le Petit colon

Le Petit Journal
Le Petit médéen
Le Petit Parisien
La Presse
Le Progrès de Mascara
Le Progrès de Orléansville
Rachidi (The Guide)
Le Radical Algérien
Recueil de législation et jurisprudence coloniales
Le Républicain de Constantine
La Revue africaine
La Revue algérienne, tunisienne, et marocaine de législation et de jurisprudence (*RA*)
La Revue de droit international privé (*RDIP*)
La Revue de l'histoire des religions
La Revue de l'Orient
La Revue des études islamiques
La Revue du monde musulman
La Revue indigène
La Revue nord africaine
Le Temps
Le Tribune Indigène
L'Union (*El Tihad*)
L'Univers israélite
La Vie algérienne
La Vigie algérienne
La Voix des humbles
Le XIXᵉ siècle

PRIMARY SOURCES

Abbas, Ferhat. *Le Jeune Algérien, 1930: De la colonie vers la province*. Paris: Gernier frères, 1981.
Abdesselem, Taleb. *L'organisation financière de l'Empire marocain*. Paris: Émile Larose, 1911.
——. "À propos des mariages musulmans en Algérie." *Journal des débats*, June 1, 1922.
——. "Le statut personnel des musulmans français." *L'Europe nouvelle* 1, no. 32 (August 17, 1918): 1516–18.
——. "Une conférence sur les musulmans." *L'Ouest-Éclair*, February 8, 1918.
Algérie: Immigrants et indigènes. Paris: Challamel, 1863.
Alloula, Malek. *The Colonial Harem*. Translated by Myrna Godzich and Wlad Godzich. Minneapolis: University of Minnesota Press, 1986.
Amar, Émile. "Projet de codification du droit musulman." *Revue du monde musulman* 6 (1908): 362–69.
Andriveau, Marcel. *De la répression pénale du duel*. Paris: A. Pedone, 1895.
Anquetil, Georges. *La maîtresse légitime: Essai sur le mariage polygamique de demain*. Paris: Les éd. Georges Anquetil, 1923.
Aumont-Thiéville, Jacques. *De l'indigénat en Algérie*. Paris: Arthur Rousseau, 1906.
Ballue, Arthur. *La question algérienne à vol d'oiseau*. Marseille: J. Doucet, 1869.
Barbet, Charles. *Au pays des burnous (impressions et croquis d'Algérie)*. Algiers: Ernest Mallebay, 1898.

——. "La femme musulmane en Algérie." *Revue algérienne de jurisprudence.* Part 1 (1903): 165–78.

Barde, Louis. *Théorie traditionnelle des statuts ou principes du statut réel et du statut personnel d'après le droit civil français.* Bordeaux: Pechade, 1880.

Barthelet, L. "Natalité et peuplement en Afrique du Nord." *Bulletin de la Société de la Géographie d'Alger et de l'Afrique du Nord* 28 (1927): 478–508.

Baudicour, Louis de. "Des indigènes de l'Algérie." *Le Correspondant* 30 (1852): 152–70, 93–211.

——. *La guerre et le gouvernement de l'Algérie.* Paris: Sagnier et Bray, 1853.

Beaumont, Tassin de. *De la consolidation de la puissance française en Algérie.* Paris: Chamerot, 1841.

Bel, Alfred. "La codification du droit musulman en Algérie." *Revue de l'histoire des religions* 96, no. 5 (1927): 175–92.

Ben Choaïb, Abou Bekr Abdesselam. "La codification du droit musulman." *Revue du monde musulman* 8, no. 5 (1909): 446–59.

Berbrugger, Louis Adrien. "La polygamie musulmane, ses causes fatales et le moyen de le détruire." *La revue africaine* 3, no. 16 (1858): 254–58.

Bertherand, Émile Louis. *Médecine et hygiène des arabes.* Paris: Ballière, 1855.

Besson, Emmanuel. "Étude comparative sur la constitution de la famille chez les Kabyles et chez les Arabes algériens." *Bulletin de la Société de législation comparée* 23 (April–May 1894): 276–97.

——. *La législation civile de l'Algérie: Étude sur la condition des personnes et le régime des biens en Algérie.* Paris: Marescq, 1894.

Bickart, Edmond. *De la naturalisation.* Paris: A. Giard, 1890.

Blocqueville, Adelheide-Louise d'Eckmühl. *Stella et Mohammed, ou Chrétienne et musulman.* Paris: E. Flammarion, 1892.

Bonnal, Marcellin. *Un amour en Algérie.* Paris: Dolin, 1848.

Bonnellier, Hippolyte. *Mœurs d'Alger—Juive et Mauresque.* Paris: Silvestre, 1833.

Bonnichon, André. *La conversion au christianisme de l'indigène musulman algérien et ses effets juridiques (Un cas de conflit colonial).* Paris: Recueil Sirey, 1931.

Boullenois, Louis. *Traité de la personnalité et de la réalité des loix, coutumes, ou status.* Paris: G. Desprez, 1766.

Bourde, Paul. *À travers l'Algérie, souvenirs de l'excursion parlémentaire (septembre–octobre 1879).* Paris: G. Charpentier, 1880.

Boyer, Samuel Abraham. *Affaire Bouïs contre Boyer.* Algiers: Fontana, 1891.

Boyer-Banse, L. "La propriété indigène dans l'arrondissement d'Orléansville." Université de Paris, 1902.

Broglie, Albert de. *Une réforme administrative en Afrique.* Paris: H. Dumineray, 1860.

Bugéja, Marie. *Séduction orientale.* Algiers: P. and G. Soubiron, 1931.

Burdeau, Auguste. *L'Algérie en 1891: Rapport et discours à la chambre des députés.* Paris: Hachette, 1892.

Cadoz, François. *Droit musulman Malékite.* Paris: Challamel, 1871.

Caise, Albert. *Teurkia.* Paris: Flammarion, 1888.

Carpentier, P. *Alger, M. le Duc Rovigo, et M. Pichon en mars et avril 1832.* Paris: Delaunay, 1832.

Cauwès, Albert. *Des rapports du mariage avec la nationalité.* Paris: L. Larose, 1901.

Chambre des députés. *Colonisation de l'ex-régence d'Alger: Documents officiels déposés sur le Bureau de la Chambre des députés. Avec une carte de l'état d'Alger.* Paris: L. G. Michaud, Delaunay, 1834.

Charbonney, Abraham. "Auvergne, Alpes maritimes." In *Récits et souvenirs de quelques-uns de ses ouvriers (1831–1881)*, 329–78. Geneva: E. Beroud, 1882.

Chevillotte, A. *De la famille musulmane en Algérie, à propos du "Statut personnel et des successions en droit musulman," par MM. Sauterra et Cherbonneau*. Paris: Balitout, Questroy, 1873.

Clavel, Eugène. "Mariage contracté devant l'officier de l'état civil français, entre un musulman algérien français et une chrétienne française." *Journal international de droit privé* (1897): 997–1009.

Codes des tribunaux mixtes d'Égypte, précédés du règlement d'organisation judiciaire. Alexandria: Impr. générale L. Carrière, 1896.

Collection complète des lois. 140 vols. Vol. 33. Paris: Recueil Sirey, 1834.

Collection des actes du gouvernement depuis l'occupation d'Alger jusqu'au 1ᵉʳ octobre 1834. Paris: Impr. Royale, 1843.

Coppolani, Xavier, and Octave Depont. *Les confréries religieuses musulmanes*. Algiers: A. Jordan, 1898.

Corre, Armand. *L'ethnographie criminelle: Les observations et les statistiques judiciaires receuillies dans les colonies françaises*. Paris: Reinwald, 1894.

Cortes, Léon. *Monographie de la commune de Médéa*. Algiers: Imprimerie algérienne, 1909.

Couchené, G. *Du mariage putatif et de ses effets en droit français*. Châtillon-sur-Seine: Imprimerie générale, 1880.

Cousin, Victor. *Cours d'histoire de la philosophie morale au dix-huitième siècle (1819 et 1820)*. Paris: Ladrange, 1841.

———. *Fragments philosophiques*. Paris: A. Sautelet, 1826.

Croabbon, A. *La science du point d'honneur*. Paris: Librairies-Imprimeries réunies, 1894.

Dain, Alfred. *Étude sur la naturalisation des étrangers en Algérie*. Algiers: A. Jourdan, 1885.

———. *Rapport sur les modifications à apporter à la loi du 26 juillet 1873*. Algiers: A. Jourdan, 1882.

Darien, Georges. *Biribi—discipline militaire*. Paris: A. Savine, 1890.

Daumas, Eugène. *La femme arabe*. Algiers: A. Jourdan, 1912.

———. *Moeurs et coutumes de l'Algérie: Tell, Kabylie, Sahara*. Paris: Hachette, 1855.

De la conversion des musulmans au christianisme, considérée comme moyen d'affermir la puissance française en Algérie. Paris: J. Lecoffre, 1846.

Delecaille, Alexandre. *De la naturalisation en droit civil et en droit international*. Paris: E. Duchemin, 1893.

Demontès, Victor. *Le peuple algérien: Essais de démographie algérienne*. Algiers: Impr. algérienne, 1906.

Depont, Octave. *L'Algérie du centenaire—L'oeuvre française de libération, de conquête morale et d'évolution sociale des indigènes—Les Berbères en France—La Représentation parlementaire des indigènes*. Paris: Recueil Sirey, 1928.

Descaves, Lucien. *Sous-Offs, roman militaire, suivi de: Misères du sabre, et des plaidoiries prononcées devant la Cour d'assises, le 15 mars 1890*. Paris: Tresse et Stock, 1892.

Desprez, Charles. *Voyage à Oran*. Algiers: V. Aillaud, 1872.

Dessoliers, Félix. *De la fusion des races européennes en Algerie par les mariages croisés et de ses conséquences politiques*. Algiers: Fontana, 1899.

d'Ivry, Fortin. "Orient et Occident." *Revue de l'Orient* 4 (1844): 209–24.

Duchêne, Ferdinand. *Ceux d'Algérie: Types et coutumes.* Paris: Horizons de France, 1929.

———. *Kamir: Roman d'une femme Arabe (Les Barbaresques).* Paris: Albin Michel, 1926.

———. *Mouna, Cachir et Couscous.* Paris: Albin Michel, 1930.

———. *Thamil'la.* Paris: Albin Michel, 1923.

———. *Thamil'la.* Paris: Supplément de *l'Illustration*, 1907.

———. *Thamilla, "The Turtle-Dove": A Story of the Mountains of Algeria.* Translated by Isabelle May and Emily M. Newton. New York: Revell, 1927.

Duchesne, Édouard Adolphe. *De la prostitution dans la ville d'Alger.* Paris: J.-B. Ballière, 1853.

Dunoyer, Léon. *Étude sur le conflit des lois special à l'Algérie.* Paris: Pedone-Lauriel, 1888.

Duval, Jules. *Réflexions sur la politique de l'empereur en Algérie.* Paris: C. Ainé, 1866.

Duvernois, Alexandre. *La question algérienne au point de vue des musulmans.* Paris: Hachette, 1863.

Duvernois, Clément. *L'Akhbar et les novateurs téméraires: Lettre à M. A. Bourget.* Algiers: Dubos frères, 1858.

———. *L'Algérie ce qu'elle est, ce qu'elle doit être: Essai économique et politique.* Bibliothèque algérienne. Algiers: Dubos frères, 1858.

———. *La réorganisation de l'Algérie; lettre à S.A.I. le prince Napoléon.* Algiers: Dubos frères, 1858.

———. *Les autolatres, lettre à l'empereur.* Algiers: Dubos frères, 1860.

Enfantin, Prosper. *La colonisation de l'Algérie.* Paris: P. Bertrand, 1843.

Estoublon, Robert. *Jurisprudence algérienne de 1830 à 1876.* Vols. 1–4 (1830–1876). Algiers: A. Jourdan, 1890.

———. "Mariages musulmans et kabyles." *Revue algérienne de jurisprudence*, part 1 (1892): 81–91.

Estoublon, Robert, and Adolphe Lefébure. *Code de l'Algérie, Vol. 1 (1830–1895).* Algiers: A. Jourdan, 1896.

———. *Code de l'Algérie, Vol. 2 (1896–1905).* Algiers: A. Jourdan, 1907.

États généraux du féminisme, Paris, 30–31 mai 1931. Paris: Conseil national des femmes françaises, 1931.

Étienne, Alphonse. "Le droit de 'djebr' et le mariage des impubères chez les musulmans en Algerie." *Journal des Tribaunaux Algériens* 13 (October 5, 1898).

Étude sur la propriété indigène et la loi du 26 juillet 1873 suivie d'un appendice (extraits de la Solidarité). Algiers: V. Pèze, 1879.

Eudel, Paul. *L'orféverie algérienne et tunisienne.* Algiers: A. Jourdan, 1902.

Exposé de l'état actuel de la société arabe, du gouvernement et de la législation qui la régit. Algiers: Imprimerie du gouvernement, 1844.

Eyssautier, Louis-Auguste. *Le statut réel français en Algérie, ou Législation et jurisprudence sur la propriété, depuis 1830 jusqu'à la loi du 28 avril 1887.* Algiers: A. Jourdan, 1887.

———. "Projet de loi sur le mariage indigène." *Revue algérienne de jurisprudence*, part 1 (1897): 93–110.

Faure-Sardet, Jeanne. *Hélia, une française en Algérie.* Algiers: Imprimerie Africa, 1932.

Féraud, Laurent-Charles. *Les interprètes de l'Armée d'Afrique.* Algiers: A. Jourdan, 1876.

Feuillide. Capo de [Jean Gabriel Cappot]. *L'Algérie française.* Paris: Plon, 1856.

Fiaux, Louis. *La police des moeurs en France et dans les principaux pays de l'Europe.* Paris: E. Dentu, 1888.

Foelix, Jean-Jacques Gaspard. "Des effets de la naturalisation." *Revue étrangère et française de législation* 10 (1843): 446–65.

Foelix [Jean-Jaques Gaspard]. *Traité du droit international privé.* Paris: Joubert, 1843.

Franclieu, Maurice. *Encore l'Algérie devant les Chambres.* Paris: La Revue algérienne, 1847.

Frégier, Casimir. *Du droit algérien, sa nature, ses éléments, son caractère: Essai d'introduction à un cours de droit algérien.* Algiers: Dubos frères, 1861.

———. *Juifs algériens: Leur passé, leur présent, leur avenir juridique, leur naturalisation collective.* Paris: Michel Lévy, 1865.

Garcin, René. *Du changement de nationalité entre époux.* Paris: L. Boyer, 1902.

Gentil, Maurice. "Administration de la justice musulmane en Algérie." Doctorat, Faculté de droit, 1895.

Godard, Léon. *La nouvelle Église d'Afrique.* Paris: Vᵉ Poussielgue-Rusand, 1858.

Godin, Annette. *L'erreur de Nedjma.* Paris: Alphonse Lemerre, 1923.

Gohier, Urbain. *L'armée contre la nation.* Paris: Éditions de la Revue Blanche, 1899.

Gourgeot, François. *Les sept plaies d'Algérie.* Algiers: P. Fontana, 1891.

Gouvernement général de l'Algérie. *Projet de codification du droit musulman.* Vol. 1, *Rapports relatifs à la codification.* Algiers: Pierre Fontana, 1906.

———. *Projet de codification du droit musulman.* Vol. 2, *Résumé des avis exprimés au sujet de la codification; texte de l'avant-projet concernant le mariage.* Algiers: Pierre Fontana, 1906.

———. *Projet de codification du droit musulman.* Vol. 3, *Procès-verbaux.* Algiers: Pierre Fontana, 1907.

Gruffy, Georges. *De l'unité de nationalité dans la famille, étude sur la naturalisation des femmes mariées et des mineurs.* Paris: E. Duchemin, 1893.

Hacoun-Campredon, Pierre. *Étude sur l'évolution des coutumes kabyles, spécialement en ce qui concerne l'exhérédation des femmes et la pratique du hobous.* Algiers: Jules Carbonel, 1921.

Hain, Victor-Arman. *À la Nation, sur Alger.* Paris: Lachevardière, 1832.

Hamel, Louis. "De la naturalisation des indigènes musulmans de l'Algérie." *Revue algérienne de jurisprudence,* no. 1 (1886): 111–19.

———. "De la naturalisation des indigènes musulmans de l'Algérie." *Revue algérienne de jurisprudence,* no. 1 (1890): 19–32.

Hamet, Ismaël. "La naturalisation des indigènes algériens." In *Congrès de l'Afrique du Nord, tenu à Paris, du 6 au 10 octobre 1908. Compte-rendu des travaux,* edited by Charles Depincé, 375–87. Paris, 1909.

———. *Les musulmans français du nord de l'Afrique.* Paris: Armand Colin, 1906.

Hamon, Augustin-Frédéric. *La France sociale et politique (1891).* Paris: Albert Savine, 1892.

———. *Psychologie du militaire professionnel.* Paris: Revue Socialiste, 1894.

Hanoteau, Adolphe, and Aristide Letourneux. *La Kabylie et les coutumes kabyles.* 3 vols. Paris: Imprimerie nationale, 1873.

Houdas, Octave. *L'Islamisme.* Paris: Dujarric, 1904.

Houellebecq, Michel. *Submission.* Translated by Lorin Stein. New York: Farrar, Straus and Giroux, 2015.

Hugonnet, Ferdinand. *Souvenirs d'un chef de Bureau arabe.* Paris: Michel Lévy, 1858.

Hugues, Albert. *La nationalité française chez les musulmans de l'Algérie.* Paris: A. Chevalier-Maresq, 1899.

Instructions du Gouverneur Général de l'Algérie pour l'exécution de la loi sur la propriété. Algiers: Allaud, 1875.

Isaac, Alexandre. *Rapport fait au nom de la commission chargée d'examiner les modifications à introduire dans la législation et dans l'organisation des divers services de l'Algérie: Justice française et musulmane; Police et sécurité.* Paris P. Mouillot, 1895.

Jacquey, Jules. *De l'application des lois françaises en Algérie.* Algiers: Imprimerie administrative, 1883.

Javary, Albert. *Études sur le gouvernement militaire de l'Algérie.* Paris: J. Corréard, 1855.

Khodja, Hamdan. *Le miroir: Aperçu historique et statistique sur la Régence d'Alger.* Paris: Sinbad, 1985.

———. *Réponse à la "Réfutation de l'ouvrage d'Hamdan-Khoja." Extrait de "L'Observateur des Tribunaux."* Paris: Dezauche, 1834.

Kocher, Adolph. *De la criminalité chez les Arabes au point de vue de la pratique médico-judiciaire en Algérie.* Paris: Ballière, 1884.

L., Ch. de. "Danses maures—Opinion sur les harems." *Revue africaine,* no. 5 (August 1837): 57–72.

Lacassagne, Alexandre. *Dictionnaire encyclopédique des sciences médicales.* Vol. 22. Paris: P. Asselin, 1886.

[Lacroix, Frédéric]. *L'Algérie et la lettre de l'Empereur.* Paris: E. Didot frères, 1863.

La Rochefoucauld-Liancourt, Frédéric Gaëtan. *Note sur l'administration d'Alger.* Paris: A. Henry, 1835.

La Sicotière, Léon de. *Rapport fait au nom de la Commission d'enquête sur les actes du gouvernement de la défense nationale.* Versailles: Cerf et fils, 1875.

Lainé, Armand. *Introduction au droit international privé, contentant une étude historique et critique de la théorie des statuts et des rapports de cette théorie avec le Code civil.* Paris: Cotillon, 1888.

———. "Le droit international privé en France considéré dans ses rapports avec la théorie des statuts." *Journal de droit international privé et jurisprudence comparée* 12, no. 3–4 (1885): 129–43.

Lamouroux. "De la polygamie en Algérie." *Revue de l'Orient* 10 (1851): 41–44.

Lanjuinais, Jean-Denis. *La bastonnade et la flagellation pénales, considérées chez les peuples anciens et chez les modernes.* Paris: Baudouin frères, 1825.

Lapasset, Ferdinand. *Aperçu sur l'organisation des indigènes dans les territoires militaires et dans les territoires civils.* Algiers: Dubos frères, 1850.

Lapradelle, Albert, and Marcel Morand. "Du mariage en France des marocains et des indigènes musulmans d'Algérie." *Revue de droit international privé* (1919): 223–33.

Larcher, Émile. "Des effets du mariage d'une femme indigène musulmane avec un indigène admis à la jouissance des droits de citoyen après la dissolution du mariage." *Revue algérienne de jurisprudence,* part 2 (1908): 209–21.

———. "Des effets juridiques du changement de religion." *Journal de droit international privé et jurisprudence comparée* 35 (1908): 375–95, 989–1001.

———. "Des effets juridiques du changement de religion en Algérie." *Revue algérienne de jurisprudence* (1910): 1–34.

———. *L'énigme, examen critique de la jurisprudence de la cour de cassation et des tribunaux algériens relativement à la compétence des tribunaux répressifs indigènes pour les délits pouvant entraîner des condamnations comptant pour la relégation.* Algiers: A. Jourdan, 1903.

——. "L'université d'Alger." In *Trois années d'études algériennes législatives, sociales, pénitentiaires et pénales (1899–1901)*. Paris: A. Rousseau, 1902.

——. *Traité élémentaire de législation algérienne*. Vols. 1–2. Paris: A. Rousseau, 1903.

——. *Traité élémentaire de législation algérienne*. 2nd ed. Vols. 1–3. Paris: A. Rousseau, 1911.

Laurent, François. *Droit civil international*. Vol. 1. Brussels: Bruylant-Christophe, 1880.

Leblond, Marius-Ary. *L'Oued*. Paris: Bibliothèque Charpentier, 1907.

Leclerc, Adrien. "De la condition de la femme musulmane." *Mémoires de la Société d'émulation du Doubs* 8, no. 1 (1907): 14–29.

——. "Des indigènes musulmans d'Algérie: De leur condition juridique et de l'orientation a donner à la législation qui les régit." Paper presented at the Congrès international de sociologie coloniale, Paris, 1900.

"Le service militaire obligatoire pour les indigènes en Algérie." *Revue africaine* 52, no. 268 (1908): 115–55.

Le Sueur, Louis, and Eugène Dreyfus. *La nationalité (droit interne): Commentaire de la loi du 26 juin 1889*. Paris: G. Pedone-Lauriel, 1890.

Letourneau, Charles. *L'évolution du mariage et de la famille*. Paris: Adrien Delahaye, 1888.

Ligue des droits de l'homme. "Le Congrès de 1917—Les droits politiques des indigènes en Algérie." *Bulletin des droits de l'homme* 18, no. 2–3 (1918): 66–109.

Loyseau, Charles. *Les œuvres de maistre Charles Loyseau, avocat en parlement: Contenant Les cinq livres du droit des offices; Les traitez des seigneuries, Des ordres & simples dignitez; Du déguerpissement & délaissement par hypothèque; De la garantie des rentes & Des abus des justices de village*. Lyon: La compagnie des libraires, 1701.

Luciani, Jean Dominique. *Traité des successions musulmanes (ab intestat) extrait du commentaire de la Rahbia par Chenchouri, de la glose d'el-Badjouri et d'autres auteurs arabes*. Paris: E. Leroux, 1890.

Lunel, Eugène. *La question algérienne: Les arabes, l'armée, les colons*. Paris: E. Lachaud, 1869.

Maine, Henry Sumner. *L'ancien droit considéré dans ses rapports avec l'histoire de la société primitive et avec les idées modernes*. Paris: Guillaumin, 1874.

Mangin, Charles. *La force noire*. Paris: Hachette, 1910.

Manuel du commissaire enquêteur pour l'application de la loi du 26 juillet 1873. Algiers: Gojosso, 1879.

Marival, Raymond [Marie Louis Raymond Vaissié]. *Chair d'ambre*. Paris: Mercure de France, 1901.

——. *Le Çof: Moeurs kabyle*. Paris: Mercure de France, 1902.

Marneur, François. "L'indigénat en Algérie: Considérations sur le régime actuel, critique, projet de réformes." Université de Paris, 1914.

Massoni, Maxime. "Fatima la répudiée." *La Revue nord africaine* 3, no. 12 (1904): 427–31.

Maupassant, Guy de. *Au soleil*. Paris: Victor Havard, 1885.

Médecine militaire—Les scandales de Médéa, mars 1891–janvier 1895. Paris: J. Allemane, 1895.

Médecine militaire—Scandales de Médéa. Paris: Toussaint Joyeux, 1892.

Mélia, Jean. *Le centenaire de la conquête de l'Algérie et les réformes indigènes*. Paris: Ligue française en faveur des Indigènes musulmans d'Algérie, 1929.

Mémoire au roi et aux Chambres, par les colons de l'Algérie (28 mars 1847). Paris: Rignoux, 1847.

Mercier, Ernest. *La propriété foncière musulmane en Algérie*. Algiers: A. Jourdan, 1898.

Mercier, Gustave. *Le centenaire de l'Algérie: Exposé d'ensemble*. Vol. 1. Algiers: P. et G. Soubiron, 1931.

Meylan, Philippe. *Les mariages mixtes en Afrique du Nord*. Collection des centres des études juridiques. Paris: Sirey, 1934.

Milliot, Louis, Marcel Morand, Frédéric Godin, and Maurice Gaffiot. *L'oeuvre législative de la France en Algérie*. Collection du centenaire de l'Algérie, 1830–1930: *Institutions de l'Algérie*. Paris: Félix Alcan, 1930.

Ministère du Commerce. *Annuaire statistique de la France*. Vols. 1–13. Paris: Imprimerie nationale, 1878–1890.

Modifications à apporter à la loi du 26 juillet 1873 sur la propriété indigène proposé par Sautayra, Robe, Vignard, Perrioud. Algiers: Imprimerie Administrative, 1882.

Morand, Marcel. *Avant-projet du Code, présenté à la Commission de codification du droit musulman algérien*. Algiers: A. Jourdan, 1916.

——. *Contribution à l'étude des réformes concernant la situation politique et économique des indigènes algériens*. Algiers: A. Jourdan, 1916.

——. *La famille musulmane*. Algiers: A. Jourdan, 1903.

Mornand, Félix. "L'algérien français." In *Les français peints par eux-mêmes—La province*. Paris: Curmer, 1842.

Morsly, Taïeb-Ould. *Contribution à la question indigène en Algérie*. Constantine: Jérome Marle et F. Biron, 1894.

Moussaud, A. *Précis pratique des maladies des organes génito-urinaires*. Paris: Delahaye, 1876.

Norès, Edmond. "Essai de codification du droit musulman algérien." *Revue algérienne de jurisprudence*, 1903–1905, part 1.

Notice sur M. Joseph Girard: Prêtre de la mission, premier supérieur du grand séminaire d'Alger. Paris: J. Mersch, 1881.

Olier, Jean. "Les résultats de la législation sur la nationalité en Algérie." *Revue politique et parlementaire* 13 (1897): 549–60.

Pavy, Louis-Claude. *La Nouvelle Église d'Afrique*. Paris: Lecoffre Fils, 1870.

Pellissier de Reynaud, Henri-Edmond. *Annales algériennes*. Vol. 2. Paris: Anselin et Gaultier, 1836.

——. *Annales algériennes (nouvelle édition, revue, corrigée et continuée jusqu'à la chute d'Abd-el-Kadr; avec un appendice)*. Vol. 3. Paris: J. Dumaine, 1854.

Pensa, Henri. *L'Algérie: Voyage de la délégation de la commission sénatoriale d'études des questions algériennes*. Paris: J. Rothschild, 1894.

Peyerimhoff de Fontenelle, Henri de. *Enquête sur les résultats de la colonisation officielle de 1871 à 1895*. Algiers: Torrent, 1906.

Pharaon, Florian. *Récits algériens*. Paris: A. Panis, 1871.

Pharaon, Joanny. *De la législation française, musulmane, et juive à Alger*. Paris: Théophile Barrois, 1835.

Pichon, Louis André. *Alger sous la domination française, son état présent et son avenir*. Paris: T. Barrois, 1833.

Piette, Paul. *De l'influence de la magistrature algérienne sur la civilisation des indigènes. Cour d'appel d'Alger. Audience solennelle de rentrée du 2 octobre 1874*. Algiers: V. Aillaud, 1874.

Pilastre, Édouard. *Du mariage putatif et de la légitimation*. Paris: E. Thunot, 1861.

Poivre, Aimé. *Les indigènes algériens, leur état civil et leur condition juridique*. Algiers: Dubos frères, 1862.

Pontier, R. *Souvenirs de l'Algérie*. Valenciennes: J. Giard, 1850.

Portalis, Jean-Étienne-Marie. *Discours, rapports et travaux inédits sur le code civil.* Paris: Joubert, 1844.

Pouyanne, Maurice. *La propriété foncière en Algérie.* Paris: E. Duchemin, 1895.

Procès-verbaux et rapports de la Commission d'Afrique. Paris: Imprimerie Royale, 1834.

Programme des instructions pour la commission spéciale à envoyer en Afrique, 22 juin 1833. Paris: A. Henry, 1834.

Qadrī Bāšā, Muḥammad. *Droit musulman. Du statut personnel et des successions d'après le rite hanafite.* Alexandria: Imprimerie française A. Mourès, 1875.

Radiot, Paul. *Notre fille de France.* Paris: Dentu, 1893.

Raffalovich. *Uranisme et unisexualité: Étude sur différentes manifestations de l'instinct sexuel.* Lyon: A. Storck, 1896.

Réfutation de l'ouvrage de sidy Hamdan-Ben-Othman-Khoja. Extrait de "L'Observateur des tribunaux." Paris: Éverat, 1834.

Richard, Charles. *De la civilisation du peuple arabe.* Algiers: Dubos frères, 1850.

———. *Du gouvernement arabe et de l'institution qui doit l'exercer.* Algiers: Bastide, 1848.

Ricoux, René, and Louis-Adolphe Bertillon. *La démographie figurée de l'Algérie: Étude statistique des populations européennes qui habitent l'Algérie.* Paris: G. Masson, 1880.

Robe, Eugène. *Propriété immobilière en Algérie: Commentaire de la loi du 26 juillet 1873.* Algiers: Juillet Saint Lager, 1875.

Roussel, Charles. "La naturalisation des étrangers en Algérie." *Revue des deux mondes* 45 (June 1, 1875): 682–95.

Sabatier, Camille. "Étude sur la femme kabyle." *Revue d'anthropologie* 12 (1883): 56–69.

Sabatier, Germain. *Études sur les réformes algériennes.* Oran: P. Perrier, 1891.

Saint-Gouric, Yvon de. *Mektoub.* Algiers: Mercure africain, 1923.

Salvador, Joseph. *Histoire des institutions de Moïse et du peuple hébreu.* Vol. 2. Paris: Michel Lévy, 1862.

Sartor, Joseph E. *De la naturalisation en Algérie (Sénatus-Consulte du 5 juillet 1865): Musulmans, israélites, européens.* Paris: Retaux Frères, 1865.

Sautayra, Édouard, and Eugène Cherbonneau. *Droit musulman: Du statut personnel et des successions.* Vol. 1. Paris: Maisonneuve, 1873.

Savary, Anne-Jean-Marie-René. *Correspondance du duc de Rovigo, commandant en chef le corps d'occupation d'Afrique (1831–1833).* Vol. 1. Algiers: J. Carbonel, 1914.

———. *Correspondance du duc de Rovigo, commandant en chef le corps d'occupation d'Afrique (1831–1833).* Vol. 3. Algiers: J. Carbonel, 1914.

Sèbe, Achille. *La conscription des indigènes d'Algérie.* Paris: E. Larose, 1912.

Simon, Frédéric. *Algérie. Les spahis et les smalas.* Constantine: L. Marle, 1871.

Société d'études politiques et sociales. "Assimilation progressive de l'Algérie à la France." *Bulletin Trimestriel* 2, no. 5 (1905).

Solus, Henry. "L'évoution de la condition juridique de la femme indigène aux colonies." *Recueil de législation et jurisprudence coloniales* (January 1934): 85–96.

Tarde, Gabriel. *Études pénales et sociales.* Paris: G. Masson, 1892.

Teissier, Charles. *Du duel, au point de vue médico-légal et particulièrement dans l'armée.* Lyon: Storck, 1890.

Tocqueville, Alexis de. *Writings on Empire and Slavery.* Edited and translated by Jennifer A. Pitts. Baltimore: Johns Hopkins University Press, 2001.

Urbain, Ismayl. *L'Algérie française: Indigènes et immigrants (1862).* Paris: Séguier, 2002.

Valette, Victor. *Un projet de loi sur la réorganisation de l'Algérie.* Algiers: Cheniaux-Franville, 1881.

Vandier, Louis. *Histoire de la Cour d'Alger—audience solennelle de rentrée (1 octobre 1896)*. Algiers: Baldachino, 1896.

Villot, Étienne. "Études algériennes." *Receuil des notices et mémoires de la Société archéologique de la Province de Constantine* 14 (1870): 349–604.

Vinet, Jules. *Le droit commun pour les indigènes en Algérie*. Paris: A. Le Chevalier, 1869.

Viviani, Édouard. *Étude sur les réformes proposées à la loi du 26 juillet 1873*. Algiers: P. Fontana, 1885.

Voirol, Théophile. *Correspondance du général Voirol, commandant par intérim le corps d'occupation d'Afrique 1833–1834*. Paris: É. Champion, 1924.

Voisin, Georges. *L'Algérie pour les algériens*. Paris: Michel Lévy, 1861.

Wahl, Maurice. *L'Algérie*. 1903.

Warnier, Auguste. *L'Algérie devant l'empereur*. Paris: Challamel, 1865.

——. *L'Algérie devant le Sénat*. Paris: Dubuisson, 1863.

Weiss, André. *Manuel de droit international privé*. Paris: Recueil général des lois et des arrêts, 1899.

——. *Traité élémentaire de droit international privé*. Paris: L. Larose, 1890.

——. *Traité théorique et pratique de droit international privé*. Vol. 1. Paris: L. Larose & L. Tenin, 1892.

Worms, Mayer-Goudchaux. *Recherches sur la constitution de la propriété territoriale dans les pays musulmans, et subsidiairement en Algérie*. Paris: A. Franck, 1846.

Zeys, Ernest. *Essai d'un traité méthodique de droit musulman (école malékite)*. Vol. 1. Algiers: A. Jourdan, 1884.

SECONDARY SOURCES

Abi-Mershed, Osama. *Apostles of Modernity: Saint-Simonians and the Civilizing Mission in Algeria*. Stanford, CA: Stanford University Press, 2010.

Adam, Jeanne. "Polémiques autour du premier Grand Prix Littéraire de l'Algérie. La situation des lettres algériennes en 1921." *Revue de l'Occident musulman et de la Méditerranée* 37, no. 1 (1984): 15–30.

Agamben, Giorgio. *State of Exception*. Chicago: University of Chicago Press, 2005.

Ageron, Charles-Robert. "Le mouvement 'Jeune-Algérien' de 1900 à 1923." *Études maghrébines, mélanges Charles-André Julien*, 217–43. Paris: Presses universitaires de France, 1964.

——. *Les Algériens musulmans et la France (1871–1919)*. Vols. 1 and 2. Paris: Presses universitaires de France, 1968.

——. *Modern Algeria: A History from 1830 to the Present*. Translated by Michael Brett. London: Hurst, 1991.

Agrama, Hussein Ali. *Questioning Secularism: Islam, Sovereignty, and the Rule of Law in Modern Egypt*. Chicago: University of Chicago Press, 2012.

Aissaoui, Rabah. "Politics, Identity and Temporality in Colonial Algeria in the Early Twentieth Century." *Journal of North African Studies* 22, no. 2 (2017): 182–204.

Aldrich, Robert. *Colonialism and Homosexuality*. London: Routledge, 2003.

Alloula, Malek. *The Colonial Harem*. Translated by Myrna Godzich and Wlad Godzich. Minneapolis: University of Minnesota Press, 1986.

Amselle, Jean-Loup. *Affirmative Exclusion: Cultural Pluralism and the Rule of Custom in France*. Ithaca, NY: Cornell University Press, 2003.

Amster, Ellen. "The Syphilitic Arab? A Search for Civilization in Disease Etiology, Native Prostitution, and French Colonial Medicine." In *French Mediterraneans:*

Transnational and Imperial Histories, edited by Patricia Lorcin and Todd Shepard, 320–46. Lincoln: University of Nebraska Press, 2016.

Andersen, Margaret Cook. *Regeneration through Empire: French Pronatalists and Colonial Settlement in the Third Republic*. Lincoln: University of Nebraska Press, 2015.

Anidjar, Gil. *The Jew, the Arab: A History of the Enemy*. Stanford, CA: Stanford University Press, 2003.

Apter, Emily "Female Trouble in the Colonial Harem." *Differences* 4, no. 1 (1992): 206–24.

Arabi, Oussama. "Orienting the Gaze: Marcel Morand and the Codification of Le Droit Musulman Algérien." *Journal of Islamic Studies* 11, no. 1 (2000): 43–72.

Arnaud, André Jean. *Les origines doctrinales du Code civil français*. Paris: Librairie générale de droit et de jurisprudence, 1969.

Arondekar, Anjali R. *For the Record: On Sexuality and the Colonial Archive in India*. Durham, NC: Duke University Press, 2009.

Asad, Talal. "Conscripts of Western Civilization." In *Dialectical Anthropology: Essays in Honor of Stanley Diamond*, vol. 1, edited by Christine Ward Gailey, 333–51. Gainesville: University Press of Florida, 1992.

——. *Formations of the Secular: Christianity, Islam, Modernity*. Stanford, CA: Stanford University Press, 2003.

——. "Reconfigurations of Law and Ethics in Colonial Egypt." In *Formations of the Secular: Christianity, Islam, Modernity*. Stanford, CA: Stanford University Press, 2003.

Assan, Valérie. *Les consistoires israélites d'Algérie au XIXᵉ siècle: L'alliance de la civilisation et de la religion*. Paris: Colin, 2012.

Asseraf, Arthur. "Foreign News in Colonial Algeria, 1881–1940." PhD thesis, University of Oxford, 2016.

Auclert, Hubertine. *Les femmes arabes en Algérie*. Paris: Société d'éditions littéraires, 1900.

Auerbach, Jeffrey A. "Imperial Boredom." *Common Knowledge* 11, no. 2 (2005): 283–305.

Autin, Jean Louis. "La législation foncière en Algérie de 1830 à 1870 ou le triomphe de la raison juridique coloniale." *Le procès* 18 (1987): 85–97.

Auzary-Schmaltz, Nada. "La magistrature coloniale." In *Faire l'histoire du droit colonial: Cinquante ans après l'indépendance de l'Algérie*, edited by Jean-Philippe Bras. Paris: Karthala, 2015.

Barrière, Louis-Augustin. *Le statut personnel des musulmans d'Algérie de 1834 à 1962*. Dijon: Éditions universitaires de Dijon, 1993.

Bassenne, Marthe, and Louis Bertrand. *Aurélie Tedjani, "princesse des Sables."* Paris: Plon, 1925.

Baubérot, Jean. *Histoire de la laïcité en France*. Paris: Presses universitaires de France, 2017.

Bayly, C. A. *Empire and Information: Intelligence Gathering and Social Communication in India, 1780–1870*. Cambridge: Cambridge University Press, 1996.

Bayly, Susan. "Racial Readings of Empire: Britain, France and Colonial Modernity in the Mediterranean and Asia." In *Modernity and Culture from the Mediterranean to the Indian Ocean*, edited by Leïla Fawaz and Chris Bayly, 285–313. New York: Columbia University Press, 2002.

Belmessous, Saliha. *Assimilation and Empire: Uniformity in French and British Colonies, 1541–1954*. Oxford: Oxford University Press, 2013.

Bendjillali, Mimoun. "L'histoire de la propriété foncière en Algérie de 1830 à 1962: Entre les lois musulmanes et françaises." *Revue des sciences humaines*, no. 26 (2006): 5–20.

Ben-Dor Benite, Zvi, Stefanos Geroulanos, and Nicole Jerr. *The Scaffolding of Sovereignty: Global and Aesthetic Perspectives on the History of a Concept.* New York: Columbia University Press, 2017.

Bennoune, Mahfoud. *The Making of Contemporary Algeria, 1830–1987.* Cambridge: Cambridge University Press, 1988.

Benton, Lauren A. "Colonial Law and Cultural Difference: Jurisdictional Politics and the Formation of the Colonial State." *Comparative Study of Society and History* 41, no. 3 (1999): 562–88.

———. *Law and Colonial Cultures: Legal Regimes in World History, 1400–1900.* Cambridge: Cambridge University Press, 2002.

———. *A Search for Sovereignty: Law and Geography in European Empires, 1400–1900.* Cambridge: Cambridge University Press, 2010.

Benton, Lauren A., and Richard Jeffrey Ross. *Legal Pluralism and Empires, 1500–1850.* New York: NYU Press, 2013.

Berenson, Edward. *Heroes of Empire: Five Charismatic Men and the Conquest of Africa.* Berkeley: University of California Press, 2011.

Berlant, Lauren. *The Female Complaint: The Unfinished Business of Sentimentality in American Culture.* Durham, NC: Duke University Press, 2008.

———. "The Subject of True Feeling: Pain, Privacy, and Politics." In *Cultural Pluralism, Identity Politics, and the Law*, edited by Austin Sarat and Thomas Kearns, 49–84. Ann Arbor: University of Michigan Press, 2001.

Betts, Raymond F. *Assimilation and Association in French Colonial Theory, 1890–1914.* New York: AMS, 1970.

Birla, Ritu. *Stages of Capital: Law, Culture, and Market Governance in Late Colonial India.* Durham, NC: Duke University Press, 2009.

Blais, Hélène. *Mirages de la carte: L'invention de l'Algérie coloniale, XIXᵉ–XXᵉ siècle.* Paris: Fayard, 2014.

———. "'Qu'est-ce qu'Alger?': Le débat colonial sous la monarchie de juillet." *Romantisme*, no. 1 (2008): 19–32.

Bland, Lucy. "British Eugenics and 'Race Crossing': A Study of an Interwar Investigation." *New Formations*, no. 60 (2007): 66–78.

———. "White Women and Men of Colour: Miscegenation Fears in Britain after the Great War." *Gender & History* 17, no. 1 (2005): 29–61.

Blévis, Laure. "Juristes et légistes au service de l'état colonial: De la mise en forme technique du statut des Algériens à sa difficile légitimation." In *Sur la portée sociale du droit.* Paris: Presses universitaires de France, 2005.

———. "Les avatars de la citoyenneté en Algérie coloniale ou les paradoxes d'une catégorisation." *Droit et société* 48 (2001): 557–80.

———. "L'invention de 'l'indigène,' Français non citoyen." In *Histoire de l'Algérie à la période coloniale*, edited by Abderrahmane Bouchène et al., 212–18. Paris: La Découverte, 2014.

———. "Une université française en terre coloniale: Naissance et reconversion de la Faculté de droit d'Alger (1879–1962)." *Politix*, no. 4 (2006): 53–73.

Boittin, Jennifer Anne. "Feminist Mediations of the Exotic: French Algeria, Morocco and Tunisia, 1921–39." *Gender & History* 22, no. 1 (2010): 131–50.

Bontems, Claude. "Coutume kabyle, jurisprudence et statut féminin (XIXᵉ–XXᵉ siè-cles)." In *La Coutume: Europe orientale, Asie et Islam*, 245–68. Brussels: Société Jean Bodin, 1994.

———. "Les tentatives de codification du droit musulman dans l'Algérie coloniale." In *L'enseignement du droit musulman*, edited by M. Flory and J.-R. Henry, 113–31. Paris: Éditions du CNRS, 1989.

Bourdieu, Pierre. "The Force of Law: Toward a Sociology of the Juridical Field." *Hastings Law Journal* 38 (1986): 805–53.

Bouveresse, Jacques. *Un parlement colonial: Les délégations financières algériennes, 1898–1945*. Vol. 1. Mont-Saint-Aignan: Universités de Rouen et du Havre, 2008.

Bowen, John R. *Why the French Don't Like Headscarves: Islam, the State, and Public Space*. Princeton, NJ: Princeton University Press, 2008.

Bowlan, Jeanne. "Polygamists Need Not Apply: Becoming a French Citizen in Colonial Algeria, 1918–1938." Paper presented at the Proceedings—Western Society for French History, 1997.

Bowler, Kimberly. "'It Is Not in a Day That a Man Abandons His Morals and Habits': The Arab Bureau, Land Policy, and the Doineau Trial in French Algeria, 1830–1870." PhD diss., Duke University, 2011.

Bras, Jean-Philippe. *Faire l'histoire du droit colonial: Cinquante ans après l'indépendance de l'Algérie*. Paris: Karthala, 2015.

Brett, Michael. "Legislating for Inequality in Algeria: The Senatus-Consulte of 14 July 1865." *Bulletin of the School of Oriental and African Studies* 51, no. 3 (1988): 440–61.

Brophy, Alfred L. "'Over and Above . . . There Broods a Portentous Shadow,—The Shadow of Law': Harriet Beecher Stowe's Critique of Slave Law in *Uncle Tom's Cabin*." *Journal of Law and Religion* 12, no. 2 (1995): 457–506.

Brower, Benjamin Claude. *A Desert Named Peace: The Violence of France's Empire in the Algerian Sahara, 1844–1902*. New York: Columbia University Press, 2009.

Brown, Wendy. "Civilizational Delusions: Secularism, Tolerance, Equality." *Theory & Event* 15, no. 2 (2012).

———. *Regulating Aversion: Tolerance in the Age of Identity and Empire*. Princeton, NJ: Princeton University Press, 2006.

Burke, Edmund. "France and the Classical Sociology of Islam, 1798–1962." *Journal of North African Studies* 12, no. 4 (2007): 551–61.

Burke, Edmund, and David Prochaska. *Genealogies of Orientalism: History, Theory, Politics*. Lincoln: University of Nebraska Press, 2008.

Burton, Antoinette. "From Child Bride to 'Hindoo Lady': Rukhamabai and the Debate on Sexual Responsibility in Imperial Britain." *American Historical Review* 103, no. 4 (1998): 1119–46.

Camiscioli, Elisa. *Reproducing the French Race: Immigration, Intimacy, and Embodiment in the Early Twentieth Century*. Durham, NC: Duke University Press, 2009.

Cantier, Jacques. "Les gouverneurs Viollette et Bordes et la politique algérienne de la France à la fin des années vingt." *Revue française d'histoire d'outre-mer* 84, no. 314 (1997): 25–49.

Carbonnier, Jean. "The French Civil Code." In *Rethinking France: Les Lieux de Mémoire*, edited by Pierre Nora, 335–60. Chicago: University of Chicago Press, 2001.

Çelik, Zeynep. "Framing the Colony: Houses of Algeria Photographed." *Art History* 27, no. 4 (2004): 616–26.

Charnay, Jean-Paul. *La vie musulmane en Algérie d'après la jurisprudence de la première moitié du XXᵉ siècle*. Paris: Presses universitaires de France, 1965.

———. "Le rôle du juge français dans l'élaboration du droit musulman algérien." *Revue internationale de droit comparé* 15, no. 4(1963): 705–21.

Charrad, Mounira. *States and Women's Rights: The Making of Postcolonial Tunisia, Algeria, and Morocco*. Berkeley: University of California Press, 2001.

Chatterjee, Nandini. "English Law, Brahmo Marriage, and the Problem of Religious Difference: Civil Marriage Laws in Britain and India." *Comparative Studies in Society and History* 52, no. 3 (2010): 524–52.

———. "Religious Change, Social Conflict and Legal Competition: The Emergence of Christian Personal Law in Colonial India." *Modern Asian Studies* 44, no. 6 (2010): 1147–95.

Chatterjee, Partha. *The Nation and Its Fragments: Colonial and Postcolonial Histories*. Princeton, NJ: Princeton University Press, 1993.

Cherchari, Mohamed Sahia. "Indigènes et citoyens ou l'impossible universalisation du suffrage." *Revue française de droit constitutionnel*, no. 4 (2004): 741–70.

Christelow, Allan. *Muslim Law Courts and the French Colonial State in Algeria*. Princeton, NJ: Princeton University Press, 1985.

Clancy-Smith, Julia. "The Intimate, the Familial, and the Local in Transnational Histories of Gender." *Journal of Women's History* 18, no. 2 (2006): 174–83.

———. "Islam, Gender, and Identities in the Making of French Algeria, 1830–1962." In *Domesticating the Empire: Languages of Gender, Race, and Family Life in French and Dutch Colonialism, 1830–1962*, edited by Julia Clancy-Smith and Frances Gouda, 154–74. Charlottesville: University Press of Virginia, 1998.

———. "La Femme Arabe: Women and Sexuality in France's North African Empire." In *Women, the Family, and Divorce Laws in Islamic History*, edited by Amira El Azhary Sonbol, 52–63. Syracuse, NY: Syracuse University Press, 1996.

———. *Mediterraneans: North Africa and Europe in an Age of Migration, c. 1800–1900*. Berkeley: University of California Press, 2011.

———. *Rebel and Saint: Muslim Notables, Populist Protest, Colonial Encounters (Algeria and Tunisia, 1800–1904)*. Berkeley: University of California Press, 1994.

Cohn, Bernard. *Colonialism and Its Forms of Knowledge: The British in India*. Princeton, NJ: Princeton University Press, 1996.

Collot, Claude. *Les institutions de l'Algérie durant la période coloniale (1830–1962)*. Paris: Éditions du CNRS, 1987.

Colonna, Fanny. *Instituteurs algériens, 1883–1939*. Paris: Presses de la Fondation nationale des sciences politiques, 1975.

Comaroff, John L. "Colonialism, Culture, and the Law." *Law and Social Inquiry* 26, no. 2 (2001): 305–14.

Conklin, Alice L. *A Mission to Civilize: The Republican Idea of Empire in France and West Africa, 1895–1930*. Stanford, CA: Stanford University Press, 1997.

Cooper, Frederick. *Colonialism in Question: Theory, Knowledge, History*. Berkeley: University of California Press, 2005.

Coquery-Vidrovitch, Catherine. "Nationalité et citoyenneté en Afrique occidentale français: Originaires et citoyens dans le Sénégal colonial." *Journal of African History* 42, no. 2 (2001): 285–305.

Cuno, Kenneth M. *Modernizing Marriage: Family, Ideology, and Law in Nineteenth- and Early Twentieth-Century Egypt*. Syracuse, NY: Syracuse University Press, 2015.

Curtis, Sarah Ann. *Civilizing Habits: Women Missionaries and the Revival of French Empire*. Oxford: Oxford University Press, 2010.

Davidson, Naomi. *Only Muslim: Embodying Islam in Twentieth-Century France*. Ithaca, NY: Cornell University Press, 2012.

Davis, Kathleen. *Periodization and Sovereignty: How Ideas of Feudalism and Secularization Govern the Politics of Time*. Philadelphia: University of Pennsylvania Press, 2008.

Dean, Carolyn J. *The Frail Social Body: Pornography, Homosexuality, and Other Fantasies in Interwar France*. Berkeley: University of California Press, 2000.

Déjeux, Jean. *Image de l'étrangère: Unions mixtes franco-maghrébines*. Paris: Boîte à documents, 1989.

———. "Le Grand Prix Littéraire de l'Algérie (1921–1961)." *Revue d'Histoire littéraire de la France* (1985): 60–71.

Delayen, Gaston. *Les deux affaires du capitaine Doineau: L'attaque de la diligence de Tlemcen (1856); l'évasion de Bazaine (1874), d'après documents inédits*. Paris: Éditions des Juris-classeurs, 1924.

Desan, Suzanne. *The Family on Trial in Revolutionary France*. Berkeley: University of California Press, 2004.

Deschamps, Damien. "Une citoyenneté différée: Sens civique et assimilation des indigènes dans les Établissements français de l'Inde." *Revue française de science politique* 47, no. 1 (1997): 49–69.

Djerbal, Daho. "Processus de colonisation et évolution de la propriété foncière dans les plaines intérieures de l'Oranie." Université Paris 7, 1979.

Djoudi, Oulhadj Nait. "L'exhérédation des femmes en Kabylie: Le fait de l'histoire et de la géographie." *Insaniyat: Revue algérienne d'anthropologie et de sciences sociales* 13 (2001): 187–201.

Dobie, Madeleine. *Foreign Bodies: Gender, Language, and Culture in French Orientalism*. Stanford, CA: Stanford University Press, 2001.

Dodman, Thomas. *What Nostalgia Was: War, Empire, and the Time of a Deadly Emotion*. Chicago: University of Chicago Press, 2018.

Dolar, Mladen. "Beyond Interpellation." *Qui parle* 6, no. 2 (1993): 75–96.

Dorlin, Elsa. "Le grand strip-tease: Féminisme, nationalisme et burqa en France." In *Ruptures postcoloniales*, 429–42. Paris: La Découverte, 2010.

Doumani, Beshara. *Family History in the Middle East: Household, Property, and Gender*. Albany: SUNY Press, 2003.

Dumasy, François. "Propriété foncière, libéralisme économique et gouvernement colonial: Alger, 1830–1840." *Revue d'histoire moderne et contemporaine*, no. 2 (2016): 40–61.

Dunwoodie, Peter. *Francophone Writing in Transition: Algeria, 1900–1945*. Oxford: P. Lang, 2005.

———. *Writing French Algeria*. Oxford: Clarendon, 1998.

Dupret, Baudouin. "De l'invention du droit musulman à la pratique juridique contemporaine." In *La Charia aujourd'hui: Usages de la référence au droit islamique*, 9–17. Paris: La Découverte, 2014.

Edelman, Lee. *No Future: Queer Theory and the Death Drive*. Durham, NC: Duke University Press, 2004.

Eichner, Carolyn J. "La citoyenne in the World: Hubertine Auclert and Feminist Imperialism." *French Historical Studies* 32, no. 1 (2009): 63–84.

El Mechat, Samia. "Sur les *Principes de colonisation* d'Arthur Girault (1895)." *Revue historique* 657, no. 1 (2011): 119–44.

Émerit, Marcel. "Le problème de la conversion des musulmans d'Algérie sous le Second Empire: Le conflit entre MacMahon et Lavigerie." *Revue historique* 223, no. 1 (1960): 63–84.

Emon, Anver M. "Codification and Islamic Law: The Ideology behind a Tragic Narrative." *Middle East Law and Governance* 8, no. 2–3 (2016): 275–309.

Esmeir, Samera. "At Once Human and Not Human: Law, Gender and Historical Becoming in Colonial Egypt." *Gender & History* 23, no. 2 (2011): 235–49.

——. *Juridical Humanity: A Colonial History.* Stanford, CA: Stanford University Press, 2012.

Esposito, John L. *Women in Muslim Family Law.* Syracuse, NY: Syracuse University Press, 2001.

Fabian, Johannes. *Time and the Other: How Anthropology Makes Its Object.* New York: Columbia University Press, 2002.

Fanon, Frantz. "Algeria Unveiled." Translated by Haakon Chevalier. In *A Dying Colonialism.* New York: Grove, 1967.

Farris, Sara R. *In the Name of Women's Rights: The Rise of Femonationalism.* Durham, NC: Duke University Press, 2017.

Fassin, Éric. "La démocratie sexuelle et le conflit des civilisations." *Multitudes,* no. 3 (2006): 123–31.

Fernando, Mayanthi L. "Intimacy Surveilled: Religion, Sex, and Secular Cunning." *Signs: Journal of Women in Culture and Society* 39, no. 3 (2014): 685–708.

——. *The Republic Unsettled: Muslim French and the Contradictions of Secularism.* Durham, NC: Duke University Press, 2014.

——. "Save the Muslim Woman, Save the Republic: Ni Putes Ni Soumises and the Ruse of Neoliberal Sovereignty." *Modern & Contemporary France* 21, no. 2 (2013): 147–65.

Festa, Lynn M. *Sentimental Figures of Empire in Eighteenth-Century Britain and France.* Baltimore: Johns Hopkins University Press, 2006.

Flory, Maurice, and Jean-Robert Henry. *L'enseignement du droit musulman.* Paris: Éditions du CNRS, 1989.

Fogarty, Richard Standish. *Race and War in France: Colonial Subjects in the French Army, 1914–1918.* Baltimore: Johns Hopkins University Press, 2008.

Ford, Caroline C. *Divided Houses: Religion and Gender in Modern France.* Ithaca, NY: Cornell University Press, 2005.

Ford, Richard T. "Law's Territory (a History of Jurisdiction)." *Michigan Law Review* 97, no. 4 (1999): 843–930.

Forth, Christopher E. *The Dreyfus Affair and the Crisis of French Manhood.* Baltimore: Johns Hopkins University Press, 2004.

Foucault, Michel. *The History of Sexuality, Volume I: An Introduction.* Translated by Robert Hurley. New York: Vintage, 1980.

Fouquier, Armand. "Le capitaine Doineau—attentat de Tlemcen (1856)." *Causes célèbres de tous les peuples* 2, no. 6 (1859): 1–48.

Francis, Kyle. "Civilizing Settlers: Catholic Missionaries and the Colonial State in French Algeria, 1830–1914." PhD diss., City University of New York, 2015.

Fredette, Jennifer. "Becoming a Threat: The Burqa and the Contestation over Public Morality Law in France." *Law & Social Inquiry* 40, no. 3 (2015): 585–610.

Frémeaux, Jacques. *Les Bureaux arabes dans l'Algérie de la conquête.* Paris: Denoël, 1993.

Freud, Sigmund. "A Child Is Being Beaten (1919)." In *Sexuality and the Psychology of Love.* New York: Collier Books, 1963.

———. "Fetishism (1927)." In *Sexuality and the Psychology of Love*. New York: Collier Books, 1963.

———. *The Psychopathology of Everyday Life*. Standard Edition of the Complete Works of Sigmund Freud. New York: W. W. Norton, 1989.

Friang, Michèle. *Femmes fin de siècle: 1870–1914, Augusta Holmès et Aurélie Tidjani ou la gloire interdite*. Paris: Éditions Autrement, 1998.

Fromage, Julien. "L'expérience des 'Jeunes Algériens' et l'émergence du militantisme moderne en Algérie (1880–1919)." In *Histoire de l'Algérie à la période coloniale, 1830–1962*, edited by Abderrahmane Bouchène et al., 238–44. Paris: La Découverte, 2012.

Fuchs, Rachel Ginnis. *Contested Paternity: Constructing Families in Modern France*. Baltimore: Johns Hopkins University Press, 2008.

Ghabrial, Sarah. "Le 'fiqh françisé': Muslim Personal Status Law Reform and Women's Litigation in Colonial Algeria (1870–1930)." PhD diss., McGill University, 2014.

———. "The Traumas and Truths of the Body: Medical Evidence and Divorce in Colonial Algerian Courts, 1870–1930." *Journal of Middle East Women's Studies* 11, no. 3 (2015): 283–305.

Ghosh, Durba. *Sex and the Family in Colonial India: The Making of Empire*. Cambridge: Cambridge University Press, 2006.

Glendon, Mary Ann. *The Transformation of Family Law: State, Law, and Family in the United States and Western Europe*. Chicago: University of Chicago Press, 1989.

Goldstein, Jan. *The Post-Revolutionary Self: Politics and Psyche in France, 1750–1850*. Cambridge, MA: Harvard University Press, 2005.

Gong, Gerrit W. *The Standard of "Civilization" in International Society*. Oxford: Oxford University Press, 1984.

Gordon, Sarah Barringer. "Our National Hearthstone: Anti-polygamy Fiction and the Sentimental Campaign against Moral Diversity in Antebellum America." *Yale Journal of Law & the Humanities* 8 (1996): 295–350.

Gouriou, Fabien. "Le sexe des indigènes: Adolphe Kocher et la médecine légale en Algérie." *Droit et cultures*, no. 60 (2010): 59–72.

Goutalier, Régine. "Les États généraux du féminisme à l'Exposition coloniale, 30–31 mai 1931." *Revue d'histoire moderne et contemporaine* 36, no. 2 (1989): 266–86.

Graebner, Seth. *History's Place: Nostalgia and the City in French Algerian Literature*. After the Empire. Lanham, MD: Lexington Books, 2007.

Grangaud, Isabelle. "Dépossession et disqualification des droits de propriété à Alger dans les années 1830." In *Histoire de l'Algérie à la période coloniale*, edited by Abderrahmane Bouchène et al., 70–76, 2014.

———. "Prouver par l'écriture: Propriétaires algérois, conquérants français et historiens ottomanistes." *Genèses*, no. 1 (2008): 25–45.

Griffiths, John. "What Is Legal Pluralism?" *Journal of Legal Pluralism and Unofficial Law* 18, no. 24 (1986): 1–55.

Grigsby, Darcy Grimaldo. "Orients and Colonies: Delacroix's Algerian Harem." In *The Cambridge Companion to Delacroix*, edited by Beth S. Wright, 69–87. Cambridge: Cambridge University Press, 2001.

Grosrichard, Alain. *The Sultan's Court: European Fantasies of the East*. Translated by Liz Heron. London: Verso, 1998.

Guénif Souilamas, Nacira, and Éric Macé. *Les féministes et le garçon arabe*. La Tour d'Aigues: Éditions de l'Aube, 2006.

Guénoun, Lucien. *L'ordonnance du 10 août 1834 sur l'organisation de la justice en Algérie*. Paris: P. Guethner, 1920.

Guiard, Claudine. "Être féministe en contexte colonial dans l'Algérie des années 1930: Les militantes de l'Union française pour le suffrage des femmes." *Revue historique*, no. 1 (2015): 125–48.

Guignard, Didier. "Conservatoire ou révolutionnaire? Le sénatus-consulte de 1863 appliqué au régime foncier d'Algérie." *Revue d'histoire du XIXe siècle*, no. 41 (2010): 81–95.

———. *L'abus de pouvoir dans l'Algérie coloniale, 1880–1914: Visibilité et singularité.* Paris: Presses universitaires de Paris Ouest, 2010.

———. "L'affaire Beni Urjin: Un cas de résistance à la mainmise foncière en Algérie coloniale." *Insaniyat: Revue algérienne d'anthropologie et de sciences sociales* 25–26 (2004): 123–42.

———. "Les inventeurs de la tradition 'melk' et 'arch' en Algérie." In *Les acteurs des transformations foncières autour de la Méditerranée au XIXe siècle*, edited by Vanessa Guéno and Didier Guignard, 49–93. Paris: Karthala, 2013.

Guillet, François. *La mort en face: Histoire du duel de la Révolution à nos jours.* Paris: Aubier, 2008.

Gury, Christian. *L'honneur musical d'un capitaine homosexuel en 1880: De Courteline à Proust.* Paris: Kimé, 1999.

———. *L'honneur perdu d'un politicien homosexuel en 1876: Des clés pour Flaubert, Maupassant et Proust.* Paris: Éditions Kimé, 1999.

Guterman, Simeon L. "The Principle of the Personality of Law in the Early Middle Ages: A Chapter in the Evolution of Western Legal Institutions and Ideas." *University of Miami Law Review* 21 (1966): 259–348.

Gutman, René, ed. *Les décisions doctrinales du Grand Sanhédrin, 1806–1807.* Strasbourg: Presses universitaires de Strasbourg, 2000.

Haffner, Jeanne. *The View from Above: The Science of Social Space.* Cambridge, MA: MIT Press, 2013.

Haj, Samira. *Reconfiguring Islamic Tradition: Reform, Rationality, and Modernity.* Stanford, CA: Stanford University Press, 2009.

Hallaq, Wael B. *Sharī'a: Theory, Practice, Transformations.* Cambridge: Cambridge University Press, 2009.

———. "Was the Gate of Ijtihad Closed?" *International Journal of Middle East Studies* 16, no. 1 (1984): 3–41.

Halley, Janet. "What Is Family Law? A Genealogy." *Yale Journal of Law and Humanities* 23, no. 1 (2011): 1–109.

Halley, Janet, and Kerry Rittich. "Critical Directions in Comparative Family Law: Genealogies and Contemporary Studies of Family Law Exceptionalism." *American Journal of Comparative Law* 58, no. 4 (Fall 2010): 753–75.

Halpérin, Jean-Louis. *L'impossible code civil.* Paris: Presses universitaires de France, 1992.

Hannemann, Tilman. "La mise en place du droit kabyle dans l'Algérie coloniale (1857–1868)." In *La Kabylie et les coutumes kabyles*, xxxi–cxxiv. Paris: Bouchène, 2003.

Hardi, Ferenc. *Le roman algérien de langue française de l'entre-deux-guerres: Discours idéologique et quête identitaire.* Paris: L'Harmattan, 2005.

Harris, Ruth. *Dreyfus: Politics, Emotion, and the Scandal of the Century.* New York: Metropolitan Books, 2010.

Hart, Ursula Kingsmill. *Two Ladies of Colonial Algeria: The Lives and Times of Aurélie Picard and Isabelle Eberhardt.* Athens: Ohio University Center for International Studies, 1987.

Hartog, Hendrik. "Lawyering, Husbands' Rights, and 'the Unwritten Law' in Nineteenth-Century America." *Journal of American History* (1997): 67–96.

Heggoy, Alf Andrew. "Looking Back: The Military and Colonial Policies in French Algeria." *Muslim World* 73, no. 1 (1983): 57–66.

Hennette Vauchez, Stéphanie. "Is French Laïcité Still Liberal? The Republican Project under Pressure (2004–15)." *Human Rights Law Review* 17, no. 2 (2017): 285–312.

Henry, Jean-Robert. "La norme et l'imaginaire, construction de l'altérité juridique en droit colonial algérien." *Le procès*, no. 18 (1987): 13–27.

——. "Le centenaire de l'Algérie, triomphe éphémère de la pensée algérianiste." In *Histoire de l'Algérie à la période coloniale*, edited by Abderrahmane Bouchène et al., 369–75. Paris: La Découverte, 2014.

Henry, Jean-Robert, and François Balique. *La doctrine coloniale du droit musulman algérien: Bibliographie systématique et introduction critique.* Paris: Éditions du CNRS, 1979.

Heuer, Jennifer. *The Family and the Nation: Gender and Citizenship in Revolutionary France, 1789–1830.* Ithaca, NY: Cornell University Press, 2005.

Hoexter, Miriam. "Qadi, Mufti and Ruler: Their Roles in the Development of Islamic Law." In *Law, Custom, and Statute in the Muslim World*, edited by Ron Shaham, 67–86. Leiden: Brill, 2007.

Hussain, Nasser. *The Jurisprudence of Emergency: Colonialism and the Rule of Law.* Ann Arbor: University of Michigan Press, 2003.

Hussin, Iza R. *The Politics of Islamic Law: Local Elites, Colonial Authority, and the Making of the Muslim State.* Chicago: University of Chicago Press, 2016.

Ihaddaden, Zahir. *Histoire de la presse indigène en Algérie.* Algiers: Enterprise national du livre, 1983.

Jansen, Jan C. "Fête et ordre colonial: Centenaires et résistance anticolonialiste en Algérie pendant les années 1930." *Vingtième Siècle*, no. 121 (2014): 61–76.

Jennings, Eric Thomas. *Curing the Colonizers: Hydrotherapy, Climatology, and French Colonial Spas.* Durham, NC: Duke University Press, 2006.

Johnson, Walter. "On Agency." *Journal of Social History* 37, no. 1 (2003): 113–24.

Julien, Charles André. *Histoire de l'Algérie contemporaine.* Paris: Presses universitaires de France, 1979.

Kaddache, Mahfoud. *Histoire du nationalisme algérien.* 2 vols. Paris: Paris-Méditerranée, 2003.

Kafka, Ben. *The Demon of Writing: Powers and Failures of Paperwork.* New York: Zone Books, 2012.

Kalifa, Dominique. *Biribi: Les bagnes coloniaux de l'armée française.* Paris: Perrin, 2009.

Kateb, Kamel. *Européens, "indigènes" et juifs en Algérie (1830–1962): Représentations et réalités des populations.* Paris: Institut national d'études démographiques, 2001.

——. "Polygamie et répudiation dans le marché matrimonial algérien pendant la période coloniale." *Cahiers québécois de démographie* 29, no. 1 (2000): 1–32.

Kauffmann, Grégoire. "L'affaire de la 'viande à soldats.' Une campagne antisémite en 1892." *Archives Juives* 47, no. 1 (2014): 28–36.

Kelley, Donald R. "'Second Nature': The Idea of Custom in European Law Society, and Culture." In *The Transmission of Culture in Early Modern Europe*, edited by Anthony Grafton and Ann Blair, 131–72. Philadelphia: University of Pennsylvania Press, 1990.

Kennedy, Duncan. "Savigny's Family / Patrimony Distinction and Its Place in the Global Genealogy of Classical Legal Thought." *American Journal of Comparative Law* 58, no. 4 (2010): 811–41.

Khelouz, Nacer. *Le roman algérien des années 1920: Entre fiction et réalité politique.* Espaces littéraires. Paris: L'Harmattan, 2011.

Kimble, Sara. "Emancipation through Secularization: French Feminist Views of Muslim Women's Condition in Interwar Algeria." *French Colonial History* 7 (2006): 109–28.

Kugle, Scott Alan. "Framed, Blamed and Renamed: The Recasting of Islamic Jurisprudence in Colonial South Asia." *Modern Asian Studies* 35, no. 2 (2001): 257–313.

Lacan, Jacques. *Seminar I: Freud's Papers on Technique, 1953–1954.* Translated by John Forrester. New York: W. W. Norton, 1988.

——. *Seminar VII: The Ethics of Psychoanalysis, 1959–1960.* Translated by Denis Porter. Seminar of Jacques Lacan. New York: Norton, 1992.

Lanasri, Ahmed. *La littérature algérienne de l'entre-deux-guerres: Genèse et fonctionnement.* Paris: Publisud, 1995.

Laplanche, Jean, and Jean-Baptiste Pontalis. "Fantasy and the Origins of Sexuality." *International Journal of Psycho-Analysis* 49 (1968): 1–18.

Lazreg, Marnia. *The Eloquence of Silence: Algerian Women in Question.* London: Routledge, 1994.

——. *The Emergence of Classes in Algeria: A Study of Colonialism and Socio-Political Change.* Boulder, CO: Westview, 1976.

Le Cour Grandmaison, Olivier. "The Exception and the Rule: On French Colonial Law." *Diogenes* 53, no. 4 (November 1, 2006): 34–53.

Leff, Lisa Moses. *Sacred Bonds of Solidarity: The Rise of Jewish Internationalism in Nineteenth-Century France.* Stanford, CA: Stanford University Press, 2006.

Lehning, James R. *To Be a Citizen: The Political Culture of the Early Third Republic.* Ithaca, NY: Cornell University Press, 2001.

Lekéal, Farid. "Entre séduction charnelle et spirituelle: Les magistrats d'Alger au coeur de la rivalité entre civils et militaires (1832–1834)." In *Figures de justice*, edited by Nicolas Derasse, Annie Deperchin, and Bruno Dubois, 705–22. Lille: Centre d'histoire judiciaire, 2004.

——. "Justice et pacification: De la Régence d'Alger à l'Algérie, 1830–1839." *Histoire de la justice* 16, no. 1 (2005): 13–30.

Levallois, Anne. *Les écrits autobiographiques d'Ismayl Urbain (1812–1884).* Paris: Maisonneuve and Larose, 2005.

Levallois, Michel. *Ismaÿl Urbain (1812–1884), une autre conquête de l'Algérie.* Paris: Maisonneuve et Larose, 2001.

——. "Le 'mariage arabe' d'Ismaÿl Urbain." *Études littéraires* 33, no. 3 (2001): 109–17.

Levine, Philippa. *Prostitution, Race, and Politics: Policing Venereal Disease in the British Empire.* New York: Routledge, 2003.

Lewis, Mary D. *Divided Rule: Sovereignty and Empire in French Tunisia, 1881–1938.* Berkeley: University of California Press, 2013.

Liauzu, Claude. "Guerre des Sabines et tabou du métissage: Les mariages mixtes de l'Algérie coloniale à l'immigration en France." *Cahiers du CEDREF*, no. 8–9 (2000).

——. *Passeurs de rives: Changements d'identité dans le Maghreb colonial.* Paris: L'Harmattan, 2000.

Lorca, Arnulf Becker. "Universal International Law: Nineteenth-Century Histories of Imposition and Appropriation." *Harvard International Law Journal* 51 (2010): 475–552.

Lorcin, Patricia. *Historicizing Colonial Nostalgia: European Women's Narratives of Algeria and Kenya, 1900–present.* New York: Palgrave Macmillan, 2012.

——. *Imperial Identities: Stereotyping, Prejudice, and Race in Colonial Algeria*. London: I. B. Tauris, 1999.

——. "Mediating Gender, Mediating Race: Women Writers in Colonial Algeria." *Culture, Theory and Critique* 45, no. 1 (2004): 45–61.

——. "Women, Gender and Nation in Colonial Novels of Interwar Algeria." *Historical Reflections / Réflexions Historiques* (2002): 163–84.

Lupoi, Maurizio. *The Origins of the European Legal Order*. Cambridge: Cambridge University Press, 2000.

Lydon, Ghislaine. "Obtaining Freedom at the Muslims' Tribunal: Colonial Kadijustiz and Women's Divorce Litigation in Ndar (Senegal)." In *Muslim Family Law in Sub-Saharan Africa: Colonial Legacies and Post-Colonial Challenges*, edited by Shamil Jeppie, Ebrahim Moosa, and Richard L. Roberts, 135–64. Amsterdam: Amsterdam University Press, 2010.

MacMaster, Neil. *Burning the Veil: The Algerian War and the "Emancipation" of Muslim Women, 1954–62*. Manchester: Manchester University Press, 2009.

Mahieddin, Mohamed N. "Le droit musulman et l'école de droit d'Alger." In *Quel avenir pour l'anthropologie en Algérie?*, edited by Nadir Marouf, Faouzi Adel, and Khedidja Adel, 67–86. Oran: Éditions CRASC, 2002.

Mahmood, Saba. *Religious Difference in a Secular Age: A Minority Report*. Princeton, NJ: Princeton University Press, 2015.

Maier, Charles S. *Once within Borders: Territories of Power, Wealth, and Belonging since 1500*. Cambridge, MA: Harvard University Press, 2016.

Mamdani, Mahmood. *Citizen and Subject: Contemporary Africa and the Legacy of Late Colonialism*. Princeton, NJ: Princeton University Press, 1996.

Mani, Lata. "Contentious Traditions: The Debate on Sati in Colonial India." In *Recasting Women: Essays in Colonial History*, edited by Kumkum Sangari and Sudesh Vaid, 88–126. New Dehli: Kali, 1989.

Mann, Gregory. *Native Sons: West African Veterans and France in the Twentieth Century*. Durham, NC: Duke University Press, 2006.

——. "What Was the Indigénat? The 'Empire of Law' in French West Africa." *Journal of African History* 50, no. 3 (2010): 331–53.

Mantena, Karuna. *Alibis of Empire: Henry Maine and the Ends of Liberal Imperialism*. Princeton, NJ: Princeton University Press, 2010.

Marçot, Jean-Louis. *Comment est née l'Algérie française (1830–1850): La belle utopie*. Éditions de la Différence, 2012.

——. "Les premiers socialistes français, la question coloniale et l'Algérie." *Cahiers d'histoire. Revue d'histoire critique*, no. 124 (2014): 79–95.

Margadant, Jo Burr. "Gender, Vice, and the Political Imaginary in Postrevolutionary France: Reinterpreting the Failure of the July Monarchy, 1830–1848." *Amercian Historical Review* 104, no. 5 (December 1999): 1461–96.

Markell, Patchen. *Bound by Recognition*. Princeton, NJ: Princeton University Press, 2003.

Marx, Karl. "Le système foncier en Algérie au moment de la conquête française." In *Sur les sociétés précapitalistes: Textes choisis, préface de Maurice Godelier*, edited by Centre d'études et de recherches marxistes, 382–400. Paris: Éditions sociales, 1978.

Masuzawa, Tomoko. *The Invention of World Religions, or, How European Universalism Was Preserved in the Language of Pluralism*. Chicago: University of Chicago Press, 2005.

McClintock, Anne. *Imperial Leather: Race, Gender and Sexuality in the Colonial Conquest*. New York: Routledge, 1995.

McDougall, James. *History and the Culture of Nationalism in Algeria*. Cambridge: Cambridge University Press, 2006.

——. *A History of Algeria*. Cambridge: Cambridge University Press, 2017.

Merad, Ali. "Islam et nationalisme arabe en Algérie à la veille de la première guerre mondiale." *Oriente Moderno* 49, no. 4/5 (1969): 213–22.

Merle, Isabelle. "Retour sur le régime de l'indigénat: Genèse et contradictions des principes répressifs dans l'empire français." *French Politics, Culture, and Society* 20, no. 2 (2002): 77–97.

Merry, Sally Engle. "Law and Colonialism." *Law and Society Review* 25, no. 4 (1991): 890–922.

——. "Legal Pluralism." *Law and Society Review* 22, no. 5 (1988): 869–96.

Messaoudi, Alain. *Les arabisants et la France coloniale: Savants, conseillers, médiateurs, 1780–1930*. Lyon: ENS éditions, 2015.

——. "Renseigner, enseigner. Les interprètes militaires et la constitution d'un premier corpus savant 'algérien' (1830–1870)." *Revue d'histoire du XIXe siècle*, no. 41 (2010): 97–112.

Messick, Brinkley. *The Calligraphic State: Textual Domination and History in a Muslim Society*. Berkeley: University of California Press, 1993.

——. "Written Identities: Legal Subjects in an Islamic State." *History of Religions* 38, no. 1 (1998): 25–51.

Meynier, Gilbert. *L'Algérie révélée: La guerre de 1914–1918 et le premier quart du XXe siècle*. Geneva: Droz, 1981.

——. *L'émir Khaled, premier za'îm? Identité algérienne et colonialisme français*. Paris: L'Harmattan, 1987.

Miller, Jacques-Alain. "Extimacy." In *Lacanian Theory of Discourse: Subject, Structure, and Society*, edited by Mark Bracher et al., 74–87. New York: NYU Press, 1994.

Moulis, Robert. "Le Ministère de l'Algérie (24 juin 1858–24 novembre 1860)." Université d'Alger, 1926.

Murray-Miller, Gavin. *The Cult of the Modern: Trans-Mediterranean France and the Construction of French Modernity*. Lincoln: University of Nebraska Press, 2017.

——. "Imagining the Trans-Mediterranean Republic: Algeria, Republicanism, and the Ideological Origins of the French Imperial Nation-State, 1848–1870." *French Historical Studies* 37, no. 2 (2014): 303–30.

Mussard, Christine. "Réinventer la commune? Genèse de la commune mixte, une structure administrative inédite dans l'Algérie coloniale." *Histoire@Politique*, no. 3 (2015): 93–108.

Nair, Janaki. *Women and Law in Colonial India: A Social History*. New Delhi: Kali, 2000.

Noiriel, Gérard. "L'identification des citoyens. Naissance de l'état civil républicain." *Genèses* 13, no. 13 (1993): 3–28.

Nouschi, André. *Enquête sur le niveau de vie des populations rurales constantinoises de la conquête jusqu'en 1919*. Saint-Denis: Bouchène, 2013.

——. "La dépossession foncière et la paupérisation de la paysannerie algérienne." In *Histoire de l'Algérie coloniale*, edited by Abderrahmane Bouchène et al., 189–93, 2014.

Nye, Robert A. *Masculinity and Male Codes of Honor in Modern France*. New York: Oxford University Press, 1993.

Oulebsir, Nabila. *Les usages du patrimoine: Monuments, musées et politique coloniale en Algérie, 1830–1930*. Paris: Maison des sciences de l'homme, 2004.

Pande, Ishita. "'Listen to the Child': Law, Sex, and the Child Wife in Indian Historiography." *History Compass* 11, no. 9 (2013): 687–701.

Pateman, Carole. *The Sexual Contract*. Stanford, CA: Stanford University Press, 1988.

Pedersen, Jean Elisabeth. "'Special Customs': Paternity Suits and Citizenship in France and the Colonies, 1870–1912." In *Domesticating the Empire: Race, Gender, and Family Life in French and Dutch Colonialism*, edited by Julia Clancy-Smith and Frances Gouda, 43–64. Charlottesville: University Press of Virginia, 1998.

Peirce, Leslie. *Morality Tales: Law and Gender in the Ottoman Court of Aintab*. Berkeley: University of California Press, 2003.

Peters, Rudolph. "Idjtihad and Taqlid in 18th and 19th Century Islam." *Welt des Islams* 20, no. 3/4 (1980): 131–45.

Phéline, Christian. *L'aube d'une révolution: Margueritte, Algérie, 26 avril 1901*. Toulouse: Éditions Privat, 2012.

Pierce, Steven, and Anupama Rao. *Discipline and the Other Body: Correction, Corporeality, Colonialism*. Durham, NC: Duke University Press, 2006.

Pilbeam, Pamela M. *Saint-Simonians in Nineteenth-Century France: From Free Love to Algeria*. Basingstoke, UK: Palgrave Macmillan, 2014.

Pitts, Jennifer. *Boundaries of the International: Law and Empire*. Cambridge, MA: Harvard University Press, 2018.

——. "Liberalism and Empire in a Nineteenth-Century Algerian Mirror." *Modern Intellectual History* 6, no. 02 (2009): 287–313.

——. "Republicanism, Liberalism, and Empire in Postrevolutionary France." In *Empire and Modern Political Thought*, edited by Sankar Muthu, 261–91. Cambridge: Cambridge University Press, 2012.

Porterfield, Todd. *The Allure of Empire: Art in the Service of French Imperialism, 1798–1836*. Princeton, NJ: Princeton University Press, 1998.

Povinelli, Elizabeth A. *The Empire of Love: Toward a Theory of Intimacy, Genealogy, and Carnality*. Durham, NC: Duke University Press, 2006.

——. "The State of Shame: Australian Multiculturalism and the Crisis of Indigenous Citizenship." *Critical Inquiry* (1998): 575–610.

Powers, David S. "Orientalism, Colonialism, and Legal History: The Attack on Muslim Family Endowments in Algeria and India." *Comparative Studies in Society and History* 31, no. 3 (1989): 535–71.

Prakash, Gyan. "Orientalism Now." *History and Theory* 34, no. 3 (1995): 199–212.

Pravilova, Ekaterina. "The Property of Empire: Islamic Law and Russian Agrarian Policy in Transcaucasia and Turkestan." *Kritika: Explorations in Russian and Eurasian History* 12 (2011): 353–86.

Prochaska, David. *Making Algeria French: Colonialism in Bône, 1870–1920*. Cambridge: Cambridge University Press, 1990.

Pursley, Sara. "The Stage of Adolescence: Anticolonial Time, Youth Insurgency, and the Marriage Crisis in Hashimite Iraq." *History of the Present* 3, no. 2 (2013): 160–97.

Rahal, Malika. "Ferhat Abbas, de l'assimilationnisme au nationalisme." In *Histoire de l'Algérie à la période coloniale*, edited by Abderrahmane Bouchène et al., 443–46. Paris: La Découverte, 2014.

Raman, Bhavani. *Document Raj: Writing and Scribes in Early Colonial South India*. Chicago: University of Chicago Press, 2012.

Ray, Carina E. *Crossing the Color Line: Race, Sex, and the Contested Politics of Colonialism in Ghana*. Athens: Ohio University Press, 2015.

Reichman, Ravit. "Undignified Details: The Colonial Subject of Law." *ARIEL* 35, no. 1–2 (2004): 81–100.

Renucci, Florence. "Confrontation entre droit français et droits indigènes: Le cas des mariages mixtes en Afrique du Nord (1870–1919)." *Cahiers aixois d'histoire des droits de l'outre mer français* 1 (2002): 147–91.

——. "La doctrine coloniale en République: L'exemple de deux juriconsultes algériens: Marcel Morand et Émile Larcher." In *La République et son droit (1870–1930)*, edited by Jean-Louis Halperin and Anna Storra-Lamarre, 461–78. Besançon: Presses Universitaires de Franche-Comté, 2011.

——. "La Revue algérienne, tunisienne et marocaine de législation et de jurisprudence (1885–1916). Une identité singulière?" In *Faire l'histoire du droit colonial cinquante ans après l'indépendance de l'Algérie*, edited by Jean-Philippe Bras, 181–201. Paris: Karthala, 2015.

——. "Le meilleur d'entre nous? Ernest Zeys ou le parcours d'un juge de paix en Algérie." In *Le juge et l'outre-mer*, edited by Bernard Durand, 67–85. Lille: Centre d'histoire judiciaire, 2010.

——. "Les juifs d'Algérie et la citoyenneté (1870–1902). Les enjeux d'un statut contesté." *Droit et justice en Afrique coloniale. Traditions, productions et réformes* (2013): 97–115.

Rey-Goldzeiguer, Annie. *Le royaume arabe: La politique algérienne de Napoléon III, 1861–1870*. Algiers: Société nationale d'édition et de diffusion, 1977.

Rifkin, Mark. "Settler Common Sense." *Settler Colonial Studies* 3, no. 3–4 (2013): 322–40.

Riley, Denise. *The Words of Selves: Identification, Solidarity, Irony*. Stanford, CA: Stanford University Press, 2000.

Robcis, Camille. *The Law of Kinship: Anthropology, Psychoanalysis, and the Family in France*. Ithaca, NY: Cornell University Press, 2013.

——. "Liberté, Égalité, Hétérosexualité: Race and Reproduction in the French Gay Marriage Debates." *Constellations* 22, no. 3 (2015): 447–61.

Roberts, Mary Louise. *Civilization without Sexes: Reconstructing Gender in Postwar France, 1917–1927*. Chicago: University of Chicago Press, 1994.

Roberts, Richard. "Representation, Structure, and Agency: Divorce in the French Soudan during the Early Twentieth Century." *Journal of African History* 40, no. 3 (1999): 389–410.

Roberts, Sophie B. *Citizenship and Antisemitism in French Colonial Algeria, 1870–1962*. Cambridge: Cambridge University Press, 2017.

Rogers, Rebecca. *A Frenchwoman's Imperial Story: Madame Luce in Nineteenth-Century Algeria*. Stanford, CA: Stanford University Press, 2013.

Rose, Jacqueline. *States of Fantasy*. Oxford: Clarendon, 1996.

Rosenberg, Clifford D. *Policing Paris: The Origins of Modern Immigration Control between the Wars*. Ithaca, NY: Cornell University Press, 2006.

Ruedy, John. *Land Policy in Colonial Algeria: The Origins of the Rural Public Domain*. Los Angeles: University of California Press, 1967.

——. *Modern Algeria: The Origins and Development of a Nation*. Bloomington: Indiana University Press, 1992.

Ruskola, Teemu. *Legal Orientalism: China, the United States, and Modern Law*. Cambridge, MA: Harvard University Press, 2013.

Saada, Emmanuelle. *Empire's Children: Race, Filiation, and Citizenship in the French Colonies*. Translated by Arthur Goldhammer. Chicago: University of Chicago Press, 2012.

———. "La loi, le droit et l'indigène." *Droits*, no. 1 (2006): 165–90.

———. "Law in the Time of Catastrophe: The 'Native Code' in Colonial Algeria." Shelby Cullom Davis Center for Historical Studies, April 1, 2016.

———. "Penser le fait colonial à travers le droit en 1900." *Mil neuf cent. Revue d'histoire intellectuelle*, no. 1 (2009): 103–16.

Saaïdia, Oissila. *Algérie coloniale: Musulmans et chrétiens, le contrôle de l'état, 1830–1914*. Paris: CNRS éditions, 2015.

Said, Edward W. *Orientalism*. New York: Vintage Books, 1994.

Sainte-Marie, Alain. "L'application du sénatus consulte du 22 avril 1863 dans la province d'Alger." *Cahiers de la Méditerranée* 3, no. 1 (1971): 15–34.

———. "Législation foncière et société rurale: L'application de la loi du 26 juillet 1873 dans les douars de l'Algérois." *Études rurales* 57 (1975): 61–87.

Sait, Siraj, and Hilary Lim. "Muslim Women and Property." In *Land, Law and Islam: Property and Human Rights in the Muslim World*. London: Zed Books, 2006.

Sambron, Diane. *Les femmes algériennes pendant la colonisation*. Paris: Riveneuve, 2009.

Samuels, Maurice. "Philosemitism and the *Mission Civilisatrice* in Gautier's *La Juive de Constantine*." *French Forum* 38, no. 1 (2013): 19–33.

Sanos, Sandrine. *The Aesthetics of Hate: Far-Right Intellectuals, Antisemitism, and Gender in 1930s France*. Stanford, CA: Stanford University Press, 2013.

Sarat, Austin, and Thomas R. Kearns. *Law in the Domains of Culture*. Ann Arbor: University of Michigan Press, 2000.

Sari, Djilali. *La dépossession des fellahs*. Algiers: Société nationale d'édition et de diffusion, 1975.

———. "Le démantèlement de la propriété foncière." *Revue historique* 249, no. 1 (505) (1973): 47–76.

Savage, Gail. "More Than One Mrs. Mir Anwaruddin: Islamic Divorce and Christian Marriage in Early Twentieth-Century London." *Journal of British Studies* 47, no. 2 (2008): 348–74.

Schley, Rachel Eva. "The Tyranny of Tolerance: France, Religion, and the Conquest of Algeria, 1830–1870." PhD diss., University of California, Los Angeles, 2015.

Schmitt, Carl. *Political Theology: Four Chapters on the Concept of Sovereignty*. Cambridge, MA: MIT Press, 1985.

Schneider, Zoë A. *The King's Bench: Bailiwick Magistrates and Local Governance in Normandy, 1670–1740*. Rochester, NY: University of Rochester Press, 2008.

Schreier, Joshua. *Arabs of the Jewish Faith: The Civilizing Mission in Colonial Algeria*. New Brunswick, NJ: Rutgers University Press, 2010.

———. "Napoléon's Long Shadow: Morality, Civilization, and Jews in France and Algeria, 1808–1870." *French Historical Studies* 30, no. 1 (2007): 77–103.

Scott, David. "Colonial Governmentality." *Social Text* 43 (1995): 191–220.

———. *Conscripts of Modernity: The Tragedy of Colonial Enlightenment*. Durham, NC: Duke University Press, 2004.

Scott, James C. *Seeing Like a State: How Certain Schemes to Improve the Human Condition Have Failed*. New Haven, CT: Yale University Press, 1998.

Scott, James C., John Tehranian, and Jeremy Mathias. "The Production of Legal Identities Proper to States: The Case of the Permanent Family Surname." *Comparative Studies in Society and History* 44, no. 1 (2002): 4–44.

Scott, Joan Wallach. *The Fantasy of Feminist History*. Durham, NC: Duke University Press, 2012.

——. *Only Paradoxes to Offer: Feminism and the "Rights of Man" in France, 1789–1940.* Cambridge, MA: Harvard University Press, 1996.

——. *The Politics of the Veil.* Princeton, NJ: Princeton University Press, 2007.

——. *Sex and Secularism.* Princeton, NJ: Princeton University Press, 2017.

——. "Sexularism." In *The Fantasy of Feminist History.* Durham, NC: Duke University Press, 2012.

Selby, Jennifer A. "Polygamy in the Parisian Banlieues." In *Polygamy's Rights and Wrongs: Perspectives on Harm, Family, and Law,* edited by Gillian Calder and Lori G. Beaman, 120–35. Vancouver: University of British Columbia Press, 2013.

Seshadri, Kalpana. *Desiring Whiteness: A Lacanian Analysis of Race.* London: Routledge, 2000.

Sessions, Jennifer E. *By Sword and Plow: France and the Conquest of Algeria.* Ithaca, NY: Cornell University Press, 2011.

——. "Débattre de la licitation comme stratégie d'acquisition des terres à la fin du XIXe siècle." In *Propriété et société en Algérie contemporaine. Quelles approches?,* edited by Didier Guignard. Aix en Provence: Institut de recherches et d'études sur le monde arabe et musulman, 2017.

Sharafi, Mitra. "The Marital Patchwork of Colonial South Asia: Forum Shopping from Britain to Baroda." *Law and History Review* 28 (2010): 979–1009.

——. "The Semi-autonomous Judge in Colonial India: Chivalric Imperialism Meets Anglo-Islamic Dower and Divorce Law." *Indian Economic & Social History Review* 46, no. 1 (2009): 57–81.

Shepard, Todd. *The Invention of Decolonization: The Algerian War and the Remaking of France.* Ithaca, NY: Cornell University Press, 2006.

——. *Sex, France, and Arab Men, 1962–1979.* Chicago: University of Chicago Press, 2018.

Shepardson, Charles. "Lacan and Philosophy." In *The Cambridge Companion to Lacan,* edited by Jean-Michel Rabaté, 116–52. Cambridge: Cambridge University Press, 2006.

Sinha, Mrinalini. *Colonial Masculinity: The "Manly Englishman" and the "Effeminate Bengali" in the Late Nineteenth Century.* Manchester: Manchester University Press, 1995.

——. *Specters of Mother India: The Global Restructuring of an Empire.* Durham, NC: Duke University Press, 2006.

Slimani-Direche, Karima. *Chrétiens de Kabylie, 1873–1954: Une action missionnaire dans l'Algérie coloniale.* Saint-Denis: Bouchene, 2004.

——. *Histoire de l'émigration kabyle en France au XXe siècle: Réalités culturelles et politiques et réappropriations identitaires.* Paris: L'Harmattan, 1997.

Smati, Mahfoud. *Les élites algériennes sous la colonisation.* Algiers: Dahlab, 1998.

Smith, Bonnie G. *The Gender of History: Men, Women, and Historical Practice.* Cambridge, MA: Harvard University Press, 1998.

Sonbol, Amira El Azhary. "Adults and Minors in Ottoman Shari'a Courts and Modern Law." In *Women, the Family, and Divorce Laws in Islamic History,* edited by Amira El Azhary Sonbol, 236–56. Syracuse, NY: Syracuse University Press, 1996.

Spieler, Miranda Frances. *Empire and Underworld: Captivity in French Guiana.* Cambridge, MA: Harvard University Press, 2011.

Spitzer, Alan B. *The French Generation of 1820.* Princeton, NY: Princeton University Press, 1987.

Spivak, Gayatri Chakravorty. "Can the Subaltern Speak?" In *Marxism and the Interpretation of Culture,* edited by Cary Nelson and Lawrence Grossberg, 271–315. Urbana: University of Illinois Press, 1988.

Stein, Sarah Abrevaya. *Saharan Jews and the Fate of French Algeria*. Chicago: University of Chicago Press, 2014.

Stephens, Julie. *Governing Islam: Law, Empire, and Secularism in South Asia*. Cambridge: Cambridge University Press, 2018.

Stoler, Ann Laura. *Along the Archival Grain: Epistemic Anxieties and Colonial Common Sense*. Princeton, NJ: Princeton University Press, 2009.

——. *Carnal Knowledge and Imperial Power: Race and the Intimate in Colonial Rule*. Berkeley: University of California Press, 2002.

——. *Haunted by Empire: Geographies of Intimacy in North American History*. Durham, NC: Duke University Press, 2006.

——. *Race and the Education of Desire: Foucault's History of Sexuality and the Colonial Order of Things*. Durham, NC: Duke University Press, 1995.

Sturman, Rachel. *The Government of Social Life in Colonial India: Liberalism, Religious Law, and Women's Rights*. Cambridge: Cambridge University Press, 2012.

——. "Property and Attachments: Defining Autonomy and the Claims of Family in Nineteenth-Century Western India." *Comparative Studies in Society and History* 47, no. 3 (2005): 611–37.

Surkis, Judith. "Carnival Balls and Penal Codes: Body Politics in July Monarchy France." *History of the Present* 1, no. 1 (2011): 59–83.

——. "Hymenal Politics: Marriage, Secularism, and French Sovereignty." *Public Culture* 22, no. 3 (2010): 531–56.

——. *Sexing the Citizen: Morality and Masculinity in France, 1870–1920*. Ithaca, NY: Cornell University Press, 2006.

Tabili, Laura. "Empire Is the Enemy of Love: Edith Noor's Progress and Other Stories." *Gender & History* 17, no. 1 (2005): 5–28.

Taithe, Bertrand. "Algerian Orphans and Colonial Christianity in Algeria, 1866–1939." *French History* 20, no. 3 (2006): 240–59.

——. "La famine de 1866–1868: Anatomie d'une catastrophe et construction médiatique d'un événement." *Revue d'histoire du 19ᵉ siècle* 41 (2010): 113–27.

Taraud, Christelle. *La prostitution coloniale: Algérie, Tunisie, Maroc (1830–1962)*. Paris: Payot, 2003.

——. "Virility in the Colonial Context, from the Late Eighteenth to the Twentieth Century." In *A History of Virility*, edited by Alain Corbin, Jean-Jacques Courtine, and Georges Vigarello, 325–45. New York: Columbia University Press, 2017.

Temimi, Abdeljelil. "L'activité de Hamdan Khudja à Paris et à Istanbul pour la question algérienne." *Revue d'histoire maghrébine*, no. 7–8 (1977): 234–43.

——. *Recherches et documents d'histoire maghrébine: La Tunisie, l'Algérie et la Tripolitaine de 1816 à 1871*. Tunis: Université de Tunis, 1971.

Thénault, Sylvie. "Le 'code de l'indigénat.'" In *Histoire de l'Algérie à la période coloniale*, 200–206. Paris: La Découverte, 2014.

——. "L'indigénat dans l'empire français: Algérie/Cochinchine, une double matrice." *Monde(s)*, no. 2 (2017): 21–40.

Thoral, Marie-Cecile. "Sartorial Orientalism: Cross-Cultural Dressing in Colonial Algeria and Metropolitan France in the Nineteenth Century." *European History Quarterly* 45, no. 1 (2015): 57–82.

Tissot, Sylvie. "Excluding Muslim Women: From Hijab to Niqab, from School to Public Space." *Public Culture* 23, no. 1 (2011): 39–46.

Trumbull, George R. *An Empire of Facts: Colonial Power, Cultural Knowledge, and Islam in Algeria, 1870–1914*. Cambridge: Cambridge University Press, 2009.

Tsing, Anna Lowenhaupt. *Friction: An Ethnography of Global Connection*. Princeton, NJ: Princeton University Press, 2005.

Tucker, Judith E. *In the House of the Law: Gender and Islamic Law in Ottoman Syria and Palestine*. Berkeley: University of California Press, 1998.

Turin, Yvonne. "Enfants trouvés, colonisation et utopie." *Revue historique* 224 (1970): 329–58.

Van der Veer, Peter. *Imperial Encounters: Religion and Modernity in India and Britain*. Princeton, NJ: Princeton University Press, 2001.

Vatin, Jean-Claude. "Exotisme et rationalité: À l'origine de l'enseignement du droit en Algérie (1879–1909)." *Connaissances du Maghreb* (1984): 161–83.

——. "Science juridique et institution coloniale: L'École de Droit d'Alger (1878–1909)." *Revue algérienne des sciences juridiques, politiques et économiques* 20, no. 4 (1983): 399–455.

Vaughan, Megan. *Curing Their Ills: Colonial Power and African Illness*. Cambridge: Polity, 1991.

Verhoeven, Timothy. *Sexual Crime, Religion and Masculinity in fin-de-siècle France: The Flamidien Affair*. Palgrave Pivot, 2018. ebook.

Viswanathan, Gauri. *Outside the Fold: Conversion, Modernity, and Belief*. Princeton, NJ: Princeton University Press, 1998.

Warner, Michael, Jonathan VanAntwerpen, and Craig J. Calhoun. *Varieties of Secularism in a Secular Age*. Cambridge, MA: Harvard University Press, 2010.

Weil, Patrick. "Le statut des musulmans en Algérie coloniale. Une nationalité française dénaturée." *Histoire de la justice* 16, no. 1 (2005): 93–109.

——. *Qu'est-ce qu'un Français? Histoire de la nationalité française depuis la Révolution*. Paris: Grasset, 2002.

——. "Why the French Laïcité Is Liberal." *Cardozo Law Review* 30, no. 6 (2008): 2699–2714.

Weiss, Gillian Lee. *Captives and Corsairs: France and Slavery in the Early Modern Mediterranean*. Stanford, CA: Stanford University Press, 2011.

Wexler, Laura. *Tender Violence: Domestic Visions in an Age of U.S. Imperialism*. Chapel Hill: University of North Carolina Press, 2000.

Wilder, Gary. *The French Imperial Nation-State: Negritude and Colonial Humanism between the Two World Wars*. Chicago: University of Chicago Press, 2005.

Wood, Leonard. *Islamic Legal Revival: Reception of European Law and Transformations in Islamic Legal Thought in Egypt, 1875–1952*. Oxford: Oxford University Press, 2016.

Yacono, Xavier. *La colonisation des plaines du Chélif, de Lavigerie au confluent de la Mina*. Algiers: E. Imbert, 1955.

——. "La colonisation militaire par les smalas de spahis en Algérie." *Revue historique* 242, no. 2 (1969): 347–94.

——. "La Régence d'Alger en 1830 d'après l'enquête des commissions de 1833–1834." *Revue de l'Occident musulman et de la Méditerranée* 1, no. 1 (1966): 229–44.

——. *Les bureaux arabes et l'évolution des genres de vie indigènes dans l'ouest du Tell Algérois (Dahra, Chélif, Ouarsenis, Sersou)*. Paris: Larose, 1953.

Yeğenoğlu, Meyda. *Colonial Fantasies: Towards a Feminist Reading of Orientalism*. Cambridge: Cambridge University Press, 1998.

Yerri, Urban. *L'indigène dans le droit colonial français (1865–1955)*. Paris: LGDJ, 2011.

Zimmerman, Andrew. *Alabama in Africa: Booker T. Washington, the German Empire, and the Globalization of the New South*. Princeton, NJ: Princeton University Press, 2010.

Žižek, Slavoj. *Tarrying with the Negative: Kant, Hegel, and the Critique of Ideology*. Durham, NC: Duke University Press, 1993.

INDEX

Note: Page numbers in *italic* indicate illustrations or tables.

Abbas, Ferhat, 6, 284
Abd el Kader, 245
Abdesselem, Taleb, 25, 219, *220*, 221–28, 237, 242, 245, 249
Abi-Mershed, Osama, 62
L'Afrique du nord illustrée (newspaper), *220*, 260
Afrique latine (journal), 259
Agamben, Giorgio, 9n21
L'Akhbar (newspaper), 86, 127
Alger (department), 19, 74
Algeria: advantages/privileges/excesses of, 56, 83–85, 134; annexation of (1834), 3, 4, 28, 47; budgetary independence (1901) of, 23; civilian rule (1870) of, 21, 22, 23; ex-Regency of Alger, *xvi*; French departments in, 19–20; judicial organization of, 3–4, 8, 19, 37–38, 41–42, 47–48, 54, 55, 61, 93, 124–25, 128, 134. *See also* colonization of Algeria
Algerian Jews: French citizenship for, 21, 74–78; judicial organization of, 48; legal status of, 68, 69, 75–82; use of French law by, 75–82. *See also* Mosaic law
Algerian men: advantages/privileges/excesses of, 1, 4, 5, 15–17, 58–60, 119, 138, 149–50, 183, 217–19, 227, 236–40, 247, 285, 291–94; conscription of, 24, 211–15, 236–39; feminist failure to find solidarity with, 289–93; French citizenship for, 5, 16, 20, 24, 74, 83, 213, 239; patriarchal authority of, 6, 28, 31, 52–54, 113, 132, 226, 235, 239–40, 291–92; political standing of, 25, 149–50, 211–15, 217, 221, 225–26, 236–44, 278, 284–85, 287, 292
Algerian Muslim Congress, 292
Alquier, Jeanne, 289–90
America, as analogy for colonization of Algeria, 42, 46
Ancey, Fernand, 244–45
Annales africaines (journal), 247, 251
Annales algériennes (journal), 258, 260, 275

Annuaire statistique de France, 182
Anquetil, Georges, 247
antisemitism, 168–69
Appeals Court of Algiers, 27, 76, 79, 134, 136, 174–75, 202, 203, 224, 263
Arab Bureaus, 20, 60–65, 67, 69, 89, 93
Arab Kingdom, 20, 71, 94, 95, 129, 195
Aragonès, Teresa, 203–5
Aron, Jules, 165
Artero, Antonia Ramona Juana, 201
Assembly of Jewish Notables. *See* Grand Sanhedrin
assimilation. *See* legal assimilation
L'Atlas (newspaper), 191
Attakadoum (Progress; journal), 284
Auclert, Hubertine, 146
L'Aurore (newspaper), 179
Aziz, Abdel, 50–51

Badho, Fathma, 266–67
Barbet, Charles, 148, 252, 261
Barde, Louis, 98
Barthou, Louis, 270
Bastien, Charles-François, 115
Bataillons d'Afrique, 160
Baubérot, Jean, 11
Baudicour, Louis de, 191
Beaumont, A. D. de, 245–46
Belkacem, Roumane, 261–66, 268–71
Bellemare, Alexandre, 130
ben Abdallah, Aoued Ould Ahmed, 201
ben Abdelaziz, Bouzid Mohamed, 254–55
ben Abd Eltif, Ali, 115
ben Abd Eltif, El Hadj Ahmed, 115
ben Abd Eltif, Mahmoud, 115
ben Abderrahman, Mohamed, 201
ben Ahmed, El Abassi, 126
ben Ali, Lhocine Mohand Boudjema, 263
ben Ali, Mohamed, 126

CPSIA information can be obtained
at www.ICGtesting.com
Printed in the USA
FSHW012115011119
63619FS